THE PARLIAMENTARY DIARIES OF
SIR JOHN TRELAWNY, 1858–1865

THE PARLIAMENTARY DIARIES OF SIR JOHN TRELAWNY, 1858–1865

edited by

T.A. JENKINS

CAMDEN FOURTH SERIES
VOLUME 40

LONDON
OFFICES OF THE ROYAL HISTORICAL SOCIETY
UNIVERSITY COLLEGE LONDON
GOWER STREET WC1E 6BT
1990

British Library Cataloguing in Publication Data
Trelawny, *Sir* John
The parliamentary diaries of Sir John Trelawny, 1858–1865.
—(Camden fourth series v. 40)
1. Great Britain. Politics. Trelawny, Sir John
I. Title II. Royal Historical Society III. Jenkins, T.
A. (Terence Andrew) *1958–* IV. Series
941.081092

ISBN 0–86193–125–4

Printed and bound in Great Britain by
Butler & Tanner Ltd, Frome and London

CONTENTS

PREFACE

My first acknowledgement is to Sir John Salusbury-Trelawny, Bt., for his kind permission to edit the diaries of his great-great grandfather.

The staff of the Bodleian Library, and in particular Mr. Colin Harris, have been exceptionally helpful in assisting me in my task of preparing the diaries for publication.

I should also like to thank the University of Southampton and the Gloucestershire Record Office, for permission to draw material from the papers of Lord Palmerston and T.H. Sotheron-Estcourt respectively.

I am grateful to Dr. Paul Gurowich, who first drew my attention to the existence of the Trelawny diaries, and to Dr. Miles Taylor, who has supplied me with some valuable references. Professor Derek Beales has continued to provide much appreciated advice and encouragement. My special thanks are also due to Dr. Agatha Ramm, for taking such immense care in scrutinising the early drafts of a novice to the art of editing historical documents. Dr. Colin Matthew has been, throughout, a most helpful and efficient Literary editor.

It has been possible for me to prepare this edition of the Trelawny diaries through the support of the British Academy, who appointed me to a postdoctoral fellowship.

INTRODUCTION

Sir John Salusbury Salusbury-Trelawny, the ninth baronet (1816–85), kept a diary for the period April 1857 to July 1865, when he was the member of parliament for the Devonshire borough of Tavistock. The first volume of the diary is unfortunately now missing, but seven volumes remain, commencing early in the session of 1858.[1] They present us with a detailed account of the day-to-day activities of a radical Liberal M.P. endeavouring to promote a number of measures, notably a bill for the abolition of church rates, as well as telling us of Trelawny's opinions on a wide range of other issues, both domestic and foreign. The diaries are of particular interest as a record of the impressions of a back-bencher during the period of political confusion between the fall of Palmerston's first ministry, in February 1858, and the reconciliation of the various sections of the Liberal party at the famous Willis's rooms meeting in June 1859, and they go on to illustrate the predicament of radical Liberals during the period of Palmerston's second ministry. Equally, however, Trelawny's accounts are of value for the way they add flesh to the dry bones of *Hansard's Parliamentary Debates* (which often, it has to be said, provide a far from complete skeleton in any case), evoking the atmosphere of the House of Commons, and throwing light on the character and mannerisms of its members, including such leading figures as Palmerston, Gladstone and Disraeli.

If the diaries have a limitation, it is that they are almost entirely concerned with proceedings in parliament: more specifically still, it is the chamber and lobbies of the House of Commons which provide the venue for most of what Trelawny chose to record. He rarely alludes to debates in the House of Lords, and has little to say about his attendance on select committees. Moreover, Trelawny only occasionally mentions Tavistock, a fact that could create a misleading impression as to the importance of the relations between the M.P. and his constituents. It was in satisfying the demands of the electors of Tavistock, after all, that Trelawny found one very good reason for

---

[1] Bodleian MS Eng Hist d. 410–16. The covers of the exercise books are marked 'vol II' to 'vol VIII'. Three more volumes cover the period 1868–73, when Trelawny was the M.P. for East Cornwall. The diaries were deposited in the Bodelian Library in 1974 by Miss Caroline Harvey, now Dr. Caroline Jackson, MEP, who discovered them in the offices of the Oxford City Conservative association. It is believed that all other Trelawny papers have been destroyed.

keeping a diary in the first place, as he was expected to give an account of his stewardship at a public meeting after each parliamentary session: – a custom which provided a subject for facetious treatment in a leading article in *The Times* newspaper in 1864.[2] In fact, a brief examination of Trelawny's connection with his constituency is essential for an understanding of the course of his political career.

The years 1857–65 marked Trelawny's second term as a member for Tavistock, which he had previously represented from March 1843 until April 1852.[3] In many ways M.P. and constituency seemed well matched. Trelawny, who had been educated at Westminster School and Trinity College, Cambridge (B.A. 1839), and called to the bar at the Middle Temple in 1841,[4] was the scion of an ancient Cornish landed family, with an estate at Trelawne, near Liskeard.[5] The first Trelawny to sit in parliament was returned for Cornwall in 1326; one John Trelawny was knighted by Edward III, and his son, also John, was granted a pension by Henry V for his services in the French wars (he fought at Agincourt); a later John Trelawny received a baronetcy in 1628, and his grandson, Sir Jonathan, bishop of Bristol, brought great fame to the family as one of the seven bishops imprisoned in the Tower by James II (he was duly rewarded, by the Whigs, with preferment to Exeter and finally to Winchester). Thereafter, the Trelawnys had tended to be whiggish in their politics, and Sir William, the diarist's father, had thus represented East Cornwall from 1832 until 1837. In a county characterised by the relative absence of great landed magnates, the Trelawnys were typical examples of the Cornish tradition of lesser aristocratic families with radical leanings; and it was appropriate that, in his first attempt to gain election to parliament, when he tried to recapture his father's old seat at East Cornwall in 1841, the young John Trelawny should have been nominated by a neighbouring baronet, and one of the leading radicals of the day, Sir William Molesworth.[6] Indeed, after his victory at the Tavistock by election, in March 1843, Trelawny described himself in *Dod's Par-*

---

[2] *The Times*, 23 Aug. 1864, p. 6.

[3] It seems likely that he kept a diary during this period as well. The *Spectator*, 16 June 1849, p. 561, noted that on a number of occasions when the Stranger's gallery of the House of Commons had been cleared, Trelawny had supplied the press with his accounts of the proceedings.

[4] He never practised law.

[5] Trelawny succeeded his father in Nov. 1856. Since 1840 he had been a deputy lieutenant of Cornwall and a captain in the Cornwall Rangers militia. In 1842 he married Harriet Tremayne, the daughter of J.H. Tremayne of Heligan, Cornwall. They had one son and two daughters. Harriet died in 1879. In 1881 Trelawny married again, to Harriet Keppel (neé Buller).

[6] *The Times*, 9 July 1841, p. 11; 17 July 1841, p. 4. The election revolved around the issue of agricultural protection.

liamentary Companion as 'an ultra Radical', declaring his support for the repeal of the corn laws, household suffrage, the secret ballot, triennial parliaments, the abolition of the property qualification for M.P.s, the payment of members,[7] and the 'voluntary principle' in religion. He also stated his willingness to resign his seat, if called upon to do so by a majority of his constituents.

The contrast between social tradition and political radicalism was reflected in the character of the borough which had elected Trelawny as its representative. Tavistock was a stannery town situated on the river Tavy, to the north of Plymouth, whose prosperity had been sustained, after the decline of tin mining, firstly by its emergence as a centre of the woollen cloth industry during the seventeenth century, and then by the development of copper mining, which became the mainstay of the town's economy from the late-eighteenth century until around 1870.[8] In accordance with its economic importance, the borough had returned two members to parliament regularly since 1331, and this privilege remained intact after the great reform act of 1832, although Tavistock was thereafter one of the smallest boroughs remaining. The registered electorate numbered just 247 in 1832, rising to 349 in 1852, during which time the population had increased from 5,602 to 8,086.[9] Almost the entire borough was owned by the Duke of Bedford, whose influence, as *Dod's Electoral Facts* noted, was 'paramount; his friends and relatives have never been rejected'. The most eminent authority on the electoral system after the great reform act has, understandably, listed Tavistock as a purely proprietary borough.[10] While this certainly was the case during the eighteenth and early-nineteenth centuries, there was nevertheless a powerful element of radical dissent within the borough, which had occasionally made itself apparent during the seventeenth century,[11] and this undercurrent rose to the surface again in the climate of the reformed electoral system, amongst a population engaged mostly in general trade and in the mines around the town. In practice, the electoral influence of the Duke of Bedford after 1832 was less than absolute, and, while one of the borough's seats was always filled by his nominee, it was found to be expedient for the second member to be a man with genuine radical credentials. Such was the case with John Rundle, who

---

[7] By 1850, however, *Dod* shows that Trelawny had changed his mind on this point.

[8] W.G. Hoskins, *Devon*, (Newton Abbot, 1972), pp. 485–9.

[9] C.R. Dod, *Electoral Facts 1832–1853, Impartially Stated*, (ed. by H.J. Hanham, Brighton, 1972). By 1853 only fourteen freeman voters remained. There are no poll books for the borough.

[10] Norman Gash, *Politics in the Age of Peel*, (2nd ed., Brighton, 1977), pp. 438–9.

[11] Cf. the entry for Tavistock in the *History of Parliament* volumes for *The Commons, 1660–1690*, (ed. by B.D. Henning, 1983), with those covering the period 1715–1820.

was first returned for the borough in 1832, and it was on his retirement in 1843 that Trelawny received a large requisition from the electors of Tavistock inviting him to fill the vacancy.[12] It had been assumed that Trelawny would be elected unopposed, but radical feeling in the borough proved to be so strong that even he was not considered suitable by everyone, and a hostile faction put up Henry Vincent, a prominent Chartist, to oppose him. Ominously, Vincent, whose candidature was represented as a challenge to the Russell influence, had a large majority amongst the non-electors who swamped the nomination meeting, and on a poll being held he secured a more than creditable sixty-nine votes to Trelawny's 113. The key to Trelawny's position at Tavistock, it would therefore seem, was that he was an earnest, yet socially respectable radical, satisfactory to the 'liberal' (as distinct from Chartist) electors of the borough, and, for the same reason, politically acceptable to the Duke of Bedford.

It was probably inevitable that the position occupied by Trelawny would prove to be a precarious one, and that he all too often risked falling between different stools. This became apparent at the time of the general election, in the summer of 1847, when Trelawny was confronted with the prospect of opposition on two fronts which threatened to squeeze him out of his seat. Not only was the renewed candidature of the Chartist, Henry Vincent, thought probable, along with that of another radical, Samuel Carter, but another contender entered the field, R.J. Phillimore, a Liberal Conservative (or Peelite) whose intervention established the existence of a significant pro-Church party within the constituency. Trelawny was thus placed in the predicament that, while on the one hand he was being attacked by the militant dissenters for having supported the Maynooth grant and Lord John Russell's education bill, at the same time he risked losing the split votes of Whiggish electors concerned for the safety of the Church of England.[13] In the event, Vincent announced at a late stage that he was withdrawing his candidature, and he recommended that his supporters split their votes between Carter and Trelawny, an endorsement that was generally recognised to be a blow to Phillimore's chances. At the poll, Edward Russell and Trelawny were returned comfortably ahead of their opponents.[14] Phillimore himself was in no doubt that it was the action of the 'beast', Vincent, that had saved Trelawny, and newspaper accounts indeed show that all but nine of

[12] See the *Plymouth, Devonport and Stonehouse Herald* (hereafter *Plymouth Herald*), 4, 11 and 18 Mar. 1843, for what follows.
[13] See the *Plymouth and Devonport Weekly Journal* (hereafter *Plymouth Journal*), 5 Aug. 1847, for what follows.
[14] Russell 153, Trelawny 150, Phillimore 86, Carter 56.

the fifty-six supporters of Carter also voted for Trelawny.[15] Without this support, the result would have been very close. Indeed Phillimore felt confident, as he wrote to his close friend, W.E. Gladstone, that he had laid the foundations for future success: he observed that he had obtained the largest number of plumpers of any candidate (twenty-six), and claimed that 'the Whig votes were in greater measure split with me'.[16] Thus, Phillimore was convinced that Trelawny's position was becoming untenable, and that 'the Duke of Bedford will have to choose between me and a Chartist next time.'[17]

Before the next general election took place, however, an unexpected development had occurred. On 15 April 1852 Trelawny issued the following address to the electors of Tavistock:

> I have resigned my seat. I propose, notwithstanding, to attend the meeting tomorrow, and to show you that I have done my duty to the popular party throughout my political career. I postpone till then all denials of erroneous statements, with which your walls have teemed for some time. I do not intend to offer myself again as a candidate for Tavistock without a requisition from a clear majority of the electors.[18]

In his subsequent speech explaining the reasons for this decision,[19] Trelawny referred to a number of instances where his conduct in parliament had incurred the displeasure of his constituents. He defended, for example, his opposition in March 1848 to Joseph Hume's amendment limiting the extension of the income tax to one year, although this action had been extremely unpopular, because he believed that the longer-term retention of the income tax was essential in order to achieve the desired reduction in indirect taxes. But the central issue in the dispute between Trelawny and his constituents, as it emerges, was that of the separation of Church and State. In the heat and anxiety of the electoral battle in 1847, when Phillimore's candidacy had threatened to deprive Trelawny of his seat, and when he had thus been under pressure to bid for radical votes, he had given a rather rash pledge that he would, if desired, bring forward a motion on disestablishment in the new parliament. That Trelawny afterwards regretted having made this promise is perhaps suggested by the fact

---

[15] *Plymouth Herald*, 7 Aug. 1847. On the other hand, Carter suffered from the fact that twenty-five 'liberal' voters plumped for Trelawny.

[16] Phillimore to Gladstone, n.d. [docketed 4 Aug. 1847], Gladstone MSS (British Library, Add MSS), 44276, fo. 129.

[17] Phillimore to Gladstone, 5 Aug. 1847, ibid, 44276, fo. 133.

[18] *The Times*, 17 Apr. 1852, p. 8.

[19] See the extensive account in the *Plymouth Journal*, 22 Apr. 1852, for the whole of what follows.

that, in recounting to his constituents the subsequent history of the matter, he claimed that he had had no personal recollection of giving any pledge. On receiving confirmation from the editor of a local newspaper that an unequivocal promise had been made, Trelawny then conferred with his radical colleagues in parliament, during the session of 1848, but was persuaded that it would be inexpedient to press a motion on disestablishment, given the disturbed state of affairs at that time. Furthermore, while Trelawny had then indicated to his constituents that he hoped to bring the subject forward in the 1849 session, the feeling amongst the parliamentary radicals against the wisdom of so proceeding still prevailed, and on issuing a letter to his constituents asking for guidance on the matter, and promising to introduce a motion if requisitioned to do so, there had been no response.

Early in 1852, however, Trelawny found that meetings were being held in Tavistock condemning him for having broken his promise to his constituents. The situation was further complicated by Trelawny's admission that his own views on the question of English Church disestablishment had by now undergone a change, at least in their practical bearing. While his abstract belief in the desirability of the separation of Church and State remained unchanged, recent events had convinced him that to pursue such a policy was to play the game of the Puseyite faction within the Church, who favoured disestablishment as a means of gaining full control over Church doctrine and the education system, which would enable them to establish a 'spiritual despotism' over the people. The outcome of the celebrated Gorham case of 1850 had impressed Trelawny with the advantages of the erastian policy of maintaining State control over a powerful ecclesiastical body, as a check against the spread of Puseyism. He therefore argued that it was better for the dissenters to focus on specific grievances such as church rates and University tests, rather than to press the demand for disestablishment.

Ironically, while Trelawny professed anti-Romanist sentiments, he was nevertheless accused of having Papist sympathies. His radical opponent in Tavistock, Samuel Carter, who was critical of Trelawny's failure to proceed with the disestablishment motion, also admitted that he had been responsible for one of the posters put up in the town – 'Popish plaster for a broken pledge' – alleging, on the basis of comments made by Trelawny in the House of Commons in defence of the Maynooth grant, that the member for Tavistock favoured the payment of the Roman Catholic priesthood in Ireland by the State.[20]

***

[20] 16 June 1851, *H* cxvii. 825–6. Trelawny claimed that he had been badly reported. What he probably meant to say was that logically, while the established Church in

In the light of the hostile meetings that had been held in the town, and of the letters he had received accusing him of a betrayal of trust, Trelawny felt that as a matter of honour he was bound to resign his seat.[21] Although a requisition was got up by his supporters, urging him to stand again (according to Carter less than 100 electors signed it), Trelawny adopted the curious position that he would not offer himself for re-election, but that he would take his seat in parliament if returned. At the ensuing by election, however, Trelawny was defeated by Carter, with Phillimore in third place.[22] No contemporary analysis of the poll is available, but it seems clear that while Phillimore's vote had held steady since 1847, thus retaining the adherence of many Whigs, Trelawny had lost a great many votes to Carter and did not obtain the split votes of Carter's supporters in the way he had in 1847.

Following his breach with Tavistock, Trelawny was persuaded to come forward as the advanced Liberal candidate at Brighton, at the general election held in the summer of 1852. His chances of success here may never have been very great, as the two sitting members, a Liberal and a free trade Conservative, were both defending their seats, but Trelawny was clearly embarrassed by the intervention of another Liberal candidate, by the name of Ffooks, who concentrated on certain populist themes, condemning the Maynooth grant, supporting the ecclesiastical titles bill, and denouncing the late-Whig government's militia bill, in each respect differing from Trelawny.[23] It cannot be asserted, though, on the basis of the poll, that Ffooks split the Liberal vote in a decisive way, as the sitting members were returned well ahead of Trelawny and Ffooks combined.[24] Two more unsuccessful attempts to get back into parliament were made by Trelawny at by elections in 1854. On the first occasion, at his home territory of Liskeard in March, where three Liberals were contesting the seat, Trelawny took a clear lead during the early hours of polling, and would certainly have won had it not been for the decision by a large number of Conservative voters to throw their weight behind the

Ireland remained, the Catholic priesthood should be paid as well. But Trelawny remained committed to disestablishment in the case of Ireland.

[21] Trelawny mentioned to the meeting at Tavistock, in Apr. 1852, that he had been approached with an offer to stand for a large metropolitan constituency. This was Lambeth, where it had seemed possible that a vacancy might occur. However, Trelawny had written to the embattled sitting member, Charles Tennyson D'Eyncourt, to assure him that he would never be a 'party to the undermining of any liberal man's seat'. 27 Feb. 1852, Tennyson D'Eyncourt MSS (Lincolnshire Archives Office), 2 T d'E/H/61 fo. 24.

[22] Carter 115, Trelawny 89, Phillimore 80. See the *Plymouth Journal*, 29 Apr. 1852.

[23] *The Times*, 10 June 1852, p. 5; 8 July 1852. p. 4.

[24] Pechell 1,924, Harvey 1,431, Trelawny 1,173, Ffooks 119.

Whig candidate, William Grey, ensuring him victory.[25] At Bedford, in December, where Trelawny was invited by the advanced Liberals to challenge a Conservative candidate, religious prejudice seems to have played a crucial part in the campaign, especially Trelawny's past record of support for the Maynooth grant, and he must have felt on uncomfortably familiar ground: 'He treated with quiet sarcasm the attempts which he said had been made to brand him as a Papist.'[26] His denials proved to be of no avail, as the Conservative candidate, Stuart, was victorious by 422 votes to 331.

An additional problem which Trelawny had encountered, at the Liskeard by election, arose from the comments made about the modest size of his purse, and the implicit concern about his ability to spend money on the constituency in the way that mid-Victorian M.P.s were often expected to do. At the hustings, Trelawny had frankly admitted that he was not a wealthy man, but argued that this should not be held to disqualify him as a suitable representative for the borough.[27] In November 1856 he was to inherit the family estate, on the death of his father, and, although only a limited amount of information is available about Trelawne, there is sufficient evidence to confirm the accuracy of the statement made at Liskeard. According to the entry in the fourth edition of John Bateman's *Great Landowners of Great Britain and Ireland* (1883), published near the end of Trelawny's life, the estate amounted to 8,000 acres and yielded a gross rental of £6,000 per annum, which included the revenue from woodland.[28] Unlike many Cornish landowners, Trelawny was not enriched through the presence of substantial mineral deposits under his land: there was in fact just one mine, Herodsfoot, producing silver-lead ore, the dues from which appear to have been worth £150 to him in 1862.[29] By the standards of the nineteenth century, then, Trelawny's income was of quite modest dimensions.

At the general election of April 1857, Trelawny, now Sir John, finally returned to parliament on being reunited with Tavistock. The situation in the borough had altered considerably since his earlier departure: at the general election of 1852, George Byng had been duly returned in the Russell interest, while the second seat had been held by Samuel Carter, who decisively defeated Phillimore.[30] However in February 1853, following an election petition, Phillimore was seated

---

[25] *Plymouth Herald*, 1 Apr. 1854, p. 8.

[26] *The Times*, 7 Dec. 1854, p. 6.

[27] *Plymouth Journal*, 30 Mar. 1854, p. 5.

[28] Trelawny had replied to Bateman that the entry was approximately correct.

[29] Cf. Webb and Geach, *The History and Progress of Mining in the Caradon and Liskeard District*, (2nd ed., 1863), and Thomas Spargo, *The Mines of Cornwall and Devon*, (1865).

[30] Byng 220, Carter 169, Phillimore 104.

in Carter's place on the grounds that the latter did not possess the requisite property qualification for a borough M.P. Thus for the next four years Tavistock was in the peculiar position of having for one of its representatives a Liberal-Conservative lawyer, quite obviously possessing only a minority following in the borough, who happened to be one of the most prominent upholders of the principle of church rates. Clearly, such a position could not be maintained for long, and by the beginning of 1856 Phillimore was aware that his days at Tavistock were probably numbered, as he reported to Gladstone: 'Tavistock must be given up – the Duke's agent means to return Trelawny and will do so.'[31] Trelawny received a requisition asking him to come forward again, and, contrary to custom, he undertook a vigorous canvass of the electors during the weeks prior to the election, agreeing to stand only after he had satisfied himself that a majority were pledged to support him. Phillimore's decision, shortly before polling day, not to defend his seat, further cleared the way for Trelawny's re-election. In these circumstances, Byng and Trelawny were returned well ahead of Carter, whose vote was down on the level of 1852.[32] Not everyone, though, was pleased to see Trelawny back: as one newspaper reported, after the result of the poll had been announced, 'Sir John was assailed by the infuriated mob. We believe that had it not been for a small band of devoted friends, who surrounded and conducted him to the hotel, his life would have been in danger. He, as well as others, received several blows, but we are happy to say that, fortunately, no great damage was done, though we firmly believe from the violence manifested that much was intended.'[33]

With the absence from the new parliament of Sir William Clay, who had promoted annual bills for the abolition of church rates in 1854–6, it was Trelawny who pressed the Palmerston government, during the session of 1857, for a statement of its intentions on the question. When Palmerston replied that a measure was being prepared, and that it would be introduced in the current session, Trelawny withdrew the motion he had placed on the order paper.[34] In spite of this clear undertaking by the government, however, no measure was forthcoming. Furthermore, when a deputation from the Liberation Society met the prime minister, in January 1858, they were informed that he could not give any pledge either to introduce a bill or to make parliamentary time available for a private member's

[31] Phillimore to Gladstone, 11 Jan. 1856, B.L. Add MSS 44277, fo. 44.
[32] Byng 242, Trelawny 198, Carter 130. See the *Plymouth Journal*, 2 Apr. 1857, p. 7.
[33] Ibid, p. 8.
[34] 4 June 1857, *H* cxlv. 1104.

bill.[35] No doubt Palmerston was preoccupied with other matters, such as the Indian mutiny and the financial crisis. As a result of the government's unwillingness to act, the Liberation Society asked Trelawny to introduce a bill on its behalf for the simple abolition of church rates.[36]

Trelawny's decision to accept the parliamentary leadership in the church rate battle, raises the question of whether he was motivated simply by constituency considerations, rather than by any genuine desire to settle the question, in the way that was alleged by the biographer of a leading radical of the time, Thomas Duncombe.[37] There can be no doubt of Trelawny's consistency in advocating the abolition of church rates, for he and John Bright had introduced a motion with this object as early as March 1849,[38] and in 1851 he had secured the appointment of a select committee to inquire into the working of church rate law.[39] Nor does it seem that his renewed concern with the question in 1857 was the direct result of a compact with his constituents. It was not until shortly after his election victory, in 1857, that Trelawny informed an audience, at a banquet held in Tavistock, that he had been approached by an organisation in London with the request that he raise the church rates question in parliament.[40] However, it is unclear whether any engagement between Trelawny and the Liberation Society extended, at this stage, beyond a motion calling for prompt action by the government, as it is known that when the Society decided to arrange for an abolition bill to be introduced, in 1858, Trelawny was not their first choice as mover. It was on the recommendation of two more senior radicals, Duncombe and Thomas Milner Gibson, neither of whom wished to take charge of the bill, that Trelawny was asked to bring it forward.[41] There was certainly good reason for Duncombe and Gibson to suppose that Trelawny would be the right man to act, as a by election had been held at Tavistock in September 1857, caused by the resignation of Byng, in which the Duke of Bedford's nephew, Arthur Russell, had been challenged by none other than Edward Miall, the editor of the *Nonconformist* newspaper and a prominent figure in the Liberation Society.

[35] Liberation Society minute book (Greater London Record Office), A/LIB/2, 30 Jan. 1858.
[36] Ibid, 5 Feb. 1858.
[37] T.H. Duncombe, *The Life and Correspondence of Thomas Slingsby Duncombe* (1868), ii. 337–8.
[38] 13 Mar. 1849, *H* ciii. 639–48.
[39] 8 Apr. 1851, *H* cxv. 1229–42. Trelawny published an *Epitome* of the committee's report, in 1852.
[40] *Plymouth Journal*, 16 Apr. 1857, p. 8.
[41] Liberation Society minute book, A/LIB/2, 5 Feb. 1858.

Once again, a by election provided an occasion for expressions of radical resentment at the influence exercised by the Duke, and Miall was only beaten by forty-four votes.[42] Whatever his original intentions may have been, therefore, it seems reasonable to conclude that, at the beginning of 1858, Trelawny must have been conscious of the expediency of sponsoring the church rate abolition bill, in view of the state of feeling in his constituency, and that force of circumstances had probably helped to dictate his decision.

The diaries record in detail the early successes and subsequent frustrations of Trelawny's leadership on the church rates issue. To the surprise of many, the abolition bill secured a substantial majority of fifty-three for its second reading, on 17 February 1858, and in the following session this was increased to seventy-four (15 March 1859). After the general election of 1859 and the formation of Palmerston's second ministry, church rates became an open question within the government, and the majority of seventy obtained for the second reading of Trelawny's bill, on 13 July 1859, included the prime minister and Lord John Russell. But this was to mark the limit of the abolition bill's progress. The problem facing Trelawny was not simply the obstacle to the passing of his bill posed by the Conservative dominated House of Lords, but the aggressive tactics adopted by the Liberation Society, which provoked a formidable reaction in favour of the Church of England.[43] A particularly potent weapon was handed to the pro-Church party by the evidence given to a House of Lords select committee by C.J. Foster and Samuel Morley, of the Liberation Society, who admitted that behind their campaign against church rates lay the ulterior motive of achieving the disestablishment of the Church of England. As a result of this confession, the majority for the second reading of Trelawny's bill, on 8 February 1860, dwindled to just twenty-nine.[44] Whereas Trelawny concluded that the way forward now lay in an attempt to seek a compromise settlement with the Conservatives, however, the Liberation Society persisted in its determination to press for unconditional abolition.[45]

It was during the session of 1861, after a majority of fifteen had been obtained for the second reading of his bill (27 February), that Trelawny opened communications with the former Conservative home secretary, T.H. Sotheron-Estcourt, with a view to encouraging a compromise measure. Consequently, on 3 June, Trelawny agreed

[42] 164:120. See the *Plymouth Journal*, 3 Sept. 1857, p. 7; 10 Sept. 1857, p. 7.

[43] Cf. G.I.T. Machin, *Politics and the Churches in Great Britain, 1832 to 1868*, (Oxford, 1977), pp. 306–7, 311–13.

[44] Diary, 8–9 Feb. 1860.

[45] Liberation Society minute book, A/LIB/2, 10 Feb., 16 Mar., and 19 Oct. 1860.

to postpone the further progress of the abolition bill for a fortnight while an alternative measure was drawn up, a decision that caused considerable annoyance to the Liberation Society.[46] (It might be added that Duncombe was also extremely critical of Trelawny's conduct,[47] and that this was probably the origin of the subsequent accusation of insincerity on Trelawny's part contained in Duncombe's biography.) Disappointment was to follow for Trelawny, though, as the Sotheron-Estcourt plan, revealed on 7 June, fell far short of the requirements of the dissenters, leaving him with no alternative but to proceed with his own bill. The division on the third reading, on 19 June, astonishingly resulted in a tie, 274:274, with the Speaker then casting his deciding vote against the bill. From this point on the cause of abolition went downhill, and in 1862 and 1863 majorities were recorded against the second reading of Trelawny's bill. His one remaining hope, in 1863, had been that the government might act by adopting an alternative plan, proposed by Lord Ebury, whereby the legal power to enforce the payment of church rates would be abolished. It was typical of the state of political paralysis fostered by the Palmerstonian regime, in which major party conflict was to be avoided as far as possible,[48] that the government proved unwilling to take responsibility for such a measure. With the defeat of the abolition bill by ten votes, in April 1863, therefore, Trelawny decided to resign his responsibility for the cause. It was not to be until 1868, while he was out of parliament, that a bi-partisan settlement of the issue was achieved along the lines of the Ebury plan.[49]

After leading on the Church rates question for six years, Trelawny was left in no doubt that there was insufficient commitment, amongst the various parties involved, for a successful compromise plan to be found. On the one hand, the Liberation Society appeared quite happy to keep the grievance alive, as a useful leverage in its more general campaign for the separation of Church and State, while on the other, the Conservative leadership, Disraeli especially, was eager to seize the opportunity offered by the issue to adopt a strong pro-Church stance.[50] Consequently, Sotheron-Estcourt and the minority of other Conservatives, such as R.A. Cross, who wished to be conciliatory, were not in a strong enough position within their own party to be able to offer terms which the dissenters could accept, and the main effect of their efforts was to erode the support for Trelawny's bill amongst the

---

[46] Ibid, 7 June 1861.
[47] 10 July 1861, H clxiv. 668.
[48] Cf. P.M. Gurowich, 'The continuation of war by other means: Party and Politics, 1855–1865', Historical Journal, XXVII, (1984), especially pp. 612–16.
[49] Machin, Politics and Churches, pp. 349–55.
[50] Ibid, pp. 317–19.

moderate Liberals, making his position even more hopeless. Ultimately, of course, it was the government's unwillingness to take the initiative that was decisive: without ministerial assistance or involvement, there was little prospect of a back-bench member being able to settle such a controversial issue as church rates.

There can be no doubt that Trelawny's championship of the cause of church rate abolition was beneficial to him for electoral purposes. At the general election of June 1859, he was returned for Tavistock for the only time without a contest, an outcome that was assisted by the fact that his Whig colleague, Arthur Russell, also supported the abolition bill. At the hustings, Trelawny's old radical opponent, Samuel Carter, could not find anyone to nominate him.[51] After 1859, however, Trelawny found that the stance he adopted on a number of other issues led to serious criticism from his constituents and renewed doubts about the security of his seat. Trelawny may have been the champion of the nonconformists with regard to church rates, but he abhorred religious bigotry and zealotry in any form, and was therefore unable to gratify the feelings of his constituents on sabbatarian issues. The most serious threat to Trelawny arose from his advocacy of the opening of museums on Sundays, a measure which he favoured as being morally beneficial for the working classes.[52] Similarly, he angered many constituents through his opposition to a bill for the closing of public houses on Sundays.[53] Nor was the other great cause with which Trelawny was associated during the early–1860s, the affirmations bill, proposing to allow atheists to give evidence in criminal cases, exactly designed to please the dissenters of Tavistock.[54] It is also possible that his campaign for a contagious diseases act, to regulate prostitutes serving the armed forces, caused offence to puritanical minds. By the summer of 1865, therefore, with the dissolution of parliament looming, Trelawny's canvass of the constituency revealed that discontent had accumulated to such an extent that he could no longer rely on the backing of many of his old supporters.[55] As his diary records, when he held a public meeting in order to gain a vote of confidence, most of the electors stayed away, leaving him to the mercy of the mob.[56] Trelawny did not trouble to stand at the general election. It was John Stuart Mill's opinion, expressed after the elections were

---

[51] *Plymouth Journal*, 28 Apr. 1859, p. 5; 5 May 1859, p. 7. Trelawny's nominator, Thomas Nicholls, had formerly supported Carter and Miall.

[52] Diary, 14 Feb. 1860.

[53] Diary, 25 Mar. 1863.

[54] Diary, 18 Feb. and 20 Mar. 1861.

[55] *Western Daily Mercury*, 6 July 1865, p. 4.

[56] Diary, 30 June and 4 July 1865.

over, that the rejection of Trelawny was 'one of the greatest of the few losses which advanced opinions have suffered'.[57]

Clearly it was both Trelawny's strength and his weakness that he was an individualistic politician, whose views did not fit into any simple category. His political antecedents lay in the rationalist tradition of philosophic radicalism,[58] and he counted amongst his friends Mill, George Grote and J.A. Roebuck, but by the time Trelawny entered politics in the 1840s this was very much a spent force as a parliamentary movement. In any case, he differed in important respects from the views of many utilitarians. While Trelawny was anxious to protect the civil rights of free thinkers, for instance, he himself was a sincere broad churchman who hoped, through his efforts on such issues as church rates, to reconcile anglicans and dissenters as far as possible; and it has already been noted that, by the early-1850s, he had moved away from his original views on the separation of Church and State towards a more Whiggish, erastian position. Trelawny was also appalled at the attitude of utilitarians like Roebuck, whose zeal for colonial expansion was so great that they lacked any humanitarian concern for the fate of natives, like the Maoris in New Zealand, who were being robbed of their lands.[59]

Nor can Trelawny simply be described as a radical of the 'Manchester School', although coming into politics in the 1840s he was naturally profoundly influenced by the campaign for free trade. From the outset of his career Trelawny was an ardent free trader, advocating the repeal of the corn laws on the grounds not so much of securing supplies of cheap bread, but as a way of expanding trade and therefore creating employment, a process which he held would be beneficial to agriculture as well as to industry: it was the system of protectionism, in Trelawny's view, that was ruining the Country's prosperity.[60] While he was generally sympathetic, therefore, to Sir Robert Peel's policies in the early-1840s, the Bank Charter act of 1844 was one measure which did not meet with Trelawny's approval, as he wished to see the principles of free trade extended to the banking system as well.[61] Where Trelawny departed from the 'Manchester School' was in his dislike of their 'little Englandism', and his diaries show that he was often critical of what he considered to be Cobden's narrow mindedness

---

[57] Mill to G.J. Holyoake, 8 Aug. 1865, Francis E. Mineka and Dwight N. Lindley (eds), *The Later Letters of John Stuart Mill, 1849–1873*, (Toronto, 1972), iii, 1086–7.
[58] Cf. *Illustrated London News*, 2 May 1857, p. 417.
[59] Diary, 10 Mar. 1865.
[60] E.g. 9 May 1843, *H* lxix. 85–90. Trelawny's maiden speech.
[61] See Trelawny's pamphlet, *Sketch of existing restrictions on banking and doubts of the soundness of the principles on which they rest*, (1847).

with respect to questions of national defence.[62] Trelawny was one of that breed of radical who was able to respond to the rhetoric of Liberal-nationalism so skilfully exploited by Palmerston, for instance with regard to the independence of Italy and Poland.[63] There is no doubt that Trelawny felt genuine admiration for the resilience of the veteran prime minister, and for his dexterity in managing parliament, if not for his political morality.[64]

Trelawny's radicalism is perhaps best defined as anti-centralist,[65] seeking to restrict the role of the State. He was an 'economist', in the tradition of Joseph Hume,[66] specialising in the harassment of ministers through the careful scrutiny of the details of departmental estimates on supply nights. One of Trelawny's constant themes, particularly during the early part of his career, was the need to systematically reduce the national debt, in order to relieve the burden on all taxpayers. It was his opinion that the country 'ought to maintain an honest and manly system of finance.'[67] In order to achieve economy in government, it was necessary to combat the system of aristocratic privilege, and the corruption which attended it. One eye had always to be kept open for cases of jobbery, therefore, and it was necessary to campaign relentlessly, as Trelawny did during the late-1850s and early-1860s, against such abuses as the privileged position of the Guards' regiments, and the enormous waste of resources which this system involved. Any proposal which seemed to be designed for the benefit of the ruling class, was sure to meet with Trelawny's disapproval: Gladstone's motion of March 1850, for instance, calling on the government to make £3,000,000 available for land drainage, was denounced as 'a great communist scheme', which would fritter away public money.[68] Trelawny's laissez faire principles applied equally to the working classes, and he was determined to resist measures which encouraged the 'habit of thinking that those things would be done for them which could only be done by themselves.'[69] He was dismissive of sentimental motions which were 'apt to lead the working classes to form expectations of millennial happiness which could never be realised', and complained that 'The House fostered socialist views too much, and then wondered at the fruits that they produced', such as

---

[62] Diary, 3 June 1862.
[63] E.g. diary, 28 July 1859; 27 Feb. 1863.
[64] E.g. diary, 30 July 1860; 31 May 1862; 20 Mar. 1863; 20 May 1864.
[65] Cf. diary, 26 May 1862.
[66] Cf. *Illustrated Times*, 1 Aug. 1857, p. 86.
[67] 4 Apr. 1851, *H* cxv. 1075–6.
[68] 18 Mar. 1850, *H* cix. 1068.
[69] 5 Mar. 1850, *H* cix. 364–6.

strikes.[70] Unsurprisingly, it was Trelawny who, in May 1847, moved the hostile amendment against the third reading of the factory bill to restrict working hours, a measure which he denounced as an invasion of the rights of property, and as inadmissible interference by the State in the relations between masters and workmen.[71] In response to such demands for 'social' legislation, what Trelawny was prepared to offer was an extension of the franchise coupled with 'a large and comprehensive system of education', which he desired to see provided free of charge and on a secular basis.[72]

At the Tavistock banquet of April 1857, Trelawny stated his adherence to the conventional nostrums of Liberalism: 'My principles are those of civil and religious liberty: my motto is "peace, retrenchment and reform"'. The qualifications which he added to this familiar Liberal motto are not without interest. Trelawny desired peace, 'so long as it can be maintained with credit to a nation whose voice is entitled to be heard among the people of the world, and whose example is a great international instruction.' Retrenchment was to be pursued, 'so far as it is compatible with the due efficiency of all our public departments', and reform had to be achieved 'without revolution'.[73]

Trelawny personally does not seem to have attracted a great deal of attention from the journalists of the day, but there is one description of him in the *Illustrated Times*, by William White, the doorkeeper of the House of Commons, who shared many of Trelawny's radical sympathies:

Sir John's place in the House is the back-bench below the gangway, where he may easily be discovered by his long light-coloured beard [...] Sir John is not an orator – does not affect to be one; but he is an able, painstaking member of Parliament, and one of the most successful tacticians in the House. He is an advanced Liberal in politics [...] The Honourable Baronet is also an independent member in the most literal acceptance of the word. Though confessedly not a rich man, it is obvious to all that he came not into Parliament for place or power, otherwise he would not have meddled with the Guards' business; for so sagacious an observer as Sir John must have known that to interfere with the privileges of this powerful body, both in court and aristocratic favour, was to close and double-lock the gates of office against him for ever;

[70] 17 Feb. 1852, *H* cxix. 686–7.
[71] 3 May 1847, *H* xcii. 306–7, 313. See also 26 Jan. 1847, *H* lxxxix. 493, and 17 Feb. 1847, *H* xc. 168–9.
[72] 6 June 1850, *H* cxi. 853–4; 22 May 1851, *H* cxvi. 1265–6.
[73] *Plymouth Journal*, 16 Apr. 1857, p. 8.

but in truth Sir John wants no office. The emoluments would be acceptable, no doubt; but the collar would be intolerable. He prefers to walk into the House his own master, unawed and uninterrupted by the "whips" who prowl at the door. Sir John belongs to a large and increasing party in the House, which the old politicians say will make stable government impossible, but which we are disposed to say will only make corrupt government difficult.[74]

At the time White was writing, in March 1859, the Liberal party was in a particularly disunited state, of course, and a large group of 'independent Liberals', with whom Trelawny was certainly associated, seemed inclined to maintain a minority Conservative administration in power rather than allow Palmerston to return to office.[75] It may be as well, therefore, to clarify Trelawny's attitude towards party. Though avowedly an 'independent' member,[76] what Trelawny understood by this term was that he was not in any way personally beholden to the party leadership; he did not mean that he was a 'non-party' politician. As the events of June 1859 show, for all his doubts about the feasibility of Liberal reunion, Trelawny acquiesced in the decision reached at the famous Willis's rooms meeting.[77] Trelawny's independence largely took the form of what has been termed 'extremist dissidence',[78] where he and other radicals found themselves at odds with a recalcitrant Whig ministerial-bench, who were unwilling to act on major issues of reform and content to rest secure in the knowledge that the Conservative opposition would not allow them to be defeated. This was not incompatible, however, with the existence of a fundamental two-party alignment in the House of Commons,[79] and when the Conservatives made what were recognised to be 'party attacks',[80] the position of radicals like Trelawny was clear. According to William White's definition, a radical was 'one who supports a Whig government in difficulties.'[81] On the rare occasions when Trelawny did go into the division lobby with the Conservatives, in defiance of the Liberal leadership, this was never undertaken in a gratuitous

[74] *Illustrated Times*, 26 Mar. 1859, p. 198.
[75] Cf. Gurowich, 'Party and Politics, 1855–1865', p. 609 and n. 45.
[76] Cf. diary, 18 and 23 Mar. 1859; 19 Feb. 1861.
[77] Diary, 3 and 6 June 1859.
[78] Hugh Berrington, 'Partisanship and dissidence in the nineteenth century House of Commons', *Parliamentary Affairs*, XXI, (1968), pp. 338–74.
[79] Confirmed by Valerie Cromwell's analysis, 'Mapping the political world of 1861: a multidimensional analysis of House of Commons division lists', *Legislative Studies Quarterly*, VII, (1982), pp. 281–97.
[80] E.g. diary, 24 July 1860; 11 Mar. 1861; 1 Aug. 1862; 18 Apr. 1864; 2 Mar. 1865; 2 May 1865.
[81] *Illustrated Times*, 9 Feb. 1861, p. 84.

spirit, but with the painful realisation that he might be considered 'almost an opponent of the party with which it has usually been my fate to act.'[82]

Trelawny would have regarded himself as essentially a 'practical' politician, content on the whole to operate behind the scenes, trying to influence those in positions of power, and caring little who got the credit for the final victory. Towards the end of his political career, he expressed his philosophy to a friend in the following way: 'what matters it who does a good work? The thing is to get the work done. I like to see good dogs laid on a scent and then find a fresh fox for myself.'[83] One further characteristic, on which all seem to have been agreed, was the great courtesy and consideration which Trelawny displayed in conducting his electoral campaigns and pursuing his political objectives; the injection of personal asperity into disputes was not a part of his style. Even the Conservative *Saturday Review* was ready to acknowledge the 'pleasant violence' of Trelawny's assault on the Church of England.[84] As William White observed, when lamenting Trelawny's decision to resign the leadership of the church rate issue in 1863, 'It is questionable ... whether the [abolition] party will ever again get so able and efficient a leader as Sir John. He was so politic, so courteous to his opponents, so wise in his generation.'[85]

---

[82] Diary, 17 June 1864.
[83] Trelawny to G.J. Holyoake, 27 May 1873, Holyoake MSS (microfilm copy, Seely History Library, Cambridge).
[84] *Saturday Review*, 20 Feb. 1858, pp. 187–8.
[85] *Illustrated Times*, 9 May 1863, p. 326.

EDITORIAL NOTE

It appears that Trelawny's practice was to make pencil notes during his attendance at parliamentary debates, and to write these up along with his other observations at a later stage, sometimes the next day. The text of the diaries was then corrected at leisure, usually for the purpose simply of improving the literary quality, and it is the corrected version that has therefore been followed in this edition. In a few cases, however, where a deletion seems to indicate a change of opinion or a significant toning down of a comment, the original version has also been included: these passages are printed within + signs. Trelawny used a facing page system, and sometimes added marginal comments on the left hand page with a symbol to indicate where these were intended to be inserted into the text: these passages have been printed within * signs.

In order to convey some of the flavour of the original document, it has been my policy to retain certain abbreviations which Trelawny used almost constantly, such as wd., shd., govt., and agt., as well as the ampersand, and to confine expansions to less familiar abbreviations which might disrupt the flow of the text. Trelawny's erratic capitalisation has also been adhered to. With regard to punctuation, however, it has been found necessary in places to make silent alterations in order to render the text more intelligible.

This edition of the Trelawny diaries contains approximately sixty-five percent of the original text. Much of the material that has been omitted is of a routine nature, or else has been judged to be unduly repetitive (he often used the diary to rehearse his arguments on the major issues with which he was concerned, such as the church rate abolition bill). Trelawny also frequently suffered from gout, and during his enforced absences from the House of Commons he relied heavily upon newspaper reports when writing up brief summaries of events in the diaries. It has therefore been possible to omit many such entries without loss to the value of the edition.

There are signs that Trelawny had it in mind that he might eventually publish his diaries, perhaps in the form of the writings of an anonymous observer, a style that was common in the journals of the day. If so, this may help to explain one peculiarity of the text: Trelawny's habit of referring to himself in the third person.

Brief biographical details of members of parliament have been included in the index, although certain information has sometimes been added in the footnotes where it seemed appropriate to do so.

The place of publication of all secondary works is London, unless otherwise stated.

The following abbreviations have been used throughout the footnotes:

H	*Hansard's Parliamentary Debates*, 3rd series.
P.P.	*Parliamentary Papers.*
B.F.S.P.	*British and Foreign State Papers.*

THE PARLIAMENTARY
DIARIES OF
SIR JOHN TRELAWNY

SESSION OF 1857–8[1]

Tuesday, 16 February: [. . .] Baillie came on with a motion on the Mutinies.[2] Palmerston appealed to him to give way. Baillie seemed to be replying to the appeal and all were looking for his withdrawal, when he at once slid into his subject. (General titter.) Members go to dinner.

8.20. Came down & found Baillie had done, and Lord John defending Dalhousie.[3] Oude for 55 years systematically broke treaties with us. Want of prudence: – not enough troops in Oudh to tread out opposition. Govt. shd. not have denuded India for Persian war.[4] He did not like the Russian war – but if the war were wise – more troops should have been sent. Dissertation on the vain phantom of 'prestige', which had ruined Napoleon at Moscow. This, too, we have been following in some of our Eastern wars.

Lord J. Manners – dull & documentary. Thin house – ominous gathering of leading Peelites. Graham, Gladstone & Herbert in eager confabulation.

9.15. Manners still shouting & throwing his arms about. House all talking – Peelites plotting. Manners proposed bravely to restore Oude to the King (oh! oh! & laughter).

Mangles on his legs. General understanding that there wd. be no division – so I went home to prepare for Church-rates.

While absent Thompson seems to have made a rash speech, expressing disbelief of Indian atrocities & characterizing our executions as acts of murder. (Oh! oh! Indignant speech from solemn Palk.) [. . .]

---

[1] Parliament had sat from 3 to 12 Dec. 1857, following the government's suspension of the Bank charter act, and reconvened on 4 Feb. 1858. The first surviving volume of Trelawny's diary begins on 15 Feb. 1858.

[2] Calling for papers relating to the annexation of Oude in 1856, with the implication that this was a major cause of the Indian mutiny; *H* cxlviii. 1477–95; agreed to.

[3] Who, as governor general of India, had been responsible for the annexation of Oude.

[4] Troops had been sent to Herat, against the Persians, in 1856.

Wednesday, 17 February: [...] I had expected that I should get a chance for Church-rates[5] – & so it proved.

I moved – & got through it pretty satisfactorily. Gen[era]l Thompson followed briefly. Then Lord R. Cecil replied in a very quiet & gentlemanly way – agreeing with many of my opinions as to the conduct of the Church of England.

Several speakers supported me – among others, Lord Stanley & Ball the tenant farmer's representative.[6]

Drummond opposed. The evil was a delusion. The House of Lords' decision was a scandalous decision.[7]

Hope they would not hear – nor Slaney. Sir Geo. Grey offered a feeble & ineffectual compromise[8] which I treated with disdain. I replied. We went to a division Ayes 213, Noes 160. So I won [...] Many people tried to persuade me not to divide. I resolved to do so – & all went well.

Drummond's line was that it is no more a grievance to pay a Church rate wh. a majority has carried than police rate under the same circumstances. Also, that it is not conscience, but money wh. is at the bottom of the grievance.

Cecil's point was of a kindred character, but he contended, also, that for 95 per cent of the Churches rates were not refused. His fallacy was exposed by Lord Stanley & Mr. Ball, the latter a dissenter, who yet for peace & because it is the law, pays his rates.

The return on wh. the 95 per cent argument is based is defective. It is so worded as to exclude large populations – 25,000 in Cambridge alone. The words are cities & 'parishes in Parl[iamentar]y boroughs'. But many parishes lie outside the boundaries of the Parl[iamentar]y Boro.

Also, many rates are only not refused because people prefer a quiet life – or dread law.

Then the return does not include a large number of Towns, where rates cannot be refused because no one thinks of asking for them.

I replied – commenting on Drummond's strong language in censure of the decision of the Lords. I said that, in the case of a minority of dissenters, he was severe enough, & yet he himself was in a minority & was not content to take the decision of the judges appointed by the

---

[5] 2nd reading of Trelawny's abolition bill; *P.P.* 1857–8, i. 341.

[6] Both Conservatives; Stanley being Lord Derby's son.

[7] I.e. in the Braintree case (1853), that the Church rate was illegal unless voted by a majority of attendants at the Vestry meeting.

[8] The home secretary repeated his proposal made at the time of Sir William Clay's bill (5 Mar. 1856), that abolition should only apply to parishes where rates had not been collected for a specified period of time, while dissenters in other parishes might claim exemption; *H* cxlviii. 1575–9.

majority & sitting in the Highest Court of appeal! I, also, addressed myself to the govt. & pointed out how the evil might be diminished by defining the legal objects of a Church rate, as dissenters might endure a rate for Churchyards – inter alia. Govt. shewed neither imagination or statesmanlike qualities.

I called Drummond a great 'Anarch' & mentioned the ratcatcher & fox-killing rates.[9] It was bad enough to kill foxes, but to kill them by a Church rate was a double desecration.

Thursday, 18 February: Postponed Church-rates to the first open Wednesday 21st April.

Mr. Speaker[10] called me to him & kindly said 'if you will permit me to say so, you made a very good speech'. I replied that he was very kind to say so, that I might, perhaps, have added more matter, but that I had a dislike to being documentary. He quite agreed.

Indian Debate[11] [...] I paired, returning at 10.50. Bulwer just finishing. Johnnie rises. 'A great crisis not the time?' We legislated three times in a crisis – Catholic question, Corn Laws, Reform Bill. The suspense an evil. Argued that some decision must be taken, & a larger force of Queen's troops sent. This virtually breaks down the Company, because you ought not to trust the Company with too large a force. Something absurd in certain proprietors of stock selecting the Govt. of a nation. He would be quite ready to join any man who proposed a practical amendment in details. His fears of the angry discussion of Indian matters in this House. There always will be men who will doubt the competence or honesty of Govt. or perhaps both; (a laugh) – but this sort of discussion is a condition of our existence. Peroration about millions & providence.

Dizzy dwelt on what he called the real point – finance, which will be the weekly subject of discussion in the House.

Palmerston laughs at the physical exertions of Bulwer & Whiteside. Whether B. excited conviction in the House by 'the speech they had just *seen*' – or not – he must certainly have excited envy in Whiteside (great laughter). Both in fact rant.

Newdegate attempts to be heard. 'Divide divide'! 'Oh! Oh'! groans.

[9] Returns from Streatham, Surrey, and Sydenham, Kent, showed that these expenses had been paid for out of church rates; *H* cxlviii. 1582.

[10] John Evelyn Denison.

[11] Continued debate on the Government of India bill, introduced by Palmerston on 12 Feb. The bill ended the system of dual control from London by the East India Company and the Board of Control, replacing it with a council of India consisting of eight nominated members, presided over by a Cabinet minister. *P.P.*, 1857–8, ii. 267.

Tremendous row, and he sat down. Speaker puts question[12] In the midst Newdegate again tries to be heard. 'Order order' – put down again.

Note: – When Vernon Smith shook his head, Bulwer should not have said, 'The Hon[oura]ble member shakes his head, but I doubt if there is anything in it'.

Friday, 19 February [...] Conspiracy Bill.[13] Pam deprecated nickname Alien Bill. + Gibson's Amendment – weak and a mere refinement. + Gibson moves a cleverly worded amendment.[14] Excellent point on the non-recommendation by the Statute Law Commission to alter the law of treason. Great speech. 55 minutes. Well heard, & greatly cheered. Gibson stronger than ever. Strong things levelled at Palmerston. His position is seriously damaged.

Baines replying 5.40. Benches at once lost most of their occupants. The rest buzz. Gave it up in $\frac{1}{4}$ of an hour.

Walpole accused Government of neglecting their duty. Liked the Bill, but first required the satisfaction of the honor of England. I hear he will support Gibson's resolution, which delays the Bill till certain opinions have been expressed by us.

Grey very warm but feeble. McMahon – lawyer – (Johnnie[15] in confab with Gibson – Tories looking on). McMahon argued ably that the bill might be as bad as an alien bill in operation. He pointed out, to his own satisfaction, how.

Byng for Gibson $\frac{1}{4}$ past 8. A neat learnt speech of $\frac{1}{4}$ of an hour.

Spooner for Bill. Peel & White dying to speak: also, Lawyer Mellor. Plot thickens.

Harry Vane – pompous platitudes. Will support the Bill – but did not think there was much in it (ironical cheers from the House– & laughter – near nine, House filling) – refining & splitting hairs.

---

[12] Thomas Baring's amendment that it was not expedient at present to legislate for the government of India, defeated 318:145; 1st reading of bill passed.

[13] 2nd reading of the conspiracy to murder bill, making conspiracy a felony rather than a misdemeanour. This was a response to demands for action by France after the assassination attempt on the Emperor Napoleon III by a group of Italian nationalists, led by Felice Orsini, who had operated from Britain.

[14] Trelawny had evidently modified his assessment of the utility of Gibson's amendment, which did not attack the conspiracy bill as such, but condemned the government's failure to give a formal answer to the despatch from Count Walewski, the French foreign minister (which was conveyed to his British counterpart and laid on the table of the House of Commons), calling for Britain's help in suppressing revolutionary movements and guaranteeing France's security. By giving no formal answer to this despatch. Gibson contended, the government had implicitly admitted that Britain was harbouring assassins; *H* cxlviii. 1745–58.

[15] Lord John Russell.

Approves of both amendment & Bill (laughter). [...] Peel.[16] A slashing English speech. Remarkable & even executive style. Genius, & occasional naivete. His very blunders full of humour. Pronunciation half French. 'Pretendant' for 'Pretender', 'Antecedent'. Very severe on Pam whom he has unmasked. Praises Lord John & the 3 Peelite chiefs Graham, Gladstone & Sidney Herbert. House in roars of laughter at his jokes & sarcasms.

Henley. Lord Advocate.[17] Neither remarkable. Gladstone. Very urgent, severe, eloquent & inflammatory. The House seems not unlikely to follow his views. Downward & backward movement in Europe. Responsibility centres in the Institutions of England.

Deprecates moral complicity with retrogressive policies.

Att[orne]y Gen[era]l[18] Would not cope in declamation but would utter a few faithful words (laugh). Long legal arguments to prove that the law would only put the foreigner in the same position as an Englishman.

Dizzy. Very good. Reserves to himself to oppose Bill on it's merits; meanwhile agrees with Gibson. Thinks it essential to the honor of England to support the resolution.[19] Very keen & caustic.

Pam. Tuquoque to Gibson. He has ransacked old newspapers. Luckily for him he has not turned over the records of his own words & deeds. Gibson's policy a policy of submission. He had even reached furious invective agst. Gibson (cries of question!). Pam in a rage. Lost himself. Calls on House calmly to consider &c. (Great laughter. 'Divide! Divide!'). He is losing himself more & more, & is laughed at more & more each sentence. Division. Hayter[20] biting his fingers in an awful frame of mind. Ayes 215. Noes 234. Govt. beaten. Great cheering.

I voted with Gibson on the ground that his motion was true in words & was the best means available of throwing out the bill. But I would have preferred to negative the bill at once.

Monday, 22 February: Great gathering to bury Palmerston's ministry. Members compelled to hear private business much agst. the grain. $\frac{1}{4}$ past 4. Roebuck presents the Petition charging I. Butt with

---

[16] Sir Robert Peel, son of the former prime minister.

[17] James Moncrieff.

[18] Sir Richard Bethell.

[19] Gibson's amendment enabled the Conservatives to oppose the government without opposing the Conspiracy bill itself. Lord Derby had earlier given ministers the impression that he would help them to pass the bill; Angus Hawkins, *Paliament, Party and the Art of Politics in Britain, 1855–59*, (1987), pp. 97–8, 104–6.

[20] Government chief whip.

corruption.[21] R. reads the substance thereof. Proposes a plan of dealing with it by a Committee.

Butt's gallant defence, demanding of the House, not out of the natural sympathy of gentlemen with a gentleman so accused, but out of justice to himself, that the foul charge should be investigated as soon as the forms of the House wd. admit (great cheers). On concluding he withdrew. [...] Names read of Committee proposed. The few first were names of leading Derbyites sure to be in the Cabinet. Their names, as severally proposed, produced much merriment, as their objections to serve let 'the cat out of the bag'. Thus, Henley & Manners could not act. The number of the Committee is to be 7. Bright advised this – & one or two of his suggestions obtained acquiescence. He seemed to see his way more clearly than the govt. or Dizzy. It was a curious thing to watch the working of a popular assembly compelled to come to a practical conclusion suited to difficult & pressing circumstances. Somehow or other, in spite of the number of talkers, the House emerged from its difficulty &, having constituted its tribunal, appointed Roebuck & Serj[ean]t Deasy as prosecutor & defender.

Palmerston now, in a firm & short speech, stated the fact of the Ministerial resignation – adding that an adjournment had been agreed upon with Lord Derby till Friday. In 2 minutes the House was all but empty. So, I went home – with my cold.

Is it not an alarming sign of the times that, in the amusement excited by circumstances arising in debate, the House should appear to have forgotten altogether the heavy charge brought agt. one of its members? One would have expected of a Senate a grave, serious – & anxious demeanour. One of two members is almost sure to be damaged in reputation, &, if the charge be proved, the character of the House must suffer. On the contrary, the House seemed to be entirely wrapt up in the present enjoyment & the anticipation of pleasure to come in the announcement the existing govt. might make [...]

Friday, 26 February: House meets whilst new govt. is in its infancy.

Droll appearance – members having generally changed places. Eccentric people assert their characteristics.

Graham adhered to his old seat – is it that he is above the accidents of party? Drummond, too, who talks on all sides, is at least determined to be constant to one thing – or is it that there is no fear lest anyone

---

[21] A petition from Edward Lees Coffey, of Sheffield, alleging that in 1856 Issac Butt, M.P. for Youghal, had entered into a corrupt agreement with the Ameer Ali Moorad Khan, by which he received money in return for advocating the recovery of the Ameer's territory (Sind), which had been annexed by the East India Company.

shd. infer his opinions from the locality he adopts?[22] Cardwell on the 1st. seat above the gangway on the bench behind the ex ministers. This looks as if he had disconnected himself from the orthodox Peelites.

After a little time, the calm, sly, half-smiling ex-attorney (Bethell) glides up the House, like 'the Jesuit in the family', & as if by inadvertence, walks to his old place on the govt. side (great laughter).

Palmerston now enters (considerable Whig cheering).

New writs are now moved.[23] Dizzy's – (silence).

Lord Stanley's – (some expressions like dissatisfied surprize).

Thesiger's[24] – (cheers of kindly congratulation from all sides) [...]

Monday, 1 March: [...] Cardwell [...] shewed symptoms of restiveness;[25] &, if I am not deceived, he will yet give the govt. trouble. As will Horsman & others. The plot thickens. We are already making preparations for aggressive movement. We are going to take up army reform in a comprehensive manner so as to divide the labor, alloting special grievances to particular members [...]

Friday, 12 March: The reappearance of the govt. on its formation & after the elections for vacant seats.

Dizzy gives a statement of satisfactory termination of the dispute with France.[26] (Great cheers – swelling from his side to ours – real satisfaction drowning party feeling.) Graham, however, looks very sulky &, also, contemptuous – this is a way of the arch Peelite.

[...] Govt. benches look very spare. Liberals in good muster.

Rich requires a statement of general policy. O'Brien in the same sense, but going further & severely criticizing the discrepancies betwn. the speeches of governmt. candidates at elections. He went in at them like an Irish mameluke – a regular enfant terrible. The Derbyites look very crestfallen. Kinglake now interposes – 'across the scent' with his Cagliari question regarding the 2 English engineers detained by the Neapolitans.[27] In matter good, he was too long – also very prosy and documentary. Patience of the House sorely tried. At length, good

---

[22] He always sat on the ministerial side, regardless of party; cf. *Illustrated Times*, 9 July 1859.

[23] Under the place act of 6 Anne c. 7 members had to gain re-election on accepting a place of profit under the Crown.

[24] Appointed Lord Chancellor (Lord Chelmsford).

[25] On the India loan bill.

[26] Arising from the Orsini affair; see the despatches in *B.F.S.P.*, xlix. 1249–52.

[27] In June 1857 the Cagliari, a Sardinian mailboat, had been taken over by carbonarists who proceeded to release a number of prisoners from the island of Ponza and then made their escape on the Italian mainland. Soon afterwards, the Cagliari, whose crew included two English engineers, Park and Watt, was arrested by a Neopolitan ship. Park and Watt were imprisoned and maltreated, the latter losing his sanity.

nature gave way – & the fatal words fell 'Read read'. Some signs of sitting down (cheers).

Dizzy replies timid, tentative, feeble & deprecatory. He declared that govt. were doing the best they could with the case as they found it & he expressed a hope that amiable language would be used [...] Roebuck very warm. 'An Englishman driven mad by illegal treatment & the Minister calls for amiable language!' *His* amiable language would be a line of battleship & cannon balls.

Horsman in the same line of business – position of England humiliating. Sardinia was doing her work.[28] (Govt. wince – they have an earnest of good things to come). He (H) demands the fullest information – on this & all other diplomatic matters (cheers).

Gladstone agrees that Horsman's proposal should be acceded to. He was ashamed that the duty of vindicating England had fallen to the hands of feeble Sardinia.

Palmerston sees no objection to the production of papers down to the time of his resignation. The facts of the capture, now known, altered the original aspect of the case.[29] Milnes supports.

Seymour Fitzgerald's (under-foreign sec[re]t[ar]y) reply not amiss – but tone still deprecatory.

John Russell rises from his seat below the gangway (cheers). Good stuff from the right post – calls for information.

Osborne unmuzzled after 5 years[30] – (tremendous cheers at the return of the old favourite – the House's jester).

Dwells upon the neglect of Tories to describe policy. They have come into power – or, rather, into office (great laughter). He intended to use most forbearing language (renewed laughter).

Dizzy was a great reformer – if he would but weed his party – among others of the premier.[31] He (B. O.) would not give any money without a programme. He would, that refused, concoct a resolution with the assistance of the great artist in motions – the hon[oura]ble MP for Ashton-under-Lyme (Milner Gibson).

Supply followed – numerous speakers to little purpose. A very ridiculous, whining & contemptible speech of Townsend MP for Greenwich who, almost a mendicant, pleaded on behalf (as he said) of his constituents. Dockyard labourers seeking increase of pay. He

---

[28] The foreign office at Turin had taken the lead in condemning the action of the Neapolitan government; *The Times*, 1 Feb 1858, p. 9, 19 Feb 1858, p. 12.

[29] It had emerged that the Cagliari had been arrested on the high seas and not, as originally thought, in Neapolitan waters.

[30] Ralph Bernal Osborne had been parliamentary secretary to the admiralty under both Aberdeen and Palmerston.

[31] Lord Derby.

entreated – he implored – he beseeched – he &c till one was ashamed to sit by him.

[...] India Loan Bill. Dizzy deprecates opposition – withdrawing 2 objectionable clauses; one giving the company power to borrow indefinitely in England; the other, making the amount in all £10,000,000. As it stands, 8 millions will be the amount. Cardwell accepts the bill, as altered, in a short, clear & cogent speech.

Saturday, 13 March: [...] Note. It seems to be thought that the new govt. have already made a capital blunder in not seizing the opportunity of insisting upon the release of the 2 engineers, afforded by the discovery that the capture was illegal. Lord P[almerston] has already cut the ground from under their feet by indicating that his course was taken under a different impression.

Monday, 15 March: [...] Report of supply. Osborne to the fore – a regular onslaught. He rallied the Derbyites in general – as having no principle or contrary principles. He produced merriment by criticizing his late chief[32] for carelessness. His speech was clever & amusing as usual, but not calculated to raise his position in the House. One good point: Disraeli had spoken of the Reform Bill as a gross Whig job, and yet Lord Derby had been one of the Ministers who carried it.[33]

He (Osborne) rallied the attorney general for almost Chartist opinions.[34] He twitted Stanley with his support of the Church rate Abolition Bill, and doubted whether the radical aeneas would be able to carry on his shoulders the Conservative Anchises. He much feared some Dido would come in the way.

He reminded the House of Disraeli's treatment of Peel – 'the organised hypocrisy' – 'the Whigs caught bathing & plundered of their clothes' – 'the great middlemen who robbed one party & bamboozled the other with the cry "no principles but fixity of tenure"'.

Disraeli. Successful enough. Congratulated the House on Osborne's release from thraldom – yet thought his wit had grown somewhat rusty & would be improved by use.

Plenty of counterhits & attacks upon opponents on the ground of their inconsistencies. Banter about Reform so often postponed. (Lord John walks up the House to Palmerston & seems to ask a question, then retires behind the Speaker's chair. Johnny returns – & then

---

[32] Palmerston.

[33] Lord Derby, as E.G. Stanley, had been Irish chief secretary in Lord Grey's government at the time of the great reform act.

[34] See *The Times*, 8 Mar 1858, p. 4, for Sir Fitzroy Kelly's speech at Ipswich.

Hayter[35] sits down in the gangway close by him in conference. What is up?)

Disraeli goes on to promise a Reform Bill, which will not be devised to bolster up a party, and will, he earnestly hoped, give *universal* satisfaction. (Great laughter.) But his government was said to be in a minority. 'Why, that's the question!' He would not admit that his party was weaker than Pam's or Johnnie's. (Sits down amid great cheering.) Horsman disagrees with Osborne. Good strong observations on the characteristics of Lord Palmerston, in relying on dexterity in managing his foes, than in conciliating friends. He should have evinced solid fidelity to great principles. H. denounced Palmerston's shabby nepotism in dispensing offices. Nothing can be worse than to have neither a liberal govt. or liberal opposition. Lord John – agreed with Disraeli so far as this: Does not consider a declaration of Policy in a new govt. necessary. Expects to disagree but will not embarrass govt [...]

Lord John observed very emphatically &, avec intention *thought* that 'We have very little security for Reform from Disraeli'. Palmerston follows, & replies to Horsman on his charge – that he looked for support to opponents. Of course he looked for it wherever he could get it. Tone conciliatory towards liberals. Claims credit for war management & for participation in all great liberal measures. Leaves his reputation to the impartial verdict of history [...] I gather that Palmerston & Johnnie are no longer irreconcilable & so says Rumour.

Tuesday, 16 March: [...] Supply. Disraeli earned credit by a frank statement that money should only be applied to the purposes for which it has been voted. Vid. 26 & 27th clauses of the approp[riatio]n act.

[...] The Tory government still yield everything demanded from them. One may move for Committees & returns ad libitum. They want to stand well with the radicals – also, perhaps, having been long out of office, they have no fear of publicity, but might derive advantage from it by comparison. Perhaps, after Easter when in the saddle, they will be less compliant. By that time they will have done something they will be glad to hush up.

Thursday, 18 March: [...] During the evening a good speech was made by Ayrton on the subject of profligate bribery at the Galway election, openly avowed in his place by Sir Thomas Burke. To what is Parliament fallen! Of what use are committees of inquiry on electoral corruption if members can accuse themselves of it in the open Senate –

---

[35] Whig whip.

amid roars of laughter? It seems Dunkellin & Clanricarde are mixed up in the business[36] *feel whether it is safe to print this.*

Monday, 22 March: [...] the Jews had a victory of nearly 2 to 1.[37] Of course I voted in the majority. [...] I think nothing very new was said – it was a regular debate of a debating society. The alterior object of the motion – ie, beyond the question of religious liberty – is the reconstitution of the liberal party & the creation of a difficulty in the way of government. A bill of this kind binds the party together – & it is time that liberals should be seen together in the same lobby.

NB. I noted, early in the evening, that Lord John went over & sat with Graham, chatting & laughing for a long time – say 20 minutes. He would not have done this last session. Something is 'looming' – as Disraeli would say.

Thursday, 25 March: Lord Lieutenant Abolition Bill.[38] Roebuck brief & rather tame, but irreproachable. House languid – & as usual sceptical. S. B. Miller moves previous question – not the time. Feeble & wordy. Colonel French – heavy & dull. House weary. Lord Naas[39] – quiet & gentlemanly. I heard only part – but I gathered that he concurred with Miller. The change must be assented to by the Irish people. Cornewall Lewis – office a relic of provincial or colonial system of government. Yet, he was averse to the substitution of a new secretary of State for Ireland. We must look to abolition when Ireland can be governed without special & local organisation. (Graham goes over to Lord John – more symptoms of approaching combinations?) Lewis splits hairs – & seems to be concluding. Several jump up – he goes on again (great hilarity) [...] Some Tory (Blackburn) M.P. for Stirling, speaks well for motion (Hayter in conference with Lord John) [...] Baxter agrees with Roebuck – indeed he wants a secretary for Scotland as he can never discover who is responsible for Scotch affairs. As a financial Reformer he is favourable to the measure. Johnny Russell goes up & shakes hands with Palmerston, & remains chatting. Disraeli looks black as thunder. Perhaps Baxter's allusion to the budget discomposed him.[40]

---

[36] For the culture of electoral corruption in county Galway, where Lord Dunkellin and the Marquess of Clanricarde exercised great influence, see K. Theodore Hoppen, *Elections, Politics and Society in Ireland 1832–1885*, (Oxford, 1984), pp. 76, 146, 155.

[37] House in committee, discussing Russell's oaths bill. Newdegate's amendment to omit the 5th clause, allowing jews to sit in parliament, rejected by 297:144.

[38] Roebuck's resolution for the abolition of the Lord Lieutenancy of Ireland and its replacement with a secretary of state; *H* cxlix. 766–9.

[39] Irish chief secretary.

[40] Baxter had described Disraeli as an 'excellent Liberal', and urged him to begin his work of reducing the estimates by ending the 'unnecessary outlay' on the Lord Lieutenancy; *H* cxlix. 749–51.

Dobbs – good, & Fortescue of Louth follow. Latter characterized Roebuck as a member of rather a destructive character (much mirth). Several speakers more, Lord John feeble. He votes with government, because by moving the previous question, they rather affirm the policy recommended.[41] This evoked Walpole,[42] who spoke for retaining the office & ought logically to oppose his own colleague Naas. Lord John put government in this difficulty. Lord Palmerston followed suit like Lord John. Roebuck replies with great humour & sarcasm – reminding Naas & Lord John, & all the late government of their former vote[43] & causing great merriment. A first rate reply & then Division.[44] I voted with Roebuck [. . .]

Friday, 26 March: Questions. India Bill (No. 2).[45] Disraeli develops govt. plan & explains why he adopted a principle embodied in the bill of the late govt. So far as the abolition of the Company is concerned The House had by a great vote decided that point.

It strikes me that White's criticisms on the mixed nominee & representative constitution of the proposed India governt. are sound. The two parties will, probably, soon be in hostile array.

Bright & Roebuck are evidently opposed to the bill. The Bill of the late Cabinet seems to be preferred by many Liberals. Will Lord Palmerston make India his battlefield? Bright spoke out very strongly agt. the return of the late govt. to power – consequently, Lord P. can hardly expect Bright's vote in order to compass that event. We shall have a row after Easter [. . .]

Monday, 12 April:[46] [. . .] Lord John recommends resolutions in committee of Whole House.[47]

---

[41] Russell affected to believe that the government was not disinclined to consider the question, and he therefore urged them to devise a measure more acceptable to the Irish than Roebuck's bill; *H* cxlix. 766–9.

[42] Home secretary.

[43] In May 1850 Russell, then Prime Minister, had introduced his own abolition bill, and Naas had spoken in favour of it.

[44] 243:116 against the resolution.

[45] The Derby ministry's alternative to Palmerston's bill, also provided for the abolition of the system of dual control. A Council of India, presided over by a minister of the rank of secretary of state, was to consist of eighteen members nominated by the Crown, five members elected by the cities of London, Manchester, Liverpool, Glasgow and Belfast, and four members elected by a constituency consisting of certain British subjects resident in India; *P.P.* 1857–8, ii. 287.

[46] The House had resumed after the Easter recess.

[47] I.e. that the government should drop its India bill and allow a committee to draw up resolutions providing the basis for a new measure. Russell's action had been pre-arranged with ministers. Originally, he had intended to oppose the bill outright, but, along with the Peelites and many Radicals, had feared that this would lead to the restoration of Palmerston to power; Hawkins, *Art of Politics*, pp. 124–30.

D'Israeli does not shrink from the idea [...] Sir C. Wood considers that this was abdication. Edward Ellice agreed. One Govt. enough at a time. Walpole – decorous platitudes, denies the abdication. Mangles says a few words in favor of E[ast] I[ndia] C[ompany].

Palmerston thinks the bill should be discussed, as usual, clause by clause in Comm[itt]]ee. Waste of time & inconvenient precedent to adopt the plan proposed. Dizzy does not like the charge of abdication. He will place resolutions on the table of the House this day fortnight.

Bouverie demurs. Govt. jump at opportunity of getting rid of Bill. The course was novel and unusual. Practical absurdities of the rival positions of bill and resolutions. It was abdication [...] Horsman – good speech, deprecates party proceeding. Delay of a year less inconvenient than premature action.

Supply. Voted agst. Williams's proposal to refer the Estimates to a Select Comm[itt]ee.[48] Gain nothing by it [...]

Tuesday, 13 April: [...] Ricardo brought on the Stade Dues[49] in a good speech. Government suggest to him to have a comm[itt]ee on the subject – to the propriety of which Palmerston demurs, as not the proper mode of proceeding. This brought down Horsman upon him. There were several speeches – no division. (Mem[orandum]: Symptoms today as in the debate of yesterday, of a tendency among the Radicals and Tories, to be mutually forebearing, in joint antagonism to Palmerston, whose criticisms seem to carry no favour, and who makes no progress in uniting the Liberal party. The truth is: the breach seems daily widening between politicians of the school of Horsman & Lord John on the one hand, and the ex-government on the other. The Manchester School especially implacable towards Palmerston.)

Sir J. Trelawny brought on his motion upon the Coffey's petition case.[50] A lively and interesting debate followed. A considerable number of the experienced members thought that a new resolution might rather tend to narrow the old principle of the House, that members ought not to vote on matters on which they are interested. So Trelawny accepted the suggestion to withdraw. A very few demurred.

[48] Defeated by 161:24; *H* cxlix. 878–82.

[49] A toll levied on goods en route to Hamburg by the Hanoverian town of Stade, on the river Elbe.

[50] See above, 22 Feb., for the allegation of corruption brought against Isaac Butt, M.P., by Edward Lees Coffey. On 12 Mar., Sir James Graham's select committee had reported that the allegation was untrue, but that Butt had received money from the Ameer of Sind; *H* cxlix. 75–6. Dissatisfied with this outcome, Trelawny now moved that rewards to members should be condemned as a high breach of parliamentary privilege; *H* cxlix. 1019–21.

Monday, 19 April: [...] The Budget. Disraeli surpassed himself. He made a lucid & comprehensive statement. He laid bare the actual difficulties of the country – discussed the diff[eren]t plans open to him – threw in a stroke of humour here & there, &, finally, proposed a plan which the country will not, I think, much complain of & which his foes in the House will be puzzled to defeat.

The fact is there is a deficit of 4 millions.[51] Of this $1\frac{1}{2}$ might be got rid of by merely suspending the operation of the sinking fund – which he considered as liable to criticism unless they are the effect of a bona fide surplus. The other 2 millions consist of exchequer bonds wh. are not to be paid at the time fixed. As to the remaining £500,000, he proposed to equalize the spirit duties (now lower in Ireland) & impose 1d. stamp on cheques.[52]

He made fun of the poor Irishmen – holding them out equal govenment, forsooth! in a 'cordial spirit' – with other jests to match – all well received. I noted that he was not long – about one hour & half.

The Irish chiefly followed – Grogan – Pat O'Brien – & so on – all very fluent and funereal [...]

Wednesday, 21 April: I presented 23 petitions agst. Church-rates. I proposed to go into Committee. Packe made a stolid amendment.[53] Considerable discussion followed. Bright made a speech in his best manner. Gladstone, also, spoke – as wordy as usual & leaving his views entirely in the dark. At last, we got into Committee. Two amendments proposed to clause one.[54] Neither successful, although no division. Lygon moved to report progress. This was evidently the game of the Tories for fear of progress and defeat on the main question. D'Israeli rose and put it to the House to get on with the Bill – the principle of which was affirmed – showing equal solemnity & fairness. He was well understood. We divided; and had an enormous majority of over 3 to 1.[55] And so the field day ended.

Thursday, 22 April: Good speech of Wise, proposing to bring diplomatic expenses under the immediate control of Parliament.[56] Some of them escaped notice, being charged on the consolidated fund. The

---

[51] Trelawny mistakenly wrote $4\frac{1}{2}$ millions.

[52] The other main provision of the budget was the reduction of the income tax from 7d. to 5d. in the £.

[53] To delay the bill for six months.

[54] Stating that no church rates should be levied in any parish of England and Wales once the bill had been passed.

[55] 346:104 against reporting progress.

[56] *H* clxix. 1496–1508.

British Public pay dearly & are ill served. Numerous consulates & missions might be consolidated. Recommendations of a parl-[iamentar]y Committee not attended to. No public school of oriental languages, as in France. Most of the good places given to the connexions of the Peerage – hard working places excepted. Diplomatic Officers do not rise gradually to the top of the tree, but new & incapable men foisted upon the service. No pupil consuls in our Service. The fine gentlemen unpaid attaches, having no interest in – or sympathy with – commerce, & little knowledge of their business. We were opposed by Lord Palmerston & Lord John – as well as the Govt; and yet we divided 114 to 142. Tremendous & protracted cheering – the Radicals making a good fight against Whigs and Tories combined. Trelawny went home, gouty, after this vote, & lost an unimportant division on an Irish row, involving a question of fact, which, being Irish, was insoluble by evidence.[57]

Friday, 23 April: [...] Navy Estimates: A very substantial point made agst. the arrangements of Haslar,[58] for hauling up 40 gun-boats. Bentinck led; Sailor Sir J. Elphinstone backed him; & scarcely any but civilians took the other side. Cost for the place for stowing these gunboats – £70,000. The gun-boats can't be launched under many weeks, as the operation depends on tide & the boats can only be launched one at a time. The proper way would be to keep them afloat, so as to be ready at a moment's notice, at little or no cost. Right being on our side, we divided; but the cowards threw us over; so we were beaten by a large majority[59] [...]

Monday, 26 April: India Question. D'Israeli moves that his resolutions[60] have precedence next Friday. He makes a speech rather applicable to his India Bill than to his motion as it stood – defending at length & with minuteness the various proposals submitted in his recent speech in explanation of his Bill. Now, most people would have thought that the less he said of his ill-starred measure the better – & that the resolutions afforded him a capital opportunity of escaping the ridicule attaching to his fantastic composition – especially, the elective portion of the project giving to the 5 great cities the selection of members of the India Board. The House fairly laughed in his face at some of his arguments – yet, he was felicitous in his sarcasm as

[57] Concerning Bagwell's motion for a select committee to inquire into the problem of destitution in county Donegal; *H* cxlix. 1525–7.

[58] In Gosport.

[59] 224:26; Bentinck and Elphinstone having declined to support Briscoe's motion to omit the vote of £5,000 for Haslar.

[60] Substituted for the Government of India (no. 2) bill.

usual & sustained attention well, producing the average amount of merriment.

Lord Palmerston was in his glory – cutting jokes & letting off cracker after cracker in the face of the govt. If the govt. bill was good, why did they kill it? was the argument of his speech.

Gladstone followed, deprecating change. He seems on the whole contented with the Company's government & most people think they have still a kick left. We might indeed go further & fare worse. The Company has done certain work not altogether amiss.

Will the new plan work any better? [...]

Tuesday, 27 April: Locke King proposes to extend the County franchise.[61] Disraeli moves previous question – holding out, however prospects of some sort of Reform Bill.

Lord John Russell & Labouchere shew some favour to the motion of L. K.

The Question is put as if the Tories really meant to divide, when no one claims a division on their side – & so, amid great cheers & laughter, the Bill is allowed to come in – in defiance of our strong government. The fact is Lord John Russell is governing.

After some other questions of little note, Puller moves his reactionary & impracticable Church rate scheme. He made a very fair speech, which was very well received by the Govt. People & naturally enough as he gave them more than they have got – viz, a certain & permanent rate – fixing the charge as a land tax on the property which has heretofore paid it [...] Puller wanted to withdraw – the radicals forced a division when we beat the mover by a prodigious majority of course[62] [...] The Tories paid the penalty for the factious course of last Wednesday, when they took advantage of the approaching hour of six o'clock & moved an adjournment in order to prevent a division on the main question. Of this I reminded them. Lygon denied that he was actuated by 'factious' motives – the word is his – I never used it – as I merely described the course pursued. The whole lesson is a good one. The radicals would not let him get a first reading of his Bill,[63] wh., returning good for evil, I was disposed (as I said) to allow him.

Wednesday, 28 April: Agricultural Statistics. Caird's Bill, not com-

---

[61] 1st reading of his annual bill to extend the £10 borough household franchise to the counties.

[62] 317:54.

[63] To exempt dissenters from payment of church rates; *H* cxlix. 1869–71.

pulsory.[64] I voted with him – induced, partly, by a very lucid & argumentative speech of Cardwell. Young Du Cane as I heard distinguished himself.[65] On the whole, it was a dull Wednesday.

Thursday, 29 April: A Maynooth motion.[66] Old Spooner & Newdegate have their annual field day. The former opened briefly – merely reading some documents in support of a few propositions. The old Man is evidently breaking up. He could scarcely read his papers – even with the aid of an enormous pair of coloured spectacles. The liberal party said nothing.

Walpole[67] gave two or three reasons agt. the motion. Newdegate & Spooner briefly followed amid very loud cries of 'divide' & we proceeded to a division, winning easily.[68] Of course, I opposed Spooner – as usual. Thank god! this question has come at last to be regarded as both ridiculous & impracticable. + May bigotry always assume that aspect! +

Friday, 30 April: We got into Committee by a large majority; and then recommenced the great Indian question.[69] Mangles and Sykes[70] stood out manfully for the Company. Horsman delivered a good set speech, more appropriate to the 2d. reading of a bill than a debate in committee. Gladstone drew several nice distinctions & was replied to with satirical elaborateness by D'Israeli who affected to entertain minute points of criticism which in his mind he really laughed at; & so the first great resolution passed[71] [...]

Tuesday, 4 May: Great debate on Gladstone's motion – to give a certain tone to the conduct of our minister who attends the conference at Paris on the Danubian principalities question.[72] The mover was

[64] His aim was to obtain voluntary returns of the acreage of land under cultivation, *H*. cxlix. 1871—9; defeated by 241:135.

[65] Opposing Caird; *H* cxlix. 1182–8.

[66] For an inquiry into the annual grant from the consolidated fund to the Catholic seminary of Maynooth, in Ireland.

[67] Home secretary.

[68] 210:155.

[69] The fourteen resolutions drawn up in lieu of the government of India bill; *H* cxlix. appendix.

[70] Directors of the East India Company.

[71] That it was expedient to transfer the government of India to the Crown.

[72] I.e. the future of Moldavia and Wallachia, formerly part of the Ottoman empire, whose position had been left unsettled at the end of the Crimean war. Gladstone's motion called for the desire for unification as Rumania, expressed by a representative assembly (divan) of the principalities, to be given due weight at the conference; *H* cl. 44–66.

very eloquent, and riveted the H. of C. for a full hour. The drift of his speech was the importance of creating a liberal power as a balance against Russia. The deliberate wishes of those peoples ought to be attended to in the conferences.

Seymour Fitzgerald replied – not unskilfully. It would be a most unusual & perhaps injurious thing to send the minister to the conferences with any bias of the kind proposed. His answer was mainly technical, questioning, too, some of Gladstone's assertions of fact.

[...] Palmerston showed, as might be expected, great knowledge of the subject, arguing that the Wallachian principalities, if treated as perfectly free & perfectly disconnected with the Suzerainty of the Porte, would never maintain themselves against Russia. There was no barrier, there were no fortresses: – it would be isolation.

Lord John combated these views, stigmatizing our conduct at the Peace as unwise.

D'Israeli was very brilliant.

Gladstone replied; & was beaten by 2 to 1.[73] [...]

Thursday, 6 May: A tedious whine on tenant-right. Motion refused by a large majority,[74] with whom I voted.

Caird proposed to introduce a Scotch 40/- franchise, in a plain business like speech. Considerable discussion. The opposition was chiefly that of whigs above the gangway – who yet said they meant to allow the first reading – wherat radicals & tories laughed sneeringly. It was said that the motion originated with a certain clerical agitator in Scotland, which was the only thing of weight I heard against it. I voted with Caird in the minority.[75]

[...] Locke King followed, with a second reading of the Property Qualification bill.[76] Bentinck feebly opposed; when up gets old Miles of Somersetshire & fairly laughs him out of court, giving up the whole case, & with it one of the great 'pillars of the British constitution'! The Whigs must have felt very uneasy, for here were the Tories admitting one point of the Charter! More remarkable still, the Home Secretary (Walpole) in a brief & unanswerable speech, shivered the law to atoms. It seemed to be generally admitted that a large number of members had no qualification at all, though they solemnly declared they had. The law does not, in fact, ensure independence in the

---

[73] 292:114.

[74] 232:43 against Greer's motion for a select committee.

[75] 103:84 against the 1st reading. In Scotland, contrary to England and Wales, there was only a £10 freehold franchise for the counties.

[76] To abolish the requirement, laid down by the Act 9 Anne c. 5, that borough M.P.s must own landed property worth at least £300 per annum and county M.P.s property worth at least £600 per annum; Royal assent, 26 June.

candidate as alleged, and as to it's preventing speculative candidates being put in nomination, they were sufficiently deterred by election expenses. One sentiment of Locke King was responded to favorably, even by Bentinck – that, if Chartists got into the House, they were better there than out of it, on the principle of a safety-valve, & because their opinions generally became modified. Bill read a second time nem:con.

Monday, 10 May: Cardwell gives notice of a great motion, wh. it is thought may oust the present govt. It is a motion in censure of the conduct of Lord Ellenborough for the Indian Despatch.[77] Evidently, there is a storm brewing [...]

Oaths Bill. Lord John proposes to the House to disagree with the Lords who have removed the words framed for the admission of the Jew.[78] Newdegate opposed + in his usual style – solemn, pompous & bigoted, as usual – his arms working exactly like those of a Semaphore. +

[...] N. Zealand. I brought on the New Zealand Loan or, rather, represented the contrariety betwn. the evidence of H. Sewell & the records of the proceedings in the New Zealand Parliament.[79] The reply was not clear or satisfactory. Though there was a great desire to screen Sewell, it was a strong condemnation to say (as Labouchere[80] said) that it was a pity Mr. Sewell had not stated certain facts. Lord Stanley[81] seemed, too, to leave him impaled – tho', as an official, he did his best to palliate the case. It wont do – & even Mr. Adderley's loss of temper & unjust attack on me will not excuse Mr. Sewell. The attempt to save him was somewhat Homeric – they raised a cloud of evasive & confusing generalities & distinctions & bore him off from the field invisible to foes [...]

---

[77] The motion, drawn up by Palmerston and Lord Granville, censured Ellenborough, the president of the board of control, for publishing his despatch severely rebuking the governor general of India, Lord Canning, for his Oude proclamation, and thus undermining the governor general's authority at a time of crisis; *H* cl. 674–86. Canning's proclamation had announced the confiscation of the people of Oude's proprietory rights to the land.

[78] Lord Chelmsford's amendment, inserted into the bill on 27 Apr., was rejected by the Commons, and Russell moved for a committee to draw up the reasons for disagreeing with the peers: *H* cl. 336–54.

[79] In his evidence to the New Zealand loan guarantees committee in 1857, Henry Sewell, the colonial treasurer, stated that the New Zealand House of Assembly had decided that it would not accept a loan of £200,000 if parliament was not prepared to offer the desired loan of £500,000. Trelawny showed that this was not the case; *H* cl. 354–7.

[80] Colonial secretary in the Palmerston ministry.

[81] Colonial secretary.

Thursday, 13 May: Report of the Oaths Bill Committee – first specimen, perhaps, of Judaic Handiwork, as Rothschild was upon it.[82] Resolutions read.[83] The Tories never heard a lesson more likely to be disagreeable to them. Each resolution in succession riveted some great argument from which they had always dissented. They seemed very much disconcerted – listening in a morose silence. At last Newdegate could hear it no longer & rose to protest. In vain. Other resolutions followed till the whole case of the Jew was fairly exhausted & formally accepted by a full House.

Limited liability followed – & then Church rates which got thro' Committee. Biggs made a very comical speech – giving us the benefit of his personal experience, which has been considerable in Church rate matters. Mellor made a good statement, too – as a lawyer retained in various great Church rate suits.

The Property Qualification Bill was delayed by an adjournment. The Tories had had enough Reform for one night.

Friday, 14 May: The Great Indian Field day.[84] Cardwell opened neatly, calmly & skilfully – perhaps his manner is too slow & phlegmatic. But he puts his points like an old debator, as, indeed, he is. His model is evidently Graham.

Deasy more warm – & less cautious. Fluent & ready, when he raised a cheer agt. him by admitting too much, he always contrived to extricate himself with dexterity. It was evident, however, that he had little solid knowledge of Indian affairs & his speech was only good nisi prius declamation to order – moreover, he has the fault of most of his race – his tone is a sort of whine, as though the conquest of his country was ever in his mind. This spoils most of the Irish speakers.

Cairns[85] made a brilliant oration, wh. was received with vehement & long-sustained applause. I lost much of it, as I went to hear Lord Ellenborough, who was also effective. Lowe followed – feebly. Then Lindsay & Dillwyn – also, Vane Tempest. D[illwyn] moved an amendment.[86]

Lord John & Lord Stanley I failed to hear. Debate adjourned.

---

[82] Baron L.N. de Rothschild had been returned for the city of London since 1847, but was unable to take his seat; there was an eighteenth century precedent for someone sitting on a parliamentary committee before he had taken the oath.

[83] *H* cl. 529–30 for the 9 resolutions establishing the reasons for disagreeing with the House of Lords.

[84] The motion of censure on Lord Ellenborough, who had already announced his resignation, on 11 May.

[85] Solicitor general.

[86] Expressing confidence in Lord Canning, the governor general of India. Dillwyn made it clear that he had no wish to see Palmerston restored to power by means of the censure motion against Ellenborough; *H* cl. 727–8.

We have a difficult vote before us. Cardwell's motion has a passage, which would appear to censure Lord E[llenborough] for publishing his despatch. I think that taken alone was a merit. Then, as to the policy – I incline to think it was good. To what, then, do I object as at present advised? Why, to the fact of allowing Lord Canning to remain for even an hour in the government of 180,000,000 of men after he had been believed by Lord E. & his colleagues to be deserving of the censure contained in the despatch. This was in my judgment a high crime & misdemeanour, & is deserving of severe reprobation.

I must qualify what I have said about the publication of the Despatch. I meant merely to express a regard for publicity of counsels. Certainly, to publish such an invective agt. a governor in the midst of a mutiny & a revolution & not recall him was dangerous at least. At this time I incline to vote with Cardwell. Yet, several of my kidney are going the other way – eg, Roebuck, Pease, Dillwyn, Bright & Gibson.

Monday, 17 May: I heard Roebuck, who opened the debate[87] in a speech of 35 minutes. He was very bitter in his criticisms of the late administration – speaking of the Govt. we had cashiered for its insolence & insisting that we were making the fate of 200,000,000 of men turn upon a question of the benches on which two parties sat. He considered that Ellenborough was right throughout – the despatch was called for & was appropriate & its production necessary, because it was already known that Canning had written a Proclamation (which had been read) & the Proclamation demanded an immediate answer [...]

I returned later, when a vehement piece of declamation was delivered by Whiteside[88] amid the frantic exultation of his party. I should, however, not omit an energetic & amusing speech of Sir R[ober]t Peel, who seems to be alternately statesman & jester. There was much that was good & generous in his matter, &, yet, he, while always well heard, does not gain moral influence & cannot be in the high road to leadership. Jesting & personality are out of place in a solemn argument on a question of immense Imperial import. No division – & I still doubt.

Tuesday, 18 May: Having ridden home to tea at Kensington I was absent during an unexpected vote, on a motion of Williams of

[87] On the censure motion against Ellenborough, continued.
[88] Irish attorney general.

Lambeth, on probate duty in respect of real & corporate property. I have little doubt but I should have voted with him[89] [...]

Members were kept waiting, because the Church rate Bill stood to be 'considered as amended'. It was thought that there might be a division – if not on its principle, at least on some permissive clause like one of which notice stood on the paper by Mr. Garnett. However, no one shewed fight – &, amid considerable cheers, our stage passed & the Bill was ordered to be read on an early day after the recess.

What do the Tories mean? Has their right hand forgot its cunning? or do they coquet with the extreme liberals? or is it that they choose to rely on the defeat of the Bill in the Lords house? Certainly, we have had sweeping majorities – & motions on adjournment – plausible compromises & other devices – all singularly unfortunate. My line has been to abstain from representing the grievance as exclusively a dissenter's grievance – shewing how injurious & discouraging the law is to Churchmen where [there] are double or treble rates. Also, I have carried the war into the enemies' country by reminding the House repeatedly of the neglect to open Churches & perform service on week days. This might be expected of a highly paid clergy. I suspect this has been felt as a deadly dig – though I say it who dealt it – which, perhaps, I shouldn't.

Thursday, 20 May: To disagree with Cardwell's motion is to condone Ellenborough & blame Canning – since E[llenborough] has severely censured C[anning.] Now, while I cannot with Dillwyn endorse C[anning]'s conduct, even up to the period named in D[illwyn]'s amendment, until I know what that conduct has been, still less am I warranted, it may be said, in visiting it with reprobation.

The terms of Cardwell's motion begin to seem to me inexorable. Still, let us hear the remainder of the discussion.

When the Conspiracy Bill was before us, I accepted Gibson's abstract resolution in order to defeat the Bill.[90] The Tories professed to vote for it on the simple ground of its truth in terms & not on that of its consequences. My vote for a true proposition helped them into office, which was not my object. Now, the tables are turned, it may be said; &, if I concur with Cardwell's language, I ought not to depart from my rule for the single purpose of keeping the Tories in. These comments *look* like voting with Cardwell – I wonder what I shall do in fact [...]

---

[89] Williams' motion, to equalise the duties on real (including corporate) and personal property, defeated by 172:68; *H* cl. 867–9.

[90] See above, 19 Feb.

Friday, 21 May: Graham has pronounced – agt. Cardwell's resolution. G. thinks the Ellenborough despatch & policy substantially right – the language & manner harsh & wrong. The substance of the Canning proclamation he disapproves. It seems Bright made a furious onslaught upon Lord John Russell[91] – & was altogether more bitter, personal & irrelevant than sagacious & statesmanlike. It is a pity Bright does not 'lie on his oars' a little. Ill health[92] is the cause of his seriously compromising a grand & well earned reputation.

We are likely to receive more information today with regard to the Canning proclamation & Outram's[93] opinion of it. Lucky for those whose votes are still undecided – or, rather, unpledged.

12.40 p.m. The Indian papers, promised, have appeared. Outram was strongly opposed to the Canning proclamation. The R[eform] club is in great commotion.

4.30 p.m. Repeated solicitations addressed to Cardwell to give way on pleas of the altered position of affairs since the arrival of information in letters from India laid on the table. Great merriment of the Conservatives at our difficulties.

Duncombe, Tite, Locke of Honiton, Clay, & White of Plymo[uth] put it to the Whigs not to press the embarrassing resolution. At first, Cardwell stood to his guns, supported by Goderich (I think)[94] & Vivian. At last, however, he went up to Palmerston & seemed, also, to confer with Lord John &, in a moment, the whole House became convinced that the game was up & that the Tories would have their triumph. People suspect & insinuate what is vulgarly called a 'cross'.[95] It certainly looked very like it. In any case the effect was an enormous relief to troubled minds. Disraeli, of course, crowed greatly & even affected to make a merit of allowing the motion to be withdrawn. Palmerston bore his defeat so good-humouredly that, when he arose to announce the surrender in a broad grin, the House received him with evident favour & a keen gusto in anticipation of the mode in which he would save his dignity. He did it as well as possible – the House laughing greatly at his transparent excuses – & so the impeachment ended in a farce.

---

[91] Bright, following Russell in the debate, considered Cardwell's motion to be unwise and expressed his resentment at the failure of the Liberal leaders to consult the party first before adopting a course of action; *H* cl. 1055–8.

[92] Thought to have been a nervous breakdown resulting from the hostile reaction to his opposition to the Crimean war; G.M. Trevelyan, *The Life of John Bright*, (1913), pp. 254–8.

[93] Sir James Outram, the military commander in India.

[94] It was William Coningham.

[95] Cardwell had earlier tried to secure Disraeli's agreement to the withdrawal of the motion; Hawkins, *Art of Politics*, pp. 142–3.

The whole result is to strengthen Ministers.

Friday, 28 May: House resumed after recess. Spar between Lord John & Disraeli with Gibson & Rich for bottleholders. All arose out of Disraeli's speech at Slough[96] [...] It appears that Disraeli, having lost an opportunity of lampooning the ex govt. thro' the withdrawal of Cardwell's resolution, could not resist the temptation to disburthen himself of his speech in the provinces. It is thought that he has made a mistake – in as much as he will probably have alienated a large section of Evangelical people who swear by Shaftesbury – & the latter comes in for the heaviest penalties inflicted by D's sarcastic tongue. The 'Saturday Review'[97] is remarkably felicitous on this point.

Monday, 31 May: Another faction fight on the topic of the Slough speech of Disraeli. Palmerston led the fray – Disraeli followed in self-defence – & so on to Lord John & Pakington [...] D'Israeli has been damaged by the joint effect of Palmerston's attack & his own defence; – the indiscretion of saying at Slough that war was a question not of days but of hours when he took office was thought to have been lamely & not ingenuously explained. Lord John's calm dissection added to his discomfiture.

Tuesday, 1 June: [...] Captain Vivian brought on the question of Divided Responsibility in the administration of the army,[98] with many instances & proofs. Gen[era]l Peel,[99] Palmerston & others opposed the motion. Division. For Vivian 106. Govt. 104. Vivian's speech was a very good one, & he carried laurels accordingly from all sides. Sidney Herbert said that, in point of fact, the Minister for War is already responsible for every act done with regard to the army. If so, Vivian's motion was a truism; & it was so in theory, but in practice a divided responsibility exists. The fact is the Court has striven to retain in its own hands the Government of the army,[100] & Ministers for War have not had courage to assert their powers. Vivian's success will be a lesson to the Court. Trelawny voted with Vivian.

---

[96] *The Times*, 27 May 1858, p. 9.

[97] 29 May 1858, pp. 554–5. Lord Shaftesbury had moved the censure motion against Ellenborough in the House of Lords, on 14 May. In his speech at Slough, Disraeli had likened Shaftesbury to 'a Pharisee of old, with broad phylactery on his brow, calling god to witness, in the voice and accents of majestic adoration, that he was not as other men'.

[98] He moved that the department of the Horse Guards and the war office should be under the control of one responsible minister; *H* cl. 1328–37.

[99] Secretary for war.

[100] The commander in chief was the Duke of Cambridge, the Queen's cousin.

Roebuck brought on his motion for leaving the Turks to decide upon its merits the question of the Suez canal,[101] a matter in which we have systematically interfered. A lively debate ensued. Roebuck defeated.[102] Trelawny in the minority. It was urged that the canal was a bubble. Roebuck said that was not the question, being within the province of the Turks. The motion seemed to me to be a very good one, Roebuck's object being apparently to lay down broadly that England is prepared to give up any policy not consistent with the interests of humanity at large; – such a declaration at the present time would remove the reproach of perpetual self seeking & interference on our part & very likely prevent future wars, in which we may be coerced into giving up the same advantages with a bad grace [...]

Thursday, 3 June: Disraeli announced that Govt. had no intention of making any alteration in the War administration or, rather, of taking any step in consequence of Vivian's motion.

I opposed the large vote for Metropolitan Police on account of the amount of the increase (£24,000) in one year, which was explained in 2 ways by the govt. & late govt. – the latter attributing it, mainly, to the increasing size of London. I took, also, an objection in principle – wishing to stem the tide of centralization. Majority 157. Minority 28.

Afterwards, we defeated a rank job detected by Cowan – a sinecure office of general & particular register of Sasines!! at a salary of £1,000 a year, filled up by the expiring Whig dynasty with a minute in their cupboards recommending its abolition! Wilson[103] asserted that new work had been assigned to the office on a plan of amalgamation, which the Lord advocate[104] roundly denied! What next?

Out of very shame & consternation the vote was disallowed [...] Subsequently, the Property Qualification Bill was, amid loud cheers, read a 3rd time – & so bedwards at $\frac{1}{2}$ past one. On the whole, the evening was a disgraceful one to the House of Commons – personality, charges of lying, exposure of neglect or duty, (2) detections of sinecures lately filled up by different Ministers (one – which I shall have to notice – of some £1,000 or £1,200 given some years since by Graham to Lord Dalhousie & held, I heard, while he was in India),[105] opposite

---

[101] I.e. that Britain should not pressurise the Sultan to withhold consent for the canal project; *H* cl. 1360–7.

[102] 290:62.

[103] James Wilson, financial secretary to the treasury under both Aberdeen and Palmerston.

[104] Charles Baillie.

[105] The 1st Marquess of Dalhousie was governor general of India, 1848–56; it is not clear what 'jobbery' Trelawny thought had occurred.

& mutually destructive excuses coolly asserted – & each exposure only received with a laugh raised at the clumsiness of rascality found out!

Friday, 4 June: [. . .] supply – Lord John R[ussell] moved the British Museum votes. I inquired whether the Trustees proposed to allow the working classes to see the Museum on Sundays after the hours of Divine Service. The reply was unfavourable. I used a few arguments & made two suggestions; one, that these buildings should be opened on weekdays for 2 hours betwn. 8 & 10 p.m. & another, that since it was considered by many that the sight of books & fossils would be destructive of the Xtian Religion, a large Hall or Chamber should be set apart & filled with works of art & remains illustrative of Scripture History. The former idea was a good deal & very favourably discussed.

[. . .] During most of the evening I was engaged in collecting names of those who had voted with Capt. Vivian & desired to hold a meeting to consider what shd. follow Disraeli's cool contempt of a vote of the House.[106] Many are doubtful whether the meeting projected will be productive of any good. We may render our position worse instead of better. The House has resolved that the army is under the control of the Minister for War. This was the theory, before we arrived at the vote, according to Sidney Herbert. If we make a feeble attempt to enforce the decision come to & be defeated, the Country will be in a worse position than before. At present, the War authorities must act under a certain dread of the consequences of contravening a formal resolution of the Commons [. . .]

Monday, 7 June: A long debate on the Indian Question – Gladstone moved a resolution proposing to constitute, till the end of next session, the present Court of directors as Council of the Minister for India. He was defeated[107] – I paired agt. him with Mr. Watson Taylor. Lord Stanley has, already, evinced marked aptitude for the branch of the administration under his charge – he seems to be a born Statesman.

Tuesday, 8 June: Morning sitting – Church rates.[108]
I moved – eschewing argument on the general Question – appealing on grounds of policy & convenience. The Question was effete. Argument exhausted. Recommended that the bill should be referred to the judicial mind of the Lords. Then, the onus of rejecting possible compromise would rest with us on the bill coming down amended.

---

[106] See above, 1 June, for Vivian's motion on divided responsibility in the administration of the army.
[107] 265:116. *H* cl. 1613, 1615–33, for Gladstone's resolution.
[108] 3rd reading of Trelawny's abolition bill.

The great fact was Graham's conversion – which was announced in an admirable speech. Gladstone opposed feebly – & eke Walpole – also, Packe & Sir Brook Brydges. Division 266 to 203. Great Victory.

Ackroyd make a speech wh. was, of course, approved by the Tories, being in their sense. He will find it difficult to reconcile his course on Church rates & Ballot with the profession of a Liberal for these times. He liked the popular manner in wh. Church rates are laid & passed – forgetting the sense of grievance in the minority coerced agt. their will. Also, he desired to leave the Church its power of taxing herself. Who would deprive her of it? Why should not the members of the Church tax themselves.

Afterwards, came the great Ballot motion. No new argument. Marsh produced much merriment by reading accounts of proceedings in the Australian Parliament – personal amenities – a member sitting in his shirt sleeves (a laugh). The fact is that, in the existing state of heat, such a sound struck the House agreeably.

I believe no first class official or ex official came over to the Ballot ranks – but the opponents have paid it the compliment of a whip – & hence a great defeat[109] in a full House of near 500. Bright made a very good speech of nearly an hour – to the evident delight of his audience. His fine & manly style – clear & racy English – & conscious power took, as usual, even with his opponents, who admire a great artist, even when engaged in dissecting them.

He reminded the Tories with irresistible force of the many false fears they had entertained – & the numerous instances in which they had predicted the irretrievable ruin of the Nation from measures subsequently productive of great & generally admitted benefit. Lords Palmerston & Russell were especially the objects at which his shafts were aimed. Lord John sat carefully concealing his expression under his hat & with the aid of his hands on which he affected to lean. Palmerston contrived to look stolid but covered as much as possible – as is the wont of some Statesmen in the Commons assailed by their critics. The fact is the light hurts their eyes. Bright paid Lord John the equivocal compliment of belief in his sincerity – from which, of course, Palmerston took nothing.

Thursday, 10 June: Locke King's £10 Country Franchise Bill – carried by a majority of 58,[110] with wh. I voted.

Du Cane (Essex) made a speech, moving the previous question. It was considered to be a speech of promise. In parts there were some racy personal passages – not ill-natured & quite legitimate.

---

[109] 294:197 against Henry Berkeley's bill.
[110] 226:168 for the 2nd reading.

Old Miles – half-laughingly – seconded. He appealed to the Palmerstonians to save the government in return for a like office in favour of their chief on a former occasion in 1857. I believe the allusion referred to the China War vote.[111] Palmerston said, in reply, that there had been an 1858 as well as 1857 – & in 1858 the Tories joined his foes & overthrew him.

No other speech of note. We divided very early by common consent – & won easily. Note, Palmerston out of office, helps onward some liberal measures, which, in office, he opposed. Graham & Sidney Herbert went with us – as well as Lord John. In short, the division lobby contained a govt. & its party ready cut & dried. Verily, too, there is a growing antagonism betwn. Lords & Commons. We send up measure after measure, Jew Bill, Church rates abolition Bill, Property Qualification Bill, & now we are preparing to send up the £10 County franchise Bill. It is true that the 2d. reading of the Prop[erty] Qual[ification] Bill has passed in the Lords – but Lord Derby says he shall oppose the franchise Bill [...]

Friday, 11 June: [...] Disraeli was loudly cheered on his announcement of the settlement of our difficulty with Naples. The Cagliari is to be delivered up & our two engineers compensated[112] [...]

The govt. had a considerable majority on the Indian Council question.[113] If they be but moderately prudent, they may long remain in office – such is the discord in the ranks of the Liberals! The chief danger of the Derby-Disraelites lies, I think, in the number of Orators they have among them – some of whom are apparently covert rivals. On dit that Derby laughed as much as any one at Palmerston's successful tilt at Disraeli.[114] The Slough speech damaged govt. Probably, Bulwer's mouth was almost shut in consequence in Hertfordshire. He did little but dwell upon the renown of his ancestors & the antiquity of his race.[115]

Tuesday, 15 June: Evening sitting – proposal to make a Scotch

---

[111] Trelawny is obviously mistaken, as the Conservatives had helped to defeat Palmerston's ministry on the China war question, in Mar. 1857. Miles may have been referring to the Conservatives' support for Palmerston against Roebuck's resolution (16 July 1857) condemning the Persian war; *H* cxlvi. 1577–1655.

[112] See above, 12 Mar., for the Cagliari affair.

[113] Palmerston and Russell's attempt to limit the membership of the Council to a maximum of twelve was defeated by 243:176. Lord Stanley then carried his resolution that there should be a minimum of twelve and a maximum of fifteen members. Trelawny was absent from these divisions.

[114] See above, 31 May.

[115] For Bulwer's empty speech at Hertford, see *The Times*, 11 June 1858, p. 12.

Secretary of State.[116] The argument seemed to me agt. it. Baxter, in moving, is said to have made a good speech.

Scotch business is somehow proverbially well done. The Lord Advocate is always a first rate man – & the duties of the office have been well fulfilled. Why make a change for the mere sake of uniformity? That were rather pedantic – &, if carried out, might be dangerous. In short I for one was not convinced.

Wednesday, 16 June: Edinburgh Annuity tax.[117] Beaten by one vote – 129[118] to 130. It struck me that the liberals brought about this by talk. Their game was an obvious one – to assume a victory on the grounds of the judgments come to in the several cases of the Ministers money Bill[119] & the Church rate abolition Bill. As it happened, talk begat talk &, meanwhile, the Tories whipt.

Horsman especially talked – long after his own party had desired to divide. But, after all, what children we all are! No one cared as much about the question as about the nearness of the numbers voting on either side. Breathless attention – & then a vehement cheering & laughing! And this is pretty Fanny's way. I voted with Adam Black.

[...] a talk agt. time on a voluminous Insurance Bill of Sheridan's of Dudley.[120] It struck me that, in gaining his point, he cut his throat. The House never likes the man the better who forces it –even with a 'douce violence'.

The mover did not lack fluency or self possession. Like many good horses in the House, he wants a jockey.

Thursday, 17 June: [...] It appears that Lord Stanley's new plan for the Indian Council[121] did not meet with general approbation. It was handled by Ld. Palmerston, Bright & others. Disraeli, seeing a storm gathering, interposed & offered to the House at once to bring in the bill to be founded on the resolutions already agreed to. This

---

[116] Rejected by 174:47.

[117] Adam Black's motion to abolish the compulsory levy of 6 percent on the occupants of houses, shops and warehouses, used to pay the stipends of Church of Scotland ministers in Edinburgh.

[118] Trelawny mistakenly wrote 128.

[119] A similar impost on the inhabitants of certain towns in Ireland for the benefit of Church of Ireland ministers; abolished in 1857.

[120] The Insurance and Assurance Institutions bill was an attempt, by a private member, to consolidate the statutes in this area. Sheridan refused to withdraw the bill, as he wanted a force a discussion. It was subsequently postponed.

[121] That it should consist of 8 members nominated by the Crown and 7 chosen by the existing directors of the East India Company, with vacancies filled alternately by Crown nomination and election by the Indian Council; *H* cl. 2221–5.

was arranged – & a bill, so brought in, was read a first time.[122] Of course, this was a dummy – which means a bit of paper tied with tape – so as to look like a Bill. Pity more of our bills are not equally innocuous!

[...] a growing disgust was exhibited in various quarters at the state of the Thames, which is now a recognized common sewer. The library of the House is nearly untenable. And, yet, the little Parliament of Thwaites & Co.[123] was created, partly, in order to abate this great nuisance! Constitutional government is still on its trial.

Monday, 21 June: Kensington Estate & dissolution of Partnership Bill betwn. govt. & Commissioners.[124] Several members raised points of detail. One proposed that the Public should receive interest, as well as principal money, paid. This seemed reasonable – & I voted accordingly.[125]

More discussion. Hints that there is some mysterious influence at work on the subject of this scheme. In short, the Prince is the person aimed at – yet, I certainly never quite understood why.[126] To prove this it is only necessary to quote what I caught in passing from some member explaining his vote to another. He said 'I can't stand Albert!' And there is certainly a prevalent sentiment of this kind [...]

Friday, 25 June: [...] The Session is waning apace. The state of the Thames is vitally affecting the destinies of 180,000,000 in India, since the House legislates with more expedition from apprehension of the noxious effect of the effluvia near home. Morning & evening sittings take place – the Thames being a standing topic – which apparent paradox is in some sense true, because the poisonous properties are supposed to float above the sea water & haunt the metropolis with a sort of love of home. Govt. seem inclined to act at last with decision & energy in this matter. Their future is in their own hands – since mere party amendments produce no impression on their position. The Country wants work – not talk – & little minds who the men are.

---

[122] The government of India (no 3) bill; *P.P.* 1857–8, ii 313.

[123] Sir John Thwaites was chairman of the metropolitan board of works, set up in 1855, which had still not produced its plan for the drainage of London.

[124] To dissolve the partnership between the government and the commissioners for the great exhibition of 1851; Royal assent, 12 July. The debate concerned the repayment of a parliamentary grant of £200,000, after which the land purchased by the commissioners in South Kensington was to be released so that the plan to establish a permanent exhibition site could be fulfilled.

[125] Blackburn's amendment was rejected, 208:99.

[126] Prince Albert had served on the commission for the great exhibition of 1851 and favoured the concentration of the national museums on the South Kensington site; Sir Theodore Martin, *Life of the Prince Consort*, (1875–80), ii. 233–7, 445–6, 569–73.

Monday, 28 June: [...] Luckily the wind has changed & so wafts the odour of the River to the Lambeth Shore, where maybe it will poison a bishop & so bring about Sanitary Legislation [...]

Tuesday, 29 June: [...] Six o'clock. Caird brought on a vote in censure of wastefulness in the expenditure of the Commiss[ione]rs of Woods in the case of Hainault Forest. It was an elaborate & well delivered statement, but very partially damaged by the reply of the Minister Hamilton.[127] The speech displayed very considerable knowledge of farming & draining & the costs at which agricultural operations are conducted. The worst part of his case, however, lay in the mover's readiness to consent not to divide. If his facts were to be relied upon, why did the case come to so lame & impotent a conclusion? As a general rule, I think a mover – especially, if his motion attacks persons – should carry it to a division. I say this with some soreness, because I have too often yielded to pathetic or crafty appeals not to divide. I withdrew my motion on the question of rewards to members at the suggestion of 3 or 4 leaders of parties &, yet, later in the session, Lord Hotham carried a still more sweeping resolution![128]

Wednesday, 30 June: I went down to the House in order to support Lord Bury's Marriage Reform Bill which would permit a man to marry his deceased wife's sister. Young Lygon signalized himself by an obstructive &, as was thought, rather factious course – that of moving repeated adjournments so as to defeat the Bill by time [...] I voted twice – once on words excluding Ireland from the operation of the measure. On this point we were mostly in a state of indecision from not understanding the effect of the question put. I looked out for Lord Bury, & learning that he considered that the success of his bill depended upon his acquiescence in the exclusion of Ireland, I voted accordingly.[129] So did many others holding my views – & I heard Gibson say we were right in so doing. But it went agt. the grain – & had I clearly known what we were about, I confess I should have hesitated. Yet, the Irish do not desire the measure (as I gathered) – so that probably no harm is done [...]
  [...] we had a vote on the member's freedom from arrest Bill [...]

---

[127] Lord Claud Hamilton, treasurer of the household.

[128] See above, 13 Apr., for Trelawny's motion that rewards to members be regarded as a high breach of parliamentary privilege. On 22 June, Lord Hotham had carried, by 210:27, the resolution that 'it is contrary to the usage and derogatory to the dignity of this House, that any of its members should bring forward, promote, or advocate, in this House, any proceeding or measure in which he may have acted or been concerned, for or in consideration of any pecuniary fee or reward'; *H* cli. 176–209.

[129] Monsell's amendment was passed, 140: 98.

I voted for it.[130] What practical evil would arise from subjecting members to the risk of arrest for debt? Would the House consist of inferior men? [...] It was argued that Burke and Sheridan might have been arrested. But those were days of Nomination. The whole case is now altered – it is hardly possible to draw comparisons wh. shall be useful for purposes of argument. We have a work to do – to purify commercial character in England – & more good will be done by keeping a certain check on persons of property & their manner of dealing with their creditors than evil by the loss of the services of indebted persons who happen to possess Statesmanlike qualities [...]

Thursday, 1 July: Scotch Universities Bill.[131] This Bill is understood to be a good & useful Bill with one exception. It has a clause relating to the future payment of professors (who may be Theological) by virtue of which Parliament will be annually asked to vote money. Baxter moved an amendment that such persons should not be *Theological* professors. On this he & others spoke & the committee divided – govt. winning by a very slender majority.[132] We then divided on the main clause, & were still more completely beaten.[133] This second division partly arose from a shout of 'No' from me. When the question, however, was again put, I forbore: but Cox shouted & thus eventually forced a division, wh. had been more prudently avoided [...] Notable, that Graham & Gladstone went with us.

Gladstone made a good proposal during the morning – viz, to raise Scotch University education by combining, for purposes of examination for degree, the several existing Universities, wh. are still little more than Colleges. He stated his case in a lucid & unpretending manner, which favourably impressed the Committee– & may succeed on the report.[134]

[...] 10 p.m. Returning to the House I found it still on the India Bill [...] I arrived just in time to vote on the omission of the word 'misbehaviour'. Councillors are by the Bill to be removable for 'misbehaviour'. This practically gives them tenure for life – subject, however, to an address for deposing them. Palmerston thought a period of 10 years shd. be fixed. Another member (Gregson) thought

---

[130] 2nd reading passed, 129:75; but Ward Hunt's bill made no further progress.

[131] To reform the government of the Scottish Universities; Royal assent, 2 Aug. *P.P.* 1857-8, iv. 713.

[132] 102:94.

[133] Clause nineteen, relating to retirement pensions, carried by 125:76.

[134] On 5 July, Gladstone succeeded in inserting a permissive clause to the effect of his proposal; *H* cli. 961-2.

5. We voted on leaving out 'misbehaviour' in order to insert other words.[135]

I voted again on the question whether or not councillors might be members of Parliament. On this point there was much discussion. I noted that Lord John R[ussell] & Graham voted with us – for allowing such privilege to councillors.[136] Why not? I confess I saw no valid reason against it. We get much valuable information regarding India from Directors – & it is well they should be capable of sitting in the House of Commons where a certain moral influence may be brought to bear on their proceedings.

Friday, 2 July: Twelve o'clock sitting – India Bill.

Collins raised a question on wh. we divided. He proposed to make the pay to councillors £500 in lieu of £1,200 a year. After hearing all the arguments, I supported £1,200.[137] [...] If you want first class intellect, you must pay for it. Educated scientific men of high character could not be induced to work daily in London except at a fair remuneration – & less than £1,200 would not cover extra-house rent & expenses. Moreover, these councillors will be required, it is understood, to give up other business.

For my part I think it due to India herself to hold out strong inducements to men of high talent, education & moral qualities. Such men will surely earn their salt. A small stipend is often made an excuse for jobbing. Indian Princes with grievances would probably address themselves to underpaid councillors instead of members of Parliament.

After I went home there was another division at the instance of Mr. Rich on the question of pensions to persons retired from the Council. I should have voted agt. Rich.[138]

[...] Note. The Church rate Bill was thrown out of the Lords.[139] The wags say the Dissenters have been sold to the Jews.

Monday, 5 July: [...] The interest in the Session is over. Amendments are discussed briefly & in a businesslike manner – & divisions are soon resorted to. Lord Derby is in danger from his own party – who are, I hear, greatly disgusted. He seems to be simply 'Palmerston redivivus'. Were Palmerston actually defunct, I should believe in the trans-migration of souls. The British Constitution must be in danger – as

[135] Gregson's amendment, limiting the tenure to five years, with the possibility of re-election, rejected by 154:118.
[136] Sir Erskine Perry's amendment was defeated, 245:121.
[137] 224:57 against Collins' amendment.
[138] Rich's amendment restricting pensions to those who had served for at least 15 years, defeated by 199:101.
[139] By 151:36.

Newdegate & Spooner have receded to Mons Sacer. As to the debates, they have become quite tranquil since we have lost those two respectable orators.

Tuesday, 6 July: [. . .] 6 o'clock sitting.[140] Several divisions – in one I supported Palmerston's motion to limit the operation of the Bill for 5 years, so that there may be a locus penitentia if we find we have been in error. My reasons: Lord Stanley expressly describes the measure as experimental. Also, the India Co. only held India by way of leasehold for years. The Bill is not very well considered. It is quite understood that the object has been not so much to produce a good Bill as to produce a Bill unlike that proposed by Lord Palmerston who gave many months to its preparation. At least, so I heard.

I voted with Lord John agt. an enactment favourable to action thro' secret instrumentality. Sir James Graham ably pointed out the doings of the Board of Control & the Secret Committee of the India House & how faithfully the whole 24 Directors had kept secrets of great importance when secrecy was really necessary. To enact secrecy is to favour misdoings & irresponsibility. Witness the ill-judged & serious Afghan War – the proceedings in Scinde *What proceedings in Scinde? Experts differ as to wisdom or the reverse of general policy in that Country* & numerous other cases.[141] Much evil might have been prevented if full & unreserved communication had always been made to the whole body of Directors.

We were well beaten on divisions.[142] It is curious to watch some of the devices of certain ex-ministers. When Lord John & Palmerston happen to concur,[143] Graham & Gladstone seem to stand aside or oppose them. When Graham & Lord John concur, then, Palmerston adroitly moves to defeat them.[144] No Liberal govt. seems possible while this system goes on. The fact is, while we think we are gravely discussing the India Bill, we are merely the stage on which a fencing match or triangular duel is taking place between the great party leaders opposed to the Ministry.

Bright made another telling speech[145] – in his best manner – calm, fluent, argumentative. What a splendid debater! It appears to me

---

[140] The Government of India (no. 3) bill, at the report stage.

[141] The ill-fated Afghan war of 1838–42, and the annexation of Sind in 1843, were both undertaken for the purpose of countering Russian expansion in Central Asia.

[142] Palmerston's motion was defeated by 149:115. Russell's motion, to omit a clause allowing the secretary of state to send orders without reference to the Indian Council, was rejected by 176:149.

[143] On Palmerston's motion.

[144] He opposed Russell's motion.

[145] In support of Palmerston's motion.

that in that quality he has attained to the highest position in the House.

Friday, 9 July: I attended in the afternoon sitting – the House was in Committee on the Civil Service estimates [...] & very tedious work we had of it. Lord Elcho was prominent. He was again & again on his legs – now, on art – now, on the Enfield Rifle & its ammunition – & so on. He quoted Russell of the Times[146] – which was discreet, since he thus ensured a reporter. There is no member of the House who possesses a more complete stock of easy & complacent assurance. To say the truth, his speeches are very fluent – & sometimes he is facetious. He is never at a loss for a word – & his English is that of a cultivated gentleman. He has, too, the great advantages of good looks & a title. He never rises above the forcible feeble, but such as his matter is, the House hears it – but, perhaps, rather from the feeling that talk must endure for several hours & that Lord Elcho's is above the average – at least on supply nights [...]

Monday, 12 July: [...] we had the Regium Donum – or the annual vote of money to nonconformist Ministers in Ireland. Baxter moved.[147] Gilpin supported in a vigorous speech of the right stamp – & was followed with equal force & effect by W.J. Fox. The Solicitor general[148] took the opposite line on behalf of govt. and I thought argued but feebly. He urged that the chapels were better when supported by State grants. But what would he say to money voted for the Irish priests? Why, he would strenuously oppose such grants, no doubt. John Locke voted & spoke agt. Baxter – and I think Locke will live to regret his course. He agreed in principle with B., but declined to make the case a special one leaving other endowments untouched. Might it not be urged that, in disendowing one sect, you make it the enemy of grants to others? Maynooth is no case. That is educational – &, by virtue of an old pledge at the Union, has been placed on the Consolidated fund. The Regium Donum is annually voted – & Ministers get the grant when a subscription has first been raised of £35. Now, it is said the Minister sometimes himself subscribes £10 of this & so ekes out the contingency upon wh. the remainder accrues to him! If this be so, it looks a little like a pious fraud, to which one

---

[146] W. H. Russell, the famous Crimean war correspondent.

[147] That the grant of £39,400 be reduced to £366 (the item for widows and orphans of ministers of the synod of Ulster); *H* cli. 1277–8.

[148] Sir Hugh Cairns.

would fain be no party. So that I rejoice at my two votes (1) agt. the main resolution; (2) agt. the increase this year.[149]

I paired till 10 o'clock with D. Jones. As we were going out, Lord Charles Russell, the Serjeant at Arms, suddenly bolted the door – & said 'now I have got you fast!' We thought we were in custody for some crime, when we heard the awful words 'Black Rod'. Sure enough three distinct taps were made at the door which the Serjeant opened – & in stalked the majestic presence of the solemn knight of the silk stocking & fat calves.

Evening sitting.[150] Returning I heard more or less of several speeches, those respectively of Palmerston, Roebuck, Gilpin, Drummond & Pakington. Palmerston full of fire & energy – & appealing to sentiments of a religious character. He even seemed to think our good fortune, since the abolition of the Slave Trade, had been due to that event. To what cause does he attribute the evils we have suffered – such as the Russian War & a Palmerston administration? He is as bad as one of the peers who attributed the potato failure to the Maynooth g[ran]t.

I take it that P. does not like to admit that, thro' his advice, we have so long & so expensively striven in vain. Clarence Paget – a practised seaman – strongly condemned our proceedings as having the effect of increasing the evils we seek to remedy – for we ruin the health of our sailors & aggravate the horrors of the middle passage. I forgot to mention Gibson's speech on the same side. On a division we were shamefully defeated[151] – ie if wisdom goes with the many. Perhaps, we may one day appear to have been the prophets. Can we afford to spare a large body of sailors for objects which, if we do not wholly fail to attain to them, we are doubtful whether we attain to them in any considerable degree? I imagine that we should act more wisely in ceasing to risk litigation with foreigners in matters where national sensibility is easily touched – such as the right to sail free from annoyance from other powers. We can only succeed in our object by making our Navy the police of Nations – are we in a condition to act consistently in the business? If so, we must go to war with America, since we can no longer legally visit or search her ships or those carrying her flag. At least, we should exercise our powers at very great risk. An imperious captain of a Man of war might at any moment plunge us in war. I voted of course with Hutt.

---

[149] The grant was passed by 165:55. Gilpin's amendment, rejecting the increase in the grant of £346. 3s. 4d, was defeated by 147:69.

[150] Hutt's resolution against the use of military force to suppress the slave trade; *H* cli. 1286–94.

[151] By 223:24.

Tuesday, 13 July: [...] It is satisfactory to learn that we sometimes produce good results. Lord Stanley asks for £20,000 for the Kaffirs instead of £40,000 – & writes a very serious letter to Sir G. Grey on the subject of the Imperial resources.[152] We, also, heard that it had been the intention of the late government to forbear to ask for the vote for the Ecclesiastical Commiss[ione]rs,[153] and another kindred estimate (I think called the Church building Com[missone]rs estimate or some such title £10,000 about) has ceased to be called for.

Friday, 16 July: [...] Jews Bill.[154] Old Tories very rabid. Straight-waistcoat applied by Lord John to Bentinck. Lord John, speaking of the Lords & the possible necessity of a wider Jew measure, hoped sons might, as was sometimes the case, prove to be wiser than the fathers. What will Lord Derby say to that?[155]

Drummond was the Cassandra of the evening. All sorts of evils to be expected. Division 156:65.[156] [...]

Monday, 19 July: I returned to the House & listened to a long debate on the Thames Purification Bill.[157] The engineers Locke & Stephenson & builder Cubitt were, as practical men, well heard & deservedly. I confess I doubt much whether legislation is not in advance of exact knowledge in this business of the Thames. It is uncertain whether three million £ will be sufficient. The Public are guaranteeing a large loan which may be squandered uselessly. It seems likely that before 5 years expire, deodorization may be so far perfected as to be applicable to the work required [...]

Tuesday, 20 July: Attended – very lame – & heard an excellent debate on Roebuck's motion regarding the territories of the Hudson's

---

[152] Trelawny had noticed, in his speech to the Commons, Lord Stanley's despatch of 5 May to Governor Grey, regarding the scale of the financial assistance given to the Cape Colony since it was granted self-government in 1853; *H* cli. 1420–1. Trelawny had moved to reject the vote altogether, but was defeated by 177:30.

[153] Indicated by Labouchere and Vernon Smith, members of the late Palmerston ministry; *H* cli. 1401. However, the government carried the vote of £3,568 by 67:61.

[154] Lord Lucan's bill (originating in the House of Lords), which enabled either House to modify, by resolution, the form of its parliamentary oath; *P.P.* 1857–8, iii. 635. The peers had passed this bill in spite of having previously (1 July) rejected Russell's oaths bill.

[155] Russell was alluding to the attitude of Derby's son, Lord Stanley.

[156] For the 2nd reading.

[157] The metropolis local management act amendment bill, granting borrowing powers to the metropolitan board of words; Royal assent, 2 Aug.

Bay Company.[158] He was brief, full & succinct. Lord Bury made a really capital speech of $\frac{3}{4}$ of an hour in seconding. He gave a complete history of the Title of the Comp[an]y & described from personal knowledge the country over which they are supposed to have authority. As to the title, he seemed to demonstrate that it was little better than waste paper. Gladstone followed – paying high compliments to Bury & concurring with mover & seconder. Several others spoke – Lord John Russell, Gilpin, Christie & Lowe, but the main speech was that of Bulwer-Lytton[159] who gave satisfaction by the frank way in which he in spirit accepted Roebuck's resolutions, which, however, were as a matter of convenience withdrawn as Govt. could not nakedly accept them without making certain qualifications & arrangements with the Hudson's Bay Comp[an]y. The debate was one of the most satisfactory of this Session. We really begin to achieve something.[160]

[...] (I omitted to mention a day or two since Lord John's notice of motion levelled at the Lords, who thought to save their dignity by rejecting the Oaths Bill with reasons amounting to objections in principle on the ground of the importance of preserving the Xtian character of the Legislature and, at the same time, passed Lord Lucan's Jew Bill which gives up the whole case.[161] Lord J.R. will move tomorrow to the effect that this House does not consider it necessary to answer the reasons of the Lords, because they have returned an answer to their own by passing a Bill providing means for the admission of the Jews to Parliament[162] [...])

Thursday, 22 July: Appropriation Bill. Sir G. Cornewall Lewis[163] enters with criticisms of the finance of the Ministry. His object was to shew that, instead of a surplus, there would be a deficit, for that Disraeli has taken into account as assets the balances in the Exchequer – thus indirectly increasing his means. Disraeli replied & seemed to prove that all is well & that we shall have a larger surplus than he had estimated – to such an extent that he expected to pay off one million of debt. Wilson[164] followed, still endeavouring to disparage the

---

[158] Roebuck, who had been brought up in Canada, moved that the privileges of the company, soon to expire, should not be renewed as they posed an obstacle to the further colonisation of Canada; *H* cli. 1788–94.

[159] Newly-appointed Colonial secretary.

[160] An act was subsequently passed creating the colony of British Columbia out of part of the company's territory previously known as New Caledonia; *P.P.* 1857–8, ii. 397.

[161] See above, 16 July.

[162] *H.* cli. 1902. Rothschild was finally able to take his seat on 26 July.

[163] Chancellor of the Exchequer in Palmerston's ministry.

[164] Financial secretary to the treasury in Palmerston's ministry.

merit of the Treasury & foreboding mercantile losses & diminished income, & to him Hamilton replied. On the whole, Disraeli had far the best of the controversy, which was a sort of fencing match with the buttons on. + The Mountain cheered repeatedly, being well satisfied with the apparent frankness & good sense of the Minister of finance. +

Willoughby rose in Committee on the appropriation act & moved the addition of words limiting the power of the Treasury to apply without vote of Parliament surplus money voted on one item to some other inadequately provided for owing to some unforeseen emergency. I forced a division – & went with Willoughby.[165] Officials held that the words we supported would defeat our object. Officials are always very technical when abuses are checked.

[...] Much discussion on Sewage followed & one division in wh. I supported a vote calculated to leave the Board free in the choice of a plan of drainage.[166] I was rather disposed to support Ackroyd's proposal to omit the guarantee clause binding the Public faith for the £3,000,000 loan. But I think I was answered by the statement that money for drainage for other towns may always be obtained through the Exchequer Loan Com[missione]rs. Still I look with suspicion at this tendency to increase the liabilities of the State by the system of guaranteeing expenditure for local objects. Where shall we stop? Are not railways works of Public utility? Must not the machinery of the Central govt. be increased? Will there be no partiality or jobs? No discontent at undue preference.

Friday, 23 July: A long morning sitting on the Corrupt practices continuance Bill.[167] Avowed purpose to defeat it by factious means – White frankly said as much. Many, however, object bona fide to the measure on the ground of words inserted by Ayrton allowing payment of travelling expenses for a voter, but not to him – of course, only rich men can afford to hire numerous vehicles for the conveyance of voters [...] Several members mentioned instances of the mode in which the Law is defeated & bribery practically resorted to. Roebuck was very severe in his private & public observations addressed to Ayrton, who, had caused words to be inserted in the Bill rather favourable to its success & tending to facilitate the maintenance of the system of

---

[165] Who was defeated by 89:41; *H* cli. 1922, for his resolution.

[166] Headlam's amendment, giving the metropolitan board of works power to undertake 'such works as may be necessary' for the purification of the Thames and the drainage of London, defeated by 81:38, *H* cli. 1929.

[167] The corrupt practices act (1854) continuance bill; Royal assent, 2 Aug.

conveying voters & therefore rendering elections expensive. This was declared to be equivalent to a new property qualification. Roebuck told Ayrton, privately & publicly, that he had done more harm by this one act than he would ever do good while he shd. continue in Parliament.

6 o'clock sitting [...] Corrupt Practices Act [...] I voted agt. the 1st clause permissive of the payment of travelling expenses.[168] Lord Palmerston took the opposite view – on wh. Bernal Osborne rose & made one of his slashing speeches, in which he seemed to imply his independence & to pronounce ag[ains]t his late chief's return to office. So unpopular is Palmerston that, when Fox & he arose together, the liberal party called loudly for Fox!

[...] There is an odd character – one Tom Collins of Knaresborough who half-amuses, half-annoys the House. He can't sit still or be quiet for 2 minutes. He constantly interrupts members, when the rest of the audience is quiet & that in a particularly loud voice which forcibly conveys the feeling of being bored. Every moment he shouts either 'agreed, agreed', or 'divide, divide' & then throws his body into a new attitude by no means respectful to the House & seems to fall asleep, when, on a sudden, he exclaims again 'agreed, agreed' & shifts his posture. Next, he gets up hastily & crosses the House – then back again to some member on his own side – &, in another minute, he seems to be asleep. They say he is a good fellow at heart – albeit a singularly ugly one & very uncouth. As to 'order, order' – whether from Mr. Speaker or the House – it might as well be shouted at a wall.

Monday, 26 July: [...] 6 pm. sitting. I went down to the House to support the Scotch members who had resolved, if possible, to reinsert a clause which the Lords had cut out of the University Bill. The effect of the clause was adverse to religious tests in the exclusive interest of the Scotch establishment.[169] As soon as I arrived, I found the govt. had already given way – which I hardly expected. Other matters followed, in which I have no pressing interest – &, being very lame & overworked, I wind up my labours for this Session.

Thursday, 29 July: Numerous questions. It is unfortunate that so many liberals are out of Town, since their absence strengthens

---

[168] The clause was carried by 94:66.
[169] I.e. clause 3, that the principals of Edinburgh, Glasgow and Aberdeen should not be deemed to be professors of divinity.

government in enforcing the amendments of the Lords on the India Bill.[170] The government party is a well disciplined phalanx.

Monday, 2 August: Prorogation of Parliament [...]

---

[170] On the following day a Lords amendment, modifying the regulation of the system of competitive examination for officers in the artillery and engineers in India, was upheld; *H* cli. 2324–47.

SESSION OF 1859

Thursday, 3 February: I heard Trefusis move the answer to the Queen's speech. An Eton boy's recitation – no hitch – & favourably received. The echo to the Queen's speech is always read in the midst of hubbub – since everyone knows that it has no novelty. Should it not be put in the Speaker's hands to be read as a form? Beecroft seconded – I heard only part – & cannot fairly estimate his success or failure.

The House was not full – its demeanour very quiet – much as if it had met in the morning.

Lord Palmerston had little to say but to criticize the style Her Majesty had been made to use – & to twit government with the word 'Rouman' instead of Moldavian or Wallachian, which word Disraeli said had been borrowed from one of Lord P's despatches.

Appearances look warlike – Disraeli could not give us more than equivocal hopes of peace.[1]

Lord John evidently wished to go further in expression of feeling for Italian liberty than any other speaker – & he, also, appears more desirous of Reform at home than his great rival, who raised merriment by pointing to the ground when speaking of Republican institutions as 'powers from below', in contrast to those from above (meaning I suppose such as the Emperor Nicholas, the E[mperor] Napoleon, King of Naples & the Bourbons) [...]

Friday, 4 February: [...] The game of the Derby Cabinet is to present themselves in the guise of administrative Reformers – with their budget of measures ready for use. All depends upon the degree in which they sustain the character. The world is more just than idle or bad people think to those who really endeavour to do good work, & the devil himself, once Prime Minister, might remain so for an indefinite period on terms of governing well.

Tuesday, 8 February: [...] Ewart divided the House on his proposal to shut up proceedings after 12 on tuesdays & thursdays. But these are the nights which belong to Independent members. Why curtail

---

[1] In Italy, where Britain was negotiating to prevent Franco-Austrian hostilities; Derek Beales, *England and Italy, 1859–60*, (1961), pp. 36–7. In reality, France and Sardinia were colluding to provoke a war with Austria; ibid, pp. 3–8.

their already rare chances? He was beaten. T[relawny] with majority.[2]

Church rates followed – tactics on both sides.

Govt. negotiate with me thro' the Whip – I think Col[onel] Taylor.[3] Would I, on condition of getting my 1st reading without opposition from govt., allow their Statement & Bill to precede my 2d. reading? Yes, if you will fix a certain period within wh. your Statement shall come on. Oh! but it is not easy to speak absolutely for a limited time. Very well, then let the chapter of accidents sway. However, I will see Walpole again.[4]

Negotiator returns; agreed.

Trelawny dreads misconception – & so asks Minister[5] 'would the 1st reading be opposed'? Minister says the question was rather irregular (cheers) – but &c (so much bosh). In short, I felt as if I had been made a fool of – & at the time had no right to complain – not in order. So I waited. My turn at last came – & I moved.

Tories – Griffith & Drummond grumbled. Former said, why had I not adopted a title admitting of alteration in lieu of Bill to abolish Church rates? Answer 'you have been in Parliament a long time & any time in the last 25 years, you might have done this.' Home Minister seems not to admit my version of an agreement with Govt. I demur & remind him of the negotiation – no reply. So I win.

Next comes question of a suitable Wednesday. Fitzroy says 'take 1st open Wednesday' – that is the way to carry a Bill agt. a government. I agree – and then the Wednesday, which Ld. Bury was supposed to be about to take, was given up to me & this I adopt [...]

Tuesday, 15 February: Questions. Crawford's Bill on a defalcation by an Union officer. Principle to throw the burthen on a larger area of parishes.[6] This the House would not stand. I voted agt. him.[7] Let parishes take care whom they employ. Why did he not go further & charge the Consolidated fund? [...]

Wednesday, 16 February: [...] Mayer de Rothschild took his seat[8] – an ineffectual growl from Newdegate.

[2] 237:28 against Ewart's motion.

[3] T.E. Taylor, a junior government whip.

[4] Trelawny is obviously relating the dialogue here.

[5] Spencer Walpole, the home secretary.

[6] In Dec. 1857 a Mr. Manini, of the city of London poor law union, had fled the country after embezzling £26,000. Although Manini had only been responsible for collecting poor rates from nine of the ninety-eight parishes in the union, the board of guardians had proposed that all the parishes should share the burden of the loss. One parish had objected to this plan, and a series of court cases had followed.

[7] Crawford was defeated by 89:57.

[8] Baron Mayer de Rothschild, the brother of Baron L.N. de Rothschild, had been elected for Hythe.

The marriage law amendment Bill read a 2d. time by a very large majority.[9] The subject, no joke to many families, amuses members. In the lobbies where they pair, one hears 'how are you about Incest?' Another, 'I must come down tonight, as I want to marry my sister.'

Drummond says we have commenced the Session with 2 measures – one, for sacrilege; another, for incest. To cap the climax, we have 3 Jews in the House or, at least, elected – & proh pudor! they decline to be sworn except on the old Testament and with their hats on! Who will believe them? And yet their Bills would be accepted as cash from Pekin to Vancouver's Island.

Friday, 18 February: [...] Memorandum. The government receive credit for several strokes of work. Hardy introduces a great Highways Bill, which, some think, will improve our roads at greatly diminished cost. The Lord Chancellor introduces a Bankruptcy & Insolvency measure of great importance &, probably, some considerable merit.[10]

Lord Stanley does his India work so well as to be able to borrow £7,000,000 for India on Indian security & make the funds rise.

Lord Malmesbury[11] states that an act of visit for the verification of a ship's Nationality is left to the responsibility of the officer making such visit. This declaration goes far to prevent future war with America.

The Solicitor-general (Cairns) introduces a bold & comprehensive measure for the simplification & security of titles to land.[12] The Whig hacks must be frantic. Why, good god! the country may learn, if this goes on, to forget the value of Whig government!

Monday, 21 February: Church-Rates. Walpole's Bill or foundation for a Bill neatly & comprehensively introduced in a conciliatory speech. He exhausted plans heretofore proposed & reduced possible changes to my plan & his. Mine could not be accepted & therefore his only was open to us.[13]

I replied & eventually entered into an arrangement to delay my

---

[9] 135:77. Lord Bury's bill was rejected by the Lords on 22 Mar.

[10] Neither bill was passed before the dissolution of parliament in May.

[11] Foreign secretary.

[12] The titles to landed estates bill; killed by the dissolution of parliament.

[13] Walpole's bill enabled owners of land to charge their property with a church rate, and to constitute the incumbent and churchwardens as a corporation. Dissenters were to be allowed to claim exemption from payment, but would then lose the right to attend vestry meetings; *H* clii. 610–29.

Bill for a few days that the govt. Bill might be printed & the sense of the House taken upon it.

Several criticized – Lord John, Hadfield, Elton, Sir Geo. Grey & others. The notion generally prevalent is that the plan will never do. It is complicated – & would probably not work. Still, it is clearly my policy to give all propositions 'rope enough'. Eventually, the House may fall on my measure of simple abolition as a featherbed in comparison to the plans as yet submitted.

The idea of making the incumbent & Churchwardens a Corporation does not appear to me Statesmanlike, since it aggravates an existing evil; viz, the disagreeable relations in which, in Church rate matters, clergymen stand to their flocks. Nor is the change necessary. Why alter an ancient machinery which would work well enough if a question of principle or a distinct point were first settled? We have no reason to desire to abolish the office of Churchwarden, we only say that Church rates ought not to be forcibly levied upon dissenters – & we see no other way of attaining our end than by abolishing rates. Churchwardens may still receive Voluntary subscriptions & that which they receive they are compellable to spend to the last shilling on Church repairs &c.

The fact is, Walpole's plan will raise more objections from both sides than he foresees.

Lord John criticized, tho' he did not see how he could do better than the government. He dwelt upon one point, that an establishment exists not for the benefit of a single sect but for that of others. The presence of a minister was indirectly beneficial even to those who do not go to the Church. The Institution, being National, requires a National provision. And he was of opinion that the exclusion of dissenters from Vestries would tend to create new heartburnings.

The more closely the subject is approached the more difficult of application seem all plans short of Total abolition.

Some would have had me proceed with my Bill without taking the terms offered of standing first after the govt. measure on the 28th inst.

I had, however, to consider how I shd. better myself. Would not the Tories have insisted on gaining delay – on fair grounds, too? Would they not have talked agt. time on Wednesday & reproached us with intolerant rejection of all compromise? Will not discussion strengthen the total-abolitionists? Do we not then gain by acceding? & how much do we lose at the worst? about a week. Then, having a majority we can always eventually force the situation.

Friday, 25 February: I went down to the house to give a notice of opposing the govt. Church rate Bill – & consulted some of the leading tacticians on our side – Duncombe, Gibson & Fitzroy. Duncombe first thought I might with advantage move to postpone the order for the govt. Bill till after mine. Fitzroy said that, where there is little doubt but that a measure is a bad or mistaken one, the best course is to move that it be read that day 6 months. My only doubt was whether I would not treat the proposers with even extra courtesy. But Gibson's remark upon that was that a resolution in amendment shews front unnecessarily. The other motion leaves your grounds dark. So I gave notice, as advised[14] – amid some cheers.

[...] I have a notice on the paper for a Committee on the Privileges of the Guards – a propos of my recent correspondence with the Times.[15] My last letter was not published – so I took the same matter to the Spectator. Some of it appears in the 'Topics of the Day' – in that journal.[16]

The Church rate Bill of Mr. Walpole appears to please no one. It prolongs controversy in some parishes – rekindles controversy in others. How many landlords will charge their land with annuities in lieu of Church rates in order to put an end to a tax of which landlords generally approve? Why postpone abolition till very improbable events have occurred? Mr. Walpole appears not to have dealt with the cases of parishes paying rates for new chapels & rates for mother churches. Nor does he say that Churchwardens, who are to be members of the new corporations, must be Churchmen. Hence Dissenters will still elect Dissenting Churchwardens – & the quarrel still remains open.

In most large towns Church rates in effect are abolished. But how will this Bill affect these towns? Zealous Churchmen will endeavour to obtain Church rates as in former days. In other cases they may succeed – in many they will try in vain – but try. When they succeed & a rate shall be made from which Dissenters may claim exemption, then dissenters will forfeit their votes & the next rate would be easily obtained. Thus is the battle re-opened.

Is it wise or just to tie up more landed property for ecclesiastical purposes? Is it just to enable a trustee or life tenant to bind either the beneficiary or the remainder man? Take the case of an Episcopal Trustee & a poor family of young children – brought up as Catholics. Is it fair to shift to their shoulders a tax now complained of by Dissenters & some Churchmen?

Again, it seems to be unwise to extrude Dissenters from Vestries. A

---

[14] That Walpole's bill be read this day six months.
[15] Trelawny's letters were published on 18 Jan. 1859, p. 10, 24 Jan. 1859, p. 12, 2 Feb. 1859, p. 6, and 10 Feb. 1859, p. 10. See below, 17 Mar. 1859, for the debate on Trelawny's motion.
[16] 26 Feb. 1859, pp. 234–5.

Dissenter may object to a compulsory tax who may not object to a Voluntary rate. He may object to a rate when a Puseyite Minister is the incumbent, & agree to pay it when a Low-Churchman is appointed. Yet, when he has once claimed exemption as a Dissenter, he may hesitate to appear again at Church. Thus the Church may be a loser; – instead of an occasional contributor to the Church funds, it may have an obstinate opponent.

[...] The fabrics of Churches are National property. At present the future question of the manner of dealing with sects & endowments is in abeyance. Churchmen are allowed to hold quiet possession – &, while they do this, Dissenters expect Churchmen to keep fabrics in good repair. But it does not follow that Dissenters shd. so far renounce their rights as to agree to give up their power of voting at Vestries, since this might have the effect of consolidating the title of one particular communion to monopolise the use of Church buildings in all future time.

I think Walpole's plan, when understood, will make mine appear a featherbed in comparison. It is better to lose your tail at once than inch by inch – which was Cobden's remark on gradual abolition of the Corn Laws.

Dissenters do not object on the score of amount, they object to a compulsory impost.

Those who know anything of party feeling in towns & parishes & who allow for the known feelings of human nature, will be prepared for the prediction that Dissenters will not largely avail themselves of the exemption offered by Mr. Walpole's Bill. Many a man would prefer payment of the compulsory tax to a formal declaration of Dissent. Pride would induce a man who had once proclaimed his dissent to continue in a state of dissidence. Exclusive dealing is sometimes practised in order to influence votes. Dissenters would not generally claim exemption, & hence the Bill is no settlement. As Mr. Bright said the objection to pay these rates is mainly sentimental. The amount is insignificant – the real grievance is the compulsoriness of the tax.

The tendency of Mr. Walpole's Bill is to draw broadly the line of demarcation betwn. Churchmen & Dissenters. The tendency of my Bill would be to fuse apparently incongruous elements. He leaves occasions of controversy & false triumph open. I endeavour to close irritating discussion & found harmony.

Monday, 28 February: Walpole has resigned – & Estcourt[17] informs me that he will probably withdraw the Church rates Bill. It appears

---

[17] T.H. Sotheron-Estcourt had replaced Walpole as home secretary.

that he has a different view of the remedy wh. shd. be proposed. We have fixed on Wednesday 9th. for both bills.

Disraeli introduced his Reform Bill[18] in a speech of more than 3 hours. I only heard a part of it. The scheme is not well received. The Liberals – almost to a man – oppose it. They call it a measure of disfranchisement. I cannot help thinking that they are somewhat unfair. The measure might more correctly be described as a moderate Reform barely worth a stir. As I now understand it – very partially however – I cannot say that the measure would be good for nothing. The enfranchisement of all the educated classes is in itself a great merit. Also, the £10 franchise in Counties is a point, which we have been endeavouring to obtain for many years. Why refuse it when proffered? [...]

Tuesday, 1 March: Walpole & Henley[19] make statements. The vice of the Reform Bill, in their view, is the equalization of the franchise in town & country. This they deem to be anti-Conservative – & to a very dangerous degree.

The opinion of many members is that the Bill will get a 2d. reading. Disraeli, in effect, bribes members to vote for it, by not disfranchising their boroughs – or only taking away one member.

The Tories are all in commotion. Interviews are frequent. Lord Derby has met a large following – some 200.[20]

Will not dread of war – difficulty of foreign relations – fear of constituents – halfheartedness of pseudo-liberals on the ex-govt. Benches (with other causes) conduce to the success of the Reform Bill?

Monday, 7 March: [...] A rumour circulated that Lord Palmerston & Lord John had agreed upon opposing the 2d. reading of the Reform Bill.[21] It was said that deputations had waited upon each of the Independent liberals – & with good results.[22]

Horsman & I had some talk on the proper course to be taken on the 2d. reading of the Reform Bill. I told him that I could not at present quite understand that we are not in danger of factious conduct

[18] Providing for a £10 household franchise in the counties, and an increase in the borough electorate of around 200,000 through a number of 'fancy franchises'. Fifteen small two-member boroughs were to lose one of their seats, and these were to be redistributed to urban and industrial areas; *P.P.* 1859 (1), ii. 649.

[19] Explaining their resignations.

[20] Cf. Gathorne Hardy's diary, 2 Mar. 1858, in A.E. Gathorne Hardy, *Gathorne Hardy, 1st Earl of Cranbrook: A Memoir*, (1910), i. 127–8.

[21] Cf. Henry Reeve (ed.), *The Greville Memoirs*, (1888 ed.), viii. 233–4 (9 Mar. 1859).

[22] The two independent liberals referred to were Horsman and Roebuck, but this was a false rumour, as their subsequent behaviour shows; see below, 18 and 23 Mar. 1859.

in opposing a 2d. reading – since, perhaps, while of course Disraeli could not ask his party to follow him in tendering a large measure of extension of suffrage, he yet might affect to be coerced in Committee by a tyrant majority & then turn round & inquire of his supporters whether upon a question of a diff[eren]ce of a few pounds in the amount of a qualification it would be wise to throw up the reins of govt. – in the midst, especially, of European complications. Horsman was evidently of this opinion – & said that he had never known an instance in which a political party had not eventually suffered from a vote which was not given on its intrinsic merits, but under personal considerations & mere hostility to men in power [. . .]

Wednesday, 9 March: Today I expect to move that the reading of Walpole's Church Rate bill be postponed till this day six months. No one can be sure what he will say in a speech. A cheer – a taunt – a casual circumstance – may altogether throw one off the scent – & the rest is very much an affair of nerve or luck. I clearly see, however, the line I propose to take.[23]

[. . .] Glorious majority – 254 to 171! I was a teller.

I think that my speech was better than that which I wrote above. The succeeding speakers amplified my grounds of objection. Pakington lost his temper. Walpole was very feeble. Hardcastle seconded creditably. Sir George Grey, Bethell & Lowe dealt heavy blows at the miserable fruits of Walpole's winter cogitations. Omissions & commissions alike damned the wretched bill. It seem to sin agt. every principle – ecclesiastical, fiscal, constitutional, politic – &, as such, was scouted by the House. I gave notice to proceed with my Bill tomorrow. This is too daring for some nerves. But objectors hardly consider the force of my situation. Members dare not absent themselves. Govt. has the same interest, as I have, in forwarding the settlement of the question for a year at least. To be in minorities night after night is to be avoided at any price. To postpone my bill till the first open Wednesday is to prevent legislation in my sense for another year. Early as we sent the bill to the Lords last year, it was complained that the period in the Session was too late.

Thursday, 10 March: Announcement of amendments of & on Reform. Miles of Somerset gave a notice of a proposal to mitigate the harshness of the Bill as regards freeholders for counties residing in Boroughs, who would be disfranchised.

---

[23] At this point in the diary, Trelawny rehearsed the speech he was about to make in the Commons, for which see *H* clii. 1567–74; see above, 21 and 25 Feb. 1859, for his arguments.

The Tories deem it to be wise to yield in time.[24]

[...] Members kept asking me all the evening if I really meant to keep them all night for Church rates. I pertinaciously replied that a division on the question or an adjournment I was resolved to have – & so I did. I then gave way to an appeal from my opponents – & put the Bill down for friday. We must force a 2d. reading.

Disraeli evidently means to give way gradually on Reform – so as, if possible, to take the wind out of the sails of the opposition & yet not lose his party. The latter are evidently not insensible of the advantages of holding office – & might be found to be more practical & less fanatically honest than some think or they pretend.

Friday, 11 March: [...] Bulwer Lytton made a stilted, pompous, seriocomic & prolix reply.[25] He has everything to learn in the art of answering questions in Parliament. Disraeli's face it was painful to behold. Lord Stanley smiled, but smiled as though it were no smiling matter. The worst is that Bulwer-Lytton, being deaf was not aware that the House was at length fairly bored with a general buzz, in wh. it was evidently impossible that the reporters could catch the orator's words – & as these will be rendered in an incorrect & disjointed form, great mischief may be done to the individuals whose character is involved. The real wit of Bulwer-Lytton certainly failed to redeem a manner unpardonable in a Secretary of State. Graham's face indicated mixed pity & contempt – which he often affects. What a falling off since he forsooth! was on that bench!

[...] I got a day for Church rates by putting on the screw – & holding out a menace of moving that my bill shd. take precedence of government orders on an early night. Scores of members beset me with unsolicited counsels – less farsighted than obstrusive. The fact is each wanted to get home to dinner or to go to the play – & no doubt many cared little enough for my responsibilities. Some, no doubt, meant to render me a kindness – & one certainly so intended – I mean that excellent old gentleman, Lord Hotham.

Lord Clarence Paget made a capital speech on a motion to require estimates before the admiralty shall again be allowed to commit the Nation to an expense over £1,000 in naval architecture.[26] He

---

[24] Under the existing law, freeholders of property worth between £2 and £10 per annum, living in boroughs, were entitled to vote in the adjoining county as 40s. freeholders. The government now agreed to reserve this right for existing borough freeholders. Trelawny was wrong to write that such freeholders were originally going to be 'disfranchised': they were to be given borough instead of county votes.

[25] The Colonial secretary, in answer to Ridley on the corruption amongst government officers in Hong Kong.

[26] *H* cliii. 39–48.

produced a very favourable impression. Pakington[27] tried to be severe in his reply, but was merely ridiculously feeble. He had done as well as it was reasonable to expect in a person placed at the head of a great Department of the duties of wh. he knew nothing – & that qualified praise the House gave him. But the implied censure on a man who accepts an office for which he is not fitted remains in full force. We divided [...] & were in a minority – 97 to 117.

The officials & ex officials – feeling sore – became rather abusive. Osborne vented virtuous indignation as tho' the character of Sir Baldwin Walker[28] had been attacked. Young Baring (T.G.) charged inaccuracy on Paget – so did others – Sir F. Baring suspected he (P) was a better navigator than calculator. However, the impression was very strong that vast sums had been wasted – & something, I think, will come out of it.

I heard one of the clerks say that Disraeli ought to have told the Speaker of the intention to have a morning sitting for Church rates on tuesday – & I received a hint to say something to Mr. Speaker, which I did, offering to take some other opportunity. This was very well received – & was evidently called for. Mr. Speaker spoke most kindly & generously – he was ready cheerfully to undertake the toil. But Disraeli might have had tact enough to render this step unnecessary [...]

Tuesday, 15 March: Twelve o'clock sitting for 2d. reading of Church Rates. Darby Griffith bored the House for one hour & by the reaction to the nonsense talked materially aided my cause. He had an amendment wholly impracticable & altogether superseded by the progress of events. At the suggestion of Estcourt, the Home Minister, he withdrew it.

Then came Hope, who made a witty & unexceptionable speech – stating his objections in a temperate & straightforward manner.

Osborne made a dashing onslaught in his vigorous style. Sidney Herbert poured out some milk & water – drawing nice distinctions & refinements. Packe twaddled lugubriously amidst a well-sustained din & then I briefly followed – having only 5 minutes left, for had I spoken longer, I shd. have lost my division by expiration of time, it being a morning sitting.[29] The division gave me a majority of 74. Numbers 242 to 168.[30]

[...] Darby Griffith tried to identify me with the Liberation

---

[27] First Lord of the admiralty.
[28] Chief constructor for the navy.
[29] Which had to finish by 2 p.m.
[30] The bill made no further progress before the dissolution.

Society – on the ground that a newspaper, mentioning a soirée thereof, stated that my absence on a certain occasion arose from ill health. The fact is, I foresaw this attack would be made – &, when I was invited to attend the meeting alluded to, I believe I declined on the ground of health – as a courteous way of escaping an embarrassment. I never was a member of the Society much as I agree with many of its opinions. It is not my custom to join societies of this description, as I well know to what dangers they lead political men, who often are called upon to accept responsibility for follies or misdeeds of others.

By the way, we got a great convert in Stuart-Wortley.[31] He threw out a suggestion as to the feasibility of introducing clauses in Committee calculated to smooth the asperities of naked Repeal. I deemed it to be politic to lend a favourable ear to this suggestion.

Wednesday, 16 March: [...] I met Mowbray[32] to whom I made a suggestion regarding Stuart-Wortley's idea of inserting palliative clauses in Committee which would save the dignity of govt. & the Lords & be accepted by the Liberal party. Of course, the principle of the measure must not be touched [...]

Thursday, 17 March: We divided on the G[uar]ds question & were triumphantly defeated.[33] Yet, I think I was not answered.

General Peel[34] made a very bad speech – & committed the grave indiscretion of throwing a slur on the Line, as if it could not be trusted with the defence of the Sovereign. He will regret his remark. Codrington replied to things I never said – so did Lord Bury. Both threw a cloud of dust in the eyes of members, who cheered inanely. We had rather a brisk skirmish. William Coningham fairly broke down – the House were not very well bred towards him. He had come in when the debate was nearly over – & consequently was hardly in a situation to speak with effect.

We only mustered 33, tellers included – but we were right. My speech was substantially what I intended to say[35] – I forgot a few

---

[31] Conservative member for Honiton.
[32] Judge-advocate-general.
[33] Trelawny's motion for a select committee, defeated by 135:31.
[34] Secretary for war.
[35] Trelawny had again used the diary to rehearse his speech. He argued that the efficiency of the army suffered as a result of the privileges enjoyed by the Guards regiments, notably in the way that Guards officers held higher ranks, and therefore received higher pay, than their equivalents in regiments of the Line. Staffing levels and allowances, in Trelawny's view, were extravagant. Guards captains were given excessive leave and they did little company duty. The Guards were generally exempted from foreign service, but when they did go abroad, their privileges excited feelings of jealousy amongst the other regiments; see *H* cliii. 276–9, 292.

points [...] I find that a number of good men paired for my motion. All honour to them!

Friday, 18 March: Roebuck called on me & mentioned a plan he had conceived of recommending to government to proceed in the matter of Reform by way of resolutions instead of by bill. He stated at some length the reasons which guided him – & asked my opinion. I replied that I could not speak hastily on a point so weighty, but that I admitted the very difficult position in which the Independent party were placed. After further conversation, he left – & this evening at $\frac{1}{2}$ past 4 he went up to the Speaker, in order, I presume, to insure priority to Cox who had on the notice paper a similar project. Roebuck proceeded – very bitterly towards the Palmerston people. Bouverie rose to order – but took nothing by his interruption but a sarcasm.

Roebuck continued. After a few more remarks he sat down – &, amid roars of laughter, Cox began. He kept his temper & spoke on the whole with propriety & discretion. A blunder, however, in language excited great merriment – he talked of the House 'changing sides' – & then, I believe, in the vehemence of his action, he rapped J.B. Smith on the head. At least so I gathered. *Smith told me this was error – yet several thought so.*

When he sat down, it was hoped that Lord John or Disraeli would speak – but the oracles were dumb [...] Roebuck's scheme failed – and eke Cox's.

Monday, 21 March: I heard Lord John move his resolution[36] – in a fresh & racy speech – not too long – & putting his points very neatly. I think I have rarely heard him speak better. It was a very full House – almost every place taken at prayers. Lots of petitions were presented – only two in favour of the Bill – these last excited much mirth.

[...] Horsman stoutly contended for the 2d. reading of the Bill.

It does not seem likely that he will have a very considerable following among the liberals though something may be said for his course – &, indeed, he said it.

[...] Lord Stanley boldly challenged the vote as one which was less whether the Bill should pass than whether power shd. pass into new hands. He cited the opinions of Mill & Holyoake[37] (murmurs) in

[36] Condemning the government's plan to interfere with the borough freeholder's right to a county vote, and calling for a greater extension of the suffrage in the boroughs; *H* cliii. 389–405.
[37] John Stuart Mill and George Jacob Holyoake were prominent radical reformers and secularists.

favour of restriction on account of an admitted unfitness of the masses for the franchise.

Tuesday, 22 March: The House put the screw on me to give way on Church Rates. When both sides pressed, I had no choice. It was evident to me that Disraeli desired to know his fate. He, at least, urged me to let the Reform Debate proceed. So did Lord John. At all events I was not wanting in a modest resistance.

There appears to be no course for me but to vote with Lord John R. as govt. have, thro' Lord Stanley, fairly accepted the issue. There appears to be no notion of a better Bill – & the proposers desire to be judged on the evidence as it stands.

These set debates give working members a little rest – the division will not be taken till the end of the week [...]

Wednesday, 23 March: [...] Horsman's opinion seems not to excite much sympathy. Members of very independent views – such as Locke King – think that a position of so much singularity is most probably wrong. Yet, very good men have been in a minority of one. If the govt. measure were but a trifle more defensible, independent members would stand in a better position. [...] Roebuck I understand meditates some new course on the Reform Bill. I heartily wish that it were possible for us to avoid an opposition to the 2d. reading of the govt. Bill. But it is difficult to see how this can be.

Every one agrees that Bulwer-Lytton's declamation was very brilliant & that Sir Hugh Cairns was very severe & personal – chiefly at Lord John's expense. Roebuck means, I fancy, to ask the government to adopt certain changes, to be proposed by him – &, failing this, he will move an amendment on Lord John's amendment. It will be many days ere we divide, I ween.

Thursday, 24 March: A House nearly full before prayers – a thing I never yet saw! Is every member going to speak? [...] Gibson now opened[38] – but in a rather dull, laboured & prosaic manner. He did not warm to his work. So, being still unwell & the House being very hot & close, I went home.

Returning to the House early in the evening I found W.J. Fox on his legs making an earnest appeal on behalf of the working classes. The matter of his speech was so good that one was provoked that he spoke in so low a voice. Still, he was listened to with the respectful attention he deserves. He always says something worth hearing.

Hope followed – & bored the House. He spoke too long by $\frac{1}{2}$ an

---

[38] Debate on the reform bill, continued.

hour. Next succeeded Bernal Osborne – whom I once called – to the delight of his father – the Murat of debate – and a Murat he was. He kept the House in roars of laughter for 37 minutes – citing most inconvenient passages from former speeches of the Colonial Minister[39] & others – &, especially, taking to task Sir Hugh Cairns for his personality to Lord John Russell.

Walpole lugubriously explained his views on the Bill, which it seems he cannot support in its present shape.[40] Sir R. Peel[41] is evidently his model – which, however, he will never realize. The organ is wanting – but the imitator has hit & exaggerates the plausibility & solemnity of the type he affects.

Bright appears to have made a good speech. Yet, I should not pronounce it one of his broadest & best. Indeed, few of the speeches yet delivered have been worthy of the occasion – the subject being no less than the requirements of the British Constitution.

Friday, 25 March: [...] Palmerston's speech[42] seems to have been very ingenious &, at the same time, defiant. It must have been 'gall & wormwood' to the government, whom he held to their bargain of conducting the administration of very difficult affairs. Lord Palmerston considered that dissolution would be improper & would probably be successfully resisted by the majority. The Bill shd. proceed despite Lord John's resolution. Why not? Whiteside seems to have acted as the Osborne of his party. It is fortunate that, in these interminable debates, all are not as dull as decorous Mr. Walpole or irreproachable & melancholic as Mr. Cardwell or 'dyspeptic' as Horsman *Osborne's epithet.*

It is considered that Palmerston has outwitted Lord John. For, after all, he does not appear to be in any degree nearer the post of Premier. Nor, indeed, is it conceivable that he should form a stable government. The people below the gangway are, as Bulwer-Lytton has it, 'bound together by a rope of sand' – & all the rank & file are distrustful not merely of leaders but of leadership. + The best chance of ruling is not to disaffect it. +

Monday, 28 March: [...] There has been an ugly report that Govt. has been keeping back a certain contract for aid to the Galway packet Line to America in order to sway votes of some Irish & English members. A judicious question hereupon was asked by Cowper – the

---

[39] Bulwer Lytton.
[40] He had resigned as home secretary because of his opposition to the bill.
[41] The prime minister, not his son.
[42] In the reform bill debate, continued.

reply being rather evasive. No vote is to be asked this year, since the contract would only begin to take effect next. Also, that the matter is still under consideration of the Admiralty. Now, this reply leaves the insinuation untouched.

[...] The great Edwin James for Marylebone opened the Ball. I heard him for a $\frac{1}{4}$ of an hour & compared him to a feebler Osborne. Yet, he drove Palmerston's barb even further in & then wriggled it about, & in his ad hominem points was not infelicitous. He will never be a man of moral weight in the House – he may be a good scold to order – & do much useful work for Ministers [...]

Several members spoke – Elcho amongst the rest. But the great speech was Graham's which was a deadly blow to the government measure. If I mistake not, Sir James means to enter the new Cabinet.[43] He, an author of the Reform Bill of 1832, very artfully argued that the Disraelite concoction was dangerously democratic. It introduced innovations deliberately rejected in the Bill of 1832, viz (inter alia), the uniformity of franchises which leads by a mere turn of a screw to electoral districts. Also, he disliked the system of voting papers[44] – as liable to fraud, injustice & intimidation. Sir James, still opposed to the Ballot, strongly expressed his view of the growing approval it gains among constituencies – & the probability of its eventual adoption. Voting papers go far to ensure this. Pakington spoke with warmth & energy [...]

Tuesday, 29 March: [...] Gladstone seems to have been as singular as people expected he would be.[45]

Thursday, 31 March: [...] The liberals are very anxious to divide – yet, how can we expect that? Peel is going to speak. Many are giving up the attempt to catch the Speaker's eye.

[...] I heard Walter & Gilpin – neither very effective.

Henley's speech was, tho' long & prosy, interesting on account of his having so recently left the Cabinet. There was much practical good sense in his notices of the Bill, but he never rises above common place. Unfortunately, too, he thinks he possesses dry wit – & affects the being quaint & arch – delivering old laws as if he were their inventor & in a manner of one who thinks he is peculiarly knowing

---

[43] While playing a prominent part in the assault on the Derby ministry, and acting as an advisor to Russell, Graham had already decided not to take office again because of his poor health; C.S. Parker, *Life and Letters of Sir James Graham, 1792–1861*, (1907), ii, 379–91.

[44] For the proposed postal votes, which would have benefited plural voters.

[45] Taking his stand neither for Russell nor the government, and pleading for the retention of the small boroughs as 'nurseries of Statesmen'; *H* cliii. 1045–67.

& sagacious – by no means likely to accept bad for good coin. The secret of Henley's rise has been the maxim 'labore'. He has worked – &, in the dearth of men, became necessary.

But the fact that such a man was ever in a Cabinet is a great fact in the History of English politics, & proves that it is high time for the country gentlemen to go to school, lest they be supplanted by pupil teachers.

Roebuck made a severe speech – passing in review Palmerston, Bright & Lord John. He put to Disraeli certain questions, would he accept particular alterations of the Bill in Committee? If so, Roebuck agreed to vote with govt.[46]

Disraeli made a very long speech – near 2 hours. He declined to pledge himself in the manner required by Roebuck.

The gist of Disraeli's speech was critical. He darkly threatened dissolution – & asserted that the course of Lord John at that particular moment had done the Public serious injury.

I could not remain to hear the whole speech – which appears to have been copious, diffuse & personal – not one of his best.

There was a great gathering of members. We defeated government. Numbers, 330 to 291.

Afterwards, amid great confusion, Wyld put a Ballot motion[47] agt. the advice of older & much wiser men. We were, in consequence, defeated ingloriously.[48] Many walked out in disgust.

What next! Dissolution or Resignation?

Various rumours fly about. I heard a county member describe what he had just heard – that Lord Derby was to go & the governt. to be cobbled up. Not the worst plan provided always that an effective Reform Bill shall pass at once.

[...] There is a curious character in the House – one John Green MP for Kilkenny. He is of the very widest school of politicians – & seems to be of opinion that the House is full of none but rogues. He was in the gallery after the first division & conceived the notion that members desired to shirk a division on the Ballot, so he amused himself by violently declaiming agt. everybody & in stentorian & almost solitary tones, & keeping up the cry exclaiming 'divide divide'. One of his neighbours, after vain remonstrance, sheered off to escape suspicion of concurrence, and then Green fastened on me – & I hardly knew what to be at. I have reason to think he is a visionary, perfectly

---

[46] He wanted to see a £6 borough franchise, a £10 county franchise and no transfer of voters from counties to boroughs; *H* cliii. 1223–30.

[47] An amendment to Russell's resolution; *H* cliii. 1261–2.

[48] 328:98; Trelawny in the minority.

honest, but seems to me to be as mad as a hatter. He has a crotchet on printing – an invention.

Saturday, 2 April: The House stand adjourned till Monday, losing Friday. We are awaiting our fate. The question of dissolution hangs in uncertainty.

It seems that had we carried Wyld's motion, as we might by abstention from voting on the part of the Conservatives, Lord John's resolution as amended would probably have been defeated. For this I certainly was not prepared; &, possibly, the vote was injudicious. At all events, Wyld should not have placed us in a position so liable to misconstruction from either of two grounds, either that one was hostile to the Ballot or hostile to the resolution. On this account it was, no doubt, that many leading liberals forbore to vote – as I understood.

[...] The Tory club is said to be opposed to a dissolution. The 'Times' seems puzzled. The funds refuse to move – a compliment, perhaps, to free Institutions & to the moderation of the existing Parliament. No compliment to the government, if the stock exchange will not even put on a suit of black.

6 pm. The opinion grows strong that government will remain in office at the earnest wish of the Queen, who is said to be in considerable anxiety.[49]

Monday, 4 April: Dissolution announced [...] Disraeli has already issued his manifesto speaking of a 'political manoeuvre'.[50] He & Lord Derby have lost no time in dissecting Lord John Russell. We must now proceed to organize our parties & our cry must be 'To your tents, O Israel.' [...]

A NEW PARLIAMENT[51]

Tuesday, 31 May: The House met about two. Pretty full [...] The usher of the black rod entered in full canonicals of blue & gold, &, as usual, advanced to the table by very slow & awe-inspired jerks & with a command of face which no other person that I ever heard of could pretend to, required the presence of the Commons in the House of Lords to hear the Queen's commiss[io]n read. Several of the more

[49] The Cabinet had already decided, on 1 Apr., to dissolve parliament; Hawkins, *Art of Politics*, p. 225.
[50] Published in *The Times*, 5 Apr. 1859, p. 12.
[51] Trelawny returned for Tavistock without a contest.

curious members went up in a body & finding nothing exciting returned immediately.

Col[onel] Wilson Patten now addressed the clerk at the table & proposed Mr. Denison[52] for Speaker, who sat 4th from the bar on the bench on the floor – & on the ministerial side, which meant 'No party man'.

Patten acquitted himself with the taste of an experienced member of good sense & unpretending manners. His allusion to the length of time he had known Denison – 50 years – was feeling enough. The speech was, perhaps, a shade longer than necessary, but well sustained & discreet in all respects. Patten, as a very valuable & painstaking private business member, was a good authority in speaking of Denison's usefulness in such matters, wh. mostly escape the Public eye. Sir F. Baring seconded – in a good speech which, however, seemed to me to advert unnecessarily to Denison's want of practice when first elected Speaker – even though the object was to shew how much he had improved.

Hereupon Denison made a speech very appropriate to the occasion & was then conducted to the chair where he personally returned thanks. So far all was a marvel of well studied art & diction – & the action was all in keeping.

Disraeli's speech followed. He was brief, fluent & epigrammatic. The contrast was not quite favourable to preceding speakers who now seemed to have lacked oil. Disraeli rarely hesitates. Lord Palmerston had little to say. All the stock phrases were exhausted – & jokes would have been out of place [. . .]

Wednesday, 1 June: We attended to take the oaths & write our names in the Book. The Speaker present. A long table down the floor of the House was covered with copies of the oath to be taken, the same posted on strong card-board & there was a copious supply of Testaments. Counties were called alphabetically. The clerk began with County members & then he called on the Borough members of each. When the table had some 40 or 50 collected around it, the oath was read by the clerk aloud & by each member who, mumbling in chorus with his fellows, helped to produce a far from harmonious or impressive body of sound. No thought of the matter or the sanction: & one I know, by mistake, kissed the oath instead of the book. The mover & seconder of the Speaker led the way in this business – I presume, by courtesy. After swearing & writing in the book, each member was introduced to Mr. Speaker by Sir D. Le Marchant,

---

[52] Speaker in the previous parliament.

Senior clerk, & received some complimentary speech in a kindly tone & a shake of the hand – & so passed on behind the chair [...]

Thursday, 2 June: [...] It was pleasant to receive the cordial greetings of men who had rarely got beyond a frozen bow before. I do not think the English gentry want feeling, they are only fearful of rejection [...]

Friday, 3 June: [...] I note that the Liberals are likely to come to some vote for the purpose of removing the government from office. Are we strong enough? Is it wise to clutch the fruit before it is ripe? Has not each premature attack strengthened our foe – discovering his weak points wh. he at once fortifies anew? Opinions on politics are falsified almost as soon as written. However that be, at this moment I think we are about to be tempted to make a rash move.

Monday, 6 June: [...] The Liberal party met at Willis's rooms.[53] I attended. Palmerston was speaking on a platform – a few others equally conspicuous – Lord John amongst them.

The general tone & feeling of the meeting were very good. Bright was remarkably discreet & moderate. Lord John & Palmerston rivalled each other in expressing disinterestedness & readiness to co-operate. The entente cordiale seemed perfect, till Roebuck threw his shell into the party – that shell being well charged with the elements of disunion. The gist of his speech was this: he disbelieved in the possibility of a cordial combination of the various sections of the Liberal party – &, in particular, he doubted whether the 2 rival Lords would long co-operate in the same Cabinet. He, also, thought that it was not good policy to turn out the existing government without some approach to certainty of securing better men. Horsman, also, opposed – Lindsay I did not hear – old Ellice spoke on the other side. Sidney Herbert & Coningham – as well as John Locke, Edwin James & Deasy made a few observations – uttering, however, nothing noteworthy. Upshot war to the Knife.[54]

Bright was hardly satisfied with Palmerston's assurances of a pacific policy – till Lord P. had spoken again, when he gave more satisfaction. Lindsay's[55] criticisms did Lord John a good turn, as he, also, replied in an assuring tone & manner – with increased explicitness.

It was a curious meeting. The force of habit threw us into the form

[53] The famous meeting marking the reunion of the Liberal party.
[54] It was agreed to support Lord Hartington's amendment to the Address expressing a want of confidence in the Queen's ministers.
[55] Another of the 'independent' Liberals.

of a real House of Commons – we formed a sort of oval with a floor
in the middle – the floor being unoccupied, altho' many still crowded
the doorways. People at the doors took our names at a table, the
Whips said we numbered 280. The crowd outside were, I heard, less
favourable to Palmerston than to Lord John.

Graham was, to use a phrase lately criticized, conspicuous by his
absence – Nor was Cobden present – but the latter has probably not
returned from America.[56]

I noted that, when Roebuck was making his onslaught, Lords
Palmerston & John Russell were very skilful in their mode of dis-
sembling their annoyance. Palmerston leant forward with a sort of
smile of half astonished curiosity – as much as to say, What can
Roebuck mean? P. affected the air of 'un homme incompris' – good
natured but puzzled. Then he used his hand as if deaf – so as to leave
it uncertain whether the worst hits reached him. Lord John bore his
share with good temper. I observed that at one passage he drew a
deep sigh. Roebuck had several interruptions – but no cheers of
approval.

Tuesday, 7 June: I went down about $\frac{1}{4}$ before one p.m. & found
many members already in the House. We were mostly anxious to
secure places by prior occupation. The rule is that one may secure a
particular place (till a division occur, I believe) by inserting a card
at the time of prayers with one's name on it in a place suited expressly
to receive it at the back of each seat. But sometimes custom over-rides
the letter of the rule – & well known members are tacitly allowed to
hold particular places. I mention this because it is the key to some
little byplay wh. followed. Roebuck took the place wh. Lord John R.
used to hold – i.e, just below the gangway on the floor. But Roebuck
was for a short time out of the House, during wh. period Lord John
came in & took his R's place in spite of the card. Next Graham
deserted his old place on the 2d. row from the floor below the gangway
on the ministerial side & made a dash at Horsman's place on the
opposition side. This he failed in getting in spite of some clever
manoeuvring – for he pretended not to know it belonged to any one,
whereas Horsman had long been allowed to retain it unquestioned. I
offered Graham my place, wh. he declined; on wh. he took Hadfield's –
but this too he lost. Eventually he took refuge with ostentatious
modesty on the back benches. However, we are lucky in getting this
great piece of artillery on our side.

Soon we are summoned to the Lords – & although, to prevent
unseemly confusion, a small number of persons who had put down

---

[56] He did not return until 29 June; Gladstone was another absentee from the meeting.

their names were called out to proceed with the Speaker, a general rush soon took place – & almost the whole House burst into House of Lords midst shouting, laughing & general hubbub. What must the Queen & her splendid band of ladies have thought of us? A goodlier sight than the scene before us was never dreamt of in fairy land – & cannot be adequately described. That scene we completely marred. The Queen's clear & melodious voice could scarcely be heard at long intervals – & we soon backed out as disgracefully as we entered – the very policemen could not help remonstrating.

[...] Mr. Egerton moved the address – with tolerable composure & ability – & was well received on both sides. Elphinstone seconded. Disraeli was unusually brilliant, as I *heard* from people present (for at this time I was at dinner).

The game of the Tories was to let our side speak. Palmerston, of course, taunted them with their disposition to let judgment go by default. He was very sparkling & facetious – creating amazing merriment – & provoking some very disconsolate oh! oh!s from the Tories. Eventually the debate was adjourned. It was said that 17 liberals were still unsworn – also, that 4 were on the Continent [...] One hears at the club[57] that the opposition will probably have a majority of about 12 or 15.

Thursday, 9 June: [...] Serjeant Deasy opened the Ball, on the adjourned debate commencing.

The only speech I heard was Graham's – which was, like most of his efforts, a work of art. It was very telling in parts – chiefly personal, however. His remarks on the conduct of government in Naval & military matters were of considerable Public value.

The government raised the allowance to Innkeepers for billets from $1\frac{1}{2}$ to 4d. and this was proclaimed just before the Election. It is true the Whigs had, also, recommended this step. But Graham dwelt upon the point of time when it was ostentatiously announced – &, in proof of animus, he produced a placard published at Devonport where the son of the Minister for War, Peel, stood – praising the liberality of government to the Innkeeper class – & contrasting the Whig $1\frac{1}{2}$ with the Conservative 4d.[58] This told immensely.

He was very severe on the subject of the dissolution – & the liberties taken by a government conspicuously in a minority – largely increasing the army & navy & settling very difficult & most important

[57] The Reform club.
[58] In spite of these tactics, A. Peel and his Conservative colleague were defeated by two Liberals.

questions of policy, like that of bounty to seamen,[59] by a stroke of a pen when no Parliament was in existence.

Whiteside replied – in a manner, as usual, more funny than Senatorial, but still, perhaps, useful for his party [...]

Friday, 10 June: Gibson opened the debate.[60] His speech, energetic as it was, did not impress me as one of his best. However, it was good, as every speech he makes is.

Lindsay followed, obtaining rapturous cheers from the Tories by promising them his vote. He dealt several damaging blows to the Liberal leaders.

3 a.m. I have just returned from the House which has divided – 323 to 310 – so government is defeated. House crammed. Many anxious faces flitting about the doorways while the process was going on – & some betting.

Cairns, who wound up, disappointed his audience, and 'divide, divide' was heard. His speech was too long & too minutely critical – rather suited to 8 o'clock in the evening than 2 a.m. in a wearied House.

Lord John & Roebuck spoke on opposite sides – with considerable effect. [...] Sidney Herbert made the best speech of the evening [...]

These party contests are very disgraceful. Great principles are forgotten amidst personal squabbles.

When the House broke up, there was vehement cheering in Westminster Hall on the part of a great multitude who appeared to be on the point of escorting us home. At least, that is the sense in which I understood the demonstration.

Saturday, 11 June: [...] Hayter[61] came down to the House at the noon sitting with a flower in his buttonhole – radiant with delight. It was whispered that the majority was in part due to the success of his efforts in endeavouring to convince certain patriots. The government people were, also, very active. One MP received a written offer of a post of an attaché for his son – of course, without stipulation – yet, on the eve of a life or death vote! For the truth of this I vouch. The tenderer of the bait has long been deemed the least-fitted of the governt. to be a Cabinet minister[62] – & this false move shews that the

---

[59] Owing to the fear of a European war, the government had recruited additional seamen by offering bounties of £10 to able seamen, £5 to ordinary seamen and £3 to landsmen.

[60] On the Address, continued.

[61] Liberal chief whip.

[62] Probably Sir John Pakington, the first Lord of the admiralty; see above, 11 Mar. 1859.

Public judgment is not far wrong. He should have more carefully studied his man. To fail was a blunder.

Friday, 17 June: [...] Several Election petitions were announced – & each announcement was followed by a sort of buzz like the responses in a litany; which buzz sounded comically. The House stands adjourned to tuesday the 21st [...]

Tuesday, 21 June: Grave doubts still exist whether government will last long. It is generally rumoured that Bright is furious. It is said that office has not been offered to him.[63] Then, Cobden will probably not accept the post assigned to him.[64] The cabinet consists of 16. If only 2 radicals receive posts, how can it be expected that the party below the gangway shd. be satisfied? It strikes me that all depends on the conduct of men in office. If they lose no time in bringing in good measures, they may create a confidence which they at present want.

I heard last night that the Tories already talk of getting some seats in the Cabinet on the extrusion of Gibson & Cobden, which some think must come. On the whole, it appears that Gibson has made a mistake.[65] I predict Cobden will not fall into the same pitfall [...]

Thursday, 30 June: [...] The new government took the benches assigned to them by the recent vote [...] Palmerston rose to sketch the intentions of Ministers with regard to Public business. There will be, he said, no time for more than routine measures. He seemed, however, to hint darkly at an autumn Session. He seemed very anxious to declare for neutrality as regards the war;[66] but did not think a tender of good offices likely to be useful yet. His speech was quiet & discreet – the speaker, however, seemed more broken & infirm than when he was last at the head of a government.

Graham sat behind Ministers just above the gangway. Roebuck was on the floor among the Tories. Horsman was low down among the independent radicals, where many others were congregated.

[...] Disraeli & Pakington looked half grim half amused – & their faces gave indications of mischief [...]

Monday, 4 July: So Cobden has declined to take office. It seems to

---

[63] Bright was excluded owing to the vehemence of his attacks on the aristocracy; Trevelyan, *John Bright*, pp. 282–3.

[64] The presidency of the board of trade.

[65] I.e. in accepting the chief commissionership of the poor law board; but see below, 30 June 1859.

[66] Austria had declared war on Sardinia, on 29 Apr., after the latter had refused to disarm. On 3 May, France intervened on Sardinia's side.

me that, unless 2 more 'advanced liberals' be taken into the Cabinet, Gibson's solitary grandeur will soon be intolerable to him. An opinion on future political events is worth little, but I cannot forbear to predict the speedy return of a Conservative government to office. There is a very angry feeling below the gangway – a feeling that faith has been signally broken with those who sit in that quarter. Men forgive offence to consistency & sound principles, but not a slight to themselves. At present the radicals are a laughing stock. However, we shall only be in truth ridiculous if we factiously neglect any duty. So whatever we may think of the Palmerston govt., let us take care to vote rightly.

5 p.m. Moderate House. Some new writs moved for. Villiers has taken the post which Gibson held till Cobden declined[67] (Sensation).

Bright asked a question of Sir C. Wood regarding Indian finance. Wood replied in that peculiar manner of his which has the air of resenting a question with addition of a hint of the folly of putting and the wisdom of the mode of answering it. Probably, he is not as self-sufficient & indiscreet as he seems – & it may be that what sounds like loss of temper is in reality nervousness. The Whigs do not shine in replies to questions.

[...] The appointment of Charles Villiers considerably improves the position of government. It will go far to engender a disposition to look upon the new Cabinet 'with interest & with hope' to use a phrase Villiers used many years ago when a liberal administration began to look with diminished disfavour on freetraders. Still the men below the gangway may complain that faith has not been kept with them – & middle class people will say Villiers is another aristocratic selection.[68]

Tuesday, 5 July: A good deal of the evening was taken up with discussion of Palk's notice on Volunteer Rifles corps.[69] The ex-minister for war & the present minister[70] made speeches. It struck me that Peel has improved in office, & merely wants practice. He has two great merits – courtesy & +the appearance of+ straightforwardness – +probably the reality.+ Sidney Herbert it is quite a relief to hear amid general dulness & commonplace.

[...] Wrightson brought in a bill to alter the law of Anne which requires members taking offices to go to their constituents to be newly

---

[67] C.P. Villiers had accepted the chief commissionership of the poor law board *vice* Milner Gibson, who now became president of the board of trade.

[68] He was the brother of the 4th Earl of Clarendon.

[69] For supplying arms and ammunition to the volunteers; *H* cliv. 678–82. Withdrawn.

[70] General Peel and Sidney Herbert respectively; the former was hostile to Palk's motion, the latter sympathetic.

endorsed.[71] Augustus Smith deemed this to be a dangerous innovation on the Constitution.

He put the possible case of a coalition betwn. a portion of a govt. & some new blood. The former might change their principles on taking higher offices in a new cabinet – &, as a check, he thought their constituents should have a voice in the arrangement. I voted with Smith – & we won by 2 votes[72] [...]

Wednesday, 6 July: A disagreeable day. Dillwyn's Bill on endowed schools was our subject. We won on a division,[73] but a stranger would have said that we had far the worst of the argument. Cairns made a short & telling speech agt. the bill. Yet, he admitted a grievance, denying however that the Bill hit the blot. Walpole was almost equally cogent. The government was vacillating, imbecile & disingenuous. They had neither the courage to oppose or support like men. Their attempts to explain their votes was scoffed at. It was in truth a sad spectacle [...] The gravamen is shortly this; – by certain rules of interpretation which obtain in Chancery, it happens that dissenters cannot act as trustees of Charities in certain cases because godly teaching or sound learning or some similar phrase is taken to mean identity of opinion with the established Church [...]

Monday, 11 July: An instructive chapter on Govt. Guarantees. Case of the India & Red Sea telegraph,[74] which appears to have been smuggled thro' Parliament from want of watchfulness. A vote was taken for postponement, but postponement was not carried.[75] Trelawny still absent. A habit has grown up of the Executive making agreements which practically bind Parliament to pay to companies large allowances in support of their undertakings [...]

Tuesday, 12 July: Great sensation on the announcement of peace[76] [...]

---

[71] To amend the Act 6 Anne c. 7 so that it did not apply in cases where existing members of the government were appointed to new offices; *H* cliv. 704–5.

[72] 53:51.

[73] 210:192 for the 2nd reading; the bill was later referred to a select committee.

[74] The government had guaranteed the company a $4\frac{1}{2}$ percent return on its capital for the next fifty years, and nominated two ex-officio directors.

[75] Sir James Graham's motion was defeated by 177:130.

[76] On 11 July France and Austria had agreed to the peace preliminaries of Villafranca whereby Austria was to retain Venetia but cede Lombardy to France, who would then hand this over to Sardinia. A confederation of the Italian states, under the honorary presidency of the Pope, was also envisaged, although this idea was dropped at the subsequent peace conference at Zurich. *B.F.S.P.* xlix. 87–8.

Wednesday, 13 July: Trelawny had requested Mr. Dillwyn to move the second reading of the Church rate abolition Bill, which was carried by a triumphant majority of seventy. Ayes 263 Noes 193. The debate was remarkable as proving that the leaders of the Whigs have succumbed – not so much to the pressure of reason, as to the voice of opinion out of doors. Yet both are right. Cornewall Lewis, Palmerston, & Lord John, have learnt to vote as wisely as Lord Stanley. Of course D'Israeli reminded Lord John & Palmerston of their past telling speeches the other way, but on the whole the opposition was languid. I fear I had no pair, though I wrote to Dillwyn to try to get me one.

Friday, 15 July: [...] Dillwyn says it was impossible to pair me satisfactorily on Church rates since it was notorious that I was ill. To pair me, as he said, with a 'dead man' would have been of no good.

Thursday, 21 July: [...] There was much discursive talk in which Disraeli, Gladstone, Bright & Palmerston took part. I note that Bright hailed Disraeli's pacific & anti-intervention views. Fraternization in that quarter were ominous for government [...]

Tuesday, 26 July: [...] An episode on private business. A member (Whalley) complained that the Lords had passed a clause in a railway Bill[77] giving a company power to take an unnecessarily large slice of his park for their purposes. I could not forbear to beg that he might receive a hint not to advocate his own case. He was obstinate, & not only failed in his object, but received a hint from Mr. Speaker that his course was not the usual one. I really felt disposed to offer to fight his battle rather than that he should be so irretrievably indiscreet [...]

Thursday, 28 July: At the morning sitting I called attention to the subject of the New Zealand (£500,000) Loan & the (as I believed) inaccurate evidence by which the House of Commons was misled into guaranteeing the same.[78] The Undersecretary of the Colonies[79] gave me credit for having taken pains to elucidate the matter, but would not allow that the Colonial office wd. have acted differently even if Mr. Sewell's evidence had not been characterized by a certain 'absence of frankness'.

In short there the matter rests. My duty is done. Let Parliament protect itself – & so I said.

[...] Evening sitting. A very interesting debate followed Lord John

---

[77] The Vale of Llangollen railway bill.
[78] See above, 10 May 1858.
[79] Chichester Fortescue.

Russell's statement on foreign affairs [...] Lord John & Palmerston spoke out manfully & in a highly liberal strain, which it did one good to hear.[80]

I believe it will be quite impracticable to get the Church Rates Bill thro' the Houses of Parliament this year. The patience of members is fairly exhausted.[81]

Friday, 29 July: [...] At the 6 o'clock sitting Horsman's motion on our National defences came on. His proposal is to treat these as the proper occasion for a loan & as of too great magnitude to be met out of income.[82] Sidney Herbert,[83] Cobden & Palmerston, among others, spoke well – & the motion was lost.[84] My health sent me home early. But I must frankly say that had I had the least idea that Horsman would have divided I might have either paired or waited till a later hour[85] – though the latter would have been wrong, as I cannot afford another late attendance.

Cobden spoke warmly in his old sense agt. the rivalry of Nations in creating immense armies & fleets. At the same time he avowed that we ought to have a commanding naval armament, & rather than peril our safety from weakness in that respect, he said he would as cheerfully vote £500,000,000 as £5,000 (or some such sum). This produced a great sensation – the Tories almost sprang from their seats for joy. They seemed to say 'why he is one of us after all, a Briton to the backbone!'

Of course, Palmerston declared his confidence in the power of the Nation – not merely the Line & Militia but the people themselves.

Bright agreed with me in thinking that the Church rate bill shd. not be further pressed. Many members had already complained of the late attendance which I required of them – & certainly I can well understand their feelings [...]

Thursday, 4 August: [...] It is very provoking to be absent so long, but I cannot help it. One might pair till the end of the session, but then an Independent member might make bad matters worse, since he might often pair with a friend. One may sometimes pair advan-

---

[80] Expressing their desire for the independence of Italy, and doubting the feasibility of a federation including the Pope and the Austrian Emperor; *H* clv. 543–55, 572–80.

[81] Trelawny had brought his bill on again, at 2 a.m., but agreed not to press it; *H* clv. 630.

[82] He urged that Britain must take immediate steps to prepare for the possibility of a war with France; *H* clv. 676–92.

[83] Secretary for war.

[84] By 167:70.

[85] Presumably Trelawny would have opposed Horsman.

tageously for a given evening, but I doubt whether it is of advantage to extend such contracts to longer periods. There is a great laxity in pairing. I have overheard a member in the Lobby inquiring for a pair for some one on a vote already given. This seems to me to be a fraud on constituencies.

Morning & evening sittings are now in full swing. Members who attend are doing the labour of cabhorses. It were well to sketch for the information of constituents, a history of an active member's life for a week at the present period.

Friday, 5 August: [...] More speeches & proceedings with reference to our naval & military armaments. It is evident that Ministers are quite alive to the urgency of our requirements. Many measures taken in consequence have been most wise.[86] Palmerston considers that we have a total military force of all arms of no less than 200,000 men – who, he said, would read an Invader a severe lesson.

Monday, 8 August: Elcho's motion on foreign affairs (particularly Italian) withdrawn after a long debate. No divisions.

It seems to me that Ministers have been much strengthened by the Elcho movement (which purports to restrain them from joining in a conference).[87] It has given them an opportunity of propounding their views in a popular sense. Elcho's proposal to forestall events – tying the hands of government under all circumstances however unusual – was very like a vote of want of confidence. And, as such, it was open to the rebuke that it was an indirect mode of proceeding. A vote of no confidence shd. not be covert, but open & straightforward. This is so obvious that Elcho will be suspected of intending to cover Ministers by leading in an unsustained attack so as to draw out their force & consolidate their defences. A vote of this kind should either not be proposed or the proposer should stand to his guns.

Elcho was followed by Kinglake who moved the previous question. Gladstone came next, & very warmly & vigorously did he rate the governments of various parts of Italy. Most of the great speakers (& some minor) were heard in turn – Seymour Fitzgerald (he is hardly in the 1st. rank – tho' near it), Horsman, Sidney Herbert, Whiteside, Lord J. Russell, Disraeli & Palmerston. One observation strikes me – as it is said that Providence favours great battalions, so it may be said it favours powerful debaters – especially, when there are many of

---

[86] On this day the House had passed through committee the reserve volunteer force of seamen bill, allowing for the enlistment of up to 30,000 men.

[87] I.e. to settle the Italian question; *H* clv. 1120–34.

them (if they agree). It is evident that weight of metal is on the side of government, who have always shot in their locker.

Tuesday, 9 August: [...] Note to the debate of the 8th. There appears to be an impression that Gladstone, in his fervid & impassioned speech on Italian affairs, rather overstepped the bounds of discretion. Maybe it was simulated indiscretion – for such indiscretion will be received with no disfavour by the Public in England. However this may be, both Disraeli &, in another place, Lord Stratford de Redclyffe [sic] have made comments on the great orator's language & sentiments.

Saturday, 13 August: [...] The Queen's speech having been read by Mr. Speaker to some half a dozen members who remained to hear it, the Session closed.

SESSION OF 1860

Tuesday, 24 January: [...] St. Aubyn moved[1] in a very nice speech. Great self-possession – judicious handling of topics – copious, yet with brevity – neat & ready diction – shy humour now & then, just to interest & carry on his audience – & only 17 minutes. Lord Henley followed – too profuse – too confident – too important. Not always judicious – &, sometimes, travelling unnecessarily into dangerous regions. His compliments to the government were injuriously lavish – & provoked laughter. His praise of Louis Napoleon was too thorough-going, besides being uncalled for. Still, had he been more brief, his speech was not the worst one has heard from a seconder of an address.

Disraeli administered a slight castigation as regarded some of the seconder's remarks – warmly commending, on the other hand, the graceful & ingenious manner of the mover (cheers). Then Disraeli proceeded to general criticisms of government – which I lost by leaving the House.

Sir Robert Peel came & sat by me & seemed disposed to talk. Some of his criticisms struck me. He is one of the plain spoken ones. He, by the way, agreed with something I said of Lord Henley – that he exemplified the misfortune of having too much confidence – a source of great danger in the House, unless you can simulate modesty.

When the Speaker read the Queen's Speech, a general removal of hats took place. I noted – a small matter, I admit – that about 7 or 8 persons retained theirs – among others, Graham, Henley,[2] Sir C. Wood, Packe & Sir R[ober]t Peel. This was, I thought, more than accident. I suspect some of them do not concur in the etiquette. When 300 men hastily remove their hats, the exceptions must strike.

Palmerston appears to have disposed easily of Disraeli, who was not brilliant. No opposition to St Aubyn's motion. House up early.

Memorandum suggested by a fault in Lord Henley's manner – never look away from the Speaker towards the lower end of the House for long together. It bears an uncourteous aspect. In speaking it looks bad to seem to think of yourself – which is the case if the consideration due to others be wanting. Nervousness might excuse one – though hardly Lord H. – & I note the point for my own guidance. ·

Disraeli failed in good taste, I thought, when he adverted to the

[1] The address to the throne.
[2] Possibly J.W. Henley, not the seconder.

Speaker's manner of reading the Speech. He once launched a regular sarcasm at poor old Ley (then Senior clerk) who had a thick & mumbling articulation, as if his mouth was full of plum pudding. Ley was called on to read a lengthy paper on a rather solemn occasion – I forget what – & distinguished himself less than usual. Disraeli, in a parenthesis, spoke of the performance somewhat as follows;– We have all heard the document read by our Senior clerk 'with all those powers of elocution for which he is so remarkable' (loud laughter). Yet, people sympathized, I think, with the clerk – one shd. not cut jokes at servants – they can't answer.

Wednesday, 25 January: I went down early to be in time to bring on Church rates. Some petitions were presented thereupon – & Sotheron Estcourt & some other members took, irregularly, these opportunities of requesting that I would not force on the bill without affording time for petitioners to prepare their petitions agt. it. I could not reply, as I should have been out of order.

[...] I had some interviews with leading Conservatives with respect to the choice of a day for a 2d. reading. Lord J. Manners, Mowbray & Sir J. Pakington discussed the point with me. Eventually, I gave them a week more, which has, apparently, satisfied them. My bill has passed it's first reading & stands for the 8th. of Feb[ruar]y [...]

Thursday, 26 January: [...] Bouverie moved that the House on fridays shd. adjourn of course to Mondays without formal motion – his expressed object being to save time now expended in discussing all sorts of matters irregularly. Plausible, but doubtful. Disraeli hit the point, when he said that rules are of less value than tact – & good sense – enforced, in fact, by the general sense of the House. A vote & Bouverie is considerably in a minority.[3] This happened while I was absent at dinner. The vote was, in my opinion, of little importance. I am inclined to think matters shd. remain as they are. Let well alone.

[...] Great activity is evinced in favour of Church rates. A packed meeting is mentioned as having taken place at Tavistock (see Plymo[uth] Journal, Jan[uary] 26). This is not the way to fight for the Poor man's inheritance.

Friday, 27 January: We had notice [...] of a Highways Bill from Cornewall Lewis. This is, in substance, Hardy's measure – projected during the Derbyite regime[4] [...] The money expended on Highways

---

[3] He was defeated by 166:48.
[4] Empowering magistrates at Quarter sessions to divide counties into districts of parishes for the purpose of repairing highways. The bill was not passed until 1862; see below, 14 Feb. and 26 May 1862 for Trelawny's views.

is over £1,260,000. The waywardens or surveyors are often unskilled farmers – &, probably, worse engineers.

Bright objected to the measure as an innovation (laughter) & uncalled for. He reiterated this complaint – & apparently failed to discover why the House laughed. Cornewall Lewis feared Bright had neglected Constitutional history. The antiqua via were encroached upon in the last century, when the ancient rights of elective bodies were transferred to magistrates & irresponsible trustees. B. was singularly unfortunate & incautious. One lesson of this kind makes a very faint impression on him. He will make a similar blunder next week very likely.

[...] I forgot to mention notice of an Irish Landlord & tenant bill. Bold men who deal with that topic. I predict that the measure will fail to satisfy the Irish Brigade. I shall watch its fate with curiosity[5] [...]

Monday, 30 January: [...] Danby Seymour & Butler attracted attention to the disturbances in St. George's in the East.[6] Cornewall Lewis very gauche in his reply – even for him. Police are to be stationed outside the Church to arrest persons who shall *intend* to make a disturbance (great laughter). It will not be easy even for detective officers to divine intentions.

The Tories heard the subject mooted – with evident alarm – & no wonder. Hadfield, however, made all laugh at his treatment of poor letter H. The solemnity of his manner & the gravity of the topic made matters worse. He said one thing usefully – that the differences betwn. Churchmen & Dissenters were less than those betwn. Churchmen & themselves. He knew what he meant & so did we, but his mode of expressing himself was not fortunate.

A measure was, afterwards, introduced by the Lord advocate[7] to abolish in 15 years the Edinburgh annuity tax. In the meantime, a sort of makeshift or compromise.[8] I doubt if it will answer. The established Church at Edinburgh seems to be left high & dry since

[5] Cardwell's Tenure and Improvement of Land (Ireland) bill, introduced on 29 Mar., established a procedure by which outgoing tenants without leases could obtain compensation for improvements made to the holding. The bill was of a permissive nature, as the landlord had the right to object to the procedure; Royal assent, 28 Aug.

[6] The ritualistic practices adopted by the Rev. Bryan King, the incumbent of St. George's in the East, in the dockland area of London, had led to regular disruptions of his Sunday services; Owen Chadwick, *The Victorian Church, vol I*, (1966), pp. 497–501.

[7] James Moncrieff.

[8] The tax was to be replaced by a levy of 8d. in the £ on householders for 15 years, so as to accumulate a fund for the support of a reduced number of Church of Scotland ministers; *P.P.* 1860, i. 139.

the New Free Church sprung up. No wonder people think a tax unjust for wh. they get no returns. The truth is, both in England & Scotland a great religious movement is in progress & we are drifting the Lord knows whither.

[...] Pakington complained of the course of the late Committee on Contracts, by which the conduct of his govt. was a little too sharply canvassed for his stomach. A lively debate ensued[9] – & Pakington had reason to wish he had thought of an unsavoury adage. A new Committee will sit on this subject. How will it be constituted? Last year this question was considered by some – but they had not power enough. The Committee, it is alleged, was virtually packed. Government people are, after all, unfit judges. They are all in league together – to plunder the masses. Tories & Whigs have their innings – apparently, by consent. Those shall rule & rob, who can best succeed in bamboozling the Public.

I note that Church rate petitions increase – & very much agt. my bill.

Thursday, 2 February: Wise moved for the annual appointment of a committee to examine & report upon the preceding year's estimates. He made a good, plain & unpretending address – supporting his case with a copious array of figures. Laing[10] replied, deprecating the motion as tending to diminish the responsibility of government. Bright made a telling speech in his best style, scattering to the winds the flimsy officialisms by which Wise's project was opposed. The Tories seemed sulky. Some of them went with us. One point of Bright's was very good. Government have constantly alleged that the House is extravagant. Well, then, here is a case of the House helping government by decreasing[11] the risk of extravagance & lax accountancy. We won.[12] I voted with Wise. I must not omit the fact that Gladstone spoke – as usual ably. It struck me forcibly at one moment that he has made Peel[13] his model as to manner, attitude, intonation & turn of sentences. The opinin of Bright – & I agree – is that Gladstone, on finance, is one of our sincerest men.

[...] Foreign policy was the subject of some interrogations. Lord John Russell seems to be acting prudently; &, I may add, with firmness & dignity. Still, there is a strong feeling that L[ouis] Napoleon will get Savoy.

[9] On Gladstone's motion for another select committee on packet and telegraphic contracts; agreed to.
[10] Financial secretary to the treasury.
[11] Trelawny accidently wrote increasing.
[12] 121:93 for Wise's motion.
[13] The former prime minister, not his son.

There are some doubts whether the Wine duties scheme[14] will not excite strong & combined opposition in the Commons. The Irish brigade are supposed to be ripe for any mischief – & some of them are said to avow frankly that the position of the Pope is the necessary measure of their integrity as members of the British Parliament. Of course, these are not their words, but the tone in which they are said to speak.

Monday, 6 February: Gladstone ill – & budget postponed. This is a great disappointment & may be a great misfortune. It is very cynical in the Public, but they never believe in the illness of political men. They must always be up to time [...]

Wednesday, 8 February: Lots of petitions agt. my bill. What are my people about?

I opened the debate.[15] Sir C. Douglas seconded me well & judiciously. A good selection. Lord R[ober]t Montagu led the opposition & was seconded by Mr. Long.

Sir G. Cornewall Lewis supported me – & Ker Seymer was agt. me. Bristow, Disraeli, Lord Fermoy, also, spoke. Majority only 29. Ayes 263 Noes 234.

The chief point made agt. my cause was founded on the alterior & avowed designs of the anti-church rate party, who have talked too much & have brought down on me a housefull of petitions & a most active & pertinacious whip. The table was flooded with petitions. Our case has retrograded.

Cornewall Lewis prosed. He seemed half asleep. Young Long committed an act of great indiscretion in an otherwise tolerable debut – in charging Lord John Russell with insincerity – in his absence, too. He was gravely rebuked.

Disraeli made the best point – contending that my bill tends to breaking up the parochial system & substituting centralization.

Fermoy was not very felicitous. Bristow was modest & briefly effective. Ker Seymer rather slipshod.

The House was full – they gave me a good hearing & Disraeli paid me a compliment – on my calmness & courtesy. I have doubts now whether my Bill will ever pass. I fear my supporters out of doors have damaged our position. + messed matters. + A majority of 29 on 2d. reading will not enable me to trample upon opposition & force my measure thro' the 2 houses. It is a bad job. Yet our numbers are the same as on a former occasion – it is the enemy wh. has been

---

[14] I.e. the Anglo-French commercial treaty negotiated by Cobden and Chevalier.
[15] On the 2nd reading of the church rates abolition bill.

reinforced.[16] I have an idea of proposing to my clients[17] to make an arrangement with Sotheron-Estcourt with a view of blending his plan with mine & passing a bill in that sense on an understanding that the Lords will accept it. Is this possible? [...]

Thursday, 9 February: [...] Now for a description of the commencement of a plan wh. may save the Church of England.

T[relawny] does not like the idea of fighting through every night of the Session – it would benefit no one. But T. has clients & opponents equally bitter. Luckily there is a man of sense on the Conservative side.

T. first goes to his clients' leader[18] – & puts his feelers out – pointing out the effect of the admissions made before the Lords[19] about alterior designs agt. the Church & the consequent flooding of the Commons table with counterpetitions & the chances of the question being put further backwards instead of making progress. At the same time, the value of Estcourt's plan was described – & the chance of getting alterations made in it in a sense more acceptable to Dissenters. That plan would abolish Church rates – & frame a new mode enabling Churchmen to tax themselves – papers being sent round to the parish[ione]rs to ask who would assent to such a tax & who would object. Dissenters would be allowed to attend the Church. The persons assenting to be taxed would be liable to a rate enforced by simple & convenient processes. The principle of centralization would be avoided – the worst of the disturbances, now so rife, would cease. The danger is of the Tories refusing to follow a wise leader – or stipulating for impracticable conditions. Our great object must be to get rid of the requirement that the papers shd. be signed by persons dissenting; for this would at once create ill feeling – & prevent conformity where men would, otherwise, be disposed to conform. I am, perhaps, too sanguine, but I cannot help thinking the scheme has some probability of success. As the matter stands, no one is bound. Tomorrow I shall hear what the Dissenters say. I am inclined to give up the point about salaries of ministers paid out of Church rates. Such salaries shd. be sacred for life, I think.

If the Dissenters will not go with me, there will be soon a new leader. The party I act with is but a section.

[16] The opponents of Church rates abolition had numbered 160 in Feb. 1858, 168 in Mar. 1859 and 193 in July 1859.
[17] The Liberation society.
[18] Dr. C.J. Foster, chairman of the Liberation society's parliamentary committee.
[19] To the select committee on Church rates, in July 1859; *P.P.* 1859 (2) v. 15. Questions 753–73 (Morley), and 1605, 1679, 1691 (Foster).

[...] There is a great sensation about my Sunday motion.[20] All Scotland is up about it, I hear. An immense deputation has been with Palmerston.[21]

Friday, 10 February: [...] Budget – what a speech for a sick man!

Well, it was not a last dying speech, which it might have become. I think the speech lasted about 4 hours. I heard the commencement & the end – having gone home in the interval. When I returned the sickman (!) was still addressing his audience in the atmosphere of an oven with an energy but little subdued – & voice but slightly toned down. Luckily I just came in for the recapitulation & peroration. The latter was of extraordinary brilliancy. It seemed as if the speaker's brain was inexhaustible. At the end of every sentence one said 'now that will do – you may spoil it'. Not so. The next sentence was better still & so the speech went on to the last word.

[...] Gladstone's budget provides for an assumed deficit of about £10,000,000.[22] He proposes to leave the Income tax (with another penny added[23] and at 7d. under £150) in force for a year – as, also, the tea & sugar duties. Then, he strikes at the paper duties – deals with the penny stamp on newspapers substituting Queen's heads & with money payable to order &c[24] – & carries out the French treaty[25] which is to favour French produce brought here & our coal, wool &c carried to France. Also, our shipbuilders will receive a physic in diminished timber duties. This is the general scheme of the budget, wh. it were hopeless to attempt to describe now. Whether it succeed or fail, it is a great budget – & still greater was the speech in wh. it was proposed. I doubt if Gladstone's achievement was ever surpassed by any effort on a similar occasion [...]

Monday, 13 February: I saw Foster who said that the Dissenters, true to their character & antecedents repudiated compromise. Their 'sentence is for open war'. They desire that the Bill be postponed in order that petitions may be obtained in its favour. I have postponed it, but my reason is that the 28th. of March is the first open Wednesday.

I am to see F. again at a later hour this evening.

Subsequently I saw E[stcourt] & read a sketch or scheme of a bill, which might be adopted. I said that, on the surface of it & so far as so cursory a perusal admitted of a judgment, the plan seemed to be

---

[20] For the opening of museums on Sundays; see below 16 Feb. 1860.
[21] *The Times*, 10 Feb 1860, p. 10, listed the deputation headed by Lord Shaftesbury.
[22] £9,400,000.
[23] Making it 10d. in the £.
[24] A penny stamp was imposed on all cheques.
[25] I.e. the commercial treaty negotiated by Cobden and Chevalier.

liberal. More conversation took place. The upshot was that, if nothing further be said, both are free to take any course. I gather that all sensible & moderate men in the House are anxious for an arrangement, before matters become worse.

My difficulty is that I lead a party which is in pursuit of prey beyond & distinct from mine. I want to settle a great question – even at the risk of getting none of the credit of doing so; at least, from others. The Dissenters see their way to an immediate separation of Church & State. The Church rate question is a good lever, & Vestries afford an excellent fulcrum. Now we are not quite in the same boat. What can I do? If I approve of E's bill (shd. it be printed) I shall appear to desert my clients. If I oppose it, I shall do violence to my convictions. Both Bills propose abolition. One would do something more[26] – & that more would sin agt. no principle & would perhaps insure the temporary support of fabrics (wh. are public property) pending the settlement of the great future of a Church establishment.

[...] I had another long conversation with F. on Church rates. T. told him at its conclusion that neither *E*. nor *T*. can be said to be in the least bound. As the case stands, the Church rates abolition bill will come on in due course on the day for which it now stands, the first open Wednesday (28 March). Meanwhile, the dissenters mean to stir heaven & earth to obtain petitions.

I said that, if the Tories should introduce a reasonable bill in the nature of a compromise, I might be in a difficulty. At the same time, I would not compromise my party without telling him.

I added that I thought, from private conversations with members on both sides, that a bill abolishing Church rates & merely allowing Churchmen to tax themselves would receive the support of the moderate Whigs & the great body of Conservatives.

F. feels very confident – & describes the party with wh. he acts as being equally so. They care little if a settlement be postponed for another year. But then, as I observed to F, they have 2 strings to their bow, for, if Church rates remain in force, they at least remain as a means of weakening an establishment. Now, I am not exactly in unison with this policy. I would prefer to leave the establishment question open.

[...] Members tell me that my Sunday motion[27] will weaken my position as mover in the Church-rate business. The truth is members are a pack of miserable cowards & dread to give honest votes – & want a loophole of escape by endeavouring to frighten me.

---

[26] Sotheron-Estcourt's plan would have allowed the Church of England to tax its own members.

[27] For the opening of museums on Sundays.

Tuesday, 14 February: [...] It is not astonishing that remonstrances & alarms should spring out of my notice regarding Sunday amusements. Several letters from constituents have reached me. It is thought that my re-election will be in jeopardy. Perhaps so. My main object is to get our Museums opened on evenings of weekdays from 8 to 10.

Thursday, 16 February: [...] It is very doubtful whether the budget will pass. The Tories are resolved, I hear, to oppose it. The Irish Brigade will probably give trouble. It is thought that they very shabbily deserted me on Church rates. What can the Pope care about Church rates – ie, about supporting them?

I had some talk with one or two of the government people & settled a form of motion with regard to a committee on Popular recreation on week days, which was eventually accepted. The Sunday question is thus put aside – & I rest contented with as much as was practicable.[28] I firmly believe that the proposal to admit the working classes to museums on Sundays was one cause of my carrying the modified resolution. To leave the largest classes without amusement, either on Sundays or weekdays, was too intolerable. I believe had govt. not conceded my point, they wd. have been beaten. Of course, I did not travel at any length into the Sunday Question – tho' my papers contained abundant proofs of its importance. There is, perhaps, no proposal which has a larger body of intellectual men in its favour than that of opening Museums on that day. A petition for it signed by 800 persons is about to be presented to the Queen. All sorts of places are resorted to now on Sundays on payment of small sums – there are fancy dog shows – not hunts – comic story tellers – music Halls – bird matches – & various distractions of wh. some at least are of a most demoralizing character. The subject is too long for treatment here.

[...] Williams moved for returns on flogging in the Navy & army. Among other objects he had one was to shew the names of officers who flog. It was proposed by govt, to withhold names. Williams divided – & was defeated.[29] I was in the minority.

Buxton had an amendment agt. all flogging – & a speech of great length – which I think he had by heart & was burning to let off. So tho' his amendment was irregular, he presented us with the Speech, which was a tedious rechauffé of very hacknied facts & arguments in most irreproachable & well balanced sentences. We sat & bore – he bored. Roebuck spoke well – as usual. Captain Vernon was not unskilful in defending an untenable cause. His points were the difficulty of devising a substitute & the frequent capital punishments of

[28] For the subsequent report of Trelawny's select committee, see *P.P.* 1860, xvi. 1.
[29] The amendment to omit the names of officers being carried by 124:46.

French soldiers. *In Sidney Herbert's[30] argument on flogging there was an unfortunate passage, which elicited a burst of derisive shouts. He said something of this sort;– the nobility & gentry underwent this punishment, the English nature was a strong nature – that we like strong wine!!*

Hennessy moved – usefully enough – for a Select Committee to inquire into the mode in wh. competitors for Civil Service exam-[inatio]ns are placed on the list. Enough was said to prove that patronage remains nearly where it was. Competition is a delusion. To apply otherwise than thro' an MP or person of influence is a farce. An MP, applying, either fails or is obliged. Govt. opposed – but Palmerston seeing the House was almost to a man against him, affected to have misunderstood Hennessy's object & succumbed most ignominiously & disingenuously.

Roebuck was very tart. His lordship (I think it was) said the existing arrangements were the cause of little men getting into office – & Roebuck said he believed him (laughter).

In my opinion Govt. is in a very insecure position. They have not the courage of their opinions. 'England does not love coalitions'. So said Disraeli. I begin to think our natural form of government is Tory with radical opposition. I do not mean that I approve of this – but I incline to think it is inevitable. If so, the Tories have but to exhibit common tact & patience.

Monday, 20 February: The state of parties is this. The government is not sure of a majority. There are many liberal frondeurs – or, at best, supporters unattached.

The fact is that when Reform is settled & the Church-Rate question disposed of, hosts of liberals will pronounce Conservatism to be true Liberalism, on the principle 'Hold fast is the best dog'. But those questions stop the way. I gather this from excellent data. As to Reform, the Conservatives shewed their hand last year. If Reform was not required, why was it offered? As to Church Rates, the same remark may be made. What the Tories fear is, that Church-rate meetings will continue to be held & at these wider questions will be discussed & the Church endangered. Now, this the philosophical, as well as religious, Tory deprecates. The former dreads a flood of revivals & varied fanaticism ending in general insanity – the latter believes that, when the human understanding rejects truth, the State should inject it. In other words the stomach may be forced – or cheated into compliance. *The Tories, also, deprecate the break up of local self-government as exemplified in the Parochial system – & regard the maintenance of

---

[30] Secretary for war.

fabrics of Churches out of property as an inheritance of the Poor. I
incline to respect this as an honest sentiment.*

Among the Tories are men who see clearly that these great questions
must be settled & settled too by very large measures. But the head is
so far from the tail that, when the head advances, there is danger of
a solution of continuity – for, after all, the head wants the tail. When
the Reform Bill of 1832 passed, hosts of satisfied liberals joined the
Conservative party. The same thing will recur. Is it the game of the
Liberals, selfishly speaking, to settle these questions? Bright says he is
prepared to wait some 4 or 5 years for Reform. How then describe it
as a crying grievance & fertile cause of class legislation? Again, the
ultra-Voluntaries are prepared to postpone the Church Rate settlement – because it is considered that the difficulty affords a powerful
lever agt. the Church. The whole situation is a riddle. Perhaps, we
are all at cross purposes. How shall we look at our own conduct some
20 years hence?

$4\frac{1}{2}$. Numerous petitions – mostly agt. parts of the budget. The
Licentious Victuallers (as they are, rather facetiously, called) are
among the most active petitioners.[31] But local Editors are equally alive
to their interest – being fully aware of the advantage to them of a
repeal of the paper duties. It was very adroit to enlist these persons
in favour of the measure – they have great power.

[...] Disraeli now commenced.[32] His object was to shew that the
proceedings of Ministers as to the treaty & budget were irregular,
contrary to the precedent of 1787[33] & unconstitutional. It was not
considered that his effort was the greatest he has made. Incidentally
he made a point – in allusion to some one who had lately spoken
disparagingly of the French legislative assembly – he reminded radicals that the Constitution of France was founded upon Universal
Suffrage, vote by ballot, & electoral districts – a system which anticipated the type of a liberal member of a Reformed House of Commons!

Gladstone is reported to have surpassed himself. It was in truth a
most brilliant reply. The Chancellor said Disraeli was wrong in his
facts & principles – & spoke of his blind superstition with regard to
mere forms without substance, adding even these he had not understood. Gladstone, further, contended that, in truth & in fact, Government were closely adhering to that which is solid & substantial in
precedent & were giving to Parliament & the Country the fullest

---

[31] Against allowing eating houses to be licensed to sell beer and wine.

[32] With his amendment against going into committee on the Customs acts until the
House had had an opportunity to consider the commercial treaty between Britain and
France; *H* clvi. 1355–75.

[33] When the House of Commons had passed a series of resolutions embodying the gist
of the Anglo-French commercial treaty of 1786.

opportunity of pronouncing opinions on the whole financial scheme. The expression of a member to me was that the speech of Gladstone was like a cat playing with a mouse. To immense memory – marvellous facility in applying principles & facts – & close logic – this extraordinary man adds genius & first class powers of declamation. It appears to me that he has now taken his place as facile princeps among the orators of his time.

Cairns, Bethell & Fitzroy Kelly spun many legal webs out of the treaty – & were exactly in their element. [...] Ayrton & Malins – a pretty pair! Energetic & vociferous. The former, deserting his party,[34] earned the equivocal approbation of the foe. These two lawyers are very much on a par. Equal volubility – prolixity & diffidence. Talk appears to be of each the Normal condition – silence irritation & disease.

[...] A very elaborate & bitter speech was delivered by Horsman – who again earned & obtained vociferous applause from the Tories.

Lord Palmerston rose to reply at 12 o'clock – & a very fine scene occurred. It was a speech of boisterous personality – which disturbed Horsman's equilibrium & elicited, by way of interruption, a contradiction of an assertion of the Minister – viz. that H's argument, if valid at all, would justify & enforce a vote of no intercourse with France. But Palmerston would not sit down – & so, amid great noise & confusion, each remained on his legs on the floor speaking inaudibly & gesticulating at the other. They looked like two fighting cocks in a cockpit.

Quiet was at length restored – when Palmerston continued. Horsman now rose to order when P. sat down & H. declared that he had never said a syllable of the sort. Palmerston – to whom Gladstone whispered (probably to confirm his recollection) – now resumed, saying 'I reaffirm all I have said' & then went on with his criticisms of his '*Rt. Honble. friend*' – & so, after making more points, the old gentleman sat down full of self laudation, jocular confidence & a firm conviction of triumph over all foes past, present & to come.

We won by 63[35] – immense applause.

My impression is that this majority is decisive. How could the Tories be so ill advised? Should they not have taken exception to some faulty item in Gladstone's budget if there be one – or, else, content themselves with general criticism? They could not have wanted to win.[36]

---

[34] Ayrton was a Liberal.

[35] 293:230 against Disraeli's amendment.

[36] Disraeli subsequently described the debates of February as 'sham battles'; W.F. Monypenny and G.E. Buckle, *The Life of Benjamin Disraeli*, (1929 ed.), ii. 12. Cf. the *Greville Memoirs*, viii, 298 (22 Feb. 1860), for Conservative indifference to their leader's defeat.

Tuesday, 21 February: [. . .] 11 p.m. Returning at this hour I found a very dull debate in progress[37] – Stafford Northcote speaking. Perhaps, he too will one day discover he has been talking prose all his life. Erudition, fluency & practical knowledge will not make a first class man – unless nature has found an organism to match. The worthy gentleman would add & subtract figures in good extempore English from this to doomsday – but he will never be a man of large & Statesmanlike views.

Ayrton followed in another speech of dreary fluency & shallow dogmatism – just so cruelly above mediocrity as to take away one's right to go to sleep. However, a small house listlessly sat it out, as it was clear some one must talk till it was decent to adjourn.

Du Cane was the mover of the amendment, but I did not hear his speech. I doubt not he acquitted himself irreproachably as he is a good speaker, about on a par with Hardy. Baxter & others filled up the evening. House adjourned at 12.

Sir J. Shelley would not let me have my Committee,[38] he is disgusted because no metropolitan members are nominated upon it. Yet, the member for Middl[ese]x[39] is one name. I do not limit myself to Metropolitan Institutions. The Hon[oura]ble baronet was very warm on the subject & appeared to me to be a little off his guard. I offered to give him my place. Could I say fairer?[40] [. . .]

Thursday, 23 February: [. . .] After Gladstone had replied to several questions – with his usual neatness, clearness & force – the Debate proceeded.[41] Hubbard, Baines, Byng, Blackburn, Sir F. Baring & some minor fry disported themselves in the early part of the evening. The great performers were Bright, Whiteside & Cardwell. Bright, by universal admission, surpassed himself. His speech shewed more genius than any speech of his I know of. And I think he avoided most of the shoals & quick sands to wh. his vessel has sometimes been driven by even too much propelling power. He quoted with great effect a passage from one of Disraeli's political novels – & paid a beautiful tribute to Cobden. Whiteside was much as he always is – amusing, sarcastic, & humorous, but not persuasive. Sometimes he is a little high flown when ridiculous effects are to be dreaded. After a long criticism of

[37] On Ducane's amendment to the motion to enter into committee of supply on the customs acts, opposing Gladstone's method of adding to the budget deficit by diminishing the ordinary revenue and then raising the income tax; *H* clvi. 1475–96.

[38] On the Sunday opening of museums.

[39] R. Hanbury.

[40] When the committee was nominated on 23 Feb., it included Roupell of Lambeth; *Commons Journals*, 1860, p. 86.

[41] On Ducane's amendment to the motion on the customs acts.

Bright, he turned to Gladstone in order to give the highest meed of praise to his great speech on the budget. We were all in anticipation of an eloquent description of it such as the effort deserved. Whiteside said, after another remark or two, something of this kind;– 'I listened, Sir, to that wonderful effort for four hours – without once winking! (Shouts of laughter in wh. Whiteside was compelled to join). Cardwell's was another of his ponderous, solemn, & irreproachable speeches – of undoubted usefulness & but not very attractive surface – especially at midnight.

I omitted to notice that Baring's speech was agt. the budget. Bright handled it with some very suitable severity. Before Peel's great policy was resorted to, the Whig remedy for deficits was increased percentage on duties on articles of consumption. Peel, on the contrary, created large chasms – & then filled them up. Now Baring was our pilot when we were on the high road to insolvency[42] & Bright noticed that the Whigs had never produced a Chancellor of the Exchequer.

Bright summed up the advantages we shd. derive from the treaty with France. His speech was a Free Trade paean.

Friday, 24 February: [...] Ducane's debate was resumed. Gibson, Walpole, D'Israeli, & Gladstone chiefly signalized themselves. The ascendancy of Gladstone is daily more conspicuous. It is also more & more evident that D'Israeli's mode of attacking the budget is unfortunate. He courted defeat, and won it. I paired – sick – with Cubitt. Majority 116![43] Walpole's position is regarded as a very singular one, since he considered the budget right, & professed to desire to keep ministers in office, on the ground of alarm at the feebleness of our executive. D'Israeli appears to me to have put his points skilfully enough in noticing Gladstone's miscalculations in past times, though of course he did not allow enough for disturbing causes, such as the Russian War.[44] Gladstone said of Walpole that he could understand his premisses without his conclusions, or his conclusions without his premisses. Walpole & Henley[45] sit just above the gangway on the 3rd bench, from which I infer their wish to be unamenable to D'Israelite discipline. Walpole seems to me to be assuming the demeanour of Peel in 1834–35, as a dispassionate critic, not immediately ambitious of office, & desiring to be regarded as a safe & respectable man.

[42] F.T. Baring had been chancellor of the exchequer from 1839 to 1841, when there was a succession of budget deficits.
[43] 339:223 against Ducane's amendment.
[44] The Crimean war had wrecked Gladstone's plan of 1853 to phase out the income tax over a seven year period.
[45] Who had both resigned from Derby's ministry in Mar. 1859 because of their opposition to that government's parliamentary reform bill.

Thursday, 1 March: [...] To-night the Reform Bill drew a very large house at prayers. To many it may be a political quietus. Or will it ever pass? Is there not a complete apathy on the subject? Will not counter interests prevail over the Statesman's prescience – unless a season of disturbance occur? I am not confident that the Bill will not be shelved.

Lord John introduced his very unambitious Reform Bill,[46] which appears to disappoint the radicals [...]

Monday, 5 March: Govt. intended to support Byng's motion to thank H[er] Majesty for the Commercial treaty with France & Palmerston proposed to give the mover precedence. Unfortunately, the terms of the motion were not made known to the House at large – tho' privately communicated to some. This gave Lindsay a handle of objection, which others, also, seized. The Savoy treaty[47] now came into the discussion & Kinglake, Seymour Fitzgerald, Bright, Roebuck, Osborne, Lord J. Russell & others made speeches. Eventually, the motion of Byng was fixed for thursday next. What will come before then? There is a cloud in the sky. The Tories are using the Savoy question in order to ride back to office, as they rode into a short lease of power on the conspiracy bill. Their speeches were almost war speeches. Roebuck was very outspoken & obtained vehement applause from the Tories & the approval of – Lord J. Manners.

Bright, Osborne & Coningham, deprecated indiscreet language. Lord John Russell's was a calm, Statesmanlike & dignified address. Even his opponents admit that he has conducted foreign affairs in a manner worthy of England's honour.

The position looks very serious. I hardly venture to hope the treaty will be carried into effect. But what is to come out of the Savoy question? Are the boundaries of the Rhine to follow? [...]

Tuesday, 6 March: [...] In the evening Sir de Lacy Evans moved a resolution agt. Army purchase.[48] He was very illheard owing to the feebleness of his voice, wh. has long been a great disadvantage to him.

His proposal called up a cloud of officers in defence of a doomed Institution. I heard a great part of Col[onel] Lindsay's speech; as, also, the speech of Col[onel] Percy Herbert, Sidney Herbert[49] & Ellice of Coventry. These 2 last speakers acquitted themselves as men who

---

[46] Providing for a reduction in the English borough franchise from £10 to £6 and the redistribution of twenty-five seats taken from small boroughs; *P.P.* 1860, v. 597.

[47] I.e. Sardinia's cession of Nice and Savoy to France.

[48] *H* clvii. 17–20. Captain Leicester Vernon moved an amendment against any extension of the seniority system; ibid. cols 24–31.

[49] Secretary of state for war.

have studied their subject. The line of Sidney Herbert was that Govt. were engaged in considering the report of a Commission on Army matters & were anxious, after due deliberation, to act upon it if possible. But rashness must, he said, be avoided in a difficulty so considerable, for vested interests were involved & great expense might be incurred if sudden changes were resorted to. He said that he went with Evans so far as the grade of L[ieutenan]t Col[onel] is concerned. Officers ought not to be allowed to purchase, without reference to qualifications, the authority to take 1,000 men into action.

His speech seemed to me to be that of a man who had no clear hold of any great leading principle to guide him. It was very easy to him to point out defects in other systems – wh. he did — & to criticize the opinions of the mover & others. At the same time, he produced the impression that he was doing his best for the Army – & this tribute was fully & most handsomely paid to him by Ellice, who said there was no depart[men]t of that branch of the Service but exhibited traces of the presence of the War Minister's head & heart.

It struck me that there can be no difficulty which would not yield to a vigorous will. There is no purchase in the Navy, wh. includes the Marines; none in the Artillery & Engineers; none in the Indian Army (except privately). The real difficulty is vested interest, which surely might be bought out.

We were told that purchase often lifts a poor man up the ladder. His Seniors buy a way up for him – & he gets death vacancies. Also, it was urged that purchase is a guarantee agt. unfair promotions, jobbery & nepotism.

But would a good man fail to rise if responsible Ministers did their duty to the public?

[...] Lord Stanley counselled the withdrawal of the amendmt. & the original motion. Evans & the mover of the amendmt. agreed. But the radicals would not. So we went to a division & were of course defeated.[50] But purchase will not bear many such defeats.

Tuesday, 8 March: [...] questions – some of them even more puerile & ridiculous than usual [...] Alderman Salomons was very impatient to hear the great bell again – & made anxious inquiries for its condition (Laughter). Cowper[51] said it had 5 cracks – one 9 inches below the rim – & others at various distances. These were supposed to have been caused in one of 2 ways – either the clapper was too heavy for the metal or the metal not tenacious enough for the clapper (Laughter).

---

[50] 213:59.
[51] Commissioner of works and buildings.

Scully seemed to be very keen on behalf of the Pope[52] &, adverting to the relative numbers of Catholics & Protestants,[53] desired to know whether non-intervention was to be inflexibly adhered to (I forget his exact words) (hilarity). Lord Palmerston replied rather incautiously that, with respect to differences in matters of religion, Her M[ajes]tys Ministers were guided in their policy by far higher considerations. (I saw Disraeli, Bulwer-Lytton & I think Whiteside in great enjoyment of this unguarded expression of indifference – as bad by the way as Lord P's dictum that all babies are born good which induced one of the Newspaper editors (Herald?) to say he had abolished the Xtian religion).

Another gentleman[54] wanted to know when the lions would be placed at the foot of Nelson's column – & another what was to be done about planting shrubs again in the Parks – & Sir A. Agnew asked some such question, which drew down laughter at his expense & cries of order.

After this, Lord Palmerston appealed to members having notices to give way to Byng.[55] This sort of appeal, on a high party trial, is rarely rejected. Young Mr. Cave &, also, Mr. Craufurd were bold enough to set the feelings of the House at nought – &, sooner or later, they will pay for it. I left Cave on his legs with the hopeful task of prepossessing in his favour a large House – early in the evening – & that House baulked of its hope of commencing an expected trial of strength!

At last Byng was allowed to move. He appears by the reports to have acquitted himself creditably.

Cairns & Gibson were the chief speakers. Cairns criticized the details of the Treaty, yet will not oppose the address. Apparently there is no fight.

I suspect the Tories feel that we are on very delicate ground. If our relations with France suddenly deteriorate, blame might be cast upon the opposition - tho' unjustly. They are, therefore, shy of the business[56] [...]

---

[52] With regard to his temporal power in the papal states.

[53] In Ireland.

[54] Thomson Hankey.

[55] Byng's motion for an address to the Queen expressing the House's thanks for concluding the commercial treaty with France; H clvii. 121–31.

[56] The American ambassador suspected that Derby had no wish to form a government on the basis of an anti-French policy; G.M. Dallas, *Letters from London*, (1870), ii. 328–30 (6 Mar. 1860). Cf. Derby to Disraeli, 4 Mar. 1860, Hughenden MSS (microfilm copy, Cambridge University Library), B/XX/S/266, observing that hostile action against the treaty would result in a poor division in the Commons, and offend the French.

Friday, 9 March: [...] Early in the evening there was a little spar between Haliburton[57] & Gladstone. The former is rather irascible &, at the same time, inexperienced. His complaint was of some real or imagined superciliousness exhibited towards him or the Canadians or both in the matter of a question on the timber duties. The old Parliamentary debater was too cool & skilful of fence for the unway-wise author. A successful writer soon finds his level in the House – which likes modesty & will not always accept a reputation without actual proofs of its title. But, still less does the House like a man who, angry without reason (as Gladstone said) takes home his wrath to nurse it & keep it warm [...]

Monday, 12 March: Yesterday, I wrote to the Chancellor of the Exchequer & suggested to him a mode of facilitating interchanges of land for stock on the principle of the interchanges of land for land now allowed before the Inclosure Commiss[ione]rs each party concerned taking the property transfered to him with the same title as he had before.

This supersedes costly investigations of title & preparations of long abstracts citing deed some of which may have ceased to operate. At the same time I threw out to the Chancellor the hint that he might levy a small sum on each use of the power if it shd. be given.[58]

Tonight the budget comes on again – or, rather, the part relating to the paper duties.[59] My feeling is that we should have so managed our financial affairs as to dispense with increase of Income tax. The budget, good on the whole, would be endangered if a Tory motion agt. a questionable part of it were supported by any of the liberals. The truth is we want not so much a master mind to readjust our burthens merely – but to curtail our growing expenditure. Here is where the shoe pinches – £70,000,000 instead of £50,000,000 – & £30,000,000 for war purposes instead of £13,000,000 – the sum required in 1835 when the Iron Duke held the reins.

[...] 10¼ pm. My pair expired at 10. On a division Govt. had a majority of 53.[60] We were very late – breaking up about 2 a.m. [...] Horsman made a very clever, bitter and personal speech. Gladstone was his object of attack on the provocation of Gladstone's having said that Horsman's sense of duty was 'inscrutable'. Some of his remarks, tho' witty, were too coarse & will be censured by his readers.

---

[57] T.C. Haliburton, a celebrated novelist who had earlier been judge of the Canadian supreme court.
[58] Not found in the Gladstone MSS.
[59] The separate paper duties repeal bill.
[60] Miles' amendment against the repeal of the paper duties, defeated by 245:192.

He tried to quote a letter from Gladstone to a clergyman, but could not read it. Too long & too angry, he at last got all abroad & thus marred an effective speech. He has shown his hand too much & is buying Tory cheers too dearly. So all seemed to agree.

Gladstone's reply was effective in its quiet dignity. He soon left the personal topic & went into argument, where he was as usual quite at home [...]

Friday, 16 March: [...] T[relawny] still absent thro' illness [...] With regard to Savoy – it seems that the transaction betwn. L[ouis] Nap[oleon] & Vic[tor] E[mmanuel] throws overboard the rights of Switzerland guaranteed by old & modern European treaties.[61] The Swiss frontier will lie exposed. The Swiss have entered a solemn protest against the proceeding wh., of course, will not be stopped except by action of the great powers.

[...] In reply to a question Lord John stated that he had just received a despatch from France (I think it was the despatch sent thence to Switzerland) on the Savoy question, which he had not had time to read; a despatch of great importance & gravity.[62] As I understand, neither Sovereign or Cabinet had seen it. There is a story going that, when Lord John stated this, Sidney Herbert leant forward with a stare of astonishm[en]t & Gladstone fell back with his hands in the air. This came, at second hand, from a Tory County member – & I believe it.

Monday, 19 March: [...] Disraeli rose [...] on the Reform Bill, the 2d. reading of which was the stage to be passed. I heard his skilful argument agt. the Bill during half an hour – his point was that the effect of the measure would be in many boroughs to double or treble the power of the most uninformed class – in short, it was a measure of class legislation. He adverted to the aptitude for combination which the working classes had frequently exhibited. Subsequently Rolt & Bright were the two main performers. The Debate was adjourned without division.

Tuesday, 20 March: A Ballot day. Speeches bad – luckily a short debate. Old Berkeley,[63] as usual, planted his battery opposite the

---

[61] Notably the Vienna settlement of 1815, which guaranteed the neutrality of Chablais and Faucigny, part of the territory now ceded by Sardinia to France.

[62] Russell was referring to the despatch from Thouvenal to Persigny, stating the French case for annexing Nice and Savoy, which he had received the previous day; *H* clvii. 761. Cf. Beales, *England and Italy*, p. 137.

[63] Henry Berkeley, making his annual motion in favour of the secret ballot.

Ministerial benches. On a division we were very severely beaten.[64] The measure makes but little progress. Lawson made an indifferent maiden speech & chose a bad time for it. Yet, I think he has qualities – & may do some day. He has calmness & temper amid unfair interruption – something of his uncle's[65] self-possession. The House had decided to dine early – & divide first – & was unusually rude.

Wednesday, 21 March: Second reading of the Endowed Schools Bill. Rejected by a considerable majority.[66] T[relawny] in the minority. The object of the Bill was stated to be thus: – not to take away from the Church of England Schools anything undoubtedly belonging to them, but to afford Dissenters equal advantages in cases where no particular opinions were expressly favored at the creation of the Trust. It is understood that another Bill is coming before the House of Commons on the same subject, making certain concessions, which however do not satisfy Dillwyn, yet have robbed him of a considerable number of his supporters.[67] Robert Lowe[68] made, they say, a capital speech agst. Dillwyn's bill, but rather high flown in Church of Englandism for a liberal. The real question at the root of this & many other bills is what religious opinions shall have the favor of the State; or whether it is competent to anyone to fix by present endowments the course of Belief for ever. It strikes me that Dissenters over-estimate their strength; & I predict that their pride will have several falls. The indisposition to entertain compromises inevitably tends to narrow the extent of their forces [. . .]

Friday, 23 March: [. . .] Gladstone carried his extra 1d. of Income tax agt. Sir H. Willoughby.[69] The truth is we could hardly help ourselves. Without the extra 1d. there would have been a deficit of £400,000 now that we have repealed the paper duties £1,400,000. I had doubts for a moment thinking we might save £1,000,000 somewhere. Perhaps so; but all we manage to save is forestalled. We have, even now, made no provision for some exchequer bonds falling due this year. I have faith in Gladstone's resolution to reduce expenditure.

---

[64] 245:147.

[65] Sir James Graham.

[66] 190:120. Dillwyn's bill sought to secure for dissenters the right to act as trustees for schools founded before the Reformation.

[67] Sir Hugh Cairns' bill, allowing dissenters to continue to act as trustees where there was an established usage going back at least 25 years; it did not proceed beyond the 1st reading.

[68] Vice president of the education board of the privy council.

[69] *H* clvii. 1219, for Willoughby's amendment against the increase; defeated by 187:132.

But we must not tie his hands too tightly. Thanking him for a budget on the whole bold & good, I, for one, am willing to share the blame with him when he asks for the necessary sacrifice. This made me support a heavy Income tax in 1848.[70] I was severely blamed about that time at Tavistock, but events justified me. Protective duties would never have been slain without a formidable direct tax. And no one has discovered much in the Income tax, which any known plans of modification would rectify.

I perceive Ld. Panmure[71] has been opposing the substitution of selection for purchase in the Army. I note this because others besides Lord P. have sounded a warning voice hereon. It is believed that, when purchase goes, the Court will job all the appointments as now it is said to job a good many – especially through the instrumentality of the Guards Privileges [. . .]

Monday, 26 March: [. . .] we had a most envenomed & elaborate attack on Ministers by Horsman[72] – every word got by heart &, as I suspected, put together after a careful study of the Invectives of Junius. Some passages seemed to bear out my idea – which I mentioned to B.[73] my neighbour.

Horsman reaped plentiful applause from the Tories, but failed to damage the Whigs; nay, he did them a service. He elicited from Lord John Russell a declaration of opinions & a simple straightforward account of past conduct & motives which commended the earnest & hearty applause of all sides. Horsman's charges looked very small – he lost the respect of the Liberals &, in competition for Tory praise, he was distanced by the foreign Minister. In fact, Horsman had not left to himself any ground to stand upon. The House seemed to think his speech was merely the studied expression of personal malevolence – indeed, it was a speech of Horsman stinging himself because he could not reach his foe.

Lord John was, perhaps, a little too keen & outspoken in some of his animadversions & prognostications. It seemed to me that the French alliance hangs by a slender thread. Ominous hints of combination between the great Powers agt. France were dropped. England could not 'stand apart' [. . .]

---

[70] See 20 Mar. 1848, *H* xcvii. 774–5, for the unpopularity of Trelawny's support for the Russell ministry's proposal to raise the income tax from 7d. to 1s. in the £ (later withdrawn) and to extend the life of the tax for a further three years. Trelawny had also opposed Hume's amendment (13 Mar. 1848) limiting the extension to one year.

[71] Secretary of state for war in Palmerston's first ministry.

[72] Denouncing ministers for allowing themselves to be deceived by Napoleon III as to his territorial ambitions; *H* clvii. 1244–52.

[73] Probably Bright.

Osborne & I – closely watching Horsman – were quite certain the speech was got by heart. We caught him transposing important words set in antitheses where the place of a word is everything. We could not be mistaken. It seems that Horsman took little by his motion on a recent evening[74] & was discomfited by calls to order from the Speaker. His speech tonight was the endeavour to reassert himself. He is a very clever man – ever recollect that he gave up an Irish Secretaryship on the alleged ground that it was a sinecure[75] & that he was succeeded, in another ministry, by Lord Naas who, in a short tenure of office, proved to be a good workman & did not quarrel with his tools. Horsman wanted the Cabinet – so the world says – & I believe it. Meanwhile, he hits hard – & amuses the House.

[...] Bright lectured Horsman with some severity – he both protected & criticized ministers – he said (in substance) that Lord John Manners' compliments to Lord John R., when most wrong, were only natural in one who was always allied to everything retrogressive or opposed to civilization. Altogether, it was a brisk evening – & not inappropriately signalized the formal breakup of the 'entente cordiale'.

Wednesday, 28 March: I presented 209 petitions agt. Church-rates. Afterwards, we went into Committee & triumphantly carried the Bill thro'. We had one division on an amendment of Newdegate's. He proposed, in parishes where a tax has been levied within the last seven years, to substitute a fixed charge on the owner for the present rate on the occupier. [...] Cross seconded Newdegate in a long dull iteration of Church rate arguments. Mellor & Morton Peto spoke well. Lord Henley followed. Division 222 to 49.

Newdegate was very angry at the desertion of his party.[76] He confided his woes to me. Of course, I commended him for sticking to his guns.

[...] Sir Geo. Grey moved several clauses empowering parishes to introduce a species of Pew rents. After I had heard his arguments & noted the temper of the House, I decided upon opposing them – & I feel quite sure that I was right. I have for a long time doubted the policy of introducing pew rents.

I said that, if a palliative of my bill were to be adopted, it should be very well considered – & should not risk the success of the Voluntary

---

[74] On the commercial treaty (11 Mar.), *H* clvii. 247–68.
[75] Cf. 3 June 1858, *H* cl. 1450–7.
[76] A meeting   of Conservatives the previous day had decided to work to defeat Trelawny's bill rather than to amend it; diary of T.H. Sotheron-Estcourt, 27 Apr. 1860, Sotheron-Estcourt MSS (Gloucestershire Record Office), D1571/F410.

Principle. If you impose a tax on family pews or faculties, voluntary efforts would be weakened. People would say a machinery exists – tax the great Pew owners.

There can be little doubt that my simple bill which stands upon its principles & merits, would have been brought into peril when linked with doubtful expedients to which the Tories were already raising very forcible objections. It was quite clear that Grey did not see his way.

The House seemed to doubt – & many liberals asked me why I rejected Grey's plan.

[...] Altogether it was a curious state of things. Gladstone & Sidney Herbert each wanted a few minutes for indispensable work – affecting the Army votes & the budget.

Both begged hard that I would finish in time. But then I might thus have lost my bill. To make matters worse, their colleague, Grey, was, as usual, verbose & ran on so long that I trembled for the result, for on Wednesdays we close at six.

His plan was particularly distasteful to the Tories who could not resist the pleasure of attacking it, yet secretly wished to send my bill to the Lords – in hopes they may thus the sooner settle the question. The more Estcourt, Manners & Selwyn spoke, the more my hopes fell. I seized the first opportunity of pronouncing agt. Grey's resolutions – & so the Whigs forebore to divide, tho' many wished it [...]

Thursday, 29 March: I left London for the Easter Holidays.[77] [...]

Monday, 2 April: [...] The Licensing plan [78] has provoked vehement opposition from the brewers, who are monopolists of the first water. Ker Seymer & Hardy took opposite sides[79] – each has a speciality hereon. Debate adjourned. I think I remember that Ker Seymer & Hardy made their reputations on a debate about beer. Certainly they speak like men full of their subject, (which sounds as if I meant *beer*, but I don't).

Tuesday, 17 April: I sparred a little with govt. in order to obtain a day for Church-rates – the new rule regarding Thursdays[80] having to

---

[77] The Easter recess lasted from 4 to 16 Apr.

[78] The Refreshment houses and wine licenses bill, allowing eating houses to be granted licenses to sell wine.

[79] Ker Seymer supported the bill, Hardy opposed it; both were Conservatives.

[80] On 2 Apr., while Trelawny was absent from Westminster, the House had agreed that government orders should take precedence over private members bills on Thursdays until whitsun: *H* clvii. 1720–40.

a certain degree affected my measure's chance of coming on at a practicable hour. Several members spoke a few words – Bright supporting me. However, I got nothing out of Ministers. I observed that, in respect of Church-rates, I was, absurdly enough, the govt. – & entitled to every aid in bringing on my measure – that Ministers ought to do the work but they had left it to an independent member. Disraeli sided with them – he, probably, having a speech on the budget of which he desires to be disburthened [...]

Friday, 20 April: Some negotiations took place between certain members of the House & myself with regard to the fixing a convenient opportunity of taking the 3rd. reading of the Church rate Bill, which, as matters stood, might come on night after night for weeks. Disraeli & Escourt took part. Eventually, an arrangement was come to with general consent to take the Bill before notices of motions on friday next. The clerk told me his brother clerk had said the only objection to such a plan was that it was entirely without precedent.

[...] I note that Lord John Russell took occasion to mention that the Reform Bill would go on in spite of Mr. Napier's insidious proposal to refer it to a Select Committee. I believe the Palmerston section scarcely disguise their objections to the measure.

Monday, 23 April: The Reform Bill was discussed at length.

Edwin James opened proceedings in a long statistical speech. Hardy was severe on Bright. Lord R. Montagu & Lord R. Cecil were funny at the expense of free Institutions. Their speeches should be carefully studied as indications of the state of education in the upper circles of Society. Lord R. Montagu's speech was, in my judgment, not devoid of a certain merit & promise. Milnes & others spoke. The conduct of both parties as regards the Reform Bill looks like that of a naturalist who has found a curious animal or vegetable previously unknown. They are engaged in examining it & turning it over & over. None seem to understand what are its attributes – whether it is to be regarded as good or bad – useful or hurtful.

Disraeli is very astute in not dealing with it. He leaves that to the liberals – & the liberals find in it plenty of fault. The situation is anamolous. Here is a great change in the Constitution chiefly opposed on the side whence it springs. The Bill has many secret foes. The Whigs of 1832 are afraid of opening a dam wh. may swamp their bantling – now an adult of some standing. The Tories have no less dread – but they can say 'why did you open the question in 1832?' The radicals are in a false position, because they do not propose general suffrage. Their principles exact this; but, if truth be told, these are, I fear, a mere pretence & a stepping stone to seats & to a confidence wh. is shamefully betrayed [...]

Tuesday, 24 April: [...] Augustus Smith & his Foreshores question came on early in the evening.[81] I think he damaged himself by his proceedings. The attorney-general[82] hit him hard in representing that he had a lease of a foreshore & was more or less concerned in this matter which he had taken in hand – & was, moreover, a most exacting person in the exercise of the powers he possessed. A Cornishman, affected by Duchy questions, can scarcely open his mouth without giving the enemy cause to blaspheme. Smith's manner is not very fortunate – indicating some temper & obstinacy. But I believe he is a deserving man & a resolute reformer. Of course, he was no match for Bethell, who would surely transfix him & leave him impaled – arms & legs sprawling – mid a derisive House. I did not vote on this[83] – absent [...]

Wednesday, 25 April: [...] I had much talk about the Reform Bill & other measures. It is one main element in House of Commons life that opinions undergo a vast deal of preliminary discussion in the form of mere conversation between small knots of 2 or more. Few would believe, without experience, the number of speeches made in this manner. Nothing can be more useful. Asperities are softened – original views sketched – untenable arguments refuted – good hints adopted or improved upon – mistakes prevented. I was struck by the tone of one-decided liberal (Dillwyn), who is opposed to Reform as fatal to the power of the middle classes. He advocates the ballot as the grand specific for our case.

A Reform debate. Bulwer-Lytton's speech is much praised. It is said that he was very brilliant. Lord John replied – effectively, I think, if one may judge from 'The Times' report.

Several liberal members are alarmed at the Reform Bill as being too democratic & likely to swamp the middle classes.[84] During the evening there was a discreditable attempt to count out the House. Violence was used, I hear, in order to keep out members coming in

---

[81] Motion for a select committee to investigate the rights of the Crown with respect to foreshores, tidal rivers, estuaries and the bed of the sea around the coast, and to examine the manner in which the department of woods and forests had asserted these rights; *H* clviii. 25–31.

[82] Sir Richard Bethell.

[83] Smith was defeated by 134:117

[84] The Liberal chief whip, Brand, later warned Russell that there was no chance of carrying a bill containing the provision for a £6 borough franchise; 30 May 1860 (copy), Broadlands MSS (Southampton University Library), GC/BR/6.

on hearing the division bell.[85] I suspect this count out was hatched by mutual arrangement in order to persuade the Country that Reform is not required. Tories would rejoice to postpone the measure – & many Whigs think the bill would not have been allowed to come on except that Lord John R. might keep faith with the Public – who would, perhaps, release him on easy terms.

I heard part of the Several speeches of Black, Walsh & Denman. Black opposed the bill & elicited Tory applause – He never gained any other since I have sat with him. He seems to me rather a puzzle headed old gentleman – & this may explain his uncertainty as to the side on which he ought to sit. If he mess Reform as much as he has messed the Annuity tax,[86] the Tories will come soon to regard him as an useful ally.

Denman was glibtongued enough – like the lawyers in general. But had I been his counsel on his proposing to speak, I should have said 'don't'. 'You are not yet a Statesman enough for the discussion of constitutional changes. Content yourself with modest handling of Law Reform in Committee – in this manner you may with patience obtain a reputation. At present you are not in your element – a mere pretender, wh. the House abhors!'

Walsh has recently published a pamphlet, at once ponderous & prolix. But 'the Times' reviewed it in several columns of large type, & therefore it must have significance of some kind.[87] He opposed the Reform of 1832 – & has some title to be heard now. His warnings on Reform were always very serious & solemn – & made one as melancholy as his jokes.

Friday, 27 April: [...] At last, the battle of the evening commenced.[88] Whiteside spoke for an hour & a half or more. He evidently knew little of Church-Rates & indulged in all sorts of vagaries, small levities, &, generally, the personalities of the question. The measure must be bad, because a certain Society asks for something else. The measure must be bad, because certain individuals have acted wrongly in their mode of advocacy. The measure must be bad because a certain member did this or that. Then some of our petitions had been got up in an unjustifiable manner – that is to say, for example, some names of children had been appended thereto.

As to his Law, it was difficult to believe a Lawyer spoke it. He

---

[85] Confirmed by the account in *The Times*, 27 Apr. 1860, p. 7.
[86] Black, the mover of abolition bills in previous years, had supported the government's compromise measure, which did not satisfy the abolitionists; see above, 30 Jan. 1860.
[87] *The Times*, 20 Feb. 1860, p. 5.
[88] Debate on the 3rd reading of the Church rates abolition bill.

was so ignorant that almost every sentence he uttered was wrong. However, he put the Tories in good heart, & they cheered lustily.

Bright made a solid & telling speech. He put my points most ably – & made no mistakes. + committed no indiscretions. + Some passages were very eloquent.

Disraeli followed – all said he made a very weak speech. He could only ring the changes on old platitudes. I sat in admiration of the ability which enabled him to string together hearable sentences on a subject on wh. he neither knew the Law or the facts.

Afterwards, I shortly replied – especially noticing certain observations relating to the Liberation Society & my supposed connexion therewith. I praised the fearless & outspoken evidence of Dr. Foster & his colleagues in the Lords, altho', undoubtedly, their evidence has weakened the conduct of my case.[89] I took care to deny that I was a member of the Liberation Society – & I further said that I was not prepared for separation of Church & State in Dr. Foster's sense, as I consider Church revenues as a trust fund under State control – & I do not see how we can safely relinquish it. In particular, I added that I should not like to trust entirely to the clergy in matters educational. I said that in a new Colony I shd. be opposed to any connexion betwn. Church & State.

We were only successful by 9 votes.[90] This fact elicited vociferous & long sustained applause from the Conservatives. And well they might cheer! The truth is we have suffered a virtual defeat, & this is attributed to the avowal of alterior designs, on the part of Foster & Morley,[91] made before the Committee of the Lords. My difficulties increased from the moment when this avowal was made. Of course, these witnesses are not to be blamed for telling the truth. Nevertheless, my case was in this manner shaken to its foundations & the probable effect will be that the great Church-Rate question will be settled by means of some new bill – I hope I have done with the conduct of the question.

I never knew the Tories more exuberant & uproarious in their exultation. It seemed that their cheers would never cease – & one lady was waving her white handkerchief in the gallery.

Knowing what I do of the feelings of the Tory party – best informed on Church Rate difficulties – I smile at the opposition of Whiteside & Disraeli & their fine set speeches. The fact is, as I said in my speech, the Conservatives raised the debate & required one more division in order to sustain their characters with the clergy who would otherwise

---

[89] See above, 8–9 Feb. 1860.

[90] 235:226. The bill was rejected by the Lords, 128:31, on 19 June.

[91] Samuel Morley, wealthy hosiery manufacturer and prominent dissenters' leader.

complain that the game had been given up without a struggle. It is the Dissenters who are most interested in not legislating. The acknowledged abuses under Church-Rate Law are a capital whereon dissenters may trade for years – & the Church would be the loser in a waiting race.

Monday, 30 April: The Reform debate resumed. Bentinck opened his heavy guns agt. the measure.

I cannot help recurring to the idea that Household Suffrage should be the Suffrage to be adopted. A change like that betwn. £10 & £6 is not one wh. lands you, after a slide, on terra firma. It were easy to give many good reasons – at least, reasons which might weigh with many persons who now seek Universal – in favour of Household Suffrage. It is much like the old fashioned scot & lot franchise.[92] Virtual representation of every human being is afforded by it thro' heads of families. Several persons agree in this [...] Household Suffrage is a word wh. has a certain hold on the imagination – & it might be made safe by limitations more or less extensive such as these: that a voter shd. have been registered for a year – shd. have resided one, two or three years – shd. have paid a direct tax. In this manner the qualification might be narrowed at pleasure. Persons, too, possessing it, would have a stake in the hedge & would be a barrier agt. democracy.

The speakers were mostly of a 2d. or 3d. rate order – B. Cochrane, Lord J. Manners, Walter, Clay, John Locke, besides A. Mills & Pollard Urquhart. Nothing new was elicited. Bright has been the chief butt of the Tories, who appear to have failed in courtesy towards him in citing passages from speeches attributed to him without inquiring first whether he avowed their authenticity. I observe that our aristocracy can act as shabbily as any other class where it has a common foe to deal with – or a common interest at heart. Cochrane's course shd. have been to ask Bright in private very courteously whether the words attributed to him were his or not – & then act accordingly [...] There is a very general opinion that Bright's speeches of late years have produced a powerful reaction in favour of Conservatism – just as the sweeping proposals of some nonconformists have favoured the stability of the established Church.

Thursday, 3 May: The Reform Bill debate recommenced. The first speaker was Kenneth Macaulay,[93] who acquitted himself well, as, indeed, he generally does. His manner is gentle & pleasing & just that

---

[92] By which any adult male assessed for poor rate and church rate was eligible to vote.
[93] Cousin of Lord Macaulay, but a Conservative.

kind of manner which constant practice & experience of the House of Commons tend to give. It struck me there was a great deal of force in some points he undertook to establish. Of course, he opposed the measure, tho' he was not prepared to divide the House, an announcement causing derisive cheers from the liberals. He affirmed that the Bill is almost uniformly condemned by thinking & well informed people in Society; &, in private, by most members of the House – wh. statement is, I think, nearly true.

I lost Gregory's speech founded on his knowledge of the abuses of Popular govt. in America, as, also, several other speeches of little note till Mr. Gladstone's came, & of this I heard only the latter part. The House was full – there was no division on the 2d. reading. There was much sarcastic cheering when the Committee on the Bill was put off till the 4th of June. This would seem to imply that the measure will not pass this year.

[...] The comment which the debate calls forth seems to me to be this – that we are none of us in possession of accurate information as to the number or kind of the persons whom the Bill wd. enfranchise. This is additional to the observation I have previously made – that we have not the advantage of standing upon any firm & distinct principle. There is little in the bill calculated to settle the Reform question. It awakens no enthusiasm – is not regarded as a boon. The enfranchised naturally feel that their power will be weakened. The working classes will not deem their power to be appreciably increased. Now the same objections would not lie in the same force agt. House-hold Suffrage well guarded by precautionary conditions. This might be a ledge on the inclined plane & one likes to see the end of a slide.

After Gladstone had finished his speech, to the extreme annoyance of the House T. Collins arose on the floor & insisted on a hearing in spite of violent interruptions. The Speaker rather feebly endeavoured to restore 'order' in the usual way. His voice was, however, scarcely heard above the din. Some unruly individuals took advantage of their position nearly behind the chair to its left & right & continued shouting 'divide divide' & so forth. The Speaker looked somewhat wrath & they made matters worse by mimicking his manner of saying 'order, order' so as to make it seem even less authoritative than it in fact was & more ridiculous. The Speaker stretched his neck to no purpose in his endeavour to detect the offenders. The scene was very comical. I mention it as a symptom of waning authority. Shaw Lefevre[94] would have quelled the mutiny by a few words mingling urbanity with awe, as good Speakers of the Commons contrive to do.

[94] Speaker, 1839–57.

Monday, 7 May: [...] Walter (of the 'Times')[95] moved the adjournment so as to be in order while he brought under notice of the House a matter personal to himself & Horsman. In substance the case stood thus. The 'Times' & Walter seemed, on a recent occasion,[96] to Horsman to unite in bringing a charge upon the honour of the H. of Commons. The charge was that, in order to delay a dissolution, many members would be willing enough to postpone Reform. Horsman wrote to Walter & apprized him that the subject would be brought before the House. Walter attended, but Horsman failed to get a convenient opportunity of speaking. Horsman would now have let the matter drop. This did not suit Walter. More correspondence occurred. H. winds up in a fierce onslaught on the 'Times' – & all its dealings. He would by no means admit Walter's argument that he had nothing to do with the actual conduct of his paper, but contended that Walter was morally responsible for every word of it. (Great cheers from the Tories, who were delighted to see this great delinquent brought to account.) Horsman mentioned by name persons connected with the paper such as Lowe & De Lane,[97] & charged the whole fraternity with alternately calumnating & adulating every man of note – saying & unsaying every proposition – setting up & pulling down every principle in Human affairs.

[...] It seems to me neither H. nor W. was very wise. Neither was capable of putting a guard upon his tongue. Horsman undoubtedly said several good things – some of them proper to be said at this juncture, for the newspapers certainly exercise a kind of tyranny.

[...] I perceive that Palmerston & Disraeli, leaders of men, wound up the Horsman & Walter episode, respectively endeavouring to throw oil on the troubled waters. Perhaps, neither liked to hear much more about the relations of Ministers or Public men with editors of newspapers [...]

Tuesday, 8 May: [...] There was considerable discussion[98] some of it rather personal & acrimonious. Mr. Ellice lectured Gladstone on the ambitious character of his finance & his improvidence especially in giving up £1,200,000 a year of paper duties at the present moment. Disraeli followed in the same sense, attacking Gladstone with more vehemence & with ad hominem arguments – alleging rashness, inconsistency, intolerance & self contradictions. These last Gladstone

---

[95] John Walter II, M.P. for Berkshire and proprietor of *The Times*.
[96] In a leading article of 30 Apr. 1860, p. 8.
[97] Robert Lowe was a leader writer for the paper; John Thaddeus Delane was the editor.
[98] On the 3rd reading of the paper duties repeal bill.

roundly denied & added that the specific instances mentioned were instances of the very opposite.

Govt. only won by 9 votes![99] Are doubts arising among the liberal party with respect to Gladstone's financial abilities? Is this another symptom of a great reaction in favour of Conservatism? Or is it that the Licensed Victuallers have succeeded in influencing a considerable number of members & in convincing them that the sellers of beer & gin are really timid lest the sale of light wines introduce a flood of debauchery & demoralization? I know this much that, if lobbying would produce change of votes, the Licensed Victuallers at least deserve great praise for the zeal & energy they have evinced in this way of business.

The gossip of the House today runs that Disraeli quite returned to his old manner in his onslaught on Gladstone, who lay back white with rage; & when he rose to correct Disraeli on a point or two of fact, the lowered tone of his voice betrayed much effort of self control. Govt. won rather ignominiously, I hear – thro' the recreancy of some half a dozen Tories unattached.[100] Ingram, who, being proprietor of the Illustrated News, is supposed to be particularly interested in the repeal of the paper duties, got into the wrong lobby – & thus cost his party two votes. I heard there was a regular hunt after him thro' the House, with a cry of 'stolen away'.

Wednesday, 9 May: [...] a long debate on the application of the factory act to bleaching & dyeing. The case stands in this way: Bleaching & dyeing are now unrestricted. Great suffering arises from long hours of labour in very heated temperatures. Harrowing details were read. The evil was palpable – & almost every one admitted that the case was one for legislation. At the same time, there was some hesitation to accept Crook's bill without more mature investigation. All bleaching is not of the same kind – some is in the open air; some in hot rooms. The trade is conducted on different principles in Ireland & England – & in Scotland quite different modes of proceeding obtain in diff[eren]t districts. One measure might not suit all cases equally. In these circumstances wise heads were laid together & we had nearly come to a vote to refer the bill to a Select Committee when Cobbett so excited the House by describing facts of wh. he had evidence that a division on the question of committing the Bill in the usual way was

[99] 219:210.
[100] According to the Saxon ambassador, 30 Conservative M.P.s had come up to town too late for the division; Henry Reeve (ed), *St. Petersburg and London in the Years 1852–1864: Reminiscences of Count Charles Frederick Vitzthum von Eckstaedt*, (1887), ii. 69–72 (11 May 1860).

insisted on & Crook triumphed.[101] The discussion was noteworthy in that Sir J. Graham recanted his former sentiments on factory legislation – admitting that the evils he had predicted had not arisen. I think the manufacturing people – Turner[102] & others – were too anxious to defend themselves, &, in doing so, they made the further mistake of uttering countercharges which they could not sustain. Thus Roebuck & Cobbett were assailed as if they had unjustly stigmatized the conduct of certain master bleachers & dyers, whereas R. & C. had merely cited evidence open to every one.

I divided for the Select Committee – and this was the course most favourable to immediate legislation, since at this season a private member has hardly a chance of getting a bill thro' the House.[103]

It struck me that Sir James Graham gave up too much in admitting that the evils he had expected from factory legislation had not occurred. Why, we have had free trade & an influx of gold – both creating large demands for British produce & tending to raise wages! How would the case have stood in famine, pestilence, commercial crises, unpopular wars – & increased taxation? Would strong men with starving families have borne the establishment of a legislative maximum of hours of work fixed to suit their less vigorous brethren?

Tuesday, 15 May: There were two divisions – one, on Lord Haddo's motion to refuse money to schools in which undraped females are employed as models[104] [...] Lord Haddo's was thought a singularly absurd speech. He seemed to be melancholy mad. He looks like a Don Quixote. Adderley, speaking with knowledge, told the House the actual case. The House was not quite as decorous as it might have been. Palmerston made fun. What were to be the limits of permissible nudity? Crinolines too, & the present 'voluminous' fashions came under his notice. Even Cornewall Lewis contrived to raise mirth, when he began by saying with great solemnity that he spoke without 'practical' acquaintance in these matters. Adderley said there was only one school in England where these models are employed. Osborne instantly shouted 'The Manchester School!' (great laughter). There was a running fire of jokes, amidst which poor old Spooner had the courage to rise & denounce the levity with which the subject was treated &, generally, to give the mover his support [...]

Thursday, 17 May: [...] we had a long evening on Wine Licenses

---

[101] By 184:147.
[102] J.A. Turner, a cotton manufacturer and merchant in Manchester.
[103] Crook's bill did receive the Royal assent, on 6 Aug.
[104] Defeated by 147:32.

& one division.[105] As usual, I supported Gladstone – my view being
to take the budget as a whole. Yet, amongst thinkers & writers very
grave doubts exist of Gladstone's practical wisdom. The Income tax
is to expire in 1861 & there will then be a heavy deficit (some
£12,500,000). We have voted the extra 1d. for a year, & have not, as
yet, even got our paper duties off.

[...] Great interest is felt on all hands in the probable course of the
Lords on the paper duties. It is more & more said, with confidence,
that the bill will be thrown out. What next? The ominous word
Dissolution is already whispered. I fear Lord Derby has too far committed himself for retrogression.

Tuesday, 22 May: 11 a.m. So the Lords have done it![106] What will
be the next move?

4.30 p.m. Rather large attendance from curiousity. Palmerston
moves an adjournment over Wed[nesda]y the Derby day – &, also,
announced his intended course of proceedings anent the paper duties.
He proposed a committee for thursday to examine journals of the
proceedings of the Lords on these Duties & a Committee for friday to
search for precedents.

The House was very tame & quiet. Whalley & Digby Seymour
talked rather grandly or meant to do so, & appeared to think – tho'
they did not say so – that a Committee of Public Safety should be the
next step & an application to the Lord Mayor for the protection of
the trained bands. The Tories laughed outright. Palmerston coolly
said, with a comical gravity, he did not see occasion to alter the line
he had designed to follow & even Cornewall Lewis raised a laugh by
the extreme brevity & dryness of his passing notice of the position put
to him and the manner in wh. he abruptly passed to the motion of
Lord Naas on convicts at Bermuda, who seem, by the way, to be in
a condition demanding instant action on the part of the executive.

[...] As to paper duties, the fact is the Lords have plausible case at
least. True, these duties will not be sustainable for long. This is
generally admitted. But, meanwhile, they bring in a growing income
now amounting to about £1,200,000 or £1,300,000 a year. It is
doubtful to some persons whether the war duties on tea & sugar[107]
shd. not first be taken off. Besides, the war in China is to go on, we
hear, &, if it be true that Gladstone's figures are inexact, we may
want money [...]

It is my present belief that the working classes in the Country would

---

[105] The bill passed through committee.
[106] I.e. rejected the paper duties repeal bill, by 193:104, the previous evening.
[107] Additional taxes on tea and sugar imposed during the Crimean war.

perfer to hear that the sugar & tea duties were reduced to hearing that penny papers could be bought for (say) a halfpenny, should that be the effect of removing the paper duties. The fact is, the repeal of these duties is rendered suspect by the connexion of the Manchester men with the Morning Star.[108] I hear the proprietors of that Journal would get £10,000 a year by the repeal. The party seeking the change have made the capital blunder of threatening the peers. Nothing is more striking than the effect of the recent bad tactics of the Bright School.

Thursday, 24 May: Palmerston moved for a Committee to search the Lords Journals on Paper Duties. Agreed to. A Committee was immediately formed from Liberals only – & those all Whigs. (At this, the Tories laughed loudly.) The Committee immediately withdrew thro' the door behind the Speaker's chair. Whalley, who rose from the Treasury Bench (!) presented, amid more laughter, a petition to the House to take care of its privileges [...] Palmerston, after a few minutes, returned to the House thro' the door behind the Serjeant at Arms with the Report of the Committee (Great laughter). The report was read by the clerk – it began 'Die Lunae &c' (more hilarity). Palmerston now gave notice of another Committee for tomorrow on the practices of the Houses of Parliament [...]

Lygon, during my absence, was somewhat discomfited. He had brought under Clarence Paget's[109] notice a rumour that he was interested in Green's shipbuilding yard, where some of the rotten gun-boats[110] were built. Paget took occasion to challenge a direct statement. Lygon stated the rumour. Paget most triumphantly refuted it. He had had a few shares in Green's Australian Line. Asked to be Secretary to the admiralty, he declined on that account. Subsequently, he sold the shares. Later still, he was again asked, & he accepted. Lygon will regret his rashness – yet, that is doubtful; he will be too much engaged in choosing & tying neckcloths. His costume is really outrageous – & why? He is a very handsome young man – & does not need embellishment – only taste [...]

Friday, 25 May: The Great Constitutional question proceeds. Lord Palmerston moves for a Committee to examine the practice of the Houses of Parliament in relation to Bills such as Paper duties repeal Bill. Many members spoke – & several amendments were proposed.

---

[108] John Bright was one of the largest shareholders in the paper; Stephen Koss, *The Rise and Fall of the Political Press in Britain, vol I, the nineteenth century*, (1981), pp. 109–11.
[109] Parliamentary secretary to the admiralty.
[110] Laid-up at Haslar; see *The Times*, 12 Mar. 1860, p. 9.

Duncombe's motion hardly seemed to be serious at first, yet Bright caught at it. Duncombe proposed that, as the Lords had only postponed the 2d. reading for 6 months, the Commons ought not 'to adjourn beyond November' by wh. time the Lords might have changed their minds.

Wyld, Whalley, James & Digby Seymour talked without weight of influence & consequently to little purpose. Lord John Russell deprecated opposition – yet spoke so gravely & ominously that he convinced the radicals of his resolution to assert the rights of the Commons. The Tories affected to be merry & defiant, but looked very serious & alarmed during Bright's speech. The Lords have, apparently, given him a strong case – & he is disposed to make the most of it.

James Clay spoke rather pertinently agt. Duncombe's motion as not bringing to an issue the legality of the course of the Lords.[111] It was complained by some members that the Committee comprehended no men below the gangway. Palmerston promised to add 2 more members – one from either side. I was astonished at the absence of Disraeli. Did he disapprove of Lord Derby's course?[112]

I incline to think that the controversy has gone too far to recede. There must be acknowledged Victory on one side [...]

Thursday, 31 May: We had a long discussion – indeed, a series of discussions – wh. lasted six hours before a vote was taken. Every topic almost connected with the Army occupied the attention of the House. The main matter before us was the appointment of Gen[era]l the Hon. Charles Grey to the 3rd Buffs. He has not been in active military service for 18 years. He has long been private secretary to the Prince Consort. There are said to be many excellent war officers who have not yet received regiments. The case is a remarkably gross & most audacious job – & so it was characterized.

The guards' privileges were the subject of notice. As to the items of votes, it was quite hopeless to produce any impression. The estimates are so voluminous that one might as well open a dictionary & take a division upon each word. I believe the question must be treated as one of confidence in a government. Of course, strong observations may be made with advantage on going into supply – & good hints may sometimes be offered when items are mentioned. But we effect

[111] The motion was withdrawn.
[112] No evidence of this, but Trelawny's remarks reflect the widespread suspicion that there were serious differences between the two Conservative leaders; cf. Robert Blake, *Disraeli*, (1966), pp. 425–8.

little good. Evans very stoutly criticized the appointment of Grey, whose emolument will be £600 a year.

The point I tried to establish – &, indeed, did establish – was that Sidney Herbert is the responsible person & not the Prince Consort. I said that to attribute such appointments to influences behind the Minister, was 'cowardly & disingenuous'. The Minister need not succumb. If he do, he is unfit. Sidney Herbert's reply did not satisfy me; nor, I think, the House. Lord Hotham spoke very gravely on the subject.

Amongst other points, I contended that the possible savings by a more economical organization of the G[uard]ds would, on the figures presented to Parliament, give the Country a full regiment of Linesmen in addition.

Wednesday, 6 June: A whole day consumed to little or no purpose in discussing the 2d. reading of an ecclesiastical Commiss[ioner]s Bill. Selwyn opened the debate, & certainly his was an able speech.[113] He has the clearness & exactness of a lawyer without that peculiar intonation & ring of cadences which so frequently become conventional in Statesmen bred to the bar. He speaks like a cultivated English gentleman.

With respect to Reform, it appears to me that it excites not feeling within or without the walls of Parliament. The working classes out of doors do not seem to believe in John Bright. Many sincere liberals in the House, noting the general corruption, have little hopes of mending it by extending the area of representation. 'More dependence – more corruption' is their view of the case. The present aspect of foreign disorders, present or imminent, makes men unusually cautious. Strikes have added to this state of mind.[114] The game of the intelligent mechanic has not been well played. I wish these questions could be settled on some self-adjusting & elastic principle, which would systematically include within the constitution the most meretorious persons of all orders as such persons present themselves. We may drift into troubled waters & be compelled to cut away our masts. This might, perhaps, be prevented by due precautions in light airs & smooth water.

Thursday, 7 June: When I went down this evening, I found a debate

[113] Criticising the centralising tendency of the bill, which vested in the ecclesiastical commissioners the real estate of bishops, deans and chapters, who were to become stipendiaries of the centrally administered fund thus created; Royal assent, 28 Aug. *P.P.* 1860, iii. 119.

[114] Cf. the leading articles in *The Times*, 23 May 1860, p. 9, 28 May 1860, p. 8, and 29 Aug. 1860, p. 8.

in progress with regard to a market at Smithfield – which drew forth from Bouverie some valuable remarks on the characteristics & treatment of Public & Private Bills & what are called Hybrid Bills.[115] He will be Speaker yet,[116] & he evidently seeks to qualify himself. I predicted this some 11 years ago. Time will shew.

[...] About 9 I returned & had the advantage of hearing several speeches.[117] The speech of the evening was certainly that of John Bright. It was more than usually vigorous & cogent – one of his greatest efforts. Disraeli, Lord Palmerston & Lord John Russell spoke. Disraeli was witty & vivacious as usual – there was something triumphant in his tone & manner, as if he were on the winning side. Lord Palmerston outdid himself in gay & sparkling fancy – & skilful banter. He was radiant. In an enormous House, after one o'clock, his stentorian voice rang thro' the anterooms where many a far younger man was stretched at length & sound sleep. Cheers & laughter followed almost every sentence. I believe he was asleep during most of the debate – at least, he generally is – & I heard he was at Ascot all day.

Bright was very fortunate in his allusion to the recent article in the Quarterly Review levelled at Disraeli, they say by Lord Robert Cecil.[118] Lord Robert looked guilty – & disguised – or appeared to disguise – his awkwardness by the use of his glasses thro' which he scanned the orator. Bright's argument was untouched by Disraeli. Disraeli's Reform Bill purported to enfranchise half a million – many of these, artizans. Is it consistent to oppose a bill purporting to enfranchise under 400,000 on the plea 'no change required – any enfranchisment dangerous,' for this is in substance the argument of the Tory party. Our majority was 21 only.[119] There was a 2d. division wh. I lost – being unaware that the opposition party meant to divide twice on motions of a formal character.[120] However, the first division was the real trial of strength.

Sidney Herbert informed me that steps were in progress respecting leave in the Brigade of guards. At present, they often manage to get 8 months leave, I hear. This is a victory for me. He adverted to one or two military topics, which I have treated lately.[121]

---

[115] I.e. public bills which affected private rights.

[116] He was not.

[117] Reform bill debate, continued.

[118] 'The Budget and the Reform Bill', in the Apr. 1860 edition of the *Quarterly Review*, was written by Cecil.

[119] 269:248 for the 2nd reading.

[120] Baillie Cochrane's motion to adjourn the House was defeated by 267:222.

[121] For Herbert's modest plans to reform the guards, and his (unsuccessful) plan to abolish the purchase of commissions for the higher ranks of the army, see Lord Stanmore, *Sidney Herbert: A Memoir*, (1906), ii. 373–5.

Monday, 11 June: As every one seemed to expect, Lord John did the deed.[122] He murdered his offspring – & in cold blood. He made a statement of considerable length – & in tones of much solemnity. He spoke of the 250 persons who opposed his project – & of the 70 amendments of which notice had been given – also, of business uncommenced & financial matters either incomplete or not even submitted to the House. Still he believed in Reform – & thought the Suffrage ought to be extended to instructed, honest & intelligent working men, if only out of regard to the safety of the Constitution. These measures are often long in progress. Thus it was with the Sacramental test – (murmurs) & Catholic emancipation – & other changes wh., eventually, took place in spite of continued & determined opposition.

The House was rather a full one. Palmerston looked rather glum & nervous. He seemed to mutter – & frequently moved his limbs. Gladstone was busy on papers – Charles Wood & Cornewall Lewis were interchanging chuckles, in evident delight – Gibson looked like a rather dignified & contented Cabinet Minister – Lords of the Treasury & such small deer were wedged in promiscuously consoling themselves for insignificance by important looks. Above sat our Deus ex Machina old Graham – calm, observant, emotionless.

Mackinnon rather quaintly congratulated Lord John on the settlement of the question (laughter) & recommended to give his attention to difficult affairs abroad.

Disraeli spoke of the dignified course of the government – & protested (in substance) that the Bill was not withdrawn thro' opposition from his side to a well considered measure tending to include more persons fit for the franchise (laughter). He evidently guarded himself agt. the charge of unfriendliness to the unrepresented.

The Reform Bill now withdrawn he characterized (as he pronounces the word) 'a coarse & vulgar expedient of degredation to the franchise'. He used phrases of compliment to Ministers – speaking of their 'honor & propriety' – & promised aid in the conduct of business.

Bright made an excellent speech. He rivetted his recent argument on the franchise – viz, that the Tories who now deem Reform uncalled for, were recently ready to enfranchise 500,000 persons. He was very ironical & contemptuous towards Mackinnon, whose support of a measure was the only thing to be dreaded from him – & he severely rebuked the insolent speeches recently levelled at working men by some Conservative members.

[...] The great speech of the evening was Horsman's – certainly it was a fierce Phillipic. It was chiefly directed at Bright & Lord John

---

[122] I.e. withdrew his reform bill.

Russell – & Reformers of the Representation generally. Still there was much wholesome satire in his invective – & his remarks deserve attentive study [...] The sting of Horsman's speech as agt. Lord John was the charge that he risked & discredited the Constitution by renewing his attempts to deal with it; as agt. Bright, that he failed to acquire the confidence of the Public – not through want of earnestness which he conceded to him, but thro' his inconsistency in supporting the chief representative of autocratic power in France[123] – & he further alleged as a motive of Bright that, in one case at least, he was biassed by hopes of larger consumption of Manchester goods.[124] But it is impossible to do adequate justice to this remarkable speech – one of the most finished & scholarly I have read for a long time – & full of gall.

Friday, 15 June: A morning sitting – Scotch Annuity tax passed thro' Committee. On a question relating to Pew rents I could not refrain from some notice of the evidence of Archdeacon Rushton[125] on the forced exclusion of the poor from Churches professedly free – & I was about to divide on words wh. I proposed to add,[126] but I found that most, if not all, the Scotchmen were agt. me – so I gave way. This annoyed me afterwards, because it does one harm to give members the trouble of racing down from Committee rooms to no purpose. Yet, I feel that my menace & the few words I said may induce clergymen in England to obtain for their flocks what is their right under act of Parliament.

[...] There is a great stir about a clause in the New Census Bill. It will, they say, compel everyone to state his religious opinions. Dissenters are furious.[127] It is said that they are afraid lest their reputed relative strength in comparison to Churchmen suffer in Public estimation. But some philosophers object on another ground – viz, that to compel a man to state his real opinions in a country where some opinions are under a legal & social ban is calculated either to cause men to lie or to place them out of the protection of courts of justice – & instances are adduced in proof. An oath of a person is not taken, if he professes incredulity on certain points, such as belief in Hell. The subject is likely to rouse a very intense quarrel.

---

[123] I.e. Napoleon III.

[124] Horsman did not specify the case, but he was presumably referring to the French annexation of Nice and Savoy.

[125] On the inadequate provision of Church places in Manchester.

[126] Trelawny wished to add a proviso to clause 29 of the bill to ensure that one-third of Church seats were reserved for public use at no cost; *H* clix. 511.

[127] For the consequent agitation, see Arthur Miall, *Life of Edward Miall*, (1884), pp. 226–8.

The first order was a Bill from the Lords agt. Sunday trading[128] [...] It is sad to think how much bigotry will arise out of these controversial subjects. Why cannot people be content to be religious without a meddling & obtrusive egotism? Is it impossible to be good without being, also, tyrannical or impertinent? Some of these Sabbath bills will be resisted – & Juries will refuse to find, or we shall make more martyrs than our prisons will hold. In all probability the difficulty of carrying such Laws out will render them virtually inoperative.

Tuesday, 19 June: Government should know its own mind. It brings in a bill on landlords & tenants & their relations to each other & then makes a compromise with the opposition giving up a most important point – that of local, in lieu of central, tribunals. Some of their party – one even in the Cabinet, Villiers – went agt. them. I joined the ranks of those who supported the Bill as it stood.[129] In adjustments of small controversies betwn. Landlords & tenants, little hopes are to be entertained of Central jurisdictions. Who will resort to them? I suppose Lord Naas & the Tories distrust local tribunals as unsafe & likely to be partial. Government should have thought of this before. Cardwell[130] made bad matter worse, since his defence was not that Naas' views were sound, but that without the compromise the measure could not pass. This was well rebuked by Lord Fermoy, who reproached him with coming into committee to fish for a principle.

When the division Bell rang, scores of members came out of breath from Committee rooms – & much was the puzzle how to vote. Was the government to be supported in its first or second proposal? [...]

Wednesday, 20 June: [...] There was a great rush for tickets for the Volunteer Levee. Two were reserved for each M.P. who could arrive in time at the place of distribution at the end of the passage where the Speaker's list is kept. We ran a race when the doors were opened after one division & the pace at wh. we all went astounded even the runners who were of all ages. One old gentleman gave me a severe contest & won it too. The turning of corners was the worse part [...]

Wednesday, 27 June: I was present for several hours[131] & supported an amendment moved by Sir H. Cairns in favour of excepting certain manufactures conducted in the open air & opposed an alteration

---

[128] The selling and hawking goods on Sunday bill was deferred until 29 June, and made no further progress.
[129] The government's amendment to its tenure and improvement of land in Ireland bill was carried by 127:51.
[130] Irish chief secretary.
[131] During the debate on the bleaching and dyeing bill, in committee.

levelled at the 10 hour principle of the bill.[132] I shd. note that the gist of the measure is to extend the factory legislation now in force to bleaching & dyeing. It is generally agreed that this legislation on the whole works well – & I think the case of women, young persons & children justifies interference where they are employed for more than 10 hours. Women are slaves – & children are not responsible for their existence.

[...] I took steps towards some settlement of the Church-Rate controversy by negotiating with various persons. There are three parties concerned – the Whigs, the Conservatives & the Dissenters. The Whigs are afraid of introducing a measure lest the others throw it out. The Conservatives are in the same difficulty. The Dissenters have no pressing desire to lose a grievance wh. brings grist to their mill.

I had two long conversations with one of our Whips & suggested various points for his consideration. I, also, conversed with a leading dissenter. I think E[stcourt] should introduce a bill from the Conservative side – & this shd. be allowed to pass if free from objectionable matter. But men are very perverse or idle. The future, which ought to concern politicians, is left to take its chance. 'Sufficient for the day is the evil thereof'. But will not this unsettled question upset the establishment?

Thursday, 28 June: [...] The Committee on privileges will soon report. This serious business baffles conjecture. I fear we are at the commencement of a train of events perilous to the Constitution. Dark & sinister words come up, again & again, in the radical Press. The unadjusted Land Tax & the unequal Succession Duties are, for example, adverted to in the Star[133] today. Then we have before us the prospect of rotten crops – famine – pestilence – & very possibly war. This is the moment wh. the Lords have selected for a contest with the Commons on a financial point. The Lords have assumed the post of Chancellor of the Exchequer – let them take, also, upon themselves all his responsibility [...]

Monday, 2 July: [...] Talking with Roebuck, I gathered that he is of opinion that the Lords were 'in their right' in rejecting the paper duties bill. He will oppose the offending clause in the Census bill,[134] but I thought his language indecisive & ambiguous, as expressive of

---

[132] Cairns's amendment was carried by 190:48; A.F. Egerton's amendment, setting a maximum twelve hour day, was defeated by 256:42.

[133] The *Morning Star*, organ of the Manchester radicals.

[134] Requiring a statement of each person's religious opinions; see above, 15 June 1860.

his opinions. I understood that his constituents[135] had determined his course for him – I was almost saying 'but is not this delegation?' [...]

Wednesday, 4 July: Palmerston's notice respecting the Lords course on Tax Bills has been printed. It seems to me to be an impotent swagger. However, discussion may alter this judgment [...]

Thursday, 5 July: The great debate on Tax Bills opened early [...] Lord Palmerston moved his first resolution (of 3)[136] in a very lucid, well arranged & able speech – perfect in manner, tone, style & delivery – but open to two serious criticisms – first, that nearly all the cheers he received came from the Tories &, secondly, that he implied some degree of hesitation with respect to the merits of the budget under present circumstances. A Minister must not even praise by halves his colleague's doings.

Collier[137] made an able speech – lucid in order & exhaustive of the argument. All concur in giving him credit.

Gladstone may be said to have raised the standard of the rebellion of the Commons. His speech was, in effect, a reply to the premier & a defiance of the Tory party, at whose silence on so great an occasion he sneered. This seems to have aroused Whiteside & Disraeli who made long orations – too jocose & laboured – but still full of clever ad captandum points. Palmerston had the satisfaction of the unqualified commendations of these orators. Stansfeld earned laurels for a very effective statement, of wh. the manner & matter were admirable. I heard Graham & Osborne pay him high compliments. The former said 'I heard your speech with sincere pleasure' or some such words. Osborne, with less polish said 'Stansfeld, boy, you'll do' – or nearly to that effect. Pretty fanny's way! S's speech seemed to revive memories of classic times & men. It was calm, clear, firm, judicious & earnest; the House seemed to feel that another Statesmen of Roman type had come upon the scene.

Coningham, Trelawny, Dillwyn, Fermoy & such like speakers + of minor order + took, in turn, their various lines. I am concerned, however, to note that I opposed the resolutions as unequal to the occasion & contemptible. Eventually we forced an adjournment by prolonging discussion. The Country must be taught to understand the magnitude of the crisis.

---

[135] At Sheffield.
[136] The first resolution affirmed the exclusive right of the Commons to grant aid and supplies to the Crown; the others stressed the infrequent exercise by the Lords of its powers, and asserted the right of the Commons, in drafting bills of supply, to guard against an undue exercise by the Lords of its powers in future. *H* clix. 1384.
[137] Counsel to the admiralty.

The House was very full. Lords Monteagle[138] & Derby were present. While Palmerston was speaking, he looked full at Lord Derby's position under the gallery – & for a moment I could not help thinking that they were two athletes. Lord Derby looked calm, without anxiety, & I observed that he smiled from time to time as if in mockery of our impotence or pleasure at our admissions of the success of the Baronial coup d'état. The general demeanour of the Tories greatly altered during the debate. At first triumphant, it gradually became serious &, perhaps, alarmed. I do not believe this matter of Privilege is going to be settled quite as easily as some suppose. But let us not be too sanguine. We have among us but few earnest men.

Lord John Russell spoke tamely & tediously – for him. The truth is, when the Lords rejected the paper duties Bill, the government shd. have resigned. The Bill would have passed.

Friday, 6 July: Sad night indeed! The Commons have tamely passed Palmerston's 3 resolutions.[139] They are a mere truism – &, no action being taken, the course of the Lords must be considered as one wh. we do not profess to be capable of resisting.

The debate was long. Digby Seymour made a speech in wh. he analysed the precedents affecting the case – Horsman made a high Tory speech in defence of the Lords & propounding many true, but irrelevant, propositions affirming the value of the House of Peers as an element of our mixed govt. – & Bright replied in a grand restatement of the argument for the rights of the representative chamber.

As to the divisions in the shape of amendments,[140] thank God! I declined to have anything to do with them. As long as there was any chance of getting a member to move the previous question I strove with that object, but failed. In commendable disgust I retired. To my mind the House of Commons has lost caste. This comes of the rule of trimming leaders + tricksters + who look to present interest as the measure of political duty & leave posterity to its fate.

Can Gladstone retain his post? Is Gibson content? + base enough? +[141]

[...] One of my points was the narrowness of the suffrage, & the

---

[138] The former Thomas Spring Rice, a Whig Chancellor of the Exchequer; he had moved the rejection of the paper duties repeal bill in the upper House.

[139] Agreed to without a division.

[140] Lord Fermoy's adjournment motions.

[141] On 1 July Gladstone had sent a memorandum to the prime minister urging legislative action against the Lords; H.C.G. Matthew (ed), *The Gladstone Diaries*, v. 501. At the Cabinet meeting on the following day, Gibson and the Duke of Argyll were the only ministers to support Gladstone; Palmerston to the Queen, 2 July 1860, in A.C. Benson and Lord Esher (eds), *The Letters of Queen Victoria*, (1st series, 1907), iii. 402–4.

duty of the House as now constituted & assuming to represent the masses, not to betray its trust. I reminded members that in a recent debate every species of insult & calumny had been cast on working men 'by persons infinitely their inferiors' – & I added that the great body of the people looked on watchfully – taking no part because they left the whole responsibility with those who pretend to be worthy of the trust reposed in them – to defend the liberties of their order [...]

Wednesday, 11 July: [...] The Census Bill came on. After going into Committee & reaching the 4th clause Baines moved, in a long sermon, his amendment in opposition to the words requiring, under penalty, a statement by each householder of his religious profession & the professions of his household & family. There was rather a smart debate. Sir Cornewall Lewis[142] made a learned-foolish speech, in which he contrived to offend dissenters very bitterly & not altogether please Churchmen. Lewis is a sort of gauche doctrinaire – he is full of knowledge, but cannot steer clear of damaging words & topics. His illustrations either provoke a smile or make the persons angry whom he desires to conciliate. It was evidently his game to get his government out of a false position – gracefully & with kindly & considerate words. He, on the contrary, laboured to prove the course right which Ministers had adopted at first – &, in doing so, he lost the good effect of timely concession by offensive insinuations & comparisons [...] The obnoxious words were withdrawn [...]

Thursday, 12 July: [...] I rose with another member[143] at an earlier moment than I had expected, thinking that others, having notices, would precede me. However, I succeeded in getting a hearing – ostensibly on the question by the Speaker 'that I do now leave the Chair' (on going into supply), but in reality on my resolution to postpone the consideration of supplies till after the paper duties Bill shd. have become Law.

I spoke shortly to this effect – that the three resolutions lately come to by the House were futile & unworthy of the occasion – yet they assumed that occasion one for censure of the Lords, but took no action [...] The House of Lords had overthrown a *usage* of 400 years. They had assumed the whole responsibility for finance. This could not be done by halves. To reject an essential part of a budget was equivalent to originating one [...] As to the House of Commons, I described it as a degraded & discredited assembly.

---

[142] Home secretary.
[143] Sir Robert Peel, moving for papers regarding the threatened annexation of Sicily by Sardinia.

On a division, we had only 13 besides tellers[144] – more than I expected at first. As I walked up the House a Tory member whispered 'here is half an hour lost'. I said to myself 'we have lost more than that'.

Bright was, I heard, present in the corridor, but left.

I remember that I warned the House of Lords that a cry of 'Privilege & Primogeniture' would next arise in lieu of our old watchwords 'Ballot, Suffrage &c' and took care to remind the Tories that they had shared in the vote which censured the Peers.

[...] The labour of attendance at the House has become almost beyond the endurance of giants. Certainly, Palmerston is of Heroic mould. Between 3 & 4 on a summer's morning, he was still at his post baffling the Irish Brigade, who hoped by factious motions for adjournmt. to get rid of the Peace Preservation Bill.[145] Maguire suggested that the House shd. go to bed, Palmerston proposed that the minority only shd. go – & when that body dwindled to 7, he observed, on giving way, that the Public would, at least, see there were still seven wise men [...]

Friday, 13 July: [...] On supply coming on, Cochrane made a very creditable speech on the China War.[146] This led to a long discussion. Willoughby, Roebuck, Bright, Palmerston, Gladstone, Lord John, F. Baring & others spoke.

The fact is, the House wanted to see daylight about this war. Here we are at war with 380 millions of people at the other side of the earth. We are associated with a dangerous ally – & it is suspected we are thwarted by a recent enemy.[147] Our accounts are many years in arrear. We are voting money without knowledge whether it is for this China war, a former one or a Persian war – & no minister can say how much is due from the Indian Exchequer, how much from the British. These points were raised – but met with no satisfactory reply.

Then, it was demanded 'what are the objects of the war?' A resident Minister at Pekin,[148] Baring said was not wanted by merchants. Their interests are dealt with at ports. It is clear that we are drifting without a definite policy.

Lord John, Gladstone & others were reproached with incon-

---

[144] Trelawny and Dillwyn were the tellers; the majority numbered 198.

[145] The bill was given its 1st reading by 53:15; Royal assent 28 Aug.

[146] In Sept. 1859 Britain and France had decided to send another military expedition in order to force the Chinese to abide by the provisions of the treaty of Tientsin (June 1858) which had ended the first war; W.C. Costin, *Great Britain and China 1833–1860*, (Oxford, 1937), pp. 287–315.

[147] I.e. Russia.

[148] One of the provisions of the treaty of Tientsin.

sistency – they having, when out of office, resolutely & eloquently opposed the China War.[149] Roebuck distinctly pressed home this charge, wh. Gladstone attempted to rebut by alleging that the two wars are different. This is true technically, false in essence. These wars are in effect the opium war of 1840 reopened – it comes to that. This Graham evidently thought. The bent of his mind was undisguised, in his bye play & asides & interchanges of talk with Bright & others near & about the place where I was sitting.

[...] It is a shameful facet, that the vote (£443,896) repayment to Indian Govt, for expenses for China war passed.[150] We are in truth a den of thieves [...] It came out that we have an army of betwn. 17 & 18 thousand men in China – & the original number has been increased without direct orders from home. Lord Canning[151] did this on the opinion of Lord Clyde.[152] So much for the way in wh. the H. of C. manage war & finance. The China war will have cost, they say, £6,000,000 by the end of this financial year.

During the debate on Cochrane's motion, while Palmerston was dwelling on the objects & grounds of the war, the lower the ground on which he put it, such as retaliation & commercial advantage &c – the more vociferous the cheers of Kinnaird. Now this Kinnaird is a very strenuous ally of the Sabbatarians & stoutly opposes projects like that of opening Museums on Sundays. He is a very obtrusive cheerer, his voice being often heard alone – & very audible it is. Sir John Shelley's eye caught mine at the very moment of one of Kinnaird's loudest exclamations, which seemed to sound oddly all things considered – the orator[153] being called by the Low church writers 'the man of God!' – the applause coming from an earnest stickler for religious observances – & the sentiments being certainly not to be found in the New Testament. Shelley & I could not help smiling – & I said aloud across Kinnaird 'Christian!' He looked daggers.

The way Palmerston talks over the Irish is amusing. A member complained that there is no Volunteer force in Ireland – which is, in reality, owing to the apprehension that they might cherish sentiments adverse to British rule or fall foul of each other. With a grave face Palmerston argued among other reasons the rapidity with which the Irish make good soldiers, so that there is not the same necessity for armed preparation long before invasion! This was, however, too gross

---

[149] I.e. the first China war, on which issue they had helped to defeat Palmerston's ministry in Mar. 1857.

[150] Agreed to without a division.

[151] Governor general of India.

[152] The former Sir Colin Campbell; he had just retired as commander-in-chief in India.

[153] Palmerston.

for Scully, who spoke as if he understood the real value of the compliment, yet very likely took it in secret after all; wh. often happens.

Monday, 16 July: [...] It had been my purpose to move my resolution again on the Privilege question & I gave at an earlier moment a notice hereon. But conversation with members proved to me that this tame, trimming, recreant House of Commons would not support me – & that it was very likely that I should do more harm than good by such proceeding.

[...] As I was leaving the House, White, our cultivated & intelligent doorkeeper,[154] observed to me that Jules Favre[155] was in the gallery. I returned to get a look of the man who has dared to criticize a budget in a French Chamber. As I was looking at him, I noted that some one called Disraeli's attention to the presence of a stranger – I conclude it was Favre, as only one other person was sitting with him – & that other was, I think, an official pointing out to him members of the House. Disraeli could not see so far (over the clock) – so he took his eye glass – licked it – wiped it on his clothes – & then got a better view at some cost of dramatic effect. + He shd. consider that the leader of a party, who studies deportment & action so carefully, should be consistent. + [...]

Tuesday, 17 July: We had a rather smart debate on Adderley's Bill to make the employment of a child under 12 without a certificate of education penal & punishable with a fine of £1 [...] The mover of the amendment was Pease.[156] On a division the Bill was rejected.[157] I voted with the noes. It seemed to me to carry interference too far & would probably make education hateful to the People. Yet, very good arguments were adduced on the other side – &, especially, the experience of the factory act was confidently relied on [...]

Evening sitting. Events pass too rapidly for comment at length [...] Fermoy [...] moved[158] neatly enough in a speech of about $\frac{1}{2}$ an hour, well heard. Palmerston proposed, in 3 or 4 sentences, the previous question. Clay affected the office of moderator betwn. Govt. & the

---

[154] William White wrote a weekly article on events in parliament for the *Illustrated Times*.

[155] The leading radical opponent of the regime of Napoleon III in France.

[156] Henry Pease, M.P. for Durham, South; a manufacturer and coal-owner.

[157] Pease's delaying amendment being carried by 122:51.

[158] His resolutions regarding the paper duties repeal bill, criticising the policy of inaction implied by Palmerston's resolutions, urging the government to assert the rights of the people by dissolving parliament if necessary, praising Gladstone, and calling on the Commons to obstruct supply until the Lords had rescinded its vote; *H* clix. 2079–80.

radicals. Osborne dashed into the fray to what purpose Osborne only knows. The effect could not mend the position of Govt. Sir Geo. Grey spoke to little purpose. Bouverie moved an adjournment, but, gaining no hearing, withdrew it. Disraeli, under pretence of healing our differences, widened them to the best of his ability. We divided on the question that the question (Fermoy's) be put – this motion the Tories could support without inconsistency & great fears existed lest govt. shd. be defeated. We were beaten[159] – & so Ministers are easier for a time. I spoke after Fermoy.

Wednesday, 18 July: [...] Much gossip was in circulation about our privilege battle of last night. It seems the Tories are furious. They consider that Disraeli made a capital blunder in dividing with us on 'the previous question'. The appearance to the Public is as if his party had supported Lord Fermoy, who was thus teller in no inconsiderable minority. So much for trickery! Here is the engineer 'hoist with his own petard'.

The Speaker was very nervous last night. I hear he was even prepared for the contingency of having to give a casting vote. His great fear was, lest, in the event of the govt. being defeated on 'the previous question', Lord Fermoy's question shd. be put, as, if he failed, the House would have affirmed in effect that nothing more shd. be done. Now, it seems the Speaker is strongly of opinion that hereon the House shd. be quite free. The Speaker is as resolute as any one agt. the Lords.

[...] Altogether a healthier feeling begins to arise – & by God! I'll help it [...]

Thursday, 19 July: The 'Times' has a leader taking me to task.[160] It is in the very sense of Wingrove Cooke's[161] talk with me at the club last night. Now W.C. writes regularly in the 'Times'.

I have had a long & interesting conversation with May,[162] one of our clerks & author of the best work on Parliamentary proceedings. He counsels 'sullen endurance' of the indignity received from the Lords – till there shall occur some more favourable opportunity of dealing with the subject. We exhausted all possible plans that we could think of. To contest payment in the Courts would not do, since the Judges would take the naked Statute. As to refusing to pass so much of the appropriation act as would involve the amount of the

---

[159] By 177:138.
[160] 19 July 1860, p. 8, criticising the continued efforts by Trelawny and other radicals to obstruct parliamentary business.
[161] George Wingrove Cooke, a leader writer for *The Times*.
[162] Erskine May, chief clerk of the House of Commons.

paper duties, that appeared not practicable in as much as money not applied would go towards payment of debt. To continue the struggle from day to day, in the form of galling motions, would be of little use in the present apathetic state of the Public mind, which is dead to Public duty, indifferent to the abstract principles of government, &, if it feel at all, rather inclined to reaction.

May described what he wished to do very early on, when the danger of the Lords taking their course first loomed. He would then have kept back the bill for a time, obtaining a calm & temperate discussion of the anticipated difficulty in both Houses. The Lords wd. then have learnt the magnitude of the step to which they were invited by their reckless leader. I believe hatred to Gladstone has been the moving cause in the whole transaction – but what madness of hate! Here we have an insoluble difficulty betwn. Lords & Commons – with possibly a long train of calamaties arising out of it – all to gratify the spite of a defeated & disappointed faction.

When the mischief had been perpetrated, May's advice was not taken. It was this – to pass a dignified protest agt. the act being drawn into a precedent. No doubt, the dignity of the H. of C. would have stood better so than it does now. It seems several of the Cabinet agreed with him, but not enough.

[...] I note in the 'Times' a speech by Ld. Derby on the conduct of Public business in the 2 Houses. One paragraph is an admission which is remarkable. I extract it, as follows:– 'There is comparatively speaking so small a number of your lordships who are disposed very carefully to consider the provisions of measures wh. may be intro-duced, or who are interested in calling attention to matters of detail, & there is so great a readiness to allow measures to be sent from this for consideration by the other House &c &c' (See 'Times' 20th July). I wonder whether the Repeal of the Paper duties Bill was one wh. their lordships were not 'disposed very carefully to consider' [...]

Monday, 23 July: I went down to the House to hear & decide upon the government proposal with respect to fortifications. Lord Palmerston made a very good speech – much applauded by two thirds of his audience – Conservative cheers preponderating. Bright was very restless – &, now & then, betrayed marks of feeling by an ironical 'hear' or some such sign.

A plan for fortifications[163] at a new known cost of £9,000,000 & a probable £24,000,000 is enough to make old Hume[164] turn in his

---

[163] Of the dockyards and arsenals at Portsmouth, Plymouth, Chatham and Cork.

[164] Joseph Hume (d.1855), a prominent radical who campaigned for retrenchment in government expenditure.

grave. Shall we ever see the end of the bill? And, when the work shall be completed – if ever – will not new discoveries in artillery require fresh outlay?

It was remarkable that Palmerston threw off all diplomatic reserve & plainly indicated where danger lies – viz, in France. The weak point seemed to me this – P. offers us a bait in saying that, in this year only £2,000,000 will be required (altho' plans to be commenced this year will involve £5,000,000) & that an appropriation act will be passed each year, so that Parliament will keep this business in its own hands. But, if we commit ourselves to £5,000,000 at once, what becomes of such control?

It seems to me that Osborne was not far wrong in questioning the wisdom of exposing our scheme of defence to hostile criticism. We spend enough for our army – & we ought to have Staff officers capable of projecting lines of defence at a day's notice. The War Office ought to have plans ready, so that invasion shd. never take us unawares. In my opinion Staff officers should be assigned to every county – which would serve without masonry.

Lord Harry Vane (speaking to me & Sir R. Peel) said convicts might be more used in this way – & I agree.

[...] It struck many persons as remarkable that the Chancellor of the Exchequer was absent.[165] Questions relating to his department were left in some doubt. Cornewall Lewis almost took his colleague's business into his own hands – at least, what Palmerston had left to be done. The Tories evidently have hopes of disagreement in the Cabinet.

The resolution on fortifications was postponed on Bright's threat of repeated adjournments on the ground of surprise.

Tuesday, 24 July: The business was the Poor Law Board Continuance Bill. A clause contained a proposed extension of that Board for 5 years & to the end of the next Session of Parliament. Bazley moved to fix the period of 1 year. A brisk debate ensued – Estcourt recommended 5 years, tho' his arguments rather appeared to incline towards a shorter time. Osborne supported Ministers. Deedes advocated 3 years & no more.[166] Wilson Patten was favourable to a short period. Villiers[167] contended that the vote proposed would be a heavy blow levelled at the government of the Poor Law Board. Palmerston stoutly defended his brother minister, but promised an inquiry by a Committee next year to be moved for by government & alleged, in

---

[165] Gladstone spent the whole day at Cliveden, conveniently missing the debate; *Gladstone Diaries*, v. 506–7.

[166] Bazley withdrew his amendment in favour of Deedes's.

[167] Chief commissioner of the poor law board.

reply to objections, that action might be taken so soon as such committee shd. have made its recommendations. Altho' I am desirous of shortening the existence of this Centralizing Board, yet, after Palmerston's undertaking, I did not think it right to oppose the proposal of Villiers & fall out with an able administration in his department on grounds of a difference of 2 years in the time laid down. The great good achieved since /34 is to be weighed in the balance, & a little time for the inauguration of a new system is not undesirable. The money saved since 1834 amounts, I heard, to some 34 million – but far more has been saved than can be estimated, for we were drifting before to ruin.

However, we were roundly beaten – & Ministers succumbed.[168] Henley was rather hard on them, for, having intended to support them, he made their concession a ground of opposition.

Evening sitting – Again in the Mill. Pakington had a question before the House on Naval retirement. Having more confidence in the Duke of Somerset[169] than Pakington, I opposed his resolution.[170] + It appeared to be a party move – &, on the ground of general fairness towards the Executive, I lent it my support. + Had a precise & matured plan been presented to us, I think I shd. have been disposed to consider it favourably.

Then came Dunlop's motion to ordain that future contracts relating to Telegraphic & Packet communications shd. be laid on the table for a certain period before they shall take effect. This Gladstone accepted with many compliments to Dunlop. Roebuck warned us how we allowed responsibility to be shifted from the shoulders of Ministers to members of Parliament in their collective capacity – & I confess I shared his hesitation [...]

Thursday, 26 July: [...] Horsman was very vicious last night;[171] he attacks the govt. almost nightly. Certainly Ministers have not the confidence of the House. Business is greatly in arrear. It is believed that dissensions are frequent in the Cabinet. Gibson must have difficulty in agreeing to the vote for fortifications. Bright has sounded a warning hereon – & means opposition. The Paper duties question is one full of troubles. Will Gladstone persist in taking off the duty now leviable on foreign paper in excess of our excise? Again, there is the budget not completed. Bright wants to know whether Gladstone intends to

---

[168] Deedes' amendment carried, 147:92.

[169] First Lord of the admiralty.

[170] For a Royal commission to investigate the system of promotion and retirement in the navy; *H* clx. 103–12. Defeated by 89–56.

[171] Trelawny was evidently writing-up his diary the following day; he is referring to the debate on the European forces India bill, on 26 July.

send up a permanent spirit duty to the Lords who have shewn that they cannot be trusted to agree to any future recommendation of the Commons that such duty be reduced or abolished. The hitch betwn. the 2 Houses evidently exists still [...] It seems to me that the Ministry will hardly live over the Session [...]

Friday, 27 July: An Irish debate – Landlord & tenant bill. I was in one division – supporting Ministers[172] [...] There is often great vivacity in Irish debates – several on their legs together – all speaking at cross purposes and in a rich brogue. And how they talk of each other in private! [...]

Monday, 30 July: My pair with Mr. Pugh counts from this day – & my knowledge of events is derived from newspapers [...] From observations in debate I gather that there is a growing feeling that Parliamentary government is not in a career of improvement in this country. Members too frequently use their extreme rights for the purpose of delay & obstruction. Is not this the result of attempting to rule with wavering purpose, miniature measures & a divided Cabinet? or is it that the Minister is unwise in his mode of introducing his proposals & the order in which they are presented? It strikes me that he shd. lay down more fixed rules of proceeding. He shd. decide at the outset 1st. to carry necessary bills & the estimates & ways & means, & 2dly. to come to bills which, though useful, may still be postponed. Acting in this manner a leader, having general confidence & a reputation for principles and resolution to enforce them would, I apprehend, overbear mere litigiousness & earn credit for his party & himself while he benefited the Nation. Now this Lord Palmerston fails to do. He is considered to be a well meaning ruler, by rule of thumb, but, if anything at all, a Tory of the old school – of great good nature & suavity – with generous sympathies & hearty English pluck – but withal a roystering contempt for formed opinions & a jaunty indifference to the future, wh. are almost sublime.

Monday, 6 August: A great debate & division – nearly 500 members. Ministers won by 33. The amendmt. was Puller's (on customs duties on paper)[173] [...]

---

[172] Trelawny helped to defeat (71:25) Sullivan's amendment adding a clause to the bill enabling tenants to remove buildings they had erected; *H* clx. 271.

[173] Against Gladstone's resolution to equalise the customs and excise duties on paper; *H* clx. 723–42. Defeated by 273:266.

Thursday, 9 August: [...] the Galway Contract[174] [...] Lord Derby, at the very crisis of his government's fate 2 days after the dissolution,[175] gave a most lucrative contract to the Galway Company & this in direct opposition to the carefully prepared opinion of Lord Colchester, his own colleague in the Post Office [...] The impression one gleans from the whole statement of the proceedings is that the contract made by the Derby govt. was one singularly disgraceful even for these times – & Lord Derby's habitual recklessness & ignorance are rather to his advantage as tending to screen him from the charge of something worse. Had the contract been properly made, it would have been submitted to Public competition according to rule & a promise made to do nothing hastily in the business would have been kept, this being a matter of great concern to Canada, wh. has expended large sums in the creation of a Grand Trunk railway & in subsidy of a Steam Line by Sea. Bouverie proposed to reject the vote.[176] From his account it appears that, to all intents & purposes, the Company obtained its grant by a fraudulent account of its property – some of it consisting of ships mortgaged to their full value [...] No wonder Lord Derby required the paper duties – the Nation must have a plentiful balance at its banker's to cover Lord Derby's misappropriation of Public money. Disraeli & Whiteside struggled to defend their leader, yet signally failed. Laing[177] made a very good speech in proposing the vote, which he did on the ground of the Country being pledged.

Friday, 10 August: [...] Bright returned to the Paper duty question & the course taken by the Lords. He appears to have made a speech which should have been delivered when the Paper duties (excise) bill was rejected. One would think he had only just discovered that violence had been done to the Constitution. Indeed, Bright's conduct has laid him open to suspicion, hinted at in the 'Times' article of the 11th instant, that it was so important to the Star[178] & the cheap Press to get the recent reduction in the Customs duties on paper that the Constitutional question, which is of infinitely greater importance, has been allowed to lie dormant till a period when it is almost futile or ridiculous to renew it. Palmerston took great advantage of Bright's false position – & pounded him rarely. Bright studiously avoided my

---

[174] On 21 Apr. 1859 the Derby ministry had signed a contract with the Atlantic Royal Mail company, worth £78,000 per annum, to operate a mail service between Galway and north America.

[175] 19 Apr. 1859.

[176] It was carried by 145:39.

[177] Financial secretary to the treasury.

[178] The *Morning Star*, the organ of the Manchester radicals.

motion to stop supplies[179] – either from want of nerve or want of knowledge or from some such notion as that suggested by the 'Times' writer.[180] It will do Bright harm. A man has no right to pretend to a lead so prominent as that to wh. Bright aspires & then throw overboard interests of such magnitude as those involved in the exclusive right of the Commons to hold the purse strings of the Nation [...]

Tuesday, 16 August: [...] The Irish education debate was a fine opportunity for – what is called in the slang of the day – 'Bunkum'. Irish members, like Maguire, conceive it to be their duty to advocate R. Catholic interests & parade their catalogue of alleged R.C. grievances. The Irish edu[cation] system works on the whole wonderfully well – & 570,000 children of all forms of religion in Ireland receive excellent instruction in mixed schools administered by a Commission. The English plan is Denominational – ie. money is given in aid of schools of ea[ch] separate body of religionists. In Ireland all children are educated together. It is remarked in America that the emigrants from Ireland have become greatly improved of late. It was thought the mixed system would lead to proselytism or indifferentism. Neither prophecy has been fulfilled. Maguire complains that undue advantages are extended to protestants. But facts & authorities appear to rebut his allegations. Deasy[181] & he were pretty well pitted one agt. the other. Each is fluent – each has a rich brogue – & the regular Irish whine – plaintive even in good fortune. But office makes the difference between them.

Friday, 17 August: [...] There was another division on the vote of £3,750 for the salaries of the ecclesiastical Com[missione]rs wh. was carried by one vote – 45 to 44. These Com[missione]rs have been in great & just disgrace in consequence of an increase of salary they gave the Dean of York, who now has £2,000 a year. The increased grant (of £1,000) is an unusually heartless & profligate job – & has been very severely noticed on several occasions. Hundreds of curates are on starvation allowance. So much for the people's Church! [...]

Monday, 20 August: [...] The House of Lords is in hot water again. They have sent down a Divorce law Amendment bill which is said to touch upon our powers of taxation. The Speaker used some very grave

[179] See above, 12 July 1860.
[180] Bright seems to have been concerned that hostile action might make Gladstone's position within the government more difficult; Bright to Cobden, 15 July 1860, in Trevelyan, *John Bright*, pp. 290–1.
[181] Irish attorney general.

language hereon. It is plain what he thinks. It appears a precedent has been in course of growth since 1854.[182] The House seemed awake at last – & the bill has been adjourned.

Friday, 24 August: Some very strong language, regarding the cession of Savoy & the conduct of all concerned therein, fell from Lord Palmerston. France may well take it as a menace [...]

Tuesday, 28 August: Parliament prorogued – the concoctors of the Queen's speech had a difficult task to prove the Session not abortive. It has been a Parliament of Magpies thus far.

[182] The Divorce court bill was the latest in a series of bills since 1854 which had been amended by the Lords to enable various classes of officials to claim particular expenses out of 'funds provided by parliament'. The Speaker stated that he had intimated to the Lords that in future he would object to such clauses on behalf of the House of Commons; *H* clx. 1629–30. The bill received the Royal assent on 28 Aug.

SESSION OF 1861

Tuesday, 5 February: About one o'clock I proceeded with difficulty, through crowds of the curious, to the House of Commons. More people than usual were collected in Parliament Street & there were two long lines extending to the Horse g[uar]ds from the House of Lords. I hear that the Queen was received with cheers. Very few policemen were required.

[...] After about an hour of pleasant chat & after many courteous greetings & friendly approximations, the Usher of the black rod[1] – a not very imposing personage to fill such an office – summoned us to the House of Lords. Names were read of members selected by ballot (I believe) to prevent a rush & to secure orderly conduct before the Queen. The selected proceeded as their names were called, but before the list was half finished, a large body of members crowded off, as usual, towards the H. of Lords.

[...] Sir T.E. Colebrooke moved the address – seconded by Mr. Paget of Nottingham. The former was not very audible – & I do not think he made a very striking speech, though I do not believe that it was inappropriate. Probably, it would be considered respectable, but commonplace. Paget was well heard in a few brief, modest, sensible, & candid remarks. The House laughed at an expression or two, which might have a double significance, as if his praise of govt. was to be understood as not wholly without alloy.

J. White of Brighton moved an amendment on behalf of Reform of Parliament. Disraeli criticized. Lord John plainly told the Nation it was their affair. Bright delivered a fiery & most caustic Philippic the force of which lay in a simple narrative of facts. I hardly know whether Ministers or opposition were more severely handled. On a division we were beaten – Numbers 129 & 46.[2] Of course, I voted with White [...]

Wednesday, 6 February: [...] With regard to Reform, as the crock should not be personal in describing the kettle, amenities on this subject as betwn. Ministers & opposition were discreetly waived. But Bright's tongue was loosened with perfect right. We voted the ejection

---

[1] Sir Augustus Clifford.
[2] Trelawny mistakenly wrote 47.

of Disraeli's govt. on a plea of the inadequacy of a Bill which purported to enfranchise only 500,000 persons & we adopted Lord John's resolution. Now, Lord John meets the question with ironical banter, some pleasantry & caustic humour. Will this do? Suppose a long war – or a famine – or a failure of cotton supply – or another Indian mutiny – or continued Indian deficit of (say) £7,000,000. The discipline of the Army & Navy is at a low ebb – & Volunteers are a power of vague future & uncertain import.

[...] Lord John R's speech on Italian affairs[3] strengthens Ministers. Seymour Fitzgerald must be mad not to see that, in identifying Derbyite policy with the success of Italian reaction, he rehabilitates the Ministry – suspect as Home Reformers – in the general approval of the People of England. I imagine that Italian affairs & the speeches of liberal statesmen thereon are the chief mainstay of govt.

Thursday, 7 February: Lord Palmerston asked for a Committee to consider whether any changes in our forms would expedite Public business. The House seemed languid & not hopeful of such a result. All are more or less conscious that the mischief lies not in our forms but in our abuse of them. Change the forms – & still the new ones will be abused. Suppose a member backed by half London in Palace yard – what forms would stop him? Unless liberty be put down, how can the discretion of representatives be fettered without risk? Horsman made a telling speech in support of an amendment to add words to the motion ostensibly directed to the object of making it more effectual, but really levelled as a vote of censure at Ministers for not having heretofore advised the Houses of Parliament prudently as to the course of proceedings & for not having divided business skilfully or presented measures with sufficient promptness & in a condition for enactment. Horsman, having made his speech, withdrew his motion.[4] These debates on saving time are a little like throwing good money after bad [...]

Friday, 8 February: [...] My subject of Church-Rates has arrived at the dignity of having 3 whips. I have also had the name of Sir Charles Douglas placed on the back of the Bill. The names of Trelawny & Dillwyn only might look too undiluted [...]

---

[3] Showing that Britain had taken a consistent stance of non-interference, allowing the Italians to settle their own destiny, but defending the king of Sardinia's intervention to prevent anarchy in Naples and Sicily; *H* clxi. 127–39.

[4] Palmerston's motion was then agreed to. The recommendations of the committee were partially implemented, notably the substitition of Thursday for Friday as a government night, and the adoption of Tuesday as a supply night; *P.P.* 1861, xi. 431.

Monday, 11 February: Questions. Trelawny asked a question of the Home Secretary relating to a recent suit in Rochdale County Court in which a plaintiff was nonsuited in consequence of the disqualification of his witness to give evidence on account of her not believing in a future state. The judge was Mr. C. Temple. Sir G. Cornewall Lewis could not reply in detail as he had not received notice, so I said I would repeat the question at the next sitting.

Mrs. Maden was to be a witness in a suit by her husband for £6.3. the value of a piano forte alleged to be detained by Mr. Catenack the husband of Mrs Maden's mother. The defence was that the article belonged to the latter lady. On Mrs Maden's coming forward Mr. Standring, counsel for def[enden]t, asked her whether she believed in a future state of rewards & punishments? She replied, that she did not. More passed – but the material point is that the Judge rejected her as a witness.

[...] The Bankruptcy & Insolvency Bill was, afterwards, introduced in a long speech from the Attorney-general. The measure seems to be a shorter & more manageable one than that of last year.[5] The Bill is intended to simplify the law & diminish the costs of winding up estates. Insolvency Com[missione]rs will be abolished – power of punishment in certain bad cases will be given to a judge – imprisonment of insolvents according to the present law will be abolished – great facilities will be afforded to creditors towards winding up estates without costly litigation in the Bankruptcy Court. Such is a very meagre outline of the Bill, which was very well received & will in substance pass[6] [...]

Tuesday, 12 February: Among the questions came mine of yesterday resumed by notice. Before my name was called, the Speaker desired to speak to me. So I went up to his chair. He observed that my printed question on the notice paper has the words 'certain speculative opinions' as being the cause of Mrs Maden's disqualification to give evidence & he reminded me that in my viva voce notice the day before I had specified that her inability to say she believed in a 'future state of rewards & punishments' was the cause. He therefore had thought it was respectful to the House to alter the notice in such sense & order a reprint thereof. I stated my reasons for the more comprehensive words I had used – saying that the witness had been called upon to reply to several questions, some by counsel, some by judge – & that it seemed to me that the altered words I had adopted were milder than those directly alluding to a future state. I added

[5] Which failed to pass through lack of time.
[6] Royal assent, 6 Aug.; *P.P.* 1861, i. 257.

that nothing could have been further from my mind than the idea of shewing disrespect to the House – & that I would readily use the words put upon the paper by Mr. Speaker's order – 'deferring to you, Mr Speaker'. He stated his intention of mentioning what he had done. Subsequently, I went up again to him – & a few more words passed not materially altering the understanding between us.

Eventually my name was called – & Mr. Speaker made his state-ment [...] Then came my questions – with Sir Cornewall Lewis's reply. First he represented that the suit was by Mrs Maden agt. her mother for a piano – which was not exact *Mem[orandu]m in Sept. 1861 (20th). I believe, after all, I am in error here. Mrs Maden was joint suitor with her husband. At least, I am nearly sure this was so* as the suit was by Mr. Samuel Maden agt. Mr. Catenack (Mrs. Maden's stepfather) for the value of a piano £6.3., & from the manner of Lewis, it seemed to me that he sought to prejudice Mrs M. as a litigious & ill conditioned woman wrangling with her own mother about a piano, or, else, why did he put the point in so invidious a manner?

He read an extract from Starkie[7] in order to establish the Law, which he described as tolerance, since not a future State in another world was necessarily the point, but in this one – whereon I doubt his position – & I think lawyers in West[minste]r Hall will have something to say on it. *I believe he was right. Sept 17/68.* When the Minister described the nonsuit of the Plaintiff under the circumstances stated there was an inane & bigoted cheer on the Tory benches, as if the witness's difficulty in believing was to be the cause of punishing the plaintiff by the loss of his action. I could not speak again without violating forms – & so I waited for a motion which I knew was about to come – a motion by Ld. P[almerston] for adjournment to 2 o'clock on Ash Wednesday, when I arose & opposed adjournment even for a moment until the claims of justice had been vindicated. I called attention to Lewis's inaccuracy about Mrs Maden's being pla[in]t[if]f when he said correct[in]g me 'her husband'. I accepted his version as a matter of courtesy – well knowing what he had in fact said – & represented that I must conclude my ears had deceived me – as was the case with the 'Times' Reporter. Coningham shortly supported me. *That wh. annoys one in Lewis is sin agt. knowledge.* I always thought him gauche & heavy – but, at least, an honest doctrinaire. But he appears to have been an apt scholar of the ways of office one of which is to get rid of difficulties by the suppressio veri or its distortion (as most convenient). The Speaker's interference was an impertinence,

---

[7] Thomas Starkie, *A practical treatise of the law of evidence, and digest of proofs, in civil and criminal proceedings*, (2 vols, 1833); a standard work on the subject.

which might, perhaps, be ascribed to timidity or inexperience. He had no right to alter my notice – the form of which I had a perfect right to change [...]

Thursday, 14 February: [...] Thanks were voted to officers & others engaged in the Chinese War.[8] Lord Palmerston, neatly but tamely, moved; Disraeli seconded. Scully recalled the Yuen Ming Yuen business,[9] wh. in my judgment disgraced our Country. Palmerston endorsed it, of course. He thought it an appropriate punishment of the Emperor to destroy his palace (even tho' the French general did not give his consent to the act) because the loss would fall on the Emperor & not the Chinese People. Will the Chinese be taxed to rebuild the palace? It would have been more satisfactory to fine the Emperor a fixed sum for any injuries done to us – & enforce payment. To burn a palace seems hardly in accordance with the usages of civilized Nations [...]

Friday, 15 February: [...] Thus far two observations occur to me with regard to this Session – first, I never knew a Session open more tamely; secondly, I never knew more subjects dealt with in so short a time with prepared measures.

Monday, 18 February: [...] Capital articles appear in the papers on my oaths questions – & I get many private letters of thanks. One Tory gentleman says I am an Atheist & ought to be hung. The Record[10] very spitefully assails me.

Tuesday, 19 February: [...] Locke King's motion on the county franchise[11] called forth some pleasant sparring. Lord Palmerston, Disraeli, Newdegate & others spoke. The Reform party in the Country will not think very highly of the earnestness either of government or opposition. Lord P. made a speech wh. might be called an opposition speech from the Treasury bench – for he threw cold water on a proposal contained in a bill of his own government. No division.
　[...] Hubbard moved for a Committee on the Income tax &

---

[8] The second China war had been ended by the convention of Peking, Oct. 1860; Costin, *Britain and China*, pp. 302–42.
[9] The punitive burning of the Chinese emperor's summer palace in Peking, where a number of captive British officers had been held.
[10] An evangelical paper.
[11] Extending the vote to £10 householders.

Ministers were defeated by 4 votes.[12] I much regret that ill health from overwork prevented my supporting Ministers. I cannot think Income tax inquiries likely to benefit credit at the present moment. Will govt. bear this defeat?

The Chancellor of the Exchequer has to sustain the prestige of our new finance still on its trial. The Paper duties difficulty is hardly put on the shelf. The Lords would have a good defence if they could say truly that those duties are rendered necessary by indecision on a source of taxation producing £13,000,000.

Baines moved a Reform bill for boroughs[13] – & read the Premier a lecture. Am I right in thinking that Ministers are insecure in their saddles? There is no cordiality with the independent liberals ⊤ & the Tories grow daily stronger. Their calmness evinces confidence [...]

Wednesday, 20 February: [...] I had an opportunity of asking for leave to bring in a bill to enable persons, desirous of making affirmations in lieu of oaths, to make such affirmations – & leave was, accordingly, granted to me.

[...] The Church-Rate question will be, I think, the great division of the Session – a sort of pivot of opinion. Sir Wm. Heathcote moves agt. me. I must look up my arguments.

Thursday, 21 February: The Bankruptcy & Insolvency bill makes rapid progress. Public opinion has produced some sense of shame in members who last year caused delay & the loss of the attorney-general's bill [...]

Monday, 25 February: I hear that a furious whip is at work among the Tories for the Church-Rate division. So there is on our side, but then it is said their Irish can be more relied on by them than ours by us. Some say Miall[14] has disgusted some of our voters by an indiscreet letter. The Nonconformist people are daily making mistakes of this kind.

The Govt. people profess to whip but not to 'double thong', as I hear, which means they do not fetch men from the continent & so forth. Thank God! No whip is ever required to bring me up. If one's vote can effect any good, what is one worth not to come up without

---

[12] 131:127 for an inquiry to find a more equitable means of levying the income tax so as to reduce the burden on those with 'precarious' (i.e. earned) incomes. The committee's report proved unfavourable to Hubbard's idea; *P.P.* 1861, vii. 1.

[13] To reduce the householder franchise to £6.

[14] Edward Miall, editor of the *Nonconformist* newspaper.

such stimulus? Is the Public weal no motive? However, as this whip is on my side, I suppose it were decent to say little about it.

[...] The Bankruptcy & Insolvency Bill in Committee followed. Much progress was made. The bill was a capital opportunity for aspiring lawyers, many of whom spoke. I copy my pencil entry at 28 m[inutes] to 9 p.m.

'Malins speaking – fluent, leather-tongued. A clause in the B[an]k-ruptcy Bill the subject. Thin house. Lawyers all have their chatter. The clerks in their wigs try to look serious. But their gravity indicates no attention. Now comes Mellor, Rolt, Selwyn. Att[orn]y-Gen[era]l[15] & the Lord Advocate[16] are evidently all alive, as if they had not all talked enough in Court during the day. Talk like dropping fire – mere gossip. Bill making great progress in a thin House' [...]

Tuesday, 26 February: [...] The Nepotism of the model evangelical Bishop of Durham[17] in giving Houghton-le-Skrene (some £1,360 a year) to Mr. Cheese, his son in law, in spite of the wishes of the inhabitants in the vicinity to make better provision for an increasing population,[18] has come most appropriately. If the Church fall, it will not be from adversaries without but from folly within. This is a pendant to the Dean of York business of last year.[19]

The Morning Herald[20] makes bitter complaints that the Laity will not petition agt. my Bill. Is it that they think it too scandalous to continue the existing law? It seems to me that Disraeli is the only stickler for it. May I recollect to tell him so. His reason is that local Govt. would suffer. Will he vote for my plan of financial boards?[21]

[...] Great efforts are made to defeat me. I think I shall be defeated by some 15. This is a guess. I heard that the Speaker had asked whether 280 would win agt. me. It will be a tremendous division. We are on velvet. If we win, away go Church Rates. If we lose, we strengthen the liberal party. Let us await the issue with calmness.

Wednesday, 27 February: We won – 281 to 266.[22] Brisk debate.

A great many petitions were presented by the Tories. A few in their sense by liberals – some informal as being printed. Of course, I noticed

[15] Sir Richard Bethell.
[16] James Moncrieff.
[17] Henry Montagu.
[18] See the leader in *The Times*, 26 Feb. 1861, p. 9.
[19] See above, 17 Aug. 1860.
[20] A Conservative paper.
[21] See below, 20 Mar. 1861.
[22] Church rates abolition bill, 2nd reading.

the fact – also, the want of imagination implied in the adoption of common forms – & the paucity of names, running from 5 upwards.

[...] The Oxford & Cambridge Essays & Reviews[23] gave us capital opportunities of contending that the Church no longer preaches uniform doctrine. Sir W. Heathcote's reply was polite, weak & inconclusive. He ought, as I told him, to have a measure embodying compromise – not vaguely hinted at, but ready to be passed. On the whole, as Fermoy whispered, it was the speech of a beaten man.

Gladstone put his course mainly on the point of honor. He is bound to Oxford[24] – & he did not feel sure that the Chancellor of the Exchequer could give to himself the Stewardship of the Chiltern Hundreds (a laugh).

Lord John went with me very heartily. Walpole attacked him for inconsistency in giving up everything (the whole rate), saying he would venture to assert that such a course, in a similar case, was without precedent – forgetting Vestry cess, Ministers money[25] (as Graham reminded me) & $\frac{1}{4}$ of the Irish tithe. I replied to Walpole, but my remarks are not in the 'Times'.[26]

Disraeli was pretty good, yet hardly up to his mark.

It was delightful to see a man so happy as Roebuck during Bright's description of the auction sale of a Church living & the visits at a Parsonage to see how near his end a very old gentleman was. The whole house laughed heartily. Disraeli hardly ever moves a muscle, but this was too much for him.

Fermoy's speech[27] appropriate to the occasion.

It amused me to see the anxiety there is on the part of members to take the post of teller with me. I am obliged to distribute my favours; taking one teller at one time, another at another.

My speech was very kindly received, & I am sure it was more than I deserved as I was obliged to read several long papers, wh. the House abhors.

I expected defeat by 15. During division I heard we were beaten by one. This was soon altered – & very merry our side became. It must have amazingly cheered the Testimonial dinner to Sir W. Hayter.[28]

[23] Ed. by Henry Wilson; an attempt to bring anglican thinking up to date by taking account of the critical and historical study of the bible going on in Germany; Owen Chadwick, *The Victorian Church*, vol. 2, (1970), pp. 75–97.

[24] As M.P. for the University.

[25] Both had been levied in Ireland.

[26] Nor in *H* clxi. 1053, which noted that 'the House was now crowded with members impatient for the division, and the hon. baronet's remarks were inaudible.'

[27] Seconding Trelawny.

[28] Former Whig chief whip.

I think it will be a case of Sauve qui peut. 'The Essays & Reviews' will frighten my opponents – & the further disclosures of ecclesiastical malpractices.

I have today sketched a plan which I propose that Govt. shall recommend in the shape of clauses to be added to my bill. Thus, Govt. would have the credit of doing something to save the self-esteem of the vanquished foe – & at least my plan might do some good.

Since writing the last paragraph I have had some conversation with an official & placed a manuscript in my handwriting in his charge.[29] I made a note at the head of it to guard myself agt. the supposition that my recommendations were more than rough ideas wh. might after all be unfit for enactment. If the Dissenters should be unreasonable when a good offer of a settlement shall be made to them if ever such be, they will have to seek for a better leader [...]

Friday, 1 March: I perceive that the Morning Advertiser which yesterday cut off my tail by calling me an unbeliever (or some such word), screws it on again today, evidently alarmed at a threat of a visit from my solicitor. I told a friend of the Editor of the pleasure which very probably awaited him [...]

Much interest is felt in my Affirmations Bill.[30] The existing state of the Law can hardly last long. The statement of a believer in religion that he is an infidel would legally disqualify him from giving evidence and such evidence might tend to convict him of crime or save an orthodox Christian from ruin. Suppose a deep laid scheme of commercial fraud; suppose a witness called to unravel the whole circumstances; suppose that, though guilty, he was falsely endeavouring to incriminate another – should he be allowed to stand down & escape further investigation by a collusive suggestion that he does not believe in a future state of rewards & punishments? or take the case of a divine of the Church, of the highest character & purest life, falsely accused of an offence fatal to reputation & social position & having but one witness capable of exculpating him & that witness an infidel – is the infidel's evidence to be rejected? And, yet, is the infidel to be believed without oath, when the preliminary question is put to him 'do you believe in a future State?'

The bishops are making sad fools of themselves in convocation.[31] Talk of the attack of liberals! We but fence with the buttons on our foils. The Church party is ruining its own cause.

---

[29] Not traced in the Palmerston or Brand papers.

[30] *P.P.* 1861, i. 17.

[31] The bishop of Oxford had presented a petition to convocation condemning the 'dangerous doctrines' contained in the *Essays and Reviews*; *The Times*, 1 Mar. 1861, p. 5.

The Essays & Reviews are the talk of society. The more they are abused, the more they are read. The attempt to point out their heresies, only proves that further divisions exist in the Church.

Besides the County Rates bill,[32] the Affirmations do & the Church Rates, I have on hand the New Zealand question. We have a serious war on our hands arising, as I think, out of the conduct of Gov[er]n[or] Browne, who purchased 900 acres of land from E. Teira a member of the Ngatihawa tribe, which as merely a subordinate member of the tribe he has no right to sell without the consent of W. Kingi & the rest of the tribe or Kingi at least on their behalf.[33] Some 3,000 troops of the Line are in New Zealand. They have little ground but what they occupy. The natives despise our soldiers – & it is said that the 3,000 men have been virtually blockaded by 1,500 natives. The missionaries think the native wronged. The governor can only blame himself, as, when representative institutions were given to the Colony, he reserved management of Native matters. *Sept 20th. 1861. Query, was it not more truly the Home govt. which made this reservation.[34] G[overnor] Browne has enough to answer for without this.* John Bull must pay for all this – & he has guaranteed a loan of £500,000 to the Colony.

Monday, 4 March: [...] I had some conversation with one of the officials[35] with regard to my suggestion that Govt. shd. propose some clauses to be added to the Church Rates abolition bill with a view to conciliation & an eventual settlement. The hopes I had ventured to entertain were not fulfilled. Govt. does not see what it can do with any prospect of success. Next a conservative friend[36] commenced a negotiation in a similar sense. I stated that I was prepared to assist (or something to the same effect). The Tories, as I believe, feel that the best course they can adopt is to ask to be allowed to march out of Gaeta[37] with the honours of war. I observed to my friend that this was my belief – & he did not deny it. Now, it is very strongly my desire to aid them in their honorable surrender. The difficulty will be to induce them to propose a plan which will give us, in substance, the

---

[32] See below, 20 Mar. 1861.

[33] In Mar. 1859 the governor of New Zealand, Sir Thomas Gore Browne, had purchased from chief Teira land in the Waitara valley, on north island, which was claimed by Wiremu Kingi. War broke out in Mar. 1860; James Rutherford, *Sir George Grey, 1812–1898: a study in colonial government*, (1961), pp. 443–52.

[34] It was; through the then colonial secretary's (Labouchere's) ruling of 10 Dec. 1856.

[35] Unidentified.

[36] Probably R.A. Cross; see below 13 Mar. 1861.

[37] In Jan. 1861 the French squadron had withdrawn from the harbour of Gaeta, leaving the King of Naples defenceless.

measure we insist upon – &, at the same time, disarm the opposition of local Church fanatics & uninstructed rural deans, who are not competent to judge of political difficulties & the state of opinion in the thinking world. There will be an obstacle in the obstinacy of Dissenters, who will look with a magnifying glass at any part of a scheme in projection bearing upon its face an indication of surrendering a principle, however minute [...]

Tuesday, 5 March: Mills moved for a committee on Colonial Military expenditure. Rather a dull speech, which elicited from Chichester Fortescue[38] a still duller reply. Indeed, it strikes one a serious thing that the defence of our Colonial govt. in the H. of C. should be committed to such hands. Fortescue may have respectable abilities, but really he has not, I think, calibre enough for the post he occupies. I could not help calling attention to the number of heads of departments who are in the house of Lords – the head of the Navy, of the Army, of the Colonies[39] – & the Exchequer, for I contended that the latter office is virtually placed in commission in the House of Lords since the decision on the Paper duties (a laugh). This paper duties business keeps recurring. The Lords have not heard the end of it.

Lord Palmerston gave Mills his Committee, evidently fearful of a defeat. P. had inferred, probably, the amount of support he would get from the expressions of opinion below the gangway, when any particular observations were made such as advanced liberals are wont to echo. But the concession weakened Ministers. How many more matters are to be taken out of their hands?

The hop duty episode followed. I voted with Ministers on the ground that the budget is not yet announced & other interests are as much entitled to consideration as those of the hop producing fraternity. Ministers won.[40]

Gladstone spoke of the 'Stout phalanx' who, having ceased to quarrel among themselves, were now combined to quarrel with the Chancellor of the Exchequer. I deprecate these associations of taxpayers. They come into court with ex parte complaints. Where are they to end? Why does not the working man come & ask for the repeal of the duties on tobacco? Why does not the farmer claim the right to distil? Because the revenue must be supported [...]

Wednesday, 6 March: [...] Church Rates (Committee).
Newdegate & Cross moved their several amendments. Lord Robert

---

[38] Colonial under secretary.
[39] The Duke of Somerset, Lord Herbert and the Duke of Newcastle respectively.
[40] 202:110 against J.G. Dodson's motion for the repeal of the duty.

Cecil distinguished himself unfavourably by a no compromise speech of remarkable bitterness, asperity & want of judgment. He seemed to revel in the continuance of the Church-rate battle – & talked as if it was quite a consolation to reflect that as it had already lasted so long, it might last 50 years more. I could not help reminding his lordship that a farseeing Statesman ought to look beyond 50 years, wh. was a long period in the life of a man but a short one in the life of a Nation. The House seemed to agree with me.

I was surprised that I got my bill thro' Committee.[41]

In the evening I dined with Mr. Speaker – & sat betwn. Sir John Hanmer & Sir Baldwin Leighton. Afterwards, there was a levée. Mr. Speaker talked to me for some minutes on riding & watercure [...] These dinners are a part of our constitution. At least they oil the wheels of government. It is impossible to meet Mr. Speaker & his numerous guests without some opening of the heart. Shy Englishmen would, perhaps, never speak without such opportunities and provocations. The truth is, we are thrown together in a way which almost necessitates friendly intercommunication. One does not like to be thought a bad fellow, when every one is trying to be or seem agreeable. Champagne, too, aids the effect. The Speaker asks all to drink with him in successive batches – & wonderful tact he displays in selecting each little compotation committee. He recollected to laugh a little at me when I was asked to drink wine, as I had just before told him I drank only water – & he seemed to call his neighbour's attention to my difficulty. After dinner we adjourned to coffee, wh. was excellent & small knots of members collected & discoursed. Thank God! our talk will never be reported.

Thursday, 7 March: [...] On motion for going into supply a long debate on Italian affairs[42] took place [...] Roebuck [...] shocked many liberals by language favourable to Austria & her retention of Venetia. Roebuck is more fearful of France than Austria as a foe to liberty. But shd. he not have seen that Venetia is the weakness of Austria? + The Roebuck mind is waning. + J. White indignantly attacked him & implied at least corrupt motives in a manner, I think, unfounded & unwarrantable.

Lord John Russell & Gladstone spoke during the evening – & seem to have made much impression. It seems to me that the foreign policy of Govt. is the sole cause of their continued tenancy of Downing Street.

I find that Selwyn & Kinnaird take my view of the New Zealand question – they have both had an interview with the Colonial Min-

---

[41] The Conservative amendments were dropped.
[42] Continued from 4 Mar.; no division.

ister – we are going to have the whole state of affairs in New Zealand on the floor of the H. of C. – & it is high time. Meanwhile, we await an opportunity & a mass of Published evidence, which ministers have in preparation & wh. C. Fortescue tells me is most interesting. But I find I have too many questions on my hands – & people bring me more and more [...]

Friday, 8 March: [...] C. Fortescue appealed to me to forbear from bringing forward my New Zealand motion till certain papers shd. have been presented to the House. This was but reasonable, & I agreed. Subsequently, Kinnaird, Selwyn & I had a long conference with C. Fortescue in order to ascertain where our issue will be with the Colonial office. It was clear that both Selwyn & Fortescue had made themselves acquainted with the subject, tho' F. is inclined to be flippant. He does not strike me as modest enough to be a man of any considerable power – he kept constantly interrupting me or Selwyn & endeavouring to treat our statements as quite unimportant or easily to be refuted – at the same time, he seemed rather inclined to favour our suggestion that a commiss[ione]r should be sent out to do justice in the case of the dispute between W. Kingi & the Gov[erno]r, whilst in the meantime our troops should continue the war till tranquillity shall have been restored.

I think we alarmed him. A hostile motion by me & seconded by Selwyn would, if successful, be a serious blow for Ministers.

Monday, 11 March: I have spent this morning in preparing for a speech in favour of the 2d. reading of my affirmations Bill. Petitions are coming in favour of it [...]

The present state of the law is untenable – especially, since a man may now be witness in his own case. In civil cases, a judge may dispense with an oath; yet, jurymen must still be sworn.

By the 6 & 7th. Vic. c. 22 may be taken, in certain Colonies, the unsworn testimony even 'of barbarous & uncivilized people destitute of the knowledge of God & of any religious belief'.

[...] The truth is, evidence of infidels shd. be taken, like the evidence of felons, for what it is worth. But the best thing would be to abolish judicial swearing on the principle, 'swear not at all.' A true Xtian, who is enlightened, will be inclined to doubt whether an imprecation of Divine vengeance in the next world as a punishment for falsehood is not a presumptuous solicitation. It seems to charge the Deity with vindictiveness, and a readiness, at the bidding of the commonest malefactor, to inflict a punishment on him – disproportionate, too, to the offence – & too late to prevent it.

You believe an infidel when he says he is one – & then reject his evidence in a cause as incredible, while, if the infidel declare he is a believer, though a liar, you accept his testimony. Because he lies, he is credible; because he speaks truth (at great risk, too, even of ruin) he is incredible [...]

Brand[43] has given notice of a party motion. Last week a motion was carried agt. Ministers (on Naval promotion & retirement).[44] We are asked to discharge the order – & then P[almerston] proposes to refer the subject to a Committee already appointed. The truth seems to be that Govt. feel their weakness – & deem the time come for gathering fresh elements of strength & Public confidence – even at a risk of a fall. I noticed, as did my next neighbour, a curious confabulation betwn. Disraeli, & 2 leaders who sit apart on a third bench just above the Tory gangway (Walpole & Henley).[45] Shortly afterwards, 3 or 4 of the next Cabinet retired together behind the Speaker's chair. Something is up, I think – or have I found a mare's nest?[46] [...]

Tuesday, 12 March: Slaney had a motion on the condition of the habitations of the poor wh. ended in nothing as his impracticable crotchets are apt to do.[47] Sykes bored the House till it became nearly demented. He read voluminous documents, greatly abusing the privileges usually accorded to a member by the courtesy & patience of the House. Osborne could ill endure him. As the house dwindled away & as another & another member got up to leave, Osborne pretended to be shocked at such want of interest & exclaimed loudly enough to be heard several benches off 'you are not going, are you?' or some such remark. Sykes is certainly too bad.

The admiralty question[48] followed – & then it came out why Osborne was so anxious to get rid of Sykes. He let off a sort of infernal machine into the shaky old craft, commanded (in the Commons) by the Sec[retar]y Lord Clarence Paget – & seriously shivered its timbers. It was not so much the Statistics of Sykes which oppressed Osborne – as the imperious wants of an exodus for his own pent up jests.

---

[43] Government chief whip.

[44] Elphinstone's motion for an inquiry into promotions, retirement, and officers' pay, carried by 102:97 on 5 Mar.; *H* clxi. 1458–65.

[45] Who had resigned from Derby's ministry, in Mar. 1859, over the question of parliamentary reform.

[46] According to Lord Malmesbury, a deal was struck by which the Conservatives supported Palmerston in omitting officers' pay from the remit of the committee of inquiry, in return for the premier's assistance in defeating Locke King's forthcoming county franchise bill; *Memoirs of an Ex-Minister*, (1884), ii. 249.

[47] Motion for a select committee withdrawn.

[48] The appointment of members of a select committee to inquire into the constitution of the board of admiralty.

Certainly, they were not amiss – & the best of them was that they pointed a moral by no means ill-timed. Lord Clarence Paget came into power like a Daniel come to judgment[49] – he turns out to be a most indifferent judge in the Nation's interest. The accuser has become the apologist of the Department.

Palmerston came down very stout & determined to take the wind out of Elphinstone's sails by discharging the order lately made for a committee on promotions &c (5th March)[50] & this he did, but he left Elphinstone the boast that, after all, the subject is to be referred to another admiralty committee. It seems to me beyond a joke that almost all business is merging in Committees – we have almost no govt. The Duke of Wellington's celebrated question recurs 'How is the King's govt. to be carried on?'

[...] By the way, I have actually forgotten to mention Duncombe's motion for pledging the House to a measure of Reform so soon as the Census shall be made.[51] The proposal was very puerile – though, as usual, Duncombe spoke in his racy & effective manner. I thought that he intended to aid Ministers, but, subsequently, my impression was not confirmed. I think he meant to tell the Finsbury[52] Chartists that there is 'work in the old dog yet'. I take Duncombe's manner for House of Commons purposes as nearly unsurpassable. His action – elocution – & knowledge of what will gain & keep his audience are perfect. He & Graham especially know the secret. Duncombe, when he speaks, is like a galvanized scare-crow – the wonder is that he lives.[53]

Wednesday, 13 March: [...] Locke King brings on his £10 County franchise. His manner may be described as quite unexceptionable. Plain, unadorned, lucid, straightforward. He has a good clear voice – & a quiet yet firm manner. His countenance is that of an honest & intelligent person – &, so far as I can judge, he is one of the best members of the House of Commons.

Augustus Smith moved an amendment[54] in a speech which was by no means bad. Indeed, he earned & received considerable commendation for it. He is a liberal MP & yet seems to think that Locke King's franchise would swamp the independent part of constituencies & increase the power of those who can influence small occupiers.

Disraeli lashed Lord John R[ussell] &, indeed, the castigation was

---

[49] See above, 11 Mar. 1859.
[50] See above, 11 Mar. 1861.
[51] *H* clxi. 1798–1803; withdrawn.
[52] Duncombe's constituency.
[53] He died in Nov. 1861.
[54] I.e. the previous question.

not quite undeserved. The conduct of Ministers, who came into office by carrying a resolution that a minor proposal or two in Disraeli's Reform Bill was open to objection & then remain content to shelve the subject, would seriously injure men either not wealthy or not connected with the aristocracy. C[ornewall] Lewis signally disgraced himself – in a Jesuitical, tortuous, inconclusive speech. He spoke agt. Locke King's measure – & then astounded the House by 'However' he meant to vote for it! Well might Osborne denounce the general insincerity of Parliament. O's speech, too facetious perhaps – I say, too facetious, because it jars to hear jests on a topic of such constitutional interest which will be read by so many unrepresented persons not deeming the House exclusively wise – was, however, much to the point, & suited to the exigency.

We were ingloriously defeated – majority 28.[55] Truly this looks like reaction towards Conservatism.

During the debate a meeting was held in the tea room – Sotheron-Estcourt in the Chair – for the purpose of hearing a plan for settling the Church-Rate difficulty. Cross told me of it & invited me to attend, wh. I did. I have always encouraged others to propound plans – & thought that in this case no harm could arise from my presence at a meeting of the kind described, as I stood committed to nothing. Tho' my attendance was again & again referred to as a good omen, the oracle was dumb. At present, I watch events & await the development of the scheme suggested. What will the clauses of a bill be like? How would they work?

My Affirmations Bill followed. House breaking up after the great party fight. Too much noise for a statement of legal technicalities. Still my story was heard in the main – but, as 6 o'clock drew near, Craufurd (Ayr), who supports me, moved an adjournment of the debate & we were beaten.[56]

The Speaker then announced that, tho' the majority 'in its wisdom' had expressed its desire not to adjourn the debate, yet the House actually stood adjourned inasmuch as it was $\frac{1}{4}$ to six. Thus the wish of the minority was carried by a windfall. So much the better, since at a future sitting bad law may be corrected, bigotry exposed, ignorance made ridiculous – & simple canting held up to Public reprobation.

Hardy, Malins, & C[ornewall] Lewis opposed me. Malins is a lawyer of ingrained prejudices. Narrow by nature, his profession has made him narrower still. Hardy is clever & wordy. Too clever one would think for the speech he made. But Lewis earned the palm for

[55] 248:220.
[56] By 183:50.

superior merit in the practice of the art of sinking. He well knows the law & the facts – he is profoundly read in philosophy & jurisprudence – & I have no shadow of doubt agrees entirely with me – yet, he opposed me – & that in a speech of the jesuitical kind of his later manner. Well, the future must decide between us. I would rather be thought to sin with Hobbes & Bentham than be right in the estimation of Hardy & Malins even with Lewis for their backer.

Monday, 18 March: [. . .] Lord Palmerston moved an address of condolence to Her Majesty on the death of the Duchess of Kent.[57] He performed his part well – & in spite of difficulties too, since his cough sadly embarrassed his elocution. It struck me that the language of feeling in the mover was not spoilt by the appearances of art. At least, he might have meant what he said – & this is no small praise, since it is most difficult to combine in such a speech the qualities to be desired.

Disraeli seconded – too much art – sentences almost too nicely balanced – too many studied antitheses – & too much exhibition of the artist's skill. He seemed very nervous – & when the prepared speech ended, the abrupt colloquial words of form such as 'I beg, Sir, to second the motion' seemed by contrast almost ludicrous, as tho' he were glad to escape from his effort. It is right to say that the speech in itself was in many respects very good [. . .]

Tuesday, 19 March: [. . .] Dunlop made a very severe speech, if one may judge from the report, on a motion relating to a garbled & mutilated description of despatches of Sir A. Burnes on the Afghan war & the conduct of Dost Mohomed.[58] It seems to me that the case was one for severe censure [. . .] I regret that the necessity of keeping myself in reserve for my County Rates motion rendered it impossible that I should remain at the House till Dunlop came on. It seems to me that Disraeli & his party saved Ministers.[59] The mutilation of the papers, if one may rely on the papers sent to one written in black & red ink, in order to shew the alterations made, is a very disgraceful

---

[57] The Queen's mother.

[58] By comparing the edited versions of the despatches from Sir Alexander Burnes, laid before parliament in 1839, with the full versions printed in 1859, Dunlop alleged that the Whig government of 1839, in which Palmerston was foreign secretary, had mutilated the despatches in order to give a misleading impression of the hostile intentions of Dost Mohommed Khan, the emir of Afghanistan, so as to justify the Afghan war; *H* clxii. 37–58.

[59] Dunlop's motion for a select committee defeated by 159:49. Disraeli had deprecated the re-opening of an old question, and opposed any inquiry into the way documents were prepared for presentation to parliament; *H* clxii. 77–85.

business – as bad as the opening of letters by Sir James Graham[60] –
& the treatment the case has received almost shews a laxer tone still.

The impression I gather is that Ministers suffered heavily in the
debate. One member told me that the Secretary to the Treasury sent
for him to come & vote just as he was going to bed. Disraeli saved the
government.[61]

Wednesday, 20 March: [...] My motion on County Rates[62] came
on in due course. After a forty minutes speech from me, Sir M. Ridley
moved the rejection of the Bill & was followed by many speakers. On
my side were Sir J. Shelley, Osborne & some others. On the other
side, were Pakington, Henley, Deedes, & a number of country gentlemen. Sir G.C. Lewis made a speech which was opposed in spirit to
all but the very naked principle of my measure & yet expressed his
intention to vote for the 2d. reading. As Osborne said it was in
effect the same speech he made on Locke King's Bill,[63] substituting
'nevertheless' for 'however'. This alluded to certain tricks of Lewis in
using particular words repeatedly in the same speech. For instance,
he says 'Well' at the beginning of each new argument.

The chief point established agt. my bill was effective. That was that
I allowed clauses on rural police matters to remain which legislation
of late years has rendered useless and absurd.[64] But it was hardly fair
to dwell on this, since I had stated that I merely wanted to get the
principle of the Bill affirmed & the bill itself referred to a Select
Committee – expressly, in order that allowance might be made for
alterations in the law since the measure was last before the House.[65]
I replied & noticed the fact that 4 or 5 county members among the
opponents of the bill had stated that there was discontent among the
ratepayers, a consolation for Lewis's *injurious* support – which was
itself balanced by Pakington's *beneficial* opposition – beneficial, because
Pakington asserted too much in describing the management of County
Finance as almost above improvement, when so many members on his
side admitted discontent & even supported the principle of connecting

[60] When home secretary in Peel's ministry, he had ordered the opening of letters
addressed to Giuseppe Mazzini, the Italian revolutionary nationalist exiled in England.
[61] Confirmed by the account in Sotheron-Estcourt's diary, 19 Mar. 1861, Sotheron-
Estcourt MSS, D1571/F411: 'Brand fetched Whitmore & Disraeli – who pulled the
Government through a most awkward scrape of Ld. Palmerston mutilating despatches'.
[62] 2nd reading of the county rates and expenditure bill; *P.P.* 1861, i. 607. Trelawny
sought an affirmation of the principle that ratepayers should have more effective
control over the management of county rates; *H* clxii. 98–104.
[63] See above, 13 Mar. 1861.
[64] The Police act of 1856 had made the creation of county police forces compulsory.
[65] Trelawny was putting forward the same bill promoted by Cobden and Milner
Gibson in Feb. 1853.

representation with taxation in matters relating to County Rates. Osborne stood up manfully as my friend & deserves my gratitude accordingly. My speech is very incorrectly & imperfectly given in the Times. Division 163 to 125.[66] T[relawny] teller.

The Country had quite a field day. They had in me a bag fox – & how they hunted me! & what a glorious scent there was! (it rained all day by the bye.) The justices, though on 2d. reading & not in Committee, revelled in minute details. Full of Sessions lore these justices (Shallow?) were in their glory. Glibtongued – fussy – important – narrowminded – what is the use of propounding sound doctrine to these gentry? The very terms used amongst thinkers & logicians are Hebrew to them – I am called an Atheist all over England, because I spoke of certain 'propositions' as 'speculative'[67] – by which I meant propositions within the domain of abstract thought. The truth seems to be that there is nothing for it but to retire from the field or sink to the low level of the general dulness & fanaticism.

[...] I forgot to mention how the Tories winced when Osborne & I reminded them that they were the especial friends of the tenant farmer & always very anxious to secure for that class a due share of representation, whereas here, when 4d. in the £ is in question, the greatest jealousy is evinced lest the tenant farmers should swamp their benefactors [...]

Wednesday, 10 April: Baines introduced his Borough franchise Reform Bill[68] in a very long statistical speech. Digby Seymour delivered a sort of tirade, in support of the measure – Cave moved the previous question in an exceedingly creditable harangue – Augustus Smith, on our side, backed him somewhat injudiciously (as some thought) – &, on the advanced liberals' part, Leatham & Stansfeld distinguished themselves. Sir John Ramsden amused the House & particularly delighted the Conservatives by frank confessions of the true motives of past party strategy by no means to the credit of the orator or his associates.[69] At least, so it struck me. That is a dangerous & perhaps demoralising form of candour & honesty which publicly dissects itself. It is not far removed from shameless shame. Disraeli & his myrmidons were evidently in ecstasies. Sir John Ramsden was verifying charges formerly preferred agt. Whig leaders &, I think, laboriously contradicted. Why did not Sir John state the truth at the

---

[66] Against Trelawny's motion.
[67] See above, 12 Feb. 1861.
[68] To reduce the household franchise to £6.
[69] He asserted that the Liberal opposition to the Conservatives' reform bill of Mar. 1859 had been a purely party move; *H* clxii. 401–5.

moment when it might have had its due effect? If the Tories were more sagacious & more straightforward than the liberals, surely the sooner this was known to the Nation the better for its interests. We were defeated on a division[70] – of course, I voted with Baines [...]

Thursday, 11 April:[71] [...] Late in the evening, my motion on New Zealand came on.[72] I did not do justice to my own cause, but succeeded in producing a useful debate. Selwyn spoke very ably & exhaustively in reply to Fortescue,[73] who was singularly Jesuitical. He seemed to presume on the House's entire ignorance of the subject. He was unmasked by Selwyn, and will, perhaps, be more cautious in future. Government foresaw defeat, so they arranged an adjournment of debate. Tomorrow, they will whip up, & we shall be swamped. Hope agreed with me in thinking that a tribunal should be constituted for adjudicating on the relative rights of Colonists & Aborigines in respect of Titles in New Zealand.

Friday, 12 April: [...] The adjourned debate on transactions in New Zealand followed. Lowe was spokesman for the government. Adderley, also, supported them, and we were defeated on a division. 38 to 24. The House had nearly been counted out, while I was absent for a short time [...] It may be asked, why were so few present. The division was taken very early in the ev[enin]g – & I imagine a great many must have paired. The division itself was not a bad one; & had I been well enough to do justice to my motion, I should have every reason – as I have many reasons – to rejoice that I brought it forward [...]

Tuesday, 23 April: A Ballot foray. This measure is coming to be a joke. The 'Times'[74] rightly says that if members voted by ballot on it, it would have but little support. It is very significant that debates on Ballot are generally over early & there are usually very few speakers. On a division the motion was lost.[75] Trelawny absent – ill[76] [...]

---

[70] 245:193.

[71] The House had resumed after the Easter recess on 8 Apr.

[72] For a special tribunal to be set-up to inquire into the title to the land at Waitara, once the Queen's authority had been re-asserted in New Zealand; *H* clxii. 479–81.

[73] Colonial under-secretary.

[74] 24 Apr. 1861, p. 8.

[75] Henry Berkeley's bill defeated, 279:154.

[76] Trelawny thus missed much of the parliamentary proceedings, from mid-April to mid-May.

Wednesday, 24 April: [...] Nonconformist Burials Bill was rejected on a division.[77] Trelawny absent – ill.

I fear the Dissenters are seeking more than their just due; & making more difficult the conduct of their case by persons acting, for example, in my position. Ill-judged aggressions lend strength to opposition; and the Church-rate cause is in danger from the numerous instances in which unsustainable ground in advance has been taken by the Dissenting Party. I think I foresee the Church-rate Bill will be rejected. I know that some habitually vote for the Second reading as a mode of expressing simply that legislation is necessary. These people can never be relied on on a third reading. Many Whigs begin to think compromise necessary or desirable. Some of these will probably fail me in division, whilst the Tories will muster in greater force than ever, being able to justify their continued opposition by the want of encouragement conciliatory measures have heretofore received.

Tuesday, 30 April: [...] Mem[orandu]m. It appears to me that the success of the budget[78] will not settle the dispute with the Lords, because a precedent has been set & this cannot be undone by a measure sent up under different circumstances.[79] Given a case like that of 1860 – and the Lords may allege the precedent for similar action on their part. The true course, I think, was that which I recommended at the time – to take no further steps as regards finance till the Lords had repealed the paper duties bill. The Commons were content to condescend to impotent bluster – & this year it is proposed that they evince their temper in the form which the budget assumes. But the precedent settled by the Lords remains where it was.

Wednesday, 1 May: [...] The religious worship Bill proposed to give clergymen power to perform services in parishes where they have no care. This was sturdily resisted by the Tories – & they won by a considerable majority.[80] Another symptom our aggressive policy is becoming more & more unfortunate. Well might Lord Derby & Disraeli boast at the Mansion House dinner of their power & forbearance.[81]

Thursday, 2 May: I managed to go down to the House & secure a

---

[77] 236:155 against Sir Morton Peto's bill to allow nonconformist services in anglican burial grounds.

[78] Introduced on 15 Apr., reducing the income tax by 1d. and repealing the paper duties; *H* clxii. 544–96.

[79] The repeal of the paper duties was tacked on to the budget.

[80] 191:145 against Locke King's bill.

[81] *The Times*, 2 May 1861, p. 9, and 3 May 1861, p. 9.

pair. There was, on a division on Horsfall's amendment,[82] a narrow majority of 18 for Ministers[83] in a very large House. Sir C. Burrell was my pair.

It seems to me that our support of Govt. must be taken to mean that, on the assumption that a certain expenditure is necessary, the Chancellor's plan is not amiss. But then liberals have generally contended for a far less expenditure & would undertake to govern with less. The paper duty being a vexatious excise duty, might, perhaps, be dispensed with with more advantage than the war tea & sugar duties,[84] but it is doubtful whether on a ballot this conclusion would have had so many supporters as it, in fact, received. The truth is, men are cautious how they on slight grounds vote on a question which might lead to a change of Ministers – especially, in the existing state of foreign politics. The Tories seem jubilant – & quite ready for office. Is the pear ripe?

Monday, 6 May: [...] I understand that virtually the opposition to the budget surrenders at discretion. There may be more talk, but Ministers will carry their point.

It is very remarkable that Palmerston's motion on behalf of Princess Alice on the occasion of her marriage[85] to grant her £30,000 & £6,000 a year passed nem. con. There was a strong feeling agt. the grant of £40,000 & £8,000 a year to the Princess Royal.[86] Are the rumours true that there are reasons why the Court shd. not be disturbed at present? or is the ready acquiescence of the Commons another symptom of reaction?

Wednesday, 8 May: [...] A meeting took place in one of the ante-rooms to consider a plan of compromise of the Church Rate dispute. When it had terminated, a friend shewed me a sketch of the plan & told me that he & others were pledged to stay away when next my bill shd. come on for a third reading.[87] This will, I fear, cause me & others much anxiety. It is doubtful whether any compromise would now be accepted. Shall I continue to make my motion? If I do not, will it not still be continued in other hands? Even if the compromise

---

[82] To the budget, proposing to reduce the duty on tea from 1s. 5d. to 1s. per lb instead of repealing the paper duties; H clxii. 1413–20.

[83] 299:281.

[84] The duties were increased during the Crimean war.

[85] To the Grand Duke of Hesse.

[86] On her marriage to the Crown Prince Frederick of Prussia, in 1858.

[87] Cf. Sotheron-Estcourt's diary for 8 May: 'meeting in Tea rooms about Church Rates. [G.F.] Heneage & 5 or 6 Liberals. If they will enable us to beat Trelawny on 3rd reading, we will engage to bring in a Bill.' Sotheron-Estcourt MSS, D1571/F411.

become Law, will it not be as much the subject of attack as the existing Law? If I do continue, I shall be in minorities, instead of majorities, for some time to come – &, perhaps, find much difficulty in separating myself from the intolerant & over-aggressive portion of my followers.

Thursday, 9 May: [...] Three rather close divisions in committee were taken – & some symptoms were shewn of a growing disposition to scrutinize estimates seriously – to oppose them with vigour & earnestness. Divisions in supply in forces such as 131 to 100 & such like[88] have heretofore been rare. Disraeli read Mellor a severe lecture on the occasion of his expressed doubts of the advantage of opposing items in detail in the usual manner. Perhaps, Mellor was a little misconceived.

[...] It is very provoking to be disqualified from more than a brief daily attendance for the sake of pairing. Yet, I am enabled to do a stroke of work now & then, making representations in private to Ministers of abuses which come to my knowledge or of practicable reforms. At present, Trotman's anchors,[89] cure for cholera, Chaff cutting for cavalry – & glanders in the 11th Hussars have afforded me opportunities of this kind.

Friday, 10 May: There is an odd story going about, that Steuart MP a lunatic was brought or escaped & came down to vote on the recent great trial of party strength.[90] If one may believe it, the case looks serious. It is not improbable that we shall hear more of it, as one gathers in conversation that it is suspected that his party could not resist the temptation to use his vote. It strikes me that had their wish been to damage the government, they shd. have induced him to vote for the budget not against it. But this is a little too refined, perhaps [...]

Monday, 13 May: When I came down, I found Roebuck addressing a full House on the case of Mr. Steuart MP for Cambridge & recommending a Committee thereupon. He made a brief & excellent speech. Macauley followed on the other side, as Steuart's colleague – deprecating unnecessary publicity & consequent pain; &, generally,

[88] On the army estimates: 131:100 for a vote of £1,000 for the precis writer and librarian; 165:75 against reducing by £3,000 the vote for clerks in the war department; and 124:103 for a vote of £196,244 to cover the costs of the departments of the secretary of state and the general commanding in chief.

[89] An anchor designed by John Trotman which, in spite of the recommendations of a committee in 1852, the admiralty had been slow to adopt; see Trotman's letter to *The Times*, 6 Apr. 1861, p. 6.

[90] Horsfall's amendment to the budget, on 2 May.

endeavouring to weaken Roebuck's case. Cornewall Lewis suggested the plan of waiting for a certain official report to him, which would very shortly be presented to the House. Bouverie weakly assailed Roebuck, the Tories loudly cheering. Several members endeavoured to shew that the MP for Cambridge was not in the state described [...] Bass stoutly defended Roebuck, whose case was virtually complete in all its parts since there had been Steuart in a division, though he was in confinement upon a certificate of 2 Physicians that he was dangerous to himself & to others. Lord H. Lennox warmly spoke of his friend of 30 years – & of the sanity he exhibited, altho' he voted differently from Lord H. (a laugh) in the division referred to. On the whole, I have rarely heard less sound reasoning in a given number of speeches than in this debate. The Public were almost lost sight of except by Palmerston, Roebuck, the Speaker & one or two more. Evidently, the Speaker agreed, in substance, with Roebuck. Here was a case which required a remedy & there was none. Kenneth Macauley was a little bitter [...] The truth is, there was some party feeling in the matter. The Tories vociferously cheered every one who hit at Roebuck & tried to establish Steuart's sanity.

Eventually Roebuck's motion was negatived without a division, but he had first accepted Lewis's proposal. Some first rate lawyers, sitting near me, could not contain their contempt for the logic of the members who appeared to be satisfied of Steuart's sanity because they forsooth! could detect no symptoms of disordered Intellect – as if it were not one of the most difficult undertakings of practiced professional men to demonstrate that condition of a witness under examination. A man might appear rational for a whole day or days, & then suddenly stick a knife in the side of his dearest friend.

[...] Mr. McDonogh & Sir James Graham made able speeches on the budget, especially on the Constitutional bearings of the question of privilege[91] [...] Two factious divisions were eventually taken in order to force an adjournment. This policy, of course, succeeded; but I note that the majorities for Ministers increase.[92] Lord Palmerston's capital temper is doing his party & the State good service. Gout has not soured him – old as he is!

Thursday, 16 May: After a smart debate, the budget bill passed its 2d. reading.[93] The opposition were in great straights, because they have admitted a surplus. Also, they are not unanimous on the con-

---

[91] Respectively against and in favour of the government's method of tacking paper duty repeal onto the budget.

[92] 247:164 and 233:145 against adjournment; Palmerston then gave way.

[93] I.e. the customs and inland revenue bill; agreed to.

stitutional question. I perceive that Walpole does not consider the budget bill objectionable as a mode of presenting ways & means [...]

Friday, 17 May: [...] A propos of John Locke – he is a facetious character & his speech on the last debate on the budget[94] appears to have nettled Disraeli by home truths – Locke spoke of Disraeli's 'flying kites', alluding, I believe, to his tactics of putting members up to take the chance of making a successful attack on Ministers & then not sharing the responsibility to the length of recommending them to go to a division. Sir S. Northcote, McDonogh & others are thus so many kites – some, perhaps, only sparrow hawks.

I had some more talk with May CB (one of our clerks) on the Privilege question. He appeared to think we have done all we could – the Lords having an extreme right to reject a bill, such as last year's Paper duties Bill, tho' it be a right which it were wiser not to exercise [...]

If the Lords were entitled to exercise an extreme right, we are a fortiori entitled to recur to the ancient practice of the Constitution – viz, to limit supplies to periods not too long & to include our budget in a great measure, if not entirely, in one bill. If the conduct of the Lords has been the occasion for this recurrence to sound principles, then we may so far echo the cry 'thank God, we have a House of Lords!'

It seemed to me, as I observed to May, that, unless the Lords put on their journals a resolution that their deed of last year was no precedent, we, the Commons have no redress. Virtually, we were taxed for a year by the Hereditary Chamber – acting, too, in the teeth of the advice of the Minister for Finance.

The Lords ran riot from personal feeling agt. Gladstone. Lord Derby had not sense enough or patriotism enough to stem the tide. The present success had too many charms for him. The long future of the British Constitution comes after his time – & – is as nothing to the jest of the moment. This shake to our Constitution would not have happened had Wellington or Peel lived.

Friday, 24 May: No house. Before a storm, a calm. We are to fight on the budget on Monday again.

Government are evidently anxious. The Flintshire Election is in progress – & a seat now is deemed to be of vast importance to them.[95]

---

[94] On Horsfall's amendment, 2 May.
[95] Lord Richard Grosvenor retained the seat for the Liberals by a majority of 300, on 30 May.

They appear to be beating up for aid in all quarters, as I have good reason to know.

French armaments are terrifying the Lieges – America is a subject of great anxiety – Syria & Suez[96] are serious causes of probable danger. The Queen's health occasions some apprehension – parties are nicely balanced – anxiety generally prevails. The budget is, by no means, lauded.

(**Sunday, 26 May:** Much alarm at the clubs lest the Irish members turn agt. Ministers on account of the withdrawal of the subsidy of some £72,000 a year to the Galway Packet Comp[an]y.[97] Irish members are apt to confess very readily, interpocula, that on some questions they must follow the orders of the papal party. So fear is felt lest the present question be a case in point. There is whispered talk, too, of ill health at Court – low spirits, at least.[98] But it is astonishing how guardedly people speak of the matter. I attribute their reticence to real sympathy.)

Monday, 27 May: [...] 'The Times' is sadly nervous about the coming division. But why has it systematically sneered at or damned with faint praise the proposals contained in the budget? We must reap as we have sown. 'The Times', I imagine, writes City views – &, probably, the City thinks a little of the dangers of change of Ministries – complicated foreign policy & other matters likely to affect commerce & credit. So 'the Times' pretends to forget for a while the increase of penny papers.

[...] About $10\frac{1}{4}$ I [...] found Ayrton hard at work. Paper was his theme. A languid House endured his commonplace sentences, irreproachably expressed, & well charged with statistics. Yet Ayrton has improved – & will improve. He learns – can speak – & has unbounded confidence in Ayrton. Also, he has health & no gray hairs or weaknesses. I do not believe, however, that he ever said or ever will say anything which will survive him. He may, nevertheless, be a useful man – & govt. shd. find a berth for him.[99]

Sir John Ramsden delivered a speech agt. the Ministerial plan – very ominous & unpleasant as coming from a Whig sitting behind the Treasury Bench. Sir John held office with the last Whig govt.[100] He,

---

[96] A French force was occupying Syria in accordance with an agreement by the Powers; The Suez Canal project also testified to French interest in the Middle East.

[97] Awarded in Apr. 1859 to operate a mail service between Galway and North America.

[98] The Queen had shown excessive grief after the death of her mother in Mar., Cecil Woodham Smith, *Queen Victoria, her life and times, vol I, 1819–1861*, (1972), pp. 411–12.

[99] Ayrton became parliamentary secretary to the treasury in Gladstone's first ministry.

[100] Under-secretary for war, May 1857 to Mar. 1858.

perhaps, wonders why he is not in the Cabinet. However, his speech was well heard – chiefly, I think, because of the quarter whence it came. There was nothing original in it. His manner is calm, and firm – slow & well poised. I shd. say he is a thoughtful, cultivated & conscientious man – &, as he is also of colossal fortune, he will make head in England.[101]

Rise next Bright & Sir R. Peel. Cries of 'Peel, Peel.' Though Bright is a hard hitter – & the Tories like a straight delivery, even in their own faces – yet, Peel afforded a better chance of fun. He would, probably, hit out everywhere – & make merriment besides – & he did, but was not quite as successful as usual. His best points are parenthetical, as when he spoke of 'the Veteran Conservative' the member for Carlisle.[102] (Much laughter.)

The debate was adjourned. I apprehend we shall be defeated. The Irish have lost the Galway Contract. To this point of degredation have we descended – the corrupt motive is assumed as a matter of course.

Peel is a sort of 'Enfant terrible' – the Whigs must tremble when he rises. There is no telling what he may do or say. He appears to have some fine qualities in a speaker – good voice, excellent manner of delivery – & speaks good terse English. Then, he is a fine looking fellow – full of nervous energy & courage. Yet, he wants a little more senatorial gravity. Too many jests – & too much merriment excited by his affected naiveté & bizarrerie. He is always well heard – perhaps, partly from the accident of his birth & curiosity as to what he will eventually turn out to be. He may become a Statesman, when he has thought & felt more.[103]

Thursday, 28 May: The Galway Contract daily becomes of more importance, being the supposed hinge on which the govt. of the Empire turns. A full house was in attendance, doubtless to hear what reply Ministers would give to the O'Donoghue's question whether the contract was really to be annulled. Palmerston's reply was to the effect that it was open to the Comp[an]y to make representations & to Ministers to consider & reply to them & that, as papers have been moved for, hon[oura]ble members would have an opportunity of judging whether the Ministerial course was right. (Great laughter.)

Now, nothing could be more adroit or corrupt. This is an offer of something very like a bribe; or, at all events, an enticement. We are

---

[101] Ramsden never held office again.

[102] Sir James Graham.

[103] Peel was appointed Irish chief secretary in July 1861, but he was not a success and held no office after 1865.

on the eve of a great trial of strength & a valuable consideration of no less than £72,000 a year is dangled over the Irish members like a cherry over a child's mouth. The Derbyites used the contract to catch Irish votes.[104] Lord P. uses doubts about its renewal to keep them. At least, the 'general laugh' meant this.

[...] I went to hear Earl Grey in the Lords on the New Zealand question. It is a great satisfaction to me to hear that Sir Geo. Grey[105] is to return to the Colony. Parliamentary action has forced Govt. to this step [...] The natives almost adored Sir Geo. Grey – & rightly did Lord Grey say that Sir George's return would be worth 10,000 men. In short, we have been to a great degree successful in our efforts for the natives & their just rights, wh. will, sooner or later, have to be re-established.

Wednesday, 29 May: Derby day. In the park the Church-Rate compromise bill was shewn to me. I had much talk with one of the promoters. May some sensible arrangement come out of it! I made suggestions – & think some of them may be attended to.

Thursday, 30 May: We are in the throes of uncertainty about the result of the Division on paper.[106] Are the Irish to be bribed? Will Ministers dissolve or resign if beaten?

I went down at $\frac{1}{2}$ past 4, when, among other questions, several Irish members asked what were Ministerial intentions with regard to the annulled Galway Contract. Both sides listened with the greatest anxiety to hear the Premier's reply. Tories watched for a blunder. Liberals wanted to hear the lie given to scandalous insinuations conveyed thro' the Press (see 'Times' 30 May).[107] The Irish hoped for some crumbs of comfort. Indeed, from their tone & manner, betraying as usual utter want of decent self respect, one would gather that they might, some of them, be bought very cheap. They seemed to put themselves in the market.

The debate now commenced. Mellor leading in a very fair speech for a lawyer, speaking on a large question. Disraeli followed. He commenced tamely.

It is a healthy symptom that many liberals have said that, if Govt. had yielded to Irish overtures, they would have voted *agt.* Government.

---

[104] See above, 9 Aug. 1860.
[105] Governor of New Zealand, 1845–53; no relation to Earl Grey or to Sir George Grey the Whig minister.
[106] I.e. the 4th clause of the customs and revenue bill, repealing the paper duties.
[107] Reporting (p. 8) the rumour that the subsidy to the Galway company might be continued for 6 months.

I paired till eleven with Mr. Legh – & went to bed, soon after dinner, in order to be fitter for a regular late night. About 11, on returning, I found Gladstone up – & heard most of his speech, in which he was very severe on Sir J. Ramsden – & rather justly so. Sir John was both conceited & indiscreet in his late tirade upon his old colleagues.[108]

[...] The lobbies were full – & a curious scene it was. One gentleman was in a wheel chair, sitting in expectation of the division. Great excitement prevailed. Some thought we shd. be defeated – some said we shd. have 3 or 5 – I said 5 majority. It was observed during division that a few were seen going out. Sir E.B. Lytton, to his honor, voted with us – many Irish voted agt. us. Our majority was 15.[109]

After division Lord Palmerston created much mirth in his account of Father – 'that is Mr.' – Daly's interview with him.[110] Daly was evidently an Ambassador from the Irish whom they could disavow or derive benefit from at their pleasure. So it appeared – indeed, it cannot be doubted that so it was. It strikes me that P. shd. have been more cautious. He shd. hardly have received Daly at all [...]

Friday, 31 May: More talk about Church Rate matters. A leading Conservative[111] & I have been in communication & have discussed possible courses. We rather frankly stated to each other our respective difficulties. On Monday I must be in attendance again at 4, when more may turn up. The Dissenters are not favourable, I hear, to the project of withdrawing the bill for this year. They would rather go on. The compromise will be a matter very difficult to achieve.

One of the liberal officials concurs with me in thinking that an adverse division on Church Rates would 'take the shine out' of the late victory over the opposition on the budget. Also, we are both rather anxious to release many Whigs supporters of my bill from the disagreeable position in which the proposal for a compromise has placed them. The truth is, this Church Rate matter is becoming excessively uncomfortable to all parties.

[...] It is thought that the recent division on Paper has prevented a Dissolution. The opposition were in a false position throughout. If we had no surplus, why did they want to sacrifice £2,500,000 in the shape of tea & sugar duties? If we had a surplus, how could Disraeli

---

[108] See above, 27 May 1861.

[109] 296:281. A number of Conservatives had absented themselves because of 'the unwished-for help of the Irish', Hardy's diary, 1 June 1861, in Gathorne Hardy, *Cranbrook*, i. 149.

[110] Daly, a roman catholic priest, had tried to persuade Palmerston to receive a deputation of Irish members; *H* clxiii. 343–4.

[111] Sotheron-Estcourt.

& Lord Stanley refuse to allow the Chancellor to apply it to the remission of an inconvenient excise tax, agt. wh. they formerly pronounced? Many liberals would have preferred to abolish the war duties on tea & sugar (Gladstone says they were not war duties)[112] rather than abolish the Paper duties, but then came the necessity of restraining the Peers for the future from interference with Finance – in fact, we had to make for them a straightwaistcoat, which they will shortly try on.

Saturday, 1 June: Altho' there is no sitting of the House, it is well to note the progress of the solution of our difficulty. One very eminent liberal MP[113] has had a quiet talk with me. He thinks that a withdrawal of my bill might lead to misconstruction & the suspicion of cowardice or lack of earnest interest in it. There is much truth in this. But what is to be done? Are we to continue to propose total abolition, year after year, without hope of success in the Lords?

Monday, 3 June: More coquetting about Church Rates. I expect I shall soon be the best abused man by my own side, being already the best abused man by the other side. Yet, my object is peace & quiet among religious bodies. A leading Conservative has called – & is coming again. I have already said I can take no step without consulting my coadjutors.

Well, the great man[114] came – & we deliberated on the course we should respectively take. At 4 I attended & consulted the representative of the Dissenters.[115] He doubted & did not wish to take any part of the responsibility of giving a fortnight's Law to the proposers of compromise.

More conversations took place with other persons. Finally, I agreed to assent to the delay required,[116] Estcourt meanwhile undertaking to prepare & put in my hand his plan. Many opinions were expressed on my course – Sir James Graham volunteered the remark that I had come to a wise judgment & assigned the very reasons which had mainly weighed with me – viz, that the Tories would fail in presenting a measure wh. would pass & that, in consequence of their failure, many waverers would join me. Duncombe passed me in my place & said 'you have done for the Church Rate Bill' or similar words. I

[112] They were originally levied in peacetime, but increased during the Crimean war.
[113] Unidentified, but possibly Sir James Graham.
[114] Sotheron-Estcourt.
[115] Dr. C.J. Foster.
[116] Sotheron-Estcourt's diary for 2–3 June indicates that Disraeli was anxious to delay the division on Trelawny's bill for fear of another poor Conservative showing so soon after that of 30 May; Sotheron-Estcourt MSS, D1571/F411.

offered to bet him 10 to 1 that I would carry my 3rd reading. He contested this, rather in a tone of reproof or, at least, implying it. The Whig Whip[117] had before told me that I shd. have been beaten on a division. The Dissenters will loudly abuse me. But they did not abuse me, when, in 1858, I forced a division in spite of advice from all quarters & won by about 40 votes.[118] There is a time for audacity & a time for caution. [...] Many members inquired why I had given way & allowed Estcourt time; I satisfied some, perhaps not all.

Tuesday, 4 June: [...] Denman's speech for a Committee on the claims of Baron de Bode.[119] Denman spoke ably for $3\frac{1}{4}$ hours – too long. He will say not, because he won. And it is not easy to refute him. But I cannot help thinking that the gist of a case like his may be stated in less time than Gladstone requires for a budget.

The Attorney General[120] began his reply by jests & sarcasms, inquiring whether the question was to be reopened whenever a 'young barrister' &c &c & which, I said to my neighbours, would cost govt. 15 votes. Able – almost unrivalled as Mr. Attorney is – he shd. condescend to cultivate the 'Suaviter in modo' a little more. What can he gain by stooping to ad hominem reproaches? Surely, he is strong enough to deal with the merits of each case, in a manner worthy of the Law Leader of the Senate of England? His insolence – for it was no less – went far, I believe, to cause the defeat of Govt.[121] I remained as long as my health permitted – & was not able to hear the whole argument. I did not vote, but believe I shd. have supported the Baron [...]

Wednesday, 5 June: A rumour was afloat yesterday that Disraeli had resigned the leadership of opposition.[122] It certainly strikes one that Sotheron-Estcourt seems to be put forward rather more frequently than formerly. It is possible that his Church-Rate policy is

[117] H.B. Brand.

[118] See above, 17 Feb. 1858; Trelawny's majority was 53.

[119] For compensation for the loss of his father's estates in France; although the revolutionary government had paid compensation to the British government in 1793 to cover such cases of confiscation, de Bode had never received any money; *H* clxiii. 571–84.

[120] Sir Richard Bethell.

[121] Select committee agreed to by 134:112.

[122] Rumours stemming from Disraeli's undoubted anger at the way his planned attack on the government over the paper duties, on 30 May, had been thwarted by the deliberate absence of a number of Conservative M.P.s; John Vincent (ed.), *Disraeli, Derby and the Conservative Party: The Political Journals of Lord Stanley, 1849–69*, (Brighton, 1978), p. 172 (3 June 1861).

thought safer than Disraeli's, for the latter made a declaration thereon in the winter too much in the 'No surrender' vein[123] [...]

Friday, 7 June: [...] The evening was big with events. First, the Lords have passed the Customs Bill on its 2d. reading.[124]

Next, Mr. Estcourt sent me his Church Rate plan.[125] It will certainly be rejected – & perhaps with scorn – by the Dissenters. In some respects it actually aggravates the existing causes of complaint. The question now is not what is wise, but what can be done. Temper – egotism – desire of Victory – are obstacles which beset the paths of prudent men. I had a long interview with one of the Whig officials[126] – a very sensible person – & he quite agreed with me as to the absurdity of Estcourt's proposal as considered to be a Peace offering. Indeed, I may say I wanted a Peace offering – & the Tories sent me a war hatchet. Yet, no doubt, Estcourt meant well. The truth is, the Dissenters have rendered it more than ever difficult for a Conservative to make a handsome offer – they sounded the Tocsin of 'No compromise' so loudly that, had a Tory offered to yield much, he would have lost his own character & not benefited them or the Public. Indeed, I cannot help thinking Estcourt's plan is less desirable than I should have expected, all things considered. I have indicated in various quarters my desire to be released from this Church Rate controversy – at least, as a leader. My point of view is not that of the Dissenters – nor is my manner of proceeding theirs. We are like incommensurable quantities in Mathematics. They have not followed my counsel in the beginning of our joint-crusade agt. Church Rates, which was to avoid the mixing up of the Separation question with that of the Special evils arising from Church Rates [...] I think I can now render the Public more service in the ranks, than as a leader, in Parliament. Total abolition will hardly succeed. The Lords are not to be coerced as at the time of the Reform Bill or of the Anti-Corn Law League. They can always say 'the tax falls on Landlords in the end – & we do not choose to untax ourselves & appropriate money which is a trust for the religious education of the Poor'. This may be a mere pretext – &, in policy for the Church, may be very unwise. But it is a strong prima facie position. Either the war must go on

---

[123] In a speech at Prestwood, *The Times*, 8 Dec. 1860, p. 10.

[124] Nem con.

[125] Published in *The Times*, 12 June 1861, p. 5; it allowed for the exemption of dissenters from paying church rates, which were still to be levied on members of the congregation subscribing in the past year, and it added a new rate of 1d. in the £ on owners for the upkeep of church fabrics. No rates were to be levied where none had been collected for 5 years.

[126] Unidentified.

indefinitely or there must be some compromise. I still think abolition the true course. But, as I have always entertained compromises on this question, I would rather remain free than be bound to do, exclusively, the work of the Dissenters. My wish has been to be the servant of Society at large. Estcourt is to receive my reply on tuesday evening. Meanwhile, the Dissenters are to be consulted on his plan.

Count Cavour's death elicited speeches from R. Peel, Lord John Russell, M. Milnes, & Lord Palmerston. All were excellent & some were of a very high order of merit – particularly, Lord Palmerston's. The O'Donoghue demurred – & attributed the great Statesman's death to a judgment of Providence. (oh, oh.) Never was more disgust expressed by the House. The orator was fairly beaten down by the indignation excited agt. him. He turned pale – looked cowed & ashamed – & concluded with one more feeble sentence [...]

Monday, 10 June: [...] More Church Rate talk. I shewed Estcourt's plan to Sir J. Graham who said 'of course, you will go on'. [...] I strongly urged Dr. Foster to endeavour to obtain some bid from Dissenters which would make concession more agreeable to the Church. I impressed upon him the sacrifice the Tories were willing to make for peace – & to consider that they were quite sincere in desiring to give dissenters bona fide relief. Dr. F. promised to endeavour to obtain some offer on our part wh. I might present to Mr. Estcourt.

Tuesday, 11 June: 11.30. Dr. Foster has brought me a letter with an offer such as he could make were he alone concerned.[127] This I am at liberty to mention to Estcourt. I have written a letter to him, declining his scheme of compromise.[128]

12.30. p.m. I had an interview with Estcourt & told him that he had not succeeded. I then read to him Dr. Foster's letter, in confidence – & presented to him the objections conceived to his plan by Dissenters. Mr. E. intimated to me that it would be well to ask me a question in the House eliciting in Public our refusal of the proferred terms – & so it was arranged, for which purpose I must be in my place at six. Estcourt was very kind in his observations regarding my conduct. On the other hand I told him of my efforts to obtain a counter proposal

---

[127] Not recorded in the minute books of the Liberation Society.

[128] Trelawny expressed his regret at the failure to produce 'a measure giving Dissenters in substance the relief which they seek, without humiliation or sense of *inferior citizenship*, in some form of words agreeable to Conservative Statesmen', but noted that 'even were the case otherwise [...] you do not speak with any confidence as to the chances of the Conservative party following you upon a division in favour of it.' Sotheron-Estcourt MSS, D1571/X86.

from Dissenters & my partial success. Also, I stated what I could undertake to support at once in the shape of measures for the exclusive benefit of the Church.

Six p.m. Estcourt put his question, to which I replied, saying that it was my intention to come on on next Wedn[esda]y week. So much for compromise. Cross's plan[129] pleases the Dissenters rather better than Estcourt's.

[...] My motion on New Zealand[130] followed – & I was counted out. Inglorious fate! The first time such blushing honours have been conceded to me. The truth is, I think, the House has come to a foregone conclusion that Gov[erno]r Browne is right. If Govt. be content with the victory of a count out, well & good. I do not think I shall reopen the case. At first, I thought of doing so.

These feats of counting out the House are cleverly managed. The Minister & a subordinate or two remain, the rest go outside the glass door, where they can still be seen. The Govt. people whip their friends out as well as in – & so important questions are left undecided. One must take constitutional govt. as one finds it & be thankful it is no worse.

Wednesday, 12 June: [...] The affirmations Bill came on – 2d. reading – an adjourned debate from some months back.[131] As my opening speech had been delivered, Dillwyn began – & very well he did his work. Many spoke. Lord R. Montagu made a great mistake, affirming that without the sanction of a future state, he should commit all sorts of crimes ('intrigues' &c.) which might tempt him. Roebuck spoke well. Cornewall Lewis, I fear, agt. his better knowledge. Many lawyers were with me. On the whole, a great body of new facts & arguments had a hearing; and, if I mistake not, will produce a great impression out of doors. Division, for my bill 66; agt. 136 [...]

Friday, 14 June: [...] A letter has come from Dr. Foster who states that the Dissenters are prepared to make certain sacrifices for peace.[132] I have replied that I will consider how they may be turned to account for our common cause.

Monday, 17 June: Every one was inquiring yesterday what is up in

---

[129] Allowing dissenters to claim exemption from payment of church rates, which were not to be levied at all in parishes where they had not been voted during the past seven years; *P.P.* 1861, i. 443.

[130] Condemning Governor Browne for using force to deprive the natives of their land; *H* clxiii. 952–3.

[131] See above, 13 Mar. 1861.

[132] Not recorded in the minute books of the Liberation Society.

the Derbyite camp – a meeting of the party being announced. Guesses were hazarded. I suspect that a victory is foreseen when the nomination of the committee on the Galway Contract shall come on. It is not impossible that concession on Church Rates is entertained. Some think it is the position of Disraeli as leader, which will be under notice.

Two o'clock p.m. Gossip in the Park ran that Church Rate compromise is the subject of the meeting.

4 p.m. So I hear that it was Church Rates wh., in fact, brought the Tories together.[133] It is confidently reported that we are to have a division on the 3rd reading, on the ground that such a course will best subserve the interests of no compromise-men & at the same time of the compromise party.

There has been a brisk debate on the appropriation of the 4 vacant seats for Sudbury & St Albans.[134] I paired all night with Mr. Lever.

It was reproached to Ministers that they left the 4 seats to be scrambled for on the floor of the House – & that they did not direct the judgm[en]t of Parliament on a matter so important as the distribution of power in this island. Bentinck said that they held a cabinet Council on the Treasury Bench – & thus adopted Middlesex in lieu of Chelsea & Kensington – & so it seemed to me.

The fray continued – &, after 2 divisions, a decision favourable to Birkenhead & the West Riding was come to[135] [...]

The Reform Bill above adverted to is a very trifling measure – & one about which Ministers seem to be so undecided & languid that interest is thrown away upon them. Government hangs by a thread – Lord Palmerston's life. Nothing else keeps out Lord Derby. As to Sir G.C. Lewis, he is unable to guide the House on Home affairs. In this matter of the distribution of seats, Sir Geo. Grey came to the rescue, but did not mend matters. The true, and comical, remark of Scully was that, as each place was mentioned & a vote taken, the chances of places not yet mentioned seemed to improve – & this Col[onel] W. Patten confirmed. The supporters of the interests of a particular candidate, borough or county would, of course, combine with others to favour their own game [...]

Wednesday, 19 June: [...] I moved on Church Rates[136] in a speech

---

[133] Cf. Sotheron-Estcourt's diary for 17 June: 'Meeting at 12 at Ld. Derby's. Spoke of the general Policy of our Party, complained of secession of some members on late occasion – Referred to Church Rates – I spoke – well – some account of my negotiation with Trelawny, which settled all doubts.' Sotheron-Escourt MSS, D1572/F411.

[134] Disfranchised for corruption in 1844 and 1852 respectively.

[135] One seat for Birkenhead, two for the West Riding; the other seat was eventually given to East Lancashire.

[136] 3rd reading.

of about $\frac{1}{4}$ of an hour. Collier seconded, dissecting Mr. Estcourt's plan of compromise. Estcourt followed in a remarkably courteous, moderate & statesmanlike speech, earning for him general praise. Lord R. Cecil, Buxton, Cornewall Lewis, Bright, Stansfeld, Whiteside & Hubbard spoke. Cecil rather waspishly. Bright was singularly conciliatory & moderate; also, very forcible & eloquent. Stansfeld made a clever speech – and I must not forget Lewis MP for Mary le bone, who made a fair debut.

Division now took place & in the midst of great excitement both pair of tellers made almost a dead heat at the table, when, to the ecstasy of the Tories, a tie was announced.[137] After stupendous cheering the Speaker gave his reasons for voting with the 'Noes' – so we were defeated.

The tone of the debate was very moderate – & more like that of men anxious to settle a difficulty than of men desirous of perpetuating it. Perhaps, Stansfeld was the only person who was opposed to a compromise. He thought such an idea vain & even mischievous. As usual of late, Cornewall Lewis made one of his undecided speeches – stating that he shd. vote with me & yet throwing discouragement on my bill. Lewis is not rising in the estimation of the House – he is gauche; &, if honest, contrives to appear dishonest. This sounds harsh – but, really, it is difficult to speak well of these temporising courses. Perhaps, weakness of character & timidity may be the more charitable explanation of some of his proceedings.

Bright rather astonished me by his statement that our side would consent to the postponement of the effect of my bill for 3 or 5 years. He further expressed approval of the plan of merely abolishing the powers of courts to enforce Church-Rates. All this proves that we have now a tolerable chance of settling the question.

In my opinion the excitement raised by the tie far threw into the shade any regard for religious or political principles. The sporting instinct far surpassed party bias – & even conscience was nowhere in the race.

Thursday, 20 June: The Speaker rode up to me in the Park & inquired, smilingly, whether he was very much in our black books? I assured him not in the least – & we agreed that the present position of the question is by no means the worst it could hold with reference to an accommodation. So, too, thought Collins MP for Knaresborough, who chanced to ride with us.

[...] It seems that the Church Rate abolition Bill would have been carried if Sir Charles Wood & Lord Bury had not been absent. Wood

[137] 274:274.

was shut out & I hear had a newspaper pair. Thirty seven liberals were absent;[138] but so, I believe, were twenty Tories.

Friday, 21 June: [...] I should mention that it is generally considered that the Speaker took the proper course in the case of the Church-Rate Bill. There is a kind of custom which rules the principle of such cases. His notion was that, accordingly thereto, he ought not to commit the House to taking a step from which it could not recede. Had the occasion been a 2d. reading, he indicated that his course would probably have been different. All this seems to me somewhat pedantic & fine-spun.

Note. Soon after the Debate Arthur Russell[139] told me that Lord John observed with respect to the Speaker's decision, that I had a perfect right if I had chosen, to move, after my defeat, to insert the words 'be read a third time, this day week' or similar words, after the word 'that'. This is as I understand him.[140]

As Ld. John has been mentioned here in connection with the subject of Church-rates, I think it right to record that the resolution which I moved for a Committee to inquire into the subject some years previously[141] was drawn up by Lord John Russell[142] himself, & conveyed to me by the Whip. It was my wish to know what form of resolution it would suit Government to support. I think Tufnell was the Whip.

[...] Facile princeps among our bores is Darby Griffith. He has a nonchalent & off-hand impudence which is peculiarly irritating. On his turn coming,[143] he ran off volubly into a speech without looking at the chair, which about tea-time the Speaker usually vacates & wh. he vacated just as Griffith rose. The House laughed – & he could not see why – until, after some time, he happened to turn towards the chair & discovered that he had [been] addressing an absent Speaker.

Monday, 24 June: [...] I have been thinking what chance Cross has of settling Church Rates by his bill.[144] It seems to me that his plan contemplates the resuscitation of Rates in all parishes where they have

---

[138] Some having been induced to stay away by a promise, made by certain Conservatives at a meeting in the tea room, that R.A. Cross's compromise bill would be introduced once the abolition bill was defeated; J. Banks Stanhope to Sotheron-Estcourt, 21 June 1861, Sotheron-Estcourt MSS, D1571/X86.

[139] Trelawny's colleague in the representation of Tavistock; Lord John Russell's nephew.

[140] The motion would have been 'that this bill do pass'.

[141] Apr. 1851.

[142] Then prime minister.

[143] Question on the Suez Canal; *H* clxiii. 1458–60.

[144] See above, 11 June 1861.

been practically abolished. How will this work? Will not some persons refuse to pay or to accept exemption on the terms offered? And, if so, will it be safe to enforce the powers given by the Bill? What would be the demeanour of a Manchester mob in the case of the forced sale of goods of a defaulter? Suppose an unpopular Minister the instigator – fine times for the devil indeed! What a glorious triumph Archdeacon Denison[145] would have! How happy the Ecclesiastical Press would be! [...]

Tuesday, 25 June: [...] There was a brisk debate & passage of arms on supply, Osborne leading & attacking Palmerston as the author of a prodigal child in the creation of Aldershot. Great fun was produced. T.G. Baring[146] reproached Osborne with his vote in past times directly inconsistent with his motion at the time being. Osborne replied that he was obliged, being in office,[147] to compromise some opinions – 'sufferance being the badge' of 'all our tribe'. (Great laughter.) Lord Palmerston commiserated him in respect of his sufferings while in office – & congratulated him on his happiness & freedom now & his opportunities of indulging his criticism to the fullest extent – & compared his explosions to Munchausen's trumpet the sounds of which, so long frozen up, were yet heard with effect at last. Osborne retorted that Palmerston had used the same joke 6 years before.

I never saw the House more delighted than with Palmerston's felicitous manner in attacking Osborne. The old school beat the young one despite difference of age [...]

Wednesday, 26 June: [...] The idea about the House is that Roundell Palmer will be Attorney general.[148] This will not be agreeable to Collier. The business is an unsatisfactory one, because the solicitor-general (Atherton) is not strong enough for the post of Attorney general.[149] Also, a seat may not be available for the new Attorney, if one shd. be selected from the class of lawyers without seats. Several unhappy faces may, perhaps, be seen at the House just now. One very unhappy one – & of a man who cannot dissemble disgust – least of all, in countenance. This gift should be cultivated. The want of it makes enemies laugh – & there is in Parliament a large, idle & jealous class who suspect weakness and look out for it.

[145] Tractarian archdeacon of Taunton, a prominent upholder of church rates.
[146] Under-secretary for war.
[147] As parliamentary secretary to the admiralty, Dec. 1852 to Mar. 1858.
[148] The vacancy arising from Bethell's succession to the woolsack. Palmer, who did not have a seat in the Commons, became solicitor general after being returned for Richmond in July.
[149] To which he was, nevertheless, appointed.

Friday, 28 June: [...] Evening sitting [...] Lord Palmerston made a strong appeal to members to allow Public business to make way. Others support the suggestion – particularly, Lord Hotham & Lord John Russell. And, no doubt, it is high time to get on. The House is sinking in Public estimation day by day. [...] I remained till $\frac{1}{2}$ past 11 and finding that nothing remained likely to produce divisions except the Wakefield & Gloucester writs,[150] I retired. Three divisions, in fact, occurred hereupon – but without issue of the writs. Several liberal members had evidently resolved to remain all night to prevent this – & the divisions were upon adjournments. The House broke up about 3 a.m. having sat about 13 hours at the end of June! and under the leadership of a man aged 77!!

I had some talk with Brand[151] on Church-rate tactics – and said to him that, in my judgment, our true course would be, could we but secure acquiescence on our side, to leave the Tories to their devices. In my opinion, a notice of opposition from me to their bill would only bind their party together – & weaken ours. While, if we let the measure go quietly into Committee, there, to use Brand's words, we may 'tear it to pieces'. And so, I think, it will turn out.[152]

Monday, 1 July: [...] The question whether Oliver Cromwell shd. have a statue was a good deal debated. I confess I could barely refrain from saying that I hoped he would never be placed among the general company of our Kings. Lord C. Hamilton, however, has rescued the Protector's reputation from all danger – having mentioned him under the designation of that 'talented individual'.

A great deal of business was got through by the fagged & jaded House, wh., at last, neither heard, nor cared to hear, the amendments read by the clerk in one of the Bills, which are intended to regenerate India[153] [...]

Tuesday, 2 July: [...] I was present during a considerable portion of the evening sitting & heard Enfield's respectable speech,[154] which was followed by some indignant remarks from Hadfield. Hadfield thought the Church of England degraded herself by seeking com-

---

[150] In both cases the election of June 1859 had been declared void on petition. When the by elections finally occurred, in Feb. 1862, the Liberals held Gloucester but the Conservatives captured Wakefield.

[151] Government chief whip.

[152] Cross finally withdrew his bill on 24 July.

[153] The East India (high courts of judicature) bill.

[154] For a royal commission to inquire into the effects of legislation banning burials in the city of London, which had resulted in a substantial loss of fees for certain clergymen; *H* clxiv. 199–201. Defeated by 59:48.

pensation for the loss of emoluments derived from burying the dead – her duty being to cure the souls of the living. But his manner, tho' earnest & honest, is not happy – & when he thinks he is rising to indignant remonstrance, he makes his opponents laugh. It may be, however, that some of the clergy have been sufferers & not enough considered [...]

Thursday, 4 July: Many motions & questions on Speaker leaving the chair that we might go into supply. Dillwyn made a noteworthy speech, shewing the rapid rise of education votes & complained of the kind of education given for it – which is not well suited to the poorer classes but rather to the middle & higher. He entertains a strong objection to the principle of education by the State except in cases of extreme poverty where education, otherwise, would be wanted, or in cases where the State stands in loco parentis. Dillwyn's matter is better than his manner. He is not an artist in speech & occasionally repeats words & phrases wh. have become habitual to him such as 'as I said before'. But he was well heard, because he is regarded as a painstaking man, having a purpose, & that well intentioned. This educational grant, wh. has rapidly grown up since 1839 from £30,000 a year to about £900,000, is matter for serious reflection. There is a danger of the clergy getting too much power thro' its means – increasing the servility of the National mind & destroying its healthy spontaneity.

[...] Scully made himself his own target & shot at it without mercy – amid the jeers of the House. His complaint was that the system of reporting is inadequate & partial – & he proposed to move for an inquiry thereon.[155] Scully appears to have some wit – plenty of words – some acuteness – but no judgment. Irish to the backbone. The usual Celtic whine characterizes his delivery. Intense conceit & uninsatiable appetite for notoriety are patent in every sentence he utters. Whether he is an earnest patriot at heart or not, I cannot judge. Bass hit him hard – speaking as his friend. + call that backing your friend? +

Supply is more attended to nowadays than was formerly the case. Disraeli was present nearly all the evening. People begin to prepare their attacks upon items with some care. Baxter, Childers, Lindsay & Augustus Smith are among the chiefs in this sort of campaigning [...]

Palmerston, who spoke several times at some length, had ridden in the morning to Harrow to lay a foundation stone. He made a speech there, too – & returned in rain!

Monday, 8 July: [...] The first business of importance this ev[enin]g was the battle of the styles in the matter of a new Foreign office,

155 *H* clxiv. 306–11; withdrawn.

which will cost about £200,000. Elcho led in his usual easy, fluent, conversational, & self-satisfied manner. The topic, being out of the region of ordinary subjects of discussion, interested by its freshness. Good speeches were made by persons understanding taste practically or theoretically. Layard's speech was good – his language & delivery excellent. Tite spoke well too – he has studied & practised architecture for 40 years. Palmerston – as usual – racy, buoyant & facetious – cleverly disguised his entire ignorance of his subject & gained the House to his side – in the selection of Scott's Palladian Plan in lieu of Gothic wh. pleased many more [...]

Osborne took exception to cost & with his view I agreed. He left the House. I remained to vote, because a vote merely went to affirm that the Speaker 'leave the chair' & did not commit me upon style. Therefore, I supported Ministers – who won.[156]

Returning again to the House later, supply was in progress – civil service estimates. There were two divisions – one, on an amendment by Caird to reduce the vote for Scotch solicitors under the office of Woods &c by £1,000. With this proposal, I could not concur, as the sum was quite arbitrary – & these solicitors have much business in recovering Crown property pillaged by landlords in old times. Therefore I opposed Caird.[157] But the whole vote for the office I agreed with Augustus Smith ought to have been withheld until we had received certain accounts, under an act of Parliament, still overdue. Sir H. Willoughby & Smith did good service & were ill answered by a mystifying speech from the Chancellor of the Exchequer who came to the rescue on behalf of Peel.[158] However, we were ingloriously defeated. Only 14 voted with us.[159] Perhaps, A. Smith was ill advised in pressing his amendment. Yet, there were good grounds for complaint – & it is difficult to see how more legitimately they could be shewn [...]

Tuesday, 9 July: [...] ev[enin]g sitting [...] supply, in which very great & unusual progress was made. Augustus Smith, Childers & Williams raised points. As to poor old Williams, his inefficiency is a standing jest. He, in point of fact, is a screen of abuses, because he has brought objections to votes in supply into ridicule. It is commonly said (in fun, of course) that he receives a salary for the aid he renders to Ministers.

---

[156] By 188:95.
[157] Who was defeated by 122:78.
[158] Frederick Peel, joint secretary to the treasury.
[159] 176 supported the vote of £18,708 to complete the costs of the office of woods, forests and land revenues.

Childers is setting to work more usefully. Smith has much to learn yet – above all, to keep his temper & not act impulsively or obstinately. Childers moved a reduction of an Irish Constabulary vote to the extent of £3,400 for printing, on the ground that the sum had been already included in another vote. The explanation was not very satisfactory. However, it did not appear to me that he made case enough. Cardwell said that, if a mistake had been made, it should be put right on the report. We divided & I supported Ministers[160] tho' somewhat doubtfully. I, also, supported them on a division relating to convicts[161] – Childers leading on the other side [...]

Monday, 22 July: [...] I have been absent for some days. Lord J. Russell is about to become a peer. Lord Herbert[162] will be compelled by health to retire. The cabinet is undergoing reconstruction. Roundell Palmer has been made Solicitor. Govt. is mainly sustained by their foreign policy & the great apprehensions most men now have of the effect of change at this moment. America, France, Italy, Poland, Hungary – danger everywhere. Who is to open the ball in this dance of death?

Thursday, 1 August: Lord Palmerston does not see his way to an agreement with foreign nations to limit the extension of naval armaments.[163] The House sits for form merely while House of Lords is completing work coming up from below – & occasion is taken to draw out Ministers – or to shew that the interrogator is still at his post – or to indicate an opinion which may be useful to some one hereafter [...]

Friday, 2 August: [...] Ewart propounded, in several resolutions, a scheme for the House's more speedy performance of its duties.[164] Respectable mediocrity will hardly succeed in shewing how this desirable end can be achieved by alteration of forms. Public opinion must act on human egotism [...]

'The Times' writes a very feeling notice in memory of Sidney Herbert.[165] An article, in the paper of a day previous, deservedly

---

[160] Who won by 76:44.
[161] A majority of 102:26 supported the vote of £15,776 to defray expenses relating to the transportation of convicts.
[162] Secretary of state for war.
[163] Speech on the 3rd reading of the naval officers of reserve bill; *H* clxiv. 1830–2.
[164] Restricting the opportunity for debates on motions for going into committee of supply, enhancing the role of select committees and ending parliamentary sittings at 1 a.m. when opposed business was being debated; *H* clxiv. 1870. Withdrawn.
[165] *The Times*, 3 Aug. 1861, p. 9, on the death of Herbert.

sounds praises of Lord Canning,[166] who, in the midst of the panic caused by the mutiny in India, would not listen to Europeans clamarous for vindictive & retaliatory measures agt. natives. He was calm amidst the greatest disasters & impending dangers; he was brave & for that reason not cruel. He sustained our name in the manner of some old Roman Consul, immortalized by Tacitus or Livy.

Tuesday, 6 August: Parliament prorogued [...]

---

[166] Governor general of India; he retired in Mar. 1862 and died in June.

SESSION OF 1862

Thursday, 6 February: A fresh session – & a tame opening. All is civility – & scarcely a semblance of a difference. Her Majesty was not present, & her speech contained no great programme. Mr. Portman & Western Wood receive compliments from 'The Times'. Unfortunately, for myself, I was too late to hear them – & the House was soon up.

Monday, 10 February: [...] I heard from good Ministerial authority that my bill was not likely to get a majority – & I was sounded about Lord Ebury's plan.[1] It seemed to me prudent to adhere to my own as so many are committed to it. Later a private hint was given to me that I might be opposed by the Tories on the first reading.

Tuesday, 11 February: Some discussion on a motion of White's on finance. He wishes that the House set apart one day a week for this subject, and that motions on going into supply be not allowed on that occasion. Ministers rather leaned towards his plan, but the Conservatives deprecated the innovation, from a liberal point of view. It is very doubtful to me whether White is right. I cannot help thinking that he may put a valuable privilege in jeopardy. Walpole argued this point well. However, Ministers gained time – & so the matter rests. White must frame his motion well – or it will never be accepted.[2]

Sir C. Douglas moved the 1st reading of the Church-Rates bill for me in my absence [...]

Thursday, 13 February: I omitted to note that the Speaker took occasion to observe on tuesday that, if any one chose to object to Douglas moving for me in my absence, the objection would be held valid. It strikes me the Speaker is getting fussy – or, rather, fussier, for we knew him fussy before. Yesterday, I spoke to him, apologizing for my brief absence – not having expected that two or three orders before mine would be so soon disposed of. He was very civil, & gave – what he considered to be – reasons for his course. I wish he would not single out the Church-Rates bill for, now for the second time, a victim – last year, indefensibly [...] I believe he is a good man – & a

[1] To abolish the compulsory part of church rate law; see below, 23 Mar. 1863.
[2] No further motion was made.

fair Speaker, but not equal to Shaw Lefevre,[3] whom it is his misfortune to succeed.

The great event today is Robert Lowe's defence of the Revised Code on education.[4] He is a very clever man – that Lowe & an odd one, too. We had a large & attentive House, much interested. Lowe stood forward – presenting, as he does, a curious appearance. He is only middle aged – yet, white as snow, with pink eyes & a face like the comb of an offended Turkey cock. He speaks fluently – & with complete mastery of his subject – being evidently a most painstaking person. It seems to me that there is much to be said for his code – & indeed he said it. The country is up in arms; or not so truly the country as certain salaried or interested classes. The subject is chiefly technical, & cannot be treated within a short compass, but it will be a theme for much debate during the ensuing session [...]

Friday, 14 February: Sir Robert Peel[5] should learn to reply to questions without losing his self-possession, making enemies among Irish members & committing his government. He & Maguire had a passage of arms – & Peel suffered +because, as in a battle with a chimney sweep, the latter, generally has the best of it.+ [...]

Cox (for Finsbury) gave notice of an inquiry whether Ministers mean to introduce a Reform Bill (much mirth). Aside, he told me that, if the reply shd. be in the negative, he meant, despite his feelings, to leave the Ministerial side of the House. On mentioning this to friends around, while he went up to the clerk with his notice, we all laughed considerably. Reform is in bad odour.[6]

The Highways Bill followed & Barrow divided.[7] Frankly I could not make up my mind to vote with him. It seemed to me that, as there was a good chance of its being referred to a select Committee, my opposition, if I oppose, shd. be on a later stage. It is said that expense would be diminished by one half if such a bill pass.

This seems likely. But why give more power to magistrates? Why not give it to Boards of guardians? Henley's speech was admirable in its way – & considerably weakened the case for the bill. Still, most

---

[3] Speaker, 1839–57.

[4] Replacing the existing system of State grants to elementary schools with a capitation grant subject to each pupil passing examinations in reading, writing and arithmetic; also making school managers responsible for paying masters and pupil teachers, with no guarantee for their payment by the State; *H* clxv. 191–242.

[5] Irish chief secretary.

[6] Palmerston informed Cox, on 18 Feb., that there were no plans for a bill.

[7] Against the 2nd reading, which passed by 141:30. The bill empowered magistrates at quarter sessions to divide counties into districts of parishes for the purpose of repairing highways; Royal assent, 29 July. *P.P.* 1862, ii. 315.

persons seemed to think the scheme shd. be entertained, at least – but I shall watch it with jealousy.

Wednesday, 19 February: [...] Marriage with Deceased Wife's Sister [...] came on. The old arguments were repeated. I voted for the Bill in the majority.[8] Collier shewed a weak point in his cuirass, in saying that all marriages are to be taken prima facie as lawful, wh. are not prohibited by Divine law. Walpole & Ld. R. Cecil seized the opening & reminded him that several kinds of marriages, universally condemned, are not in terms forbidden in Scripture. It was noteworthy that even Spooner was favourable to these marriages, upon social grounds and from experience; & he could not recognise any Scriptural interdiction of them. No one dared to argue the question apart from the religious sanction, which was all along implied [...]

Monday, 24 February: The O'Donoghue's escapade. Breach of privilege.[9] He sent a hostile message to Peel; and desired that his second, Major Garvin, should be referred to a friend. Palmerston, anticipating mischief, had desired that, in the event of a friend being required, Peel should refer to him. Accordingly Major Garvin waited on him to arrange the preliminaries, when he found that he had caught a Tartar, as Palmerston at once lauded him upon the outraged privileges of the House. The whole story came out in debate. Lookers on will say that Peel was injudicious, & not fit to be Secretary for Ireland; that the O'Donoghue was quite safe in proposing a resort to arms, that ordeal having been long since voted ridiculous; and that Pam acted very judiciously & has even made a better story of the transaction than he did of his business with Father Daly.[10] I speak, of course, of the comical effect. But people doubt the fairness of leading Garvin into the cul de sac. *Poor fellow! thorough Irishman & officer he acted as he said, in 'the only way he could understand'.*

Wednesday, 26 February: Two divisions, one on Collier's Conveyance of Voters Bill which was lost[11] [...] T[relawny] absent ill. The Times,[12] I observe is severe on the Govt. as if their courses of last year were in repetition in this. They give a half support to small measures, & become involved in the discredit of defeat. Collier's Bill

---

[8] 144:133 for the 2nd reading.

[9] Palmerston explained the circumstances surrounding the challenge made to Peel, the Irish chief secretary, following remarks he had made on 21 Feb. The O'Donoghue was obliged to apologise to the House; *H* clxv. 617–26.

[10] See above, 30 May 1861.

[11] 160:130 against the 2nd reading.

[12] 27 Feb. 1862, p. 8.

is ludicrous as a measure of Reform. It were waste of time to discuss it. It is enough to say that his object was to make the payment of expenses of voters coming to the Poll in carriages illegal, in the case of boroughs.

Friday, 28 February: [...] The Church Rates question cannot come on well before the first open Wednesday after Easter.[13] In my absence, Sir C. Douglas has been conversing thereon with many persons of opposite politics – & I quite approve of what he has done. The common object of sensible people shd. be, I think, to obtain some such concession as that contained in a bill of Lord Ebury's. It appears that even Mr. Estcourt inclines to it, but does not believe his party would follow him in supporting it.

The battle of the Codes[14] is the only thing which disturbs men's minds much. Endless will be the webs spun out of this material. The fact is, Ministers have touched one of the great interests of this country – & there is no interest wh., in a good or bad cause, cannot shew a good deal of fight.

Tuesday, 4 March: A debate on Mill's motion – he deems the Colonies bound to aid in the costs of their defence. His resolution was, with amendment,[15] agreed to. There is a growing feeling for his view.

Whalley brayed about the Maynooth College condolence – exciting odium theologicum & pandering to vulgarminded ultra Protestantism – Osborne chastised him deservedly, nailing his long ears to the table & leaving him in the pillory – an unpitied object of laughter & contempt – & so, I think, he will remain.

Thursday, 6 March: Army estimates – a tissue of minute criticisms, imbecile objections, inefficient attempts at small reductions, some sound, some absurd, & all ridiculous when considered in relation to the enormous waste going on everywhere & in everything. Osborne was the clown of the Pantomine – & disported himself to the delight of the Committee [...]

Friday, 7 March: Sir R. Peel again too wordy in reply[16] – at least, so the report reads. He is not the man for Irish Secretary. Tact & temper & discreet reticence are the qualities required – to which

---

[13] The Liberation Society had decided to give the Conservatives time to put forward an alternative measure; minute book, A/LIB/2, 20 Dec. 1861.

[14] I.e. the revised education code.

[15] By Buxton, so as to recognise the colonies' right to protection against dangers arising from imperial policy; *H* clxv. 1038–44.

[16] To Lefroy, regarding the rioting at the county Longford by election.

add perfect indifference in respect of quarrels betwn. Xtian sects & churches. The last quality he may have.

Gregory raised the blockade question – & elicited a fine speech from Palmer, solicitor general.[17] This will hedge loss of prestige recently suffered by Ministers. No division.

Monday, 10 March: Crawling to my duty, I was in time for an important vote. Ministers suffered a defeat on an item for Sandhurst the other night[18] – & so it was necessary to take a line. C[ornewall] Lewis notified that, in effect, the vote was only a revote – the money having been granted last year – & partly expended. He proposed a postponement & reconsideration on thursday. The postponement was agreed to, but stout opposition was raised to the reconsideration. Selwyn & Col[onel] Dickson very strongly contended agt. it – & alleged sharp practice & unconstitutional courses as to the same vote last year. It seemed to me that an enemy to Ministers might have a good excuse for reading them a lesson, for certainly the case had disagreeable features – but then, as the House sober is appealed to from the House on an ordinary supply night – when few attend & those not always the wisest – my decision was for another hearing. Bright, Douglas, White & Ayrton judged differently, but the division list shews that, if I erred, it was in very good & numerous company[19] [. . .]

Tuesday, 11 March: There was a division on Lord R. Montagu's motion on Finance.[20] In this I did not vote – being still out of health. Had I been present, I could not have supported him, as it seems to me that, in proposing to arrogate to the House powers for the control of the purse strings, he only weakens that control. Our control depends not so much on rules as upon the completeness of the responsibility of Ministers. Undoubtedly Lord R. M. shewed that our financial affairs are in a most defective condition – sums of money voted for one purpose are often expended for others – & our audit by the Board is only as to a small branch of our expenditure, several of the departments, in fact, auditing their own accounts. The evil is one thing – the remedy another. Lord R. does not appear to have hit it [. . .]

[17] Recognising the rights of belligerant states, and therefore the impossibility of breaking the blockade of the confederate ports in the United States; *H* clxv. 1209–25.
[18] On 6 Mar., the increase of £10,787 in the vote for Sandhurst had been rejected, 81:53.
[19] The voted was agreed to, on 13 Mar.
[20] For an annual committee to revise all estimates or accounts laid before parliament; *H* clxv. 1306–28. Defeated, 96:31.

Wednesday, 12 March: The deceased wife's sister was today's victim. The Tories resolved upon an early division & won cleverly by 32.[21] I sent to a friend at the outset to pair me, but such was the run for pairs that he only succeeded in getting me a newspaper pair, which I would not have taken had I had the option. As it is, one is bound by one's agent.

The defeat arose chiefly out of the mover's[22] indiscretion in including Ireland & Scotland in his bill. There is a fanatical feeling in Scotland upon the subject, & the Irish would, at present, seize any pretext for thwarting a measure supported by the bulk of the liberal party. The active people who work up the case out of doors have been a little dictatorial & have perhaps overstated the really strong points on wh. it rests.

Thursday, 20 March: [...] Little can now be done at Westminster. Advanced Liberalism is in bad odour. America[23] has lent false reasoners an appearance of argument or of that which will do as well for the purpose of convincing a large number of persons. Be that as it may, we Radicals are compelled to be comparatively quiet.

Friday, 21 March: [...] It may be worth while to mention that Baxter renewed the question of Colonial expenses – particularly, as regards fortifications.[24] Some debate followed. Parliament has shewn symptoms, several times this year, of a desire to divest itself of some portion of a heavy liability incurred on behalf of persons in high prosperity across the seas.

Tuesday, 25 March: Sir C. Douglas called to confer with me on anti-Church Rate tactics. Did I think that a question shd. be put to Estcourt as to his intentions to move? My reply was that, in my judgment, we should remain entrenched in our strong position. We have given our opponents every opening. They have failed in their ideas of compromise – & the fact of their failure is now a main part of my case. Douglas agreed.

Tonight begins the battle of the codes. The Tories only mean, I hear, to shew their strength. There is to be a bloodless session. But who can foresee what a moment may bring forth?

Hobbling down to the House, I was enabled to present 2 petitions

---

[21] 148:116 against motion to go into committee.
[22] Monckton Milnes.
[23] I.e. the civil war.
[24] Motion against such 'useless expenditure', *H* clxv. 1894–1901; withdrawn.

from Tavistock agt. the Revised code. Then came Walpole's speech,[25] wh. in the main seems to give up the case of the opposing party. He put himself in the position of a person speaking on the 2d. reading of a bill of which he approved of the objects, dissenting only as to the means in some details. It soon became pretty clear that there was to be no real fight – at least, nothing vital, & hearing that the division wd. not be that evening, I saved myself and retired. The speech of Walpole was not very impressive. He is very solemn & oracular – & mostly when he is most trite. He never rises much above respectable mediocrity. Sir R. Peel[26] is his model. Walpole is a goodnatured person in debate, but legal training crops out too much & mars his impressiveness in the House wh. has a manner of its own & likes it. Even Roundell Palmer's slip the other day,[27] when he addressed 'my Lord' or 'my Lud', was a momentary injury to the effect of a great speech on Maritime Law.

Walpole's English did not strike me as being classical. Whalley & I, chancing to sit side by side, exchanged remarks on this at the same moment – & with equal surprise. I think W[alpole] spoke of some proposition as a point which had been 'stood up for' – or some such slipslop, wh. jarred upon one in a speech of a member for an University[28] & was the more unfortunate in an orator whose voice, manner & ability arrest & retain attention – deservedly.

As to the codes, Lowe is said to be a little too cast-iron. Still, the Revised code is considered as being right in principle. The 40,000 interested persons, who presume to dictate to Parliament & openly threaten members with loss of votes at elections, will find that, while their case will be fairly heard on its merits, our paid servants are not omnipotent – & the great un-complaining mass of poorer taxpayers will not want friends. The grant is large – say £800,000 a year – Lowe thinks it is time to be sure that the Public gets corresponding results. His mode may require to be softened – &, probably, this will be the end of the business. Were I Lowe, I shd. put a guard on my tongue, in the matter of epigrams. Tact is the great quality in your official.

Thursday, 27 March: [...] Health must be economized, or I must leave Parliament. In justice to myself I ought, strictly speaking, to accept the Chiltern hundreds.

---

[25] Moving for a select committee to consider 11 resolutions criticising details of the revised code; *H* clxvi. 21–54.
[26] I.e. the former Conservative prime minister.
[27] 17 Mar. 1862, *H* clxv. 1669–83.
[28] Cambridge.

Friday, 28 March: No fight after all.[29] So I thought, some weeks since, & suggested as much to Brand,[30] who shook his head. Writing to Dr. Tancock,[31] I, also, said I expected the disagreement would be arranged. It seems to me that Lowe eats a large help of humble pie.

Many of his army were ready to fight for him & suffer wounds &, perhaps, political death – when, on a sudden, the General commanding announces a capitulation.

Still, there is comfort for his troops. They felt that, after all, the *amended*-Revised Code was susceptible of further revision – & that rather rough justice, if justice at all, had been meted out to pupil teachers & others having something like vested interests. It is pleasanter to succumb than fight in a doubtful cause.

Mutual amenities wound up the business, which stands postponed pro forma. Meanwhile, the proffered terms will be considered. The Tory party shd. rest contented with their victory as it stands. If they insist on further concessions, those made may be put in jeopardy. There is a great silent & patient body – the hardworking masses – who have, at least, a vested interest in their earnings & are intitled to know that the taxes they pay are fairly spent. The lively, quickwitted & bustling schoolmaster & pupil teacher interest has great advantage in the general scramble. It is not very creditable to the House of Commons that the deliberate judgment of the executive shd. have yielded not to arguments, but menace. Such is constitutional government + let us take the good the gods vouchsafe to us – & be thankful things are no worse dans ce meilleur des mondes possibles. Let me admit, however, that I boasted too soon of the virtue of the House of Commons in my notice of the 25th of March. +

Monday, 31 March: [...] a division on the appointment of the newly-devised Public monies Committee,[32] wh., I fear, will become a screen for the executive.

The Revised code business is postponed till May 5. Palmerston was at the House – looking as if he had suffered severely[33] – his arm in a sling [...]

Tuesday, 1 April: A debate & division on Hennessy's motion in

---

[29] Robert Lowe announced to the House the concessions made by the government to its revised education code, notably the provision of attendance grants as well as grants based on examinations, and a guarantee to make up any deficiency in the stipends of masters and pupil teachers from the State grant; *H* clxvi. 240–2.

[30] Government chief whip.

[31] Vicar of Tavistock.

[32] Gladstone's motion for a standing committee of public accounts, passed 63:11.

[33] From gout.

favour of open competition for the Civil Service.[34] Lord Stanley spoke ably. Interesting speeches were made by several members. Govt. moved the previous question & won.[35] I went with them. My reasons: – Hennessy went too far in saying that the 'best mode' was that expressed in his resolution. On the whole, the partial application of the competitive principle now in force seems to me better. After all, the responsibility of the executive for the proper selection of officials is a point of first rate importance. If for this, the authority of a board of examiners be substituted, so far that board becomes the executive. Now, a divided executive – with a doubtful or mixed responsibility – is not constitutional. We ought, always, to be able to say to the minister 'you chose your tools – it is your fault if they wont work'. Not so, if particular tools be forced upon them by a board, who may become corrupt or partial. The present system, as described by C[ornewall] Lewis, seemed to me better than Hennessy's. Govt. nominate a small number, who are examined & the fittest man is appointed.

Fire Insurances followed. Sheridan beat Ministers by 11.[36] T[relawny] paired for them with Sir E. Lacon. I disapprove of pledging the House before the budget. The tax may be very bad – but so are other partial taxes. No doubt, my vote will be unpopular.

Monday, 7 April: D'Israeli attacked the Budget, on going into a Committee of Ways & Means[37] – spitefully & pungently but not very successfully [...]

Thursday, 10 April: Courts of Justice (money) bill. This was a project for an extensive scheme of new Law buildings; & Ministers, after a smart debate, underwent a defeat[38] [...] The cost seems to be on a lavish scale, some £1,500,000 to be appropriated from the surplus of Interest fund & Suitors Fee fund, & certain risk, of considerable amount, were to be taken by the taxpayers. The House begins to be a little cautious, & high time too!

Friday, 11 April: Bowyer raised the Italian question in a sense defensive of the Papacy. Among many other speeches Palmerston's

[34] H clxvi. 336–9.

[35] 87:66.

[36] 127:116 for leave to bring in a bill to reduce the duty levied on fire insurances; not proceeded with.

[37] Accusing Gladstone of extravagance and of adding to the national debt, while having sacrificed the revenue from the paper duties; H clxvi. 639–57.

[38] 83:81 against the 2nd reading of the bill to concentrate the courts of law and equity on one site.

was notable for its bold criticisms of the conduct of France.[39] England
will be regarded by Italy as her best friend.

Monday, 28 April: The House assembled after the Easter recess. Ill
as I was, I contrived to crawl to my place, & remained about 2 hours
[...] Dr. Foster & Sir C. Douglas held a colloquy with me under the
gallery on Church Rate tactics – & it was diverting to perceive that
the Tory whips were laughingly eying us from the opposition Bench
(first row). The Church Rate fight will, I think, turn out to be the
great battle of the Session. But, perhaps, some accident may dispose
of the affair.

Tuesday, 29 April: Cochrane wanted to get a Commission to inquire
into the manner in which our Public buildings during the last 20 years
have been executed & whether something more like unity of design
might not be attained in future. A debate ensued. Manners, Cowper,
Morton Peto & others spoke. Cochrane was defeated.[40]
  My vote agt. him was determined by my dislike to the appointment
of commissions which are too apt to screen & so diminish the responsibility of governments. Several liberals were in the minority. One was
going away & met me. He made inquiries as if in doubt. I said 'if you go
there, we shall soon have all the business of ministers in commission – I
want to hang a minister if he misbehave'. My friend liked the sound
of this & changed his purpose to the infinite amusement of some
members who overheard our hurried conversation.

Thursday, 1 May: [...] The Dissenters are anxiously engaged in
preparation for the coming Church-Rates struggle. For sometime
there have been doubts whether or not it would be prudent to fight
this year. In point of fact, there is on our side a considerable apprehension of a defeat. My sentence has been for battle – thinking that
the policy of not fighting would damage us more than a fight followed
by a defeat, provided such defeat were not inglorious [...]

Monday, 5 May: I attended & heard Walpole's speech on the Re-
Revised Education Code.[41] The long & short are this: the Conservatives have been a little alarmed at their own success & have

---

[39] Criticising the French occupation of Rome, which was upholding the temporal
power of the Pope, and predicting that Rome would become the capital of the Kingdom
of Italy; *H* clxvi. 964–70.
[40] *H* clxvi:49.
[41] Withdrawing his resolution against State aid to elementary schools being based
solely on examination of each pupil; *H* clxvi. 1204–13.

accepted the Ministerial Capitulation.[42] The speech of Walpole was very prosy & rather pompous. His solemnity reminded a friend sitting near me of Osborne's jest, when he compared W. to a high stepping Undertaker's horse. Henley followed; &, as usual, entirely agreed with his late colleague with whom he usually concurs [...]

The Dissenters are working hard, & so are the Tories, in preparation for the Church-Rate fight. I wish it were over. Nothing can come of it this year, &, yet, we had no choice but to fight. I think the Whigs would be glad to hear that we were not coming on – whether they have been pulling the strings in that sense I have no evidence, but some suspicions. In Clay's time,[43] I recollect having fancied that the business was skilfully managed for the sake of keeping the liberal party 'in with' the dissenters – retaining a convenient grievance & never seriously attempting to redress it [...]

Thursday, 8 May: A grand conflict between a quartett of first bench men of more or less celebrity, topic finance.[44] Sir S. Northcote attacked Gladstone's conduct. His measures had been faulty, inefficient, delusive, inconsistent, unconstitutional & unfair to his colleagues. The last charge contained the most verius & plausibility, & was levelled at Gladstone's target in a weak place. He has, frequently, denounced our expenditure in strong terms – & has seemed to imply reproach to his government. His reply was a marvel of word manufacture – but I noted that he had comparatively few – & those not enthusiastic – cheers from members behind him. I do not think the Whigs like him or his schemes. The radicals are more inclined to approve of them. Disraeli left the House for a short time & so managed matters as to follow Gladstone. Forsooth D's absence had been 'momentary & accidental'. (Ironic cheers.) Rogue, this was regularly preconcerted, no doubt. Northcote drew the badger, & then his leader assailed it when at a disadvantage. Tricky business this – & wrong if only because transparent! Gladstone's fluency seemed to exceed itself. In one of his sentences, in wh. he simply desired to express that he repudiated a statement made by Northcote upon newspaper authority as understood by N., Gladstone contrived by ringing the changes of his vocabulary to compose a sentence which seemed from its length, fluency & fecundity to take the House's breath away. The substance of his defence touching our immoderate expenditure was that much of it was incurred in the shape of unwise contracts made by former

---

[42] See above, 28 Mar. 1862.
[43] Sir William Clay had introduced annual bills for the abolition of church rates in 1854–6.
[44] 2nd reading of customs and inland revenue bill.

governments – & of this he might complain without injustice to his colleagues [...] Palmerston was the last of the 4 orators – he followed Disraeli. Everyone speaks highly of P's effort.

Friday, 9 May: [...] The papers agree in giving Palmerston the greatest credit for his recent speech in reply to Disraeli, whom he has almost annihilated. I think D. will have lost caste among Tory land-lords by his denunciation of 'bloated armaments'. In other respects the speech was singularly injudicious. Still he found weak places in the Gladstonian policy. G. defended the remission of the paper duties on the ground of having a balance of revenue wh., however, did not exist – a debt in respect of exchequer bonds of £1,000,000 being left unliquidated. Also, he spoke of the present as a transitional & exceptional period – heavy temporary calls pressing – war bills – possible wars menaced – change of armaments – alterations in fiscal policy & other matters – & said that Peel would have borne with a deficit in a similar case. Yes, but says D., 'you said, when the Russian war loomed, that it ought to be paid for out of current income'. Of course, I do not mean to give actual words, but the substance of arguments.

G. was obliged to speak first, because the Speaker actually began to put the question in D's absence, who glided in, like a snake, from behind the chair in 2 or 3 minutes after the Chancellor commenced. In the interval afforded by a long cheer G. took a hurried draught from some small vessel, which was neatly stowed in an angle formed by some of the usual articles on the table. + Strong drink, I suspect. + [...]

Monday, 12 May: The Customs & Inland Revenue bill filled up most of the evening – & well it might, since in order to prevent interference by the Peers, it contains taxation to the extent of 25 millions. Newdegate demurred on constitutional grounds.[45] D. Griffith obtruded more of his garrulous & conceited inanity in his usual slipshod & discursive style – & drew out the master of boredom, the Renowned Tom Collins, who came over & sat amongst us; & ever & anon cried 'hear, hear' in a particularly penetrating voice & in the affected tone of a person who earnestly agreed with the member addressing the House, but always at the most unfortunate moments – e.g. when he uttered the weakest, or most useless, remark. Collins does this as no other man can – & is, so far, a Public benefactor. There was much mirth excited by him – &, at last, Griffith gave in.

---

[45]Opposing an 'omnibus' bill which prevented separate consideration of the income tax, customs, excise and stamp duties; *H* clxvi. 1561–4.

Wednesday, 14 May: A defeat on Church Rates by one vote 287 to 286. A second division followed on Estcourt's resolution,[46] when numbers were 288:271. I had guessed that we shd. have won by about 9. However, this was a crude conjecture. Both parties strained every nerve. Some think that I was unfortunate in the circumstances of my seconder, Mr. C. Buxton, being for compromise. Bright observed that the 2d. division was an error in tactics – that we shd. have moved the adjournment of the debate. I dont think this would have mended the case.

Estcourt was, as usual, moderate & fair. Cornewall Lewis proved that he did not understand the law & he did not feel much heart in the cause in hand. He is in the habit of sneering at arguments of members who have motions & then voting for them. This he consistently did in my case; – without effect, however, for his observations were hazy & inaccurate & rather told in a sense opposite to his intentions. Macdonough, an Irish lawyer, set him right in his law.

Bright made one of his best speeches, as all agreed. Disraeli spoke briefly & not to much purpose.

Great excitement attended the finale – & uproarious cheers followed the announcement of the Tory triumph [...] As we were standing at the table announcing the division, I observed old Palmerston watching, with pen & a slip of paper in hand, to catch the result & put it on record, which I thought typical of the old gentleman's interest in affairs & youthful feeling – every paper will print the result in a few hours.

Disraeli made two sneers at a member, wh. told well because he was a subaltern minister G.[47] & had affected on a notorious occasion to know cabinet secrets (on Reform)[48] & had lately attended, as chairman, a meeting of dissenters. D. accused him of having presided at a meeting of the Liberation Society. The member went to D. who was ready to make an apology, but reserved the right of making some other observations on certain proceedings therewith connected. This course seemed hardly agreeable, so the aggrieved man went to consult Pam who said 'you had better do nothing, for, if you defend yourself, it will be said that you are in the case of a lady who, charged with having had twins, urged in defence that she had only had one'. Of course these were not P's exact words, but the sense. The best of the thing, however, is that the relator did not appear to see the rebuke

---

[46] Against the abolition of church rates until parliament had agreed on an alternative provision for the Church; *H* clxvi. 1684–93.

[47] Charles Gilpin, secretary to the poor law commissioners.

[48] Reference not found.

conveyed by the ready Premier – ie, in regard to the leakiness of the man who prated about Ministerial intentions during vacation.

The Tory whip told mine that he had got up all his men but one, who is mad (Ker), & that he had got the madman of last year (Steuart for Cambridge). All sorts of odd things are reported with reference to the division. One man told me (W. of W.)[49] that he had gone to see a sick sister at Hastings – & had returned next day by an afternoon train, thus arriving too late, & he added, by way of defence, that he had formerly voted with me 4 out [of] 5 times!! Pretty excuse, when a tie was thought likely. It is said the Speaker would, in such case, have voted on his principles, with us.

It is observed (& Brand[50] agrees) that we shd. have avoided the 2d. division[51] by talking agt. time. But, on the whole, it is thought we stand well, as more voted for abolition than ever so voted before, & the responsibility for action now rests with Estcourt.

The O'Donoghue had the measles, & several others had valid excuses for absence. We were, in short, unlucky.

Friday, 16 May: A sort of fools day [...] Sir W. Gallwey raised a topic not agreeable to W. Cowper,[52] who was charged with having ill-treated Sir E. Pearson by first giving him an appointment over the Westm[inster] improvement Com[missio]n [...] & then, upon new information, giving it to Mr. Tite MP. The case was a stupid proceeding – & made infinitely worse by the defence, wh. was that the letter conveying an offer of the post to Pearson was not an appointment. (Oh, Oh from all sides). Cowper in substance said he never considered that the appointment was actually complete till ratified technically by some instrument. Palmerston backed 'his Rt. hon. *friend*'[53] stoutly enough, but did not raise the credit of either principal or second. Still, I could not vote with G[allwey] for his proposed committee, as it was hardly fair to the Public to stop supplies because Cowper had been a block head & had defended his course by special pleading (to say the least). We saved Ministers by 11 votes.[54]

Then, came various topics – among the rest the Alderney profligacy. About one million has been wasted on a fraudulent pretence of making a Harbour of refuge – really an advanced fortress near French waters – & at last convinced, Govt. desire money to complete so much of the work as to save the Nation from downright ridicule. Now, we who

[49] Woods of Wigan.
[50] Government chief whip.
[51] On Estcourt's resolution.
[52] Commissioner of works and buildings.
[53] His son-in-law.
[54] 139:128 against appointing a select committee.

always opposed the vote in its infancy were still agt. it, in its growth, refusing to throw more good money after bad, but we were defeated by a few votes.[55]

Osborne's asides agt. Cowper were funny. While the latter was attempting to defend himself by subtleties O. said C. was 'tinkering, not coopering'. O. kept up a running fire of such jocularities throughout C's long speech. Macauley wriggled about the barb Gallwey had planted in C's side. The house was much disgusted. + The moral is let Ministers beware of putting a weak man in a high Public office. + [...]

Monday, 19 May: [...] Disraeli made another onslaught upon Ministers[56] alleging that they have been bad financiers. Deficits & undue expense in armaments were the chief heads upon which he dilated. I heard the speech, wh. was diverting enough but not very practical. He took occasion to complain of Palmerston's 'happy audacity' &, specially, of his habit of giving flat contradictions, serving their purpose for the occasion but easily exposed & rebutted upon reference to authorities. Palmerston made one of his usual joyous & jaunty replies – which Disraeli says are not witty in the sense of any kind of wit described in Addison's enumeration but are more correctly described by 'banter' – or by a word still shorter which fortunately has not, he added, been as yet adopted within this House (cries of 'Chaff, chaff' & laughter) [...]

I never saw Disraeli's countenance more animated or exultant than upon his resuming his seat after his speech. He looked like a 'vivacious viper'– at least, that expression occurred to me afterwards. He evidently felt he had had a success; &, undoubtedly, he made some pretty hits at us and our Ministers. We had renounced Reform & abandoned retrenchment – such was the burthen of his song. His speech had more than usual of the old epigrammatic point which he used to employ agt. Peel.

Wednesday, 21 May: A lively discussion occurred on bills of Irish Law Reform, Whiteside leading. He obtained a little triumph over Ministers, taunting them, moreover, with their dependence upon the opposition for legal work. It seems no Irish lawyer represents Govt. policy in the House. This I had not known. What folly! – or weakness!– in these times, too[57] [...] The Tories – leaders I mean – seemed in some bustle. Disraeli went up & conferred with Henley on his 3d. bench just above the gangway, where he usually sits with Walpole.

[55] 138:130 against Baxter's motion to omit the vote of £90,000 for Alderney.
[56] On the customs and inland revenue bill, 3rd reading.
[57] The Irish attorney general, Thomas O'Hagan, was found a seat in May 1863.

Estcourt, Pakington & others seemed to be engaged on some interesting matter – I suspect, Ch. Rates, whereon more is to be heard in
a day or two.

Thursday, 22 May: The first thing I see in the notices is that
Pakington is going to ask Ministers today whether they propose to do
anything on Ch. Rates. Consciences seem uneasy.

Pakington has asked his question – would Palmerston introduce a
measure, as it was the general wish. No, P[almerston] said. If it were
the general wish, it was, also, generally known at this time how
surrounded with difficulties the question is. This was the substance of
what passed. We shall now hear what Estcourt's specific this year is
to be. We are about to be asked to 'try' the remedy of a doctor, who
prescribed last year – & this year says he would not now offer the
medicine which he last year thought would save the patient.

[...] I heard at the door that Disraeli had had a very long conference
with Lord Derby – somewhere within the House. Something is up.
Church Rates? Perhaps.

Friday, 23 May: Estcourt presented his Church Rates resolution[58] to
be moved if the House agree to go into Committee for the purpose.
It is understood that he had but very few followers. The plan will
never do. One man may take a horse to water – ten cannot make it
drink [...]

Monday, 26 May: The Highways Bill[59] was first carried into Committee after discussion. A vote on clause 5 was rejected. Sclater-Booth
moved a sort of rider to the effect of giving Vestries a negative on the
proposal to apply the Bill to a given district: for this addition thereto
I voted, as the only opportunity open to me of expressing my desire
to avoid the undue extension of the principle of centralization. So I
found myself in a lobby nearly full of Tories![60]

[...] I spoke a little on the Highways Bill & said that, in my
judgment, the Poor Law Boards shd. have the management of the
Highways. These Boards are strong enough to contend with country
gentlemen – disposed, for example, arbitrarily to shut up parish roads.
The magisterial interest, if that be desirable, is sufficiently represented
by ex officio guardians.

It was urged by some of us below the gangway & by many Conservatives that the Bill tended too much to centralization. Sir Geo.

---

[58] Not to the Commons, presumably to Trelawny himself; see below, 24 June 1862.
[59] See above, 14 Feb. 1862.
[60] Sclater Booth's amendment defeated, 138:66; *H* clxvi. 2206–7.

Grey[61] said that the justices already had the control of Police & other matters, as if that observation met our argument. I pointed out that, with this system, we, anti-centralists, are already discontented – so that the cause of existing discontent becomes a ground for still more! + logical? This were ultra official logic! with a vengeance. + [...]

Tuesday, 27 May: We all anticipated a Ballot field day – & this drew a considerable number of members [...] We, mostly, took dinner pairs – the Ballot not being expected at an early hour. I paired with St. Aubyn till nine; the Ballot came off at 1/4 before that hour in a catch division. Berkeley had a thin House – & it was suggested to him to divide without a speech – or, after only a few words. This advice he took & won – 83 to 50. Augustus Smith, also, carried his proposal to apply secret voting to Municipal Elections.[62] The truth is the Ballot has come to be treated as a joke – and a serious joke to candidates & members, since Ballot fanatics are everywhere dividing the liberal party. The measure maybe good, but is not worth that [...]

Thursday, 29 May: My affirmations bill stands for this day, postponed from last tuesday. It is doubtful if it will come on. Craufurd of Ayr drew it for me & it seems to be a skilfully devised production.

In effect, my bill was postponed till tuesday June 17th. There was hardly a chance of getting it on in the gray of morning.

[...] A thoroughly mad evening. Hours upon hours of wordjangling & inanity. Bad jokes – asperities relating to religion – false logic – ridiculous trifling.

The main point discussed was, what religion a child shd. receive, if casually found exposed & brought to an Union. Should it receive the religion of the guardians or of the finder? Of course, this opened a fine field for the Scullys, Newdegates, Grogans, Whitesides, O'Briens, Bradys, Hennessys, and a host of others. Some of these are men of talent & success, and it is curious to reflect how small a great intellect may make itself appear when it allows itself to be swayed by bigoted emotions. The least cultivated member of the House, who chances to be free from that virus, is sometimes bigger than an intellectual giant, if a religious question arise. The giant reels at once like a drunken man. How refreshing it was to hear a few calm words from Peelite Cardwell! in three or four sentences he cleared away whole skies of fog.[63] Religious differences will ruin this country in the end. So I fear.

---

[61] Home secretary.

[62] 82:48 for leave to bring in the bill, which lost its 2nd reading on 18 June.

[63] Sir Edward Grogan's amendment to the poor relief (Ireland) bill, that orphans should be brought up in the religion of the State, defeated 97:69.

Berkeley's catch victory on the Ballot[64] has already lost its shine. He obtained leave to bring in his bill by forbearing to deliver his annual budget of pent up jokes – a wonderful effort of self denial! But, it is said, the House can & will refuse to him the next step, upon which, by rule, a speech cannot be made. So much for tactics! Note, that in the House of Commons a man cannot be too simple, straight, and considerate of opponents. These, generally, have a case wh. deserves a hearing and ought to have it. No surprizes are of much use, when you can only get one stage out of some score. State great principles – and, for the rest, trust to time.

Friday, 30 May: The debate of the evening was on Sir de Lacy Evans' motion on army purchase.[65] The present Ministers are pledged to make the post of Lt. Colonel the subject of selection so far to the exclusion of the purchase system. Sidney Herbert was the organ of their undertaking, which was chronicled, amongst other places, in this diary.[66] So far from carrying it into effect, it was coolly disposed of as a plan not suitable & even open to grave objections.

There is nothing equal to the indifference with wh. Lord P[almerston] treats an obligation he has entered into, except the facility with which to serve an immediate purpose, he is ready to incur it. The promise to introduce a Church Rates bill in 1857 was a case in point. He is, no doubt, a great manager of the House, but it is clear that his political morality is by no means in advance of Sir R. Walpole's.

Gen[era]l Peel[67] replied to Evans, & Lord Stanley to Peel. Stanley, rather comically, asked Peel to fetch him a glass of water to make his elocution easier. Peel sat by Lord S., and they have been cabinet ministers together. It seemed funny enough to batter a friend's case to pieces – &, in the heat of battle, ask him for a service in support of his opponent's physical stamina. Stanley's elocution, always difficult, is becoming almost painful to his hearers. Some malformation. Osborne, sitting by me, said 'that man might be prime minister' – and he will.[68] + But the Tories do not disguise their impatience of his company. + Peel's arguments were plausible, but the case will not bear analysis. T[relawny] voted with Evans.[69]

Stansfeld's motion[70] looms large. Palmerston has framed an

---

[64] On 27 May.

[65] Against further delay; *H* clxvii. 196–9.

[66] See above, 7 June 1860.

[67] Secretary of state for war, Mar. 1858 to Jun. 1859, defending the system of purchase.

[68] He was not.

[69] Motion defeated, 247:62.

[70] For a reduction in national expenditure; *H* clxvii. 315.

amendmt. intended to defeat S. by incorporating his followers with Ministerialists as if both sections of liberals were substantially in unison[71] [...]

Monday, 2 June: [...] Friends of Ministers openly canvas for votes on the coming motion. Are the Tories about to spring upon their prey – long spared from policy?[72] or is old Palmerston going to outwit them again – & carry an endorsement in his pocket to his plantations at Broadlands, which it is said he prefers, after all, to political life? A few hours may, perhaps, decide – unless, indeed, the debate be adjourned.

Tuesday, 3 June: The ball opened with an appeal from Ld. Palmerston to members having intermediate motions betwn. Stansfeld's & Walpole's – or any motion putting in issue the real question – viz, the fitness of Ministers to hold office (loud cheers) to give way to him. This led to numerous personal explanations, qualifications, conditions, deprecations &c. Nearly every speech was irregular, as the Speaker, without much tact, frequently pointed out. Bright, Horsman, old Ellice, Walpole & others spoke. A sort of preliminary beating about the bush. Walpole, in very solemn tones, seemed to hesitate about accepting Palmerston's issue – & claimed leave to consider his position. After much delay, the Speaker called upon Stansfeld, who, in a very full House, commenced his speech.

+ Stansfeld, carefully adjusting his necktie & posing himself with considerable grace, proceeded to address himself. + His manner & elocution are admirable. His appearance is most prepossessing – features singularly well modelled – fault, that of their being almost feminine. His eye is full of fire & energy; he has, however, the advantage of speaking with perfect calm & composure. He seems too delicate an orator in a popular assembly – I regretted to observe how soon & often the glass of water was required. As to the substance of his speech, it must be confessed it was a signal failure. He appears to have mistaken declamation for argument. For half an hour he indulged in generalities & one kept saying to one's neighbour 'when will he enter upon the matter of his discourse? when will he point out in which direction a diminution of expenditure might be safely adopted?' At length, when he had spoken for 50 minutes, he rather abruptly con-

---

[71] Palmerston's amendment stressed the need to ensure national security, expressed satisfaction at recent reductions achieved in expenditure and looked forward to further reductions when possible; *H* clxvii. 333.

[72] An opposition meeting at the Duke of Marlborough's had agreed that Walpole should move an amendment to the effect of Stansfeld's motion, so as to avoid voting for a radical motion; *Stanley Journals*, p. 186 (2 June 1862).

cluded with a neat sentence. Now, however great an orator Stansfeld may be, he has to learn that the House of Commons requires more than this from a gentleman who assumes to lead on a great question. Still, no one can deny that he is an orator of remarkable promise – & that his *delivery* is hardly surpassed in the House. I know of nothing so dramatic. As to incidental points, he laid himself open by his allusions to foreign policy – & it was retorted upon him that, if he succeeded, we shd. be at war with all the world.[73] Palmerston followed in a dexterous speech, wh. I have only read – not heard. Disraeli then spoke at much length. Adverting to Walpole's weak withdrawal, he observed, allusively to the coming Derby, that his favourite had bolted (much laughter). In short D. & W. will not love each other much during the next few days, I think.

Horsman, in a caustic speech of great power, impartially distributed his severities in all directions. Sometimes, he gave warm praise, as, for example, to Gladstone for his early & useful interest in Italy. In a few sentences later, Gladstone was bitterly reviled. H. maintains the thesis – that we have not expended too much on defence.

Cobden rose after Horsman – whom he reprimanded rather savagely quoting a description of Horsman by Sheil[74] in 1843 *Horsman was described as 'possessing faculties wh. peculiarly qualified him to be the exponent of dissatisfaction and the mirror of discontent'* (oh! oh!). Cobden's physical power has become impaired, &, as to his mind, it does not appear to have gained in breadth of view, so as to compensate for want of vital force. When, however, he warmed, he became more like the Cobden of League days. But one wishes he had either retired to private life – or got out of the groove of mere peace-at-any-price principles. Osborne was witty as usual and raised shouts of laughter. Several unlucky members interrupted him – & regretted it. For each he had something not very agreeable. *Little Cox was one – &, by way of parenthesis, his borough[75] was described as containing an unusual number of men of sense.* Even Disraeli could not resist O's jokes. Roebuck's face beamed with delight. Old Hayter[76] stood near the bar, & thoroughly enjoyed the fun, altho' Whigs were sometimes rather rudely handled. *Hayter's face quite haunts me. He stood on the left side of the House in the gangway in front of the seats occupied by Peers & sons of members. It did one good to see so much genuine feeling, in old Whipper in!* Meanwhile, I have my doubts

---

[73] Notwithstanding his call for retrenchment, Stansfeld favoured British intervention in support of Liberal movements abroad.

[74] Richard Lalor Sheil (d. 1851), Irish Liberal M.P., playwright and journalist.

[75] Finsbury.

[76] Sir William Hayter, ex Liberal whip.

how the story will be read in Cheshire & Lancashire among starving operatives. Could not the British Senate conduct itself with some gravity for one evening in the midst of National Disaster?

The Tories dreaded the being too victorious.[77] The radicals were untrue to themselves. We divided – &. in the minority, we were but 65 to 367. But I think the day will come when it will be a question with constituencies how did our member vote on Stansfeld's motion?

The Speaker was unusually fidgetty & garrulous. The explanations made at the commencement of the even[in]g required some motion to make them regular. The Speaker was on his legs, making some remarks thereon, when D. Griffith, to put the matter right, rose and said 'I move the adjournment of the debate'. In such case Shaw Lefevre[78] would have sat down & accepted the motion as solving a difficulty. But Mr. Denison was sensitively afraid of more loss of dignity (not much remaining as it is) – so he reminded Griffith that the Speaker was in possession of the House. The consequence was that succeeding speakers were out of order, till old Ellice, understanding the case, moved the adjournment.

The ex-Speaker was in the gallery looking down with the calm expression of a Lucretian deity. I wonder what he thinks of his successor.

The lobbies were somewhat crowded. A custom has of late grown up of shewing the House to ladies from behind the glass doors at the entrance. Crinoline is so copious that there is some difficulty in passing. As to the ladies gallery, it was quite full of splendidly-dressed occupants, visible thro' the grating, whose presence may, to a certain extent, influence the tone of debate. At least, I feel confident that some members, when they rise, have in their minds the thought that their audience is not exclusively male.

I noticed, at one moment, that Sir Geo. Grey made an observation from his seat to the Speaker still on his legs, as though setting him right. This was in the early part of the evening when the disorderly business occurred. I was scanning the demeanour of the Treasury bench from the gallery opposite to them – and I note Grey's interruption because it confirms what I have heard & witnessed that Grey is apt to prompt both Speakers & his own colleagues. He has, I believe, a great knowledge of routine – & a fund of ready means of escaping casual mischances in debate. I should say that his type is that of a very respectable Solicitor thrown away upon the Home office.

Gladstone steadily eyed Stansfeld thro' several sentences & then lay his head back – & looked up towards the windows with a fixed, stony,

[77] Cf. Malmesbury, *Memoirs*, ii. 273–4.
[78] Speaker, 1839–57.

corpse-like countenance & an eye which seemed to be of glass. He was pale as death. Near him was Lord Palmerston who betrayed little emotion – taking things coolly, as usual, which is, in part, the secret of his longevity. At his side was his anxious A.D.C. Brand – below were Gibson & several subordinate officials sitting almost one upon another for want of room like toes in a narrow boot – & above the premier was C. Wood looking somewhat contemplative, with a tinge of anxiety – & near him G. Grey, C[ornewall] Lewis & Cardwell, who, I mean the 2 last, once or twice appeared to notice to e[ac]h other points which arose in debate. I suspect Gladstone was not allowed to speak, lest he might say too much.[79] He would have been dangerous in reply to Disraeli reminding him of the late Manchester speech & the apparent want of fidelity to his colleagues.[80]

Wednesday, 18 June: [81] [...] The Clergy Relief Bill[82] [...] we divided on 3 questions. 1st. whether certain words shd. stand which would tend to unnecessarily embitter the feelings of clergymen leaving the Church under sense of duty, & hereon I took the milder view;[83] 2dly. whether the bill, shd., in effect, enact a penalty by depriving of their posts persons who entered upon them on terms of them holding communion with the Church,[84] & 3dly. whether unfrocked ministers – unfrocked by their own choice – shd. be allowed to sit in Parliament.[85] On these last 2 questions I voted from the liberal point of view – agreeing with Dillwyn, as to the last, that constituents may well settle for themselves questions relating to trustworthiness of candidates. *The clause was aptly described by someone as dismissing clergy from the church – with a kick. The truth is the Tories are desirous of passing the Bill, because it will dispose of a thorn in the side of the church, but they desire, also to make such terms as to maintain unimpaired the theory of Church ascendancy.*

[...] I described the Bill as being, in one provision, a 'Penal bill' – & Dillwyn clenched my point. As the law now stands, a man holding

---

[79] Not the case, but Gladstone had wanted to move resolutions of his own; Philip Guedalla (ed), *Gladstone and Palmerston: Being the correspondence of Lord Palmerston with Mr Gladstone, 1851–1865*, (1928), pp. 221–8 (27–29 May 1862).

[80] See *The Times*, 25 Apr. 1862, p. 7, for Gladstone's speech criticising the nation for forcing heavy expenditure upon the government.

[81] The House had adjourned for whitsun on 5 June, and resumed on the 12th; Trelawny was absent until the 17th.

[82] Bouverie's, to relieve seceding churchmen from penalties; *P.P.* 1862, i. 249.

[83] Trelawny voted for Lord Henley's amendment to prevent bishops passing the penalty of excommunication on seceding clergymen; *H* clxvii. 710. Defeated, 173:75.

[84] 203:24 against Dillwyn's amendment to allow seceders to remain e.g. trustees of schools; *H* clxvii. 712.

[85] 166:67 against Dillwyn's amendment; *H* clxvii. 713–4.

an office to accept which communion with the Church of England is an indispensable qualification may continue to hold his office, in some cases at least, after changing his opinions. The clergy Relief Bill, if it pass, will oust such an one – wh. is not what was intended by many of its supporters. Perhaps, such a law shd. be adopted, but it is hardly fair to do this inadvertently. So we voted to exclude the word 'member'. The word 'Minister' we were prepared to leave – so that where an office required that the holder shd. be a clergyman of the Church of England, things would continue as at present. But what a convocation Parliament has become! Enter it when you will, the chances are members are discussing Theology [. . .]

Thursday, 19 June: Cotton, Cotton, Cotton. This is the cry of the day. And no wonder! But one notes that, whereas in Anti Corn Law League days it was constantly said that trade is a matter which should be left to the unfettered will of each individual, the Cotton Manufacturers are anxiously appealing to Parliament for aid. *Basically, I understand they seek for a reduction of certain Revenue duties upon British products.[86] The relief will come at the expense of taxpayers in some shape or other. It would be, in effect, a new distribution of property by the State. A protective duty were a different case.*

We had a division on the Merchant Shipping Bill, on the question whether anchors shd. be tested as a condition of their being sold at all. The subject was well discussed, when the old Free Trade & Protection doctrines, of course, came up again. The balance of argument was on the side of Free Trade, as I judged – & I voted accordingly[87] [. . .]

The Fortifications vote[88] is likely to embarrass government. A meeting thereon will be held this day in the smoking room. Osborne seems busy. He, Lord H. Lennox & Sir F. Smith were in communication on some thing wh. interested them & I suspect fortifications were the subject matter. Disraeli & Estcourt were very closely engaged – heads well together – evidently in confidential talk, nearly behind the Chair on their front bench.

[86] J. A. Turner, M.P. for Manchester, called for the abolition of the 'odious' duties imposed to protect Indian manufactures, arguing that increased exports of British manufactures to India would stimulate the supply of Indian cotton. He had led a deputation to the government the previous day; *H* clxvii. 774–6.

[87] I.e. helping to defeat Laird's proposed clause (*H* clxvii. 740) by 188:101. Royal assent, 29 July.

[88] A further £10 millions for the defence of royal dockyards and arsenals, and of the ports of Dover and Portland.

Friday, 20 June: [...] At the ev[enin]g meeting Maguire spoke at length on a motion in censure of the refusal to allow the 'Britannikosaster' to travel thro' the Post Office.[89] This is a Greek newspaper – & the Turks object to its circulation *fearful lest it propagate revolutionary sentiments. It appears that the Turks allow us to have a private Post Office at Constantinople.* The debate was disagreeably marked by personalities betwn. Maguire & Layard.[90] It is difficult to say which carried away the palm. Layard should not have spoken of Maguire as 'such a man' – still less after repeatedly describing him as his 'hon[oura]ble friend'. Disraeli benevolently mentioned this anomaly, in a speech in wh. he professed to aid them in making peace. Maguire may boast that he had first blood, as he charged Layard with having been influenced by his connexion with the Ottoman Bank, insinuating something like rigging the market – & Layard may claim the distinction of including in his rebukes 6 millions of unoffending Catholics as well as his opponent in the debate. It is to be presumed from his tone & that of Peel that Ministers hope to live by quarrelling with the whole Catholic world. Really the House of Commons is becoming proficient in the art of sinking! [...]

I heard that the smoking room meeting was attended by only about 27 members. Osborne, I observe, has given notice of an amendment to Lewis's resolution on Fortifications.

Monday, 23 June: [...] Osborne's motion.[91] C[ornewall] Lewis began, moving his resolution in Committee – a most portentously-heavy speech. He read long extracts from reports & went deeply into figures, almost exhausting the patience of the Committee before business had well commenced. However, one very important step he did take, & that was to withdraw the Spithead proposal for the present – till next Spring.[92] Osborne, Gregory & Monsell seemed to act together, & I think all these gentlemen seemed to be much disconcerted by the altered position of affairs. There was little left assailable; at least, comparatively speaking.

Osborne spoke ably, & the House concurred with his statement

[89] Maguire's amendment for the production of correspondence relating to the 'British Star', withdrawn; *H* clxvii. 810–23.

[90] Foreign under-secretary.

[91] Amendment to Lewis's motion for the fortifications vote, urging that the navy should be the mainstay of Britain's defences; *H* clxvii. 882–907.

[92] Palmerston had earlier been warned, by the chief whip, Brand, that the Conservatives and Radicals would probably unite in opposition to an extensive fortifications bill, so strong was the feeling in the Commons in favour of retrenchment, and that the Spithead proposal had therefore better be suspended; 7 June 1862, Broadlands MSS, GC/BR/13.

that he had mastered the subject. Perhaps, the House was a little too generous towards their favourite. Still, he has studied the question to good purpose & deserves considerable credit. After several speeches in a very full house, the motion was withdrawn – to the astonishment & indignation of many members [...]

Tuesday, 24 June: At the morning sitting a Scotch Police Bill of 466 clauses was carried thro' Committee. How well these men do their work! [...]

Ev[enin]g sitting [...] The noteworthy points were – Estcourt's attempt to deal with Church Rates;[93] also, Hodgkinson's.[94] Considerable discussion ensued. Heygate made a temperate & sensible speech enough. Lord R. Cecil & Grey spoke – as did Dillwyn. I studiously avoided all interference, convinced that the several plans proposed would collapse, one after the other. In truth, it is of no use to interfere. Had I spoken agt. Estcourt, it would have been said, 'how intolerant these men of one idea are! they are determined to prevent the success of any one who endeavours to compass a settlement in any way but theirs!' The gift of silence is in these cases, like others, as valuable as the gift of speech, and I have been reminded of Talleyrand's mention of the man, who was silent 'en sept langues'.

After Church Rates came my affirmations bill, which led to good & useful discussion. J. Locke & Roebuck distinguished themselves. Both spoke ably. I was tired, & so was the House. Yet, I was able to make good a few points. We divided & won[95] – & I was much pleased at not having spent my summer night, in bad air, in vain [...]

Friday, 27 June: A very lively dispute occurred on the subject of information accidentally communicated to a Mr. Higgins by Mr. Cowper,[96] a member of the Thames Embankment Committee, but intended for another & more celebrated Mr. Higgins, the Great J.O. of the Times.[97] Lord R. Montagu & Horsman appear to have baited

---

[93] Motion for a measure to enable vestries to transfer from occupiers to owners their liability for the repair of the parish church and churchyard, to repeal the existing legal process for enforcing the compulsory rate, and to provide facilities for the collection of voluntary rates; *H* clxvii. 989–97. Withdrawn.

[94] An amendment in favour of pew rents, but with no further appropriation of seats for that purpose than at present; *H* clxvii. 997–1000. Withdrawn.

[95] 88:59 for the 1st reading.

[96] Commissioner of works and buildings.

[97] Matthew Higgins, who wrote for *The Times* under the pseudonym 'Jacob Omnium'.

Cowper,[98] who is often turned down + as a sort of bag fox + for an evening's sport. In this, as in some other cases, he has not acted very wisely – & this is I think a mild statement.

[...] Lawson brought on the Great beer topic in a very fair speech.[99]

His object is to carry a bill supported by a Great body called the United Kingdom Alliance who, in order to restrict the number of houses for the sale of intoxicating liquors, desire that ⅔rds. of the Ratepayers of a district shd. decide upon the requirements of a neighbourhood in the matter of such drinks instead of the justices possessing & exercising that function.

I chatted on this point with a great oddity, Scully, who said he never liked to have any transactions with a person who did not drink his liquor, on the ground that his head was always cool and he was sure to get the upper hand. I could not help remarking that, if one comes to interference, there were other cases in which, perhaps, it might be called for more imperiously than even that of the excessive use of strong drinks. Of course, I alluded to the health of our rising generation wasted & undermined by prevalent abuses in great cities – & the want of a sanitary police [...]

Monday, 30 June: [...] Sir F. Smith's amendmt., on the Fortifications bill, for certain returns. This seemed to me to be an irregular mode of opposition, & hardly legitimate. However, I was too unwell to remain all night, & so went home to prepare for a necessary attendance next day. Smith, I perceive, withdrew his resolution, & a division followed on the 2d. reading,[100] which I lost. In my judgment the bill deserved opposition. My opinion regarding this Fortification mania remains unchanged. Earthworks, guns & staff officers shd. be our resource, if the channel fleet be defeated. Mind, money & mud are the great requisites of defence. *Bold doctrine for a layman to dogmatize on, when so many experts hold otherwise.* [...]

Tuesday, 1 July: [...] At the 6 o'clock sitting I hoped to bring on my Affirmations bill, but we were counted out. It will be withdrawn for this year, I believe.

Wednesday, 2 July: The Great Ballot motion on 2d. reading. Berk-

---

[98] Alleging a breach of confidence on Cowper's part by sending marked extracts from the Thames Embankment committee's report in order to encourage *The Times* to take a hostile view of the committee's recommendation that the length of the proposed embankment be shortened so as not to interfere with the property leased from the Crown by the Duke of Buccleuch and others; *H* clxvii. 1138–50.

[99] Urging the government to act.

[100] Carried by 158:56.

eley made a speech full of humour & not wanting in grave argument.
He made much more impression than usual. It is a whim of his to
speak from the opposition benches on the Ballot question, as if he were
a determined foe to Ministers, but for this occasion only. *Note. I am
now of opinion (July 19) that his reason is to seem consistent with his
theory that the Ballot is a conservative measure.* We divided & were
defeated – somewhere about 2 to 1.[101] I put off the affirmations Bill;
virtually for this Session, & begged Brand to pair me off – & high
time! I remained for some time in hopes of a chance turning up for
this bill, but in vain. So we must wait.

Nothing struck me more in Berkeley's speech than when he said, as it
were apologetically, that, as the advocate of the Ballot, he 'graduated
under Geo. Grote'.[102]

B. argued elaborately from American, as well as English, facts, that
the Ballot is a conservative engine. After all, his audience looked as if
they admired the rhetorician but rejected the cause. A certain moral
sense was agt. him. I say this as one of his supporters & speak of his
opponents. The truth is the question, justly or unjustly, has shared in
the discredit of the late American shipwreck.

Friday, 18 July: [...] To my mind it occurs to say that old Palmerston
seems to evince more skill & pluck as he approaches the goal of his
days. Whether fit or not to govern men, he appears to have governed
one man well. Otherwise he would hardly evince the qualities he does
at his time of life.

Wednesday, 23 July: A brisk debate on the night poaching bill[103]
[...] Take care, ye country gentlemen of England! These are not the
middle ages. There is widespread distress in the Cotton districts – a
bad harvest seems to impend – are you sure you will be able to obtain
convictions?

Thursday, 24 July: [...] The night poaching Bill was under discussion till 3 a.m. & 9 divisions were taken on it in committee.
*Mem[orandum.] Noteworthy attendance of country gentlemen in
the dogdays to pass this Bill – & all night at it. Is not this a sort of
night poaching by the squires?*

Thursday, 31 July: A power to borrow, for purposes of Poor Relief

---

[101] 211:126

[102] The leading advocate of secret ballot in the 1830s (d. 1871). A friend of Trelawny.

[103] In committee; a House of Lords bill providing for increased police powers to search
and apprehend suspects. Royal assent, 7 Aug.

in certain cases of pressure, proposed & accepted.[104] In short the Govt. has been driven to act agt. the dictates of its intellect, whether fortunately or otherwise I will not venture to say [...]

Friday, 1 August: Cobden reviews the Session. Five more divisions on the night poaching Bill, wh. was read a third time.[105] The Tories will thus have a good cry for the next election.

Lord Palmerston's reply to Cobden was very able. It was like a cat playing with a mouse. To the charge that Reform had made no progress under P's rule, he replied that this was the effect of Cobden's & Bright's indiscreet advocacy – as to Bright, a most bitter truth! To the charge that great expense has been incurred in providing for National defences at P's instance, he replied that, in attributing so much to him, C. did him more honour than he deserved. But the cruellest thing was that he would not be annoyed – & wound up with conciliatory language & expressions of his conviction that during the recess Cobden wd., on reflection, become more tolerant & considerate; & that, after all, it wd. turn out that the differences between the two great sections of liberals were less than he seemed to imagine. Disraeli followed; driving in the wedge to increase the separation. In my judgment he should, as a matter of tactics, have held his peace. He too easily discovers his hand & thus re-enlists the liberals under the same flag.

Thursday, 7 August: Queen's speech & prorogation. The speech was but moderately boastful – & has somewhat to shew – not the least thing being peace still with all the world! – but how long will peace last?

It occurs to me to note some points which have struck me during the late Session. The House has been a sort of Convocation attended by persons of every shade of religious belief. Almost every evening some matter relating to religion is a topic of discussion. This is a growing evil. *I do not think that the Irish character and antecedents are sufficiently considered. The Irish may be led by a line of a single hair. Cardwell & Peel[106] understood them pretty well. An even dispassionateness & a ready accessibility would go far towards disarming hostile feelings pervading opposite sections in Ireland. A

---

[104] The union relief aid bill, through committee; it enabled poor law unions in Lancashire, Cheshire and Derbyshire to borrow from the public works loan commissioners once their rates exceeded 3s. in the £. Royal assent, 7 Aug; *P.P.* 1862, v. 491.

[105] 84:29.

[106] Cardwell had been Irish chief secretary, 1859–61; Sir Robert Peel had held the same office, 1812–18.

little geniality & good fellowship thrown in would be so much the better. There are unfortunately some English members who are to the full as provoking as the Irish themselves.*

Great armaments in time of peace – war taxes – debts for fortifications – & a deficit in spite of an expenditure of £70,000,000 – are matters which ought to awaken reflection. What say constituencies?

[...] Lord Palmerston's extraordinary energy & readiness on all occasions have made his position unassailable.

[...] My mission appears in the House to be that of an exponent of the opinions of minorities, who cannot otherwise get a hearing. People come to me on all occasions to pick the 'chestnuts out of the fire' – the oaths question is a case in point: Guards' privileges another.

The Indian Revenue is in a greatly improved condition – but the battle betwn. Laing & Wood[107] is a curious phenomenon. *Note (2). It looks like the case of a small & obstinate mind irritated at the superiority of a subordinate. Wood should take Laing's place, as he affects to understand it better than Laing. Laing should take Wood's – for obvious reasons. We all recollect Wood at the office of Chancellor of Exchequer.[108] He was, I think, the Personification of deficit. Perhaps, he has a mortal horror of a balance in whatsoever manner produced.*

The sufferings of the cotton spinners have been a subject of debate, & a bill has passed to mitigate pressure arising from want of the raw material of their industry.[109] I doubt if the old League party ring quite true to their theory of commerce taking care of itself. What has Parliament, on their shewing, to do with supply & demand?

Looking to the greatness of the changes which happen from day to day – such as those in 1848, in India, in Italy & America – the hourly falsification of Theories of Govt. & the mortification of the pride of human Intellect – I rejoice, at least, at any cases in which I have doubted enough to be moderate in regard to men or opinions. Oftentimes doubt has painfully beset me, and it may be useful to remind constituents that they are sometimes apt to confound hesitation with inconsistency & indecision with untrustworthiness. To doubt boldly – & admit doubt at personal risk – is a quality of which the want would be a serious drawback to a politician's usefulness. Lord Holland[110] used to say 'I am so confident that I must be wrong'.

The House grumbles at the cost of our Colonies – with reason.

---

[107] On 10 July Wood, the secretary of state for India, had made a statement regarding his criticisms of the details of the accounts produced by Samuel Laing, the finance minister in India. Laing's errors cancelled one another out, and the Indian accounts were nearly in balance after several years of large deficits; *H.* clxviii. 27–59.

[108] 1846–52.

[109] See above, 31 July 1862.

[110] The 3rd baron (d. 1840), leading exponent of the Foxite tradition of whiggery.

One consolation suggested by the American struggle is that it must tend at last to make Nations perceive, with unusual distinctness, how much they are mutually dependent – & what insanity war is, unless inevitable. The fact, always self-evident to abstract thinkers, is rarely brought home so prominently as now to producers & consumers in general.

Disastrous is the war, however in this way that liberal measures, sometime feasible, here can no longer be submitted to the Legislature with any hope of their being adopted – &, if successful, the Conservative party would have greater apprehensions than ever of their effects on our happiness.

The lesson to us is to beware of division for the sake of division – to eschew self-seeking – to make no proposals except on grounds of improving a system, wh., in very many particulars, works well.

It may be a small matter, but it is not insignificant, that Disraeli has boldly adopted the name of 'Tory'.

American proceedings are now a very fertile topic of Reflection. The moral seems to be this – that a Nation must, like a ship, have ballast. The States were flighty & conceited.

Old Institutions – even though imperfect or, in part, mischievous – give a country, at least, a backbone. An ever-changing swarm of men of all Nations & languages, engaged in creating money & having often no home feelings or fixed abodes, have all their work to do before they can become an amalgamated People, with whom consistent relations may be hoped for. In England the wildest changes may be broached & discussed with little harm, because no action can be taken in haste, inasmuch as a host of defenders is sure to spring up for things as they are. Not a town or village exists which is not interested for its long-established rights. If these be attacked in one particular, common cause may at once be made with others in equal danger. The Americans appear to be less a body of men bound together in a polity than an aggregation of persons without mutual confidence or dependence.

On Church Rates, I have designed that my course should be moderate and conciliatory. To the Conservatives, anxious to mend the law, I have practically said 'Gentlemen, propose your plan – & let us see what merit it has'. To the dissenters I have preached the doctrine 'suaviter in modo – fortiter in re' – and patience. The danger, on one side, is from obstructiveness till too late – on the other, from impulsiveness & activity too soon. I claim from both sides the credit of desiring to be just to both – & from my followers I exact confidence whilst I lead.

[...] The rashest of the rash things I have witnessed in my day has been the mode of dealing with fortifications & iron plated ships. If it were of the least use to advise people who never doubt and well know the apathy of the taxpayer, I should caution the admiralty, as I have often done before, how they deal with the reconstruction of our fleet [...] The sea is a field on wh. Genius upsets in a moment the most skilful devices.I think, were I at the admiralty, I should preserve an attitude of observation – at the same time collecting materials. Any ship may be iron-plated in an extempore manner. But if ships are built with fixtures of this kind, such ships will be useless for long expeditions. They would not stow men, supplies, ammunition & guns, & could not be fought in bad weather. Our ships shd. be available, either for carriage or for defence at home, by a preconceived scheme of conversion at trifling cost. *Again what say the experts?*

The Church seems determined to scare scholars from her portals and reward dullness, real or affected, by confining patronage to men who either can't, won't or don't think. There are, at least, greater enemies of the Church than Church-Rate Repealers. Perhaps, some recent proceedings relating to Prosecutions & Patronage may be a caution for the future. Mr. Lear's case, for example.[111] Bishop Beresford may have been a good bishop – yet he was, perhaps, a dear bargain at an aggregate cost of £700,000.[112]

The Church wants conformity, not conviction; not so much Truth, as submission. Its members, holding preferment, are under a temptation to shut their eyes to the light, lest they see things which, in faithful witnesses, it were as bad as blasphemy to conceal. *They remind one of the ostrich, burying its head in the sand.*

American experiences may make a reaction beyond what is due. Tories will say 'all comes of secret & general suffrage'. And yet, they, also, say that the American Ballot is not secret – and Trollope[113] says the suffrage in America is limited. A ship may be thrown on her beam ends by a Typhoon – &, yet, her lines may be irreproachable. Let those who read accounts of American Institutions observe what has been done in America for Education alone (see Trollope) & compare the state of the negro with that of our working men. Also, read descriptions of the Lowell factories.[114] *Would it be right to argue that limited Monarchy must be a defective Institution because the Wars of the Roses lasted 30 years. And, as to American finance, let us not forget the South sea scheme – & our theory of a sinking fund –

---

[111] Lear had been given a canonry, worth £600 p.a., in addition to a living worth £1,000 p.a., by his brother-in-law, the bishop of Salisbury; *The Times*, 12 Aug. 1862, p. 8.

[112] The total value of the patronage disposed of by J. G. Beresford, archbishop of Armagh 1822–62.

[113] Anthony Trollope, *North America* (2 vols, 1862).

[114] Ibid, i. 380–93, for the superior condition of the calico workers in the town of Lowell.

or our dockyard management – or our debt of £800,000,000 mostly incurred at the behests of a narrow, obstinate, yet respectable, bigot.[115] Wrongheaded tho' both sides may be in America, note one thing – that, since the World began, so many men in a commonwealth were never yet arrayed in deadly struggle for principles. Our volunteers have exhibited virtue & self-denial, but they have fortunately experienced no fire baptism. What they would do, we may conjecture. Luckily proof is not yet exhibited.*

The Bicentenary of the desertion of 2,000 Ministers from the establishment, on account of the stringency of the act of Uniformity, shd. be a lesson to the opponents of Bouverie's Bill,[116] but it will hardly be taken.

[...] Lord Palmerston has the happy gift of saying tonight what no one expects, but a great majority will agree to tomorrow morning. He has a manner, too, which conciliates his bitterest opponents. While his geniality cannot fail to please, it is not quite satisfactory to those who have been in the habit of attaching great importance to laws, customs, Institutions or policy, in affecting the current of a Nation's History, to reflect that the personal qualities of one man carry every one captive [...]

---

[115] I.e. George III.
[116] The clergy relief bill, defeated on its 3rd reading, 9 July; see above 18 June 1862.

SESSION OF 1863

Thursday, 5 February: At one o'clock I was at my post & did not regret my punctuality. Members shd. lose no opportunities of studying their colleagues or brethren in council under favourable circumstances. The Saxon ice thaws for a moment at times like these + & good nature is found where it was least supposed to dwell. + Two members very kindly came over to me and spoke more warmly & generously than I dare describe – but let me think of them with gratitude & keep their names – Admiral Walcott & Col[onel] Gilpin.[1]

The attendance was large. The speech was delivered by Commiss[ione]rs & was nearly inaudible – so I was content with the expectation of seeing it in print.

[...] mover & seconder, the Hon. F.W. Calthorpe & Mr. Bazley, delivered their speeches. The former was nervous & forgetful for a moment, but recovered himself well & would have achieved success could he have abstained from a bitter attack on the Federals in America. Could Ministers have suggested this? Hardly. Bazley, so far as I heard, was irreproachable.

Dr. Foster & Sir C. Douglas seem to think that our division upon Church Rates will be more favourable this year than last. I told Mr. Brand[2] that I thought the subject would be noticed in the Queen's speech, & added that Ministers evidently used me to pluck the chestnuts out of the fire. Why did not Disraeli taunt them with having no policy on a point, whereupon legislation is imperiously called for?

Disraeli's speech was clever & pungent. Ministers, however, appear to stand well in spite of it, and are in great measure uncommitted. The Tories are at issue upon the policy of acknowledging the South.[3]

Friday, 6 February: The Reply to 'the speech of the Commiss[ione]rs', as Disraeli called it, was brought up, discussed & passed. A few points struck me. It is evident that Disraeli would not win in a direct trial of strength with Palmerston. Darby Griffith is often the occasion of mirth & is, certainly, still oftener very trying to the patience of the House. On this occasion he uttered some sentences which found a ready echo, & in substance he avowed the hopelessness of an attack

---

[1] J.E. Walcott of Christchurch and R.T. Gilpin of Bedfordshire, both Conservatives.
[2] Government chief whip.
[3] I.e. the confederate government of Jefferson Davis.

on the leader of govt. to whom almost every one had been compelled to promise substantial support * Darby Griffith a sort of Palmerstonian * [...]

Wednesday, 11 February: [...] I had a conference with Brand. Would I aid in the event of a bill being proposed to take away the compulsory power under the existing law of Ch. Rates? Yes. Would the dissenters concur? I thought, yes. Would my influence be favourable? Yes, but in the event of danger of failure, I shd. fall back on my lines – wh. I called my 'material guarantee'. This, in substance, passed. I reminded him of Bright's tender of a compromise to the effect alluded to by Brand.[4] Also, I mentioned Dr. Foster's tender of a compromise thro' me[5] [...]

Thursday, 12 February: After conference with Sir C. Douglas & Mr. Brand – the former having already talked to Dr. Foster – a day Ap[ril] 29th was fixed for Ch. Rates.
The Tories in high delight, having won Devonport.[6]
[...] Hardy[7] is, evidently, rather alarmed at the possible effect of refusing to pass my affirmations Bill, but he desires the Bill shd. not seem to give countenance to infidelity. I begin to think that the Bill may hereafter be so shaped as to pass. I hear that the Att[orne]y & Sol[icitor] gen[eral] are going to examine the Bill to see what can be done. Of course I shall not oppose moderate alteration provided I get my principle [...]

Monday, 16 February: [...] Irish illegitimate children Bill. Discussion in Committee. Oddly enough, Lewis criticized R. Peel's Bill.[8] Cannot these colleagues agree? In the middle of L's speech, he proved that he was not acquainted with an important feature of Irish bastardy law – & one of his assertions was met with cries of 'no no & laughter'. Lewis looked embarrassed – & then, as is his wont, took refuge in his favourite word 'well' – & spun more words in clouds of wh. he escaped further exposure. Remark around 'Lewis is making a mess of it' [...]

---

[4] 14 May 1862; *H* clxvi. 1704–15.
[5] See above, 11 June 1861.
[6] Captured from the Liberals by W.B. Ferrand with a majority of 30.
[7] Conservative under-secretary at the home office, Mar. 1858 to June 1859.
[8] The Irish chief secretary's bill (Royal assent, 8 June) enabled boards of guardians to recover the cost of maintenance from the putative father through proceedings at quarter sessions. Lewis, the war secretary, preferred the extension of the system established in England in 1844 whereby the mother was allowed to take proceedings against the father; *H* clxxix. 346–7.

Tuesday, 17 February: Cession of the Ionian Islands.[9]

Roebuck asked Palmerston whether he could not answer a question wh. R. had put a few nights since – viz, whether any despatch had come from Austria respecting the cession. To this question P. had then said he could not reply 'offhand'. R observed that this was a curious answer – & he now repeated the question. P. said there was no such despatch. R., still sitting, audibly said 'I have seen it' (much laughter) wherein P. joined, & he then proceeded with a pretty good walk – wh. was watched & noted by many – to the Bar whence he brought up a message from Her Majesty. Immediately afterwards, he moved a resolution in reply, & announced for Thursday a more substantial resolution, in the shape of a provision for the P[rince] of Wales & his bride [...]

Sir Geo. Grey privately announced to me that he shd. oppose my affirmations Bill. Humbug! [...] I exhibited a great deal of indignation at Grey's intended course, not believing that a Minister, at the Home Office, really thought that witnesses could safely be allowed to affirm, & jurors not; because this Grey distinctly stated to me at the door of the dining room. He is canting, I fear, I went over to the opposition side, & began to talk openly, even to Brand, of a motion on Ch. Rates wh. would put Govt. in a minority [...]

Wednesday, 18 February: [...] I have had much talk about Ch. Rates & my policy. Sir Geo. Grey's course on the affirmations bill has disgusted me, & I feel diminished interest in Ministers & begin to think that I shall move a resolution on Ch. Rates before my Bill shall come on for a 2d. reading or even instead of proceeding by bill at all.

[...] The Ministry are using us as a screen for censure upon them for not bringing in a Ch. Rate Bill. My bill is not supported by Govt. as such, since Gladstone, R. Peel & Bury oppose me, or do not vote for me.

'The Times[10] has evidently deserted me. Will not many timid men follow the Times lead? Am I not more likely to promote the success of the principle for which I contend by a general resolution agreed to by a large majority than by a bill, doomed as it stands, to an annual failure?

Such a motion, carried, would defeat the Ministry. But, probably, the Sun would rise as usual.

---

[9] To Greece, agreed with the European Powers on 14 Nov. 1863; *B.F.S.P., liii.* 19–23.

[10] 13 Feb. 1863, p. 8, arguing that the bill had no chance of success and was not worth the disturbance and annoyance it caused.

Thursday, 19 February: A long conference betwn. Douglas, Dr. Foster & me on the question whether we shd. proceed by resolution. We canvassed reasons on either side. Dr. Foster is going to consult some of his party.

5 p.m. Committee on Prince of Wales's allow[an]ce.[11] Palmerston's was a clever well-prepared speech. Willoughby criticized. Gladstone & Disraeli spoke, the former was in error on a point of Duchy law.

Disraeli desired an agreement nem. con.

Augustus Smith spoke, & with some effect. T[relawny] supported him, replying to Gladstone, who, by the way, had followed Smith. Neither Gladstone or the House knew that the property of the Duchy, in the event of the duke's death, goes to the Crown for life.[12] I mentioned Burke's proposal in his speech on economical reform[13] to sell the property of the Duchies of Cornwall and Lancaster & apply the proceeds to the Public service. No effective opposition [...]

Friday, 20 February: [...] Several members begin to think that the proceedings in regard to the Prince's allowance have been hasty & ill-considered. a boy with £100,000 a year & half a million in hand will be in some danger. Shd. we not have bargained with him to settle his capital? Was it necessary to add £40,000 a year out of the consolidated fund to £60,000 from the duchy[14] estate, wh. is highly improvable? Should not the Prince have purchased a perpetuity with his capital saved & thus spared new & heavy charge upon the Public?

Tuesday, 24 February: [...] Palmerston, in a reply to Newdegate who inquired whether the Princess Alexandra was a protestant, said she was young, handsome, amiable, well brought up & a protestant [...]

Thursday, 26 February: [...] I had much discussion about Church Rates tactics with Dr. Foster, Sir C. Douglas, Brand, & with Newdegate who wanted to get a 2d. reading of his Bill[15] & take it to a select committee.

I have some hope of getting a compromise by means of a bill abolishing the compulsory power of enforcing rates. Work enough & so home.

---

[11] On his forthcoming marriage to Princess Alexandre of Denmark.
[12] Trelawny's interpretation of the Duchy charter was subsequently challenged by Gladstone; 23 Feb., *H* clxix. 648–9.
[13] In 1778.
[14] Of Cornwall.
[15] Transferring the liability for the rate from occupiers to owners; see below, 6 May.

Friday, 27 February: The delinquent, Mr. Reed,[16] attended, & made a full & humble apology in carefully prepared language. The senior clerk stood with the bar down across the entrance, as it were on sentry's duty, & Reed entered the House. There was a titter at the clerk's appearance before R. came in wh. was immediately checked just in time to save our dignity (so far at least). * One of the newspapers reports that Mr. Headlam raised this hilarity by walking into the House as if he had been the expected man & escaping abruptly on discovering how matters were. * Then came a question or two from Mr. Speaker, the offender's apology & Sir F. Smith's intercession for him, on wh. he was released. As usual, when privilege questions promising a scene occur, the attendance was rather large, & I noticed Visct. Eversley[17] under the gallery. The old war horse I suppose heard sounds of battle and could not resist the temptation to be present at it.

Afterwards, Poland & its affairs occupied us for several hours. Rarely has more unanimity been witnessed in Parliament. Russia & Prussia have had a lesson. Lord Palmerston's language was grand.[18] Some passages in his speech were among the finest sentences I have ever heard spoken.

Hennessy acquitted himself ably,[19] & received many compliments. He was advised not to divide, & he prudently abstained from division accordingly.

[...] The subject of the cession of the Ionian Islands was again referred to, as well as Palmerston's statement that no communications had passed upon the matter betwn. Austria & England. This he repeated. Roebuck declared that he had seen the actual despatch, wh. was shewn to him in consequence of inquiries he had made of the Austrian Govt.; & that the subject of the despatch was exceedingly well argued. He added that he would like to see it on the table of the House. Palmerston then explained that a paper had been read to Lord Russell, but no copy was left with him. It is very difficult to understand in what manner Palmerston reconciles to himself, if he can reconcile, these incongruous statements; nor did the charge seem to trouble him for a moment.

[16] E.J. Reed, chief constructor for the navy, ordered to appear before the House for a breach of privilege, having sent a menacing letter to Sir Fredrick Smith, M.P. for Chatham, who had criticised Reed's appointment.

[17] The ex-Speaker, Shaw Lefevre.

[18] Condemning the Russian authorities, whose rounding-up of suspected revolutionaries under the guise of conscripting them into the army had sparked off the Polish insurrection, and trusting that the Prussian Landtag would not ratify the convention by which Prussia had agreed to lend assistance to Russia; *H* clxix. 932–9.

[19] His motion called for intervention by Britain in fulfilment of her obligations under the treaty of Vienna; *H* clxix. 879–92.

There were parts of Lord P's speech on Poland, wh. were almost worthy of Tacitus or Livy. It was a grand speech & must raise the House of Commons in the estimation of the world. He stigmatized the conscription, more properly a 'proscription', as *'barbarous'* a bitter word to Russians, who are peculiarly sensitive upon the point of being so deemed; &, evidently alluding to the effect of diplomatic hints of consequences, he added that the acts of Prussia had been 'stopped' '& had ceased' (sensation). The last words fell in a singular tone lower in sound but more impressive. The whole speech was very studied & diplomatic. Speaking of the Emperor's (Russia) difficulties, he said it was always a terrible calamity to be the inheritor of a 'triumphant wrong' a phrase, which produced considerable effect. To epitomize his speech is to mar it; it shd. be read at length, as it will be historical.

Monday, 2 March: [...] The corrupt Practices bill led to a debate of some length. Two close divisions occurred, & on one Ministers appear to have suffered a defeat.[20] The Bill little interests me.[21] Machinery will effect little towards the purification of morals. Any scheme such as that proposed will fail to diminish the power of wealth in the race for seats [...]

Tuesday, 3 March: [...] there was an apparition of two singular beings clad in pied dresses or long robes & tippets of alternate black & white, & wearing preposterous wigs. These curious creatures were judges; – I heard, Colin Blackburn & Williams – & brought a message from the Lords.[22] They approached the table attended by the Serjeant carrying the mace, & seemed rather shy & very awkward. As they began their walk, some members, struck with the absurdity of the scene, exclaimed, as if to carry out the farce, 'bow! bow!' & at each mandate – down went one or other of the heads, but never in time; & the malicious House, noting this, & the nervousness out of which it arose, cried 'bow! bow!' again, & down went the heads many times oftener than the proper number, 3, amidst shouts of very irreverent laughter. The poor judges hardly knew how to take it, & escaped in rather undignified plight each inclining his head from time to time in backing out to see what his neighbour was doing or, perhaps, to prevent a catastrophe. A few members, recollecting what was due to

---

[20] Cave's amendment, to omit clause 2 relating to the disqualification from voting of election agents, carried by 110:103.

[21] In the form in which it passed on 8 June, the bill provided for the punishment of electors who accepted bribes and enabled parliament to temporarily suspend the writs of corrupt constituencies; *P.P.* 1863, i. 649.

[22] Agreeing to the Prince of Wales's annuity bill.

the English Bench, exclaimed 'order, order', in reply to 'bow, bow' but this only made matters worse, since the wickedly-inclined again cried 'bow' as a thing duly in order [...]

Wednesday, 4 March: Gladstone objects to declarations 'of civil inequality'. What about Church rates? – 'no dangers to the Church from the influence of dissenters'. These too were words used in his speech on Hadfield's bill – (qualifications for offices)[23] – carried to-day on 3rd. reading. Very remarkable they seemed in a speech from him, & so people thought.

Newdegate's face of ineffable contempt at Gladstone's distinctions & doctrine respecting the supposed compact in 1828[24] was a subject of some amusement. He kept tossing his head aside with a jerk, assuming the contortions of a man taking physic, & accompanying his movements with an ironical 'hear hear' in tones like those of an old raven. Yet, he is a good & genuine man, anxious to do his duty. All honour to him! Walpole replied to Gladstone, feebly. There had been a most determined whip, & many had been summoned from the provinces to vote. But Hadfield won by 3. Division 175 to 172. I conceive that Gladstone's language almost intitles me to ask for his vote on the Church-rates Bill [...]

Thursday, 5 March: Sir C. Douglas informs me that the Dissenters think that we must persevere with the Bill as it stands – we cannot mend our position; & so it now seems to me. We must fight the old ship 'Abolition'.

Before supply, Cobden spoke for about an hour with great energy on the assumed waste in the naval administration, founding his argument on the knowledge which the Admiralty possessed many years ago, that the days of wooden ships were numbered. In spite of this knowledge, numerous wooden ships have been built or completed; & Cobden estimated our loss at at least £10,000,000. Fallacious, I think, because ironclad vessels could not have been built under several years, & the best size & form were unsettled. Cobden argued that the numbers (76,000) of seamen could not be necessary, as the wooden ships for which they are to be used are unfit to cope with an enemy. Another fallacy! It may be that the men must be kept ready for war, & no adequate numbers of iron ships are ready to receive them.

---

[23] Abolishing the declaration retained in 1828 by which members of municipal corporations were required to declare that they would not use their power to assail, weaken or spoilate the Church of England. Rejected by the House of Lords, 24 April.

[24] I.e. Gladstone rejected the claim that the repeal of the test and corporations acts represented an unalterable settlement of the relations between anglicans and nonconformists; *H* clxix. 1047–50.

Cobden was very fierce, severely censuring Pakington & Clarence Paget.[25] Not quite justly, I think. I observed twice to Mr. Steel who sat next to me that Cobden's speech would be answered & so it turned out. Clarence Paget & Pakington had an easy victory. Not that Cobden's speech was not in many parts effective, but unpractical men do not hit the right blots. Cobden is not a seaman. He is hardly aware of the difficulty of manufacturing ABs,[26] & the necessity of keeping a large stock of that article in hand. His speech was full of fallacies, & yet he might have urged an unanswerable case agt. each & every Admiralty past & present. As the case stands, he has lent strength to abuses by failure in his mode of attack & choice of points to be assailed. The worst of Cobden is his conceit. His victory over the protectionists spoilt him. By the way, what has he been doing with his diction of late? He used to be correct above the average. He spoke of cŭp-ŏlă ships, the Hūzză, Rō-mănce & Cōn-cise. The sensible House made no comment. Nor should I, but that I feel regret that so able a man should mar his vigorous style & usually skilful oratory by the adoption of an eccentric accentuation. A friend of mine, correcting my faulty & careless phraseology said lately to me & truly: 'we are all trustees for the preservation of the English language, which bad example may easily corrupt', – & I hope I may yet take the hint.

Friday, 6 March: A good speech of Collier's on Bramley Moore's Brazil motion.[27] Earl Russell was under the gallery for a short time. Seymour Fitzgerald & Layard spoke. Also, Lord R. Cecil – he rather waspishly, yet wittily. The Conservatives cannot put their horses heads together.[28]

Collier's manner is improved, but is still too forensic. While he was speaking, he used the address 'Gentlemen', wh. though immediately corrected, was remarked. But it confirmed the estimate formed by the House of the style & character of C's speaking, wh. is in the tone of an advocate speaking from a brief. Why, by the way, does he say 'nōt-ĭfȳ' & 'ĕpo' for ēpōch. Odd very in a scholar, who is rather a censor!

[...] Why does Cobden always say 'b'lieve' for 'believe' and 'diplom-acy'?

---

[25] Paget was parliamentary secretary to the admiralty, Pakington had been the first lord in Derby's ministry.

[26] Able-bodied seamen.

[27] Regretting the interruption of friendly relations between Britain and Brazil and hoping for an honourable settlement, *H* clxix. 1130–9. Collier, the counsel to the admiralty, defended the reprisals taken by Britain against Brazil after natives had plundered the shipwreck and murdered the crew of the 'Prince of Wales', in June 1861.

[28] Cecil's speech in support of Moore's motion was marred by its bitter tone; *H* clxix. 1151–8.

The debate was animated, but almost all the argument with Ministers. The mover desired to withdraw his motion. This was refused, & the motion was negatived.

[...] My thoughts are occupied with the subject of the affirmations Bill, wh. stands for Wednesday.

A short statement of the general scope of the Bill must be given, which in the main consists of two parts (1) to extend to the Scotch the principle of the common Law procedure act (1854) as to affirmations & of John Locke's Act of 1861. At present, this principle has operation only in civil cases in Scotland under an act of 1855, so that there is one state of law for England & Ireland, & another for Scotland. The principle is that persons, having religious opinions, may affirm in lieu of taking oaths. (2) To enable any persons in England, Scotland or Ireland (or, indeed, anywhere within H.M.'s possessions) to make affirmations in all cases where there is inability to take an oath from defect or want of religious belief &c (See terms of Bill).[29]

Then, I must state that it is not necessary that I shd. discuss at length the policy of requiring oaths at all, as it is only in exceptional cases that it will be necessary to substitute affirmations. Still, to account for considerable existing disinclination to take oaths, it may be well to remind the House that, if the language of Scripture were our exclusive guide 'swear not at all' would be our rule. I prefer, however, to avoid Theological arguments wh. are dangerous in the House & lead to much & unseemly controversy.

With regard to the use of oaths, there are authorities on both sides. Some barristers say that it is not the oath which educes truth but dread of the effect of cross examination & of the punishment inflicted upon prevaricating witnesses. Others say so necessary is the oath, that witnesses only kissing their thumbs consider themselves unsworn & hesitate not to lie to any extent.

It will be of little use to plead for tolerance of the infidel, on the broad ground of liberty of Conscience. Fortunately, an adequate basis for my Bill exists independently. My contention is that the State has a complete right to the testimony of every citizen, who is bound on requirement to describe with regard to every transaction the truth, the whole truth & nothing but the truth.

As I do not propose to abolish oaths, it is not necessary to open that argument. The Legislation of England on that subject has always been elastic.

As opinions have rendered change necessary, so the good sense of Parliament has supplied the want which has arisen. Thus, special law exists for Quakers, Moravians & Separatists. Again for Jews. By the

[29] *P.P.* 1863, i. 49.

act of 1854, affirmations were allowed, in lieu of oaths, to persons holding a religious belief. Locke's act of 1861 went a little further[30] &, thus, a new case, being apparent, demands a corresponding adjustment of the law.

[...] What word epitomizes most completely the great objects of all legislation? What is the quality, which, if it existed everywhere without law, would almost render all law useless – which would have little occasion for standing armies or coercive means of insuring justice betwn. man & man? That word, & that quality, is truth. In the sublime language of our litany, we pray that our magistrates may have 'grace to execute justice & maintain truth'. What if our law obliges them to execute injustice & maintain lies? This, I fear, is the effect of the existing law of oaths. The cause is adjudged to the hardest swearer.

Monday, 9 March: [...] Lewis moved the army estimates. One million less than last year. Cost altogether £15,060,237. Men 148,242: a reduction, therefore, of 4,161 men.

Williams proposed a reduction of 10,000 men; this I opposed & stated my reason afterwards. The language used with respect to the Polish insurrection could only be of value if backed by power. It is necessary to be able to bite as well as bark. (77 to 19.)[31]

Gen[era]l Peel proposed to reject an item of £38,000 for certain Indian regiments employed in China. This amendment I supported; for constitutional reasons. The men had been employed without a vote of Parliamt. We were defeated. Ayes 58 Noes 64. Majority 6.

Sir M. Peto proposed to reduce the estimates by £255,156, being the excess of cost on Vote 1[32] for this year compared with last. He shewed no adequate reasons why this precise sum shd. be the sum taken, and, therefore, I voted with Ministers.[33] This is an arithmetical way of dealing with State policy. Peto shd. have pointed out what particular sums together constituted the excess of that total which the due efficiency of the Public service requires.

About ¼ before 12, we, radicals, agreed that it was time to report progress. We urged that many topics demanded discussion – of these I named some. New Zealand, the office of Inspector General of Guards, & the three sinecure Lieutenant-Colonels of Guards. We

---

[30] The criminal proceedings oath relief act permitted christians to make affirmations in lieu of oaths in criminal cases in England and Wales; *P.P.* 1861, i. 771.

[31] Against Williams's amendment.

[32] The sum to defray the cost of the general staff, regimental pay, and allowances and charges of land forces excluding India.

[33] Peto defeated 96:22.

divided once, & were defeated.[34] Soon after Ministers gave way – & so ended a desultory & not very satisfactory evening, either to spectators or persons engaged.

Wednesday, 11 March: Another Wednesday fight. I moved the 2nd. reading of the Affirmations Bill. My speech lasted during 40 minutes, well cheered at the end; & the Att[orne]y Gen[era]l[35] followed in a speech of one hour. He moved in opposition to me [...] his was a regular lawyer's speech. Civil towards me, as he spoke of my correctness in stating the law, & said my statement was able. He has not breadth of views enough for a law Reformer. He stated, however, that he only spoke for himself; hence I inferred that qua Government the question was open.

Roebuck was effective & original. Was he a trifle too near the wind in his line of argument? The House was here & there a little frightened, especially when he said that belief was not an affair of the will, & that no educated man believes in special interpositions.

Douglas was very useful. Some of my points had not been put, & it was necessary to reply to the Att[orne]y Gen[era]l. Douglas took some of my papers & used them with great skill & readiness.

Division 142-96. So we lost [...] The whole debate lasted with division about 3 hours, & was certainly very lively & not ill sustained.

Looking back on my speech, I recollect that, as usual, I said much that I had not purposed to say, omitted points I ought to have made, & put many passages in the wrong places. In short I have not taken pains enough, or, else, I want certain qualities. I did not cite the passage from Sir W. Ashurst, that no man is so low as to be beneath the protection of English law;[36] nor that of Whately, who said it is not enough to believe what we maintain, but we must maintain what we believe & because we believe it.[37] Provoking!

How well & dramatically Roebuck speaks! No fumbling of papers there. He spins everything leisurely from his brain, & every word tells. He is an orator; & I was going to say among our last few.

Speaking of practising lawyers, he said they were usually the last to adopt reform. He compared them to metal which has run in a molten state into a mould, & there congealed. The debate will make men think.

The newsmen certainly spoil the debate in their reports. The fact

---

[34] 80:25.

[35] Sir William Atherton.

[36] A dictum cited in *Truth or Justice: or law as it is, contrasted with what it is said to be. Written in Dec. 1792 by Jeremy Bentham*, (1823).

[37] Richard Whately, archbishop of Dublin, *A view of the scripture revelations concerning a future state*, (1829).

is, the Sceptic is a character, in whose fate the Public have no interest, & the Public has not found out that the Sceptic's testimony is often a main link in the title of Christians to property, liberty & life [...]

Thursday, 12 March: I could not vote with Lindsay, on his motion, by way of amendment on going into supply, with the object of pledging ministers not to build ships of particular materials, for, besides other reasons, experience is far from being conclusive as to the relative merits of iron & wood. On division we beat him.[38] Sir F. Baring[39] well stated the obvious objections to Lindsay's proposal involving a principle, which, if it were universally applied, would be destructive of Ministerial responsibility. Good speeches were made by several great contractors &c – such as Laird, Peto & Jackson, & many useful facts & arguments were advanced. Pakington, Henley & Palmerston spoke. The economists in the House of Commons have not yet discovered the weak places in our finance; or, rather, they cannot hit the weak places.

It often happens that excellent speeches in the House are made, which contain many of the premisses essential to a wise conclusion but not all. So it was in the shipbuilding debate. Peto is not a seaman;[40] Lindsay is a shipowner, not a shipbuilder. Laird is a shipbuilder, not a constitutional lawyer. Yet, each of these men said useful things. This is the use of a Parliament. We educate each other. All knowledge is brought to account. Arguments are weighed. Garrulity propounds them in season & out of season. Fanaticism ensures their prominence. Even prejudice has a certain use in checking excess in another direction. The decision is taken in the main by a number of shrewd & silent judges, whose ears are ever open & minds are ever at work.

Friday, 13 March: [...] We had a division on a part of the sum to be voted for Colonial defence. I was a little puzzled at first. When we divided, Brand came up, bowing to the chair which was empty (great laughter) – Massey[41] having retired. We win. I went with Ministers,[42] because (1) we have voted the men & can hardly refuse the supplies for food &c (2) If we throw the army now in the Colonies on the Colonial exchequers, then, as Roebuck suggested, the Colonies may claim the right of moving the British army. Also, it will be almost impossible to divide the incidence of the sum newly to be charged on

---

[38] 154:81 against the motion opposing the construction of wooden ships if they were to be iron-cased; *H* clxix. 1333–45.

[39] First lord of the admiralty, Jan. 1849 to Mar. 1852.

[40] He was a railway contractor.

[41] Chairman of committees.

[42] Mills's motion to reduce the vote by £80,000, defeated 71:66.

the Colonies (some £80,000) as our Colonies are by no means in similar circumstances in relation to the mother country & the Crown. At the same time, one wants a legitimate occasion of opposing the policy of continuing to charge the British taxpayer with the duty of supporting armies to defend persons who are suspected of an interest in war agt. savage tribes. These tribes are destroyed & their lands taken. The presence of British troops brings numerous advantages to resident colonists, social & pecuniary [...]

Monday, 16 March: [...] A division in supply, on a begging motion in favour of certain army officers wanting forage for their horses, took place. This vote I lost.[43] This system by wh. military members use their Parl[iamentar]y position in order to obtain better terms for their confraternity, has an ugly aspect. It may be conscientious, but it may not be. It were wiser, I think, to leave the matter to the Minister for War; or, at least, to civilians having no interest.

Tuesday, 17 March: A smart little debate, with good attendance, on Forster's motion for a committee on the game laws. We were defeated by 19 votes.[44] Of course, I voted with Forster [...] It is noteworthy that, when Sir Geo. Grey[45] was speaking, the House was very impatient & repeated cries of 'divide' occurred. It is high time to introduce new blood into the Whig party. Grey is worn out, like Whiggism itself. There is little or nothing manly & progressive above the gangway. Nearly all action is with the advanced liberals. Soon the Tories will be in office, & then people will be ranged under their legitimate distinctions. [...] A full house shewed how much the country gentlemen care about the preservation of game.

Thursday, 19 March: The Chancellor of the E[xchequer] appealed to Ayrton to raise his objections to the Tobacco Bill[46] in Committee rather than before going into Committee. Ayrton declined, & the tone of his speech was rather bitter. Nor can one wonder. The Chancellor had used his powerful tongue, not long before, in endeavouring to heap ridicule on Ayrton in a manner by no means deserved. Ayrton, if not very popular, is a very painstaking person, & he has decidedly mended his manner in the House. He may not always adopt prudent courses; but the House, if he shd. leave it, would lose a man, who

[43] Bartellot's motion against stoppages from the pay of cavalry and artillery officers for forage, defeated 107:75.
[44] 176:157.
[45] Home secretary.
[46] Ayrton represented the interests of British cigar makers, concerned by the revised duties on tobacco and snuff; *H* clxix. 1611–16.

has, by perseverence, become signally useful. We beat Ayrton on a division,[47] as the Chancellor was right, I believe, on the merits [...]

Friday, 20 March: [...] Baxter moved agt. the grant of £70,000 towards the Galway packet line in a remarkably able speech. In parts he was very amusing. Shame it is to record that he was defeated by a large majority![48] I was among the pairs, being paired with Col[onel] Davie. Palmerston atempted to defend this gross job, but I am much mistaken if the National conscience has become degraded to the point of acquiescing in his self-acquittal. The Derbyites, first, perpetrated the act of turpitude in order to buy the Irish members.[49] The delinquents were found out & stigmatized. Still there was a danger lest, if the present ministers failed to carry out the proceeding, their foes would still enjoy some favour with the corrupted party. So Palmerston has courageously hedged – he sacrificing character & the Public being required to find cash for the transaction. The case reminds me of Parliamentary govt. in the days of Walpole; or, as Baxter put it, in the lobbies at Washington.

Disraeli's countenance was a study. He kept his hat well over his eyes * D. generally sits with his hat off * & looked gloomy & ill at ease. The fact is the story told by Baxter was very injurious to the Conservatives, & Bentinck was wise in steering clear of all complicity with the business. Brand's face of delight, while Baxter was dissecting the Derbyites, was a curious contrast to Disraeli's. I looked at each & studied their thoughts. Brand stood alone near the door; Disraeli sat on the Treasury Bench [...]

The Church Rate question looms. It is a real puzzle to me what line shd. be taken on the 2d. reading. How can I make a speech which will not be chargeable with 'damnable iteration'? Sometimes it occurs to me to move the 2d. reading without a speech. That would not satisfy dissenters; or, perhaps, our failure on a division might be ascribed to my neglect to submit the merits of our case. Former statements are long since forgotten.

There is a fertile theme in the incompatible prescriptions of the rival doctors who have come in as amateurs. * The different schemes put together would make something like a harlequins jacket. * Newdegate's bill would raise disturbance all over England. Exemption of dissenters in any form hitherto tendered would be no boon.

The present mode of raising funds to repair fabrics is directly at variance with the genius of Protestantism. Nothing can be more

---

[47] 170:87 against referring the bill to a select committee; Royal assent, 27 Mar.
[48] 109:46.
[49] See above, 9 Aug. 1860.

clumsy. It offers a minimum of results in return for a maximum of irritation. Church Rates are the mosquitoes of the Church of England – always teazing & inflaming.

If Church Rates are as old as the Common Law & grew up with it, can this be said of Protestantism? The right of private judgment is a part of its essence, & that right does not exist in perfection while any compulsory charge is enforced upon dissenters from the establishment [...]

Monday, 23 March: [...] Trelawny wanted explanations of the recent departures from the rule that officers of the Staff shd. only hold their appointments for 5 years unless such officers are reappointed. Brisk debate. C[ornewall] Lewis hardly defended his tolerance of such departures – in the case of the Field Marshall com[mandin]g in chief, the adj[utan]t gen[era]l & Quarterm[aste]r gen[era]l. Lewis is very superficially informed on military matters. So some of us begin to think. He is industrious & good tempered, & takes censure patiently. But really he is not apt enough for sudden attack & defence of estimates in detail. He is like a 300 pounder in a bog surrounded by sharpshooters who lie concealed in a woody country. There he sticks, every one plying him with small arms; killing his men & horses. Palmerston wants more skirmishers.

Two divisions on (1) flogging & (2) branding under the Marine Mutiny Act. T[relawny] in minorities[50] [...] An unusual thing chanced which almost made me for a time rather uncomfortable. While members were engaged in going to the lobbies on one division, the attendant, thro' an error of mine or his, directed me into the wrong lobby & I found the glass door, near the radical end of the liberal benches, shut. What could I do? If I remained, I, an old member, would have occasioned a scene & a Public correction of the lists. So to avoid this I commenced knocking at the glass, when, luckily, the man who had locked me out returned on seeing me & I got back into the house. The next question was, how shall I get told in the right lobby, it being apparently too late to file in in the regular way? So I bethought myself to try what a little force would do, the situation being urgent. I met the stream coming in from the lobby entrance (behind the Speaker's chair), where I found Brand telling; &, no one opposing, I got into the place, where the 2 clerks check the names of voters – & there got marked & then returning to the door got, also, told. Strictly speaking, I suspect I committed – & several others each committed – a breach of privilege. Suppose many persons could thus vote, would there not be a means of falsifying a division?

[50] 86:31 for corporal punishment, and 97:22 for marking deserters.

I trust I may hear no more of the matter; but I may. The Speaker is rather fussy sometimes. It is to be hoped he will not rate me at his dinner tomorrow.

Lord Enfield wished to know, privately inquiring, whether, on our possible defeat on Ch. Rates, I would be disposed to support him in moving Lord Ebury's Bill, wh. would abolish the compulsory part of Ch. Rate Law.[51] I asked for time to consider. Subsequently I threw out, without any agreement, that it might be a subject of doubt whether it were not better that he shd. move his bill first & let me keep my bill in reserve so as to have lines to fall back upon. Sir G. Grey[52] had instructed him to ask. I took care to remain unpledged – except to consider & consult. Were I to say now that I would support E[nfield], many half-hearted persons would desert me. The knowledge of my readiness to take a less bid would be sure to leak out thro' my own friends in council [...]

Tuesday, 24 March: Hubbard moved a resolution for amendmt. of the Income tax & alteration of its incidence. He proposes to charge net Income wh. he does not define, & he further desires that 'the net amounts of Industrial earnings shd, previous to assessment, be subject to such an abatement as may equitably adjust the burthen thrown upon intelligence & skill as compared with property'. what next? – and next?

He was defeated, tho' he took some 70 votes[53] [...] The worst of Hubbard's motion is its tendency to excite illusory hopes & uselessly disturb minds [...]

Wednesday, 25 March: [...] Some Tavistock people appear to be annoyed at my vote agt. the 1st. reading of the Sabbath Bill.[54] Such a bill would very likely produce riots. How curious it seems that one generally reaps most censure for one's most disinterested or most virtuous conduct. I knew that I need not have voted on the 1st. reading, or that I might have voted in the majority without being committed to the Bill. But, deeming it to be right to preach the truth by an open & downright opposition, I recorded my name with the minority [...]

Thursday, 26 March: [...] It seems to me that Ministers underwent

---

[51] Ebury never introduced his own bill in the Lords.
[52] Home secretary.
[53] 118:70.
[54] Somes's bill to close public houses on Sundays; 1st reading carried by 141:52 on 17 Mar.

some rather damaging criticism during the lengthened debate in committee of supply. Henley dealt them some heavy blows, the liberals backing him – & Cornewall Lewis could do no better than admit the force of complaints made of the novelty &, 'perhaps', 'inconvenience', of the mode of proceeding adopted by Ministers – wh. I take it consisted in obtaining money on a/c in one part of an ev[enin]g & then at a later hour asking for the main vote leaving the House in ignorance of the course intended.[55] Lord Palmerston's life is a very valuable one, but I doubt if, in order to keep him in office, we do not pay too dearly in allowing all sorts of abuses to creep in.

[...] There was an evident attempt to prevent a division on Dodson's motion.[56] When it was put, Augustus Smith & I took care to cry out 'No' very loudly, & I think Dodson was silent. Yet, he told me he intended to divide. There are several of us who are resolved to allow of no sham motions.

Friday, 27 March: Many questions arose either upon adjournment till the 13th Ap[ril] or before report on supply.

The seizure of the Peterhoff[57] by the Americans was one. Forster of Bradford tried to prove that Ministers had not dealt fairly with the Northern Americans in the matter of the fitting out of the Alabama,[58] & called forth a splendid speech from the solicitor-general,[59] who triumphantly sustained the conduct of the Govt. Palmerston very cleverly met Forster, & I may add Bright, who, I heard, was very warm in his tone. Altogether the N. Americans took little advantage from the discussion. It appears that they have received a large amount of arms & supplies from England. Laird added good reasons for believing this [...]

Dr. Foster brought me a letter on Church Rate matters[60] containing the substance of the reply to be made to the overture I lately received thro' Lord Enfield from Sir Geo. Grey. I shewed the letter to Brand & Lord E[nfield]. All agreed that it was as favourable as we could have expected. The first thing to be done is to get a victory on the

[55] The complaint was that the House was being asked to agree to vote the balance of the money when the former vote on account had not been reported, so that there was nothing to show what the second vote related to; *H* clxix. 1967–70.

[56] That all expenses of the diplomatic service should be voted annually, and that estimates should be submitted to parliament so as to permit of effective supervision; *H* clxix. 1936–8. Defeated 136:65.

[57] A British trading vessel, suspected by the federals of trying to beat the blockade of the confederate ports.

[58] A warship built at Birkenhead and supplied to the confederates before an order by the British government for its seizure had been carried out.

[59] Sir Roundell Palmer.

[60] Not recorded in the minute books of the Liberation Society.

29th of Ap[ril]. Lord Ebury's plan seems now to have a fair chance of success. The House was counted out – & we stand adjourned to the 13th of Ap[ril]. Palmerston's holiday is to be spent in making speeches at dinners in Scotland. Fine old fellow! What a slave to his duty! & how he shames our Spanish aristocracy & political aztecs! [...]

Monday, 13 April: [...] Estimates occupied the House this evening. I took the opportunity of the motion that the Speaker leave the chair to mention a recent mutiny at Sandhurst which it is said arose out of an impolitic restraint of the liberty of cadets & a departure from good faith in a new rule relating to the granting of commissions. No reply, as the Secretary for War was absent. Two packets of anonymous letters have reached me upon this subject, and their contents appear to be in substance identical. It is said that cadets were required to parade during the fall of the year for one hour (from 4 to 5 p.m.) after 8 hours of study[61] [...]

Tuesday, 14 April: So poor Cornewall Lewis is dead! he is a great loss. Well may the Times writer say he did the work of 20 men.[62] He appeared to me greater in his books[63] than in his capacity as a minister. Perhaps, my acquaintance with him as an author was the cause of my expecting very much of him. It has struck me that Horsman may become a member of the Cabinet[64] [...]

Wednesday, 15 April: Sir M. Peto moved his burials bill, wh. wd. have given to dissenters, under certain conditions, the right of being buried in parish Ch[urch]yards according to their own forms. In certain cases at least the consent of Ministers would have been required, a fruitful source of litigation & heartburning. Every exercise of the clergyman's discretion would be misconstrued. Some sects would use forms of prayer & ceremonies wh. might create serious offence & perhaps produce breach of the peace. Catholic ceremonies, for example. A right to one sect, dependent upon a discretional act of the minister of another, is not a very comfortable idea. It seemed to me that the arguments of Lord Robert Cecil & Newdegate were very forcible. Gladstone went, under some qualifications, with Peto. Upon the whole, I thought that it would compromise my leadership in the

---

[61] Trelawny did not raise the matter again.

[62] 15 Apr. 1863, p. 8.

[63] E.g. *An essay on the influence of authority in matters of opinion*, (1849), and *A treatise on the methods of observation and reasoning in politics*, (1852).

[64] He did not. Earl de Grey and Ripon became the new secretary for war.

Ch. Rate battle, if I shd. vote with Peto. Our contention is that dissenters consider that they derive no good from the ministrations of the Church; & that, therefore, they ought not to be subject to Ch. Rates. But if they derive even one undoubted benefit, shd. they not pro rata contribute towards its cost? I spoke shortly in this sense, merely to prevent misconstruction. Several members on both sides thought that my course was logical. We won by an immense majority.[65] A few Radicals were with us – Roebuck agt. us.

Thursday, 16 April: I went down to hear the Chancellor of the Ex[chequer] who introduced the budget. He appeared to be in less force than usual & far more frequently referred to M.S. matter.

He lately had a severe fall, of wh. he bore a mark on his countenance in the shape of a black patch on the nose between the eyes. He looked ghastly, & repeatedly had recourse to some stimulus, of wh. he had 2 pretty little dressing case bottles in his despatch box; each bottle having, apparently, a burnished silver cover. He was very deft in getting a drink, waiting for a moment when he had established pleasure or surprize in his audience. So it seemed to me. His budget upon the whole was well received.[66] Once or twice, his audience were on the point of demurring to some ingenious detail; but, in this hesitation to go with him, he revelled the more, as he had raised interest & rewarded it by further explanation, wh. brought with it conviction. [...] Ch. Rates. I think I must earnestly appeal to members to forget party differences & honestly endeavour to do a good & memorable deed for the benefit of the Church & that large number of the English people who use, & on the whole are contented with, her ministrations. The notion that the separation of Church & State is the point really levelled at is a complete delusion, so far as I am concerned. Hon[oura]ble members shd. allow one at least one privilege of longevity, viz, that of learning somewhat of the merits of questions really difficult but seeming easy at first. Such is the question of Church establishments. That wh. is commonly called connection of Ch. & State is in truth subjection of a great corporation to the civil power. I should be very disinclined to relinquish our hold on those who are recipients of the income accuring from Ch. property. Yet, undoubtedly I desire great changes – such as the abolition of many anomalies & incrustations upon the Xtian system as it existed in

---

[65] 221:96 against the 2nd reading.

[66] Gladstone reduced the income tax by 2d., with additional relief for those earning between £100 and £200 per annum, and reduced the duty on tea to 1s. per lb. He also proposed to reform the system of licences for the sale of wine and spirits, and to withdraw the exemption from income tax of corporate trust property and charitable endowments; H clxx. 200–51. These latter proposals were subsequently dropped.

Apostolic times; &, in particular, the emancipation of the clergy themselves from many disagreeable subscriptions by no means vital to their usefulness as a class. It seems to me that the terms of joining the Church shd. be made as broad & easy as possible. The true bond of communion shd. be community of desires, & adhesion to the same canons of right. Desire is prayer, & prayer, if not a kind of blasphemy, is desire. No difference however wide ought to exclude a man from our Church, if he concur as to the objects to be desired, & the sins to be surrendered. It shd. be the pride of the Church to be so gentle & tolerant as to evoke one's inmost thoughts without the sentiment of fear, wh. is the parent of lies.

Friday, 17 April: [...] The Church Rates question obtrudes itself continually on my mind. Have I anything worthy of the attention of the House of Commons? [...] Certain Parl[iamentary]y reports & papers will be very useful e.g. the recent report of the Ecclesiastical Com[missione]rs & the Episcopal & Capitular estates com-[missione]rs exhibiting the valuable results wh. are indirectly due to Church Rate agitation, for it was John Thorogood who first made Ch. Rates notorious[67] & caused the casting about to find available funds within the Ch. in lieu of these payments. Every move of the dissenters has done service to the Ch [...]

Monday, 20 April: Illness prevented my attendance this day & I fear I shall not be able to do much for some time as gout generally attacks me in Spring [...]

Tuesday, 21 April: There are curious things noticeable in the division list relating to chaplains for Catholic prisoners. Dissenting liberals are to be found pretty equally balanced on either side.[68]

The business of this day involved nothing very noteworthy. The political world seems to be dead – intending resurrection after Palmerston's death, whenever that event may come – & may it be very distant! Not that his influence is entirely good. But we may go further & fare worse. In politics, too, it is far from easy to discern even part of the results of a change, however small. Now his death would be a fact of magnitude [...]

---

[67] The Chelmsford shoemaker imprisoned in Jan. 1839 for refusing to pay the rate.
[68] 2nd reading of the Prison ministers bill, passed by 152:122 on 20 Apr. *The Times*, 22 Apr. 1863, p. 7, noted that the bill had been supported by such dissenters as Edward Baines and George Hadfield, but opposed by J.R. Mills and Sir Morton Peto, as well as by most of the Scottish members.

Thursday, 23 April: [...] A long interview with Sir C. Douglas, who has been in communication with Brand, Enfield & Dr. Foster with reference to the Ch. Rates Bill. It appears that Sir Geo. Grey cannot offer ministerial support to Lord Ebury's plan. In short, the sort of hopes we had founded on some of the overtures made to me at various times are evidently illusory. I told Douglas that I thought the time was come for a new move; – viz, a resolution affirming that her Majesty's advisers ought to deal with the subject; wh. resolution, skilfully framed, would probably be carried. He has gone to bring Dr. F. to a meeting with me at the H. of C. this evening. I think that the management of the cause shd. now be transferred to other hands. The Burials Bill has greatly altered my position for the worse. The Dissenters are grasping and not wise in their tactics. Ministers do not with to settle Ch. Rates. The Irish Catholics are, probably, not very anxious to co-operate with our Low Church people or dissenting bodies. The Question of separation of Ch. & State was, always, imprudently mixed up with my measure, & the whole case in my conduct is now brim-full of difficulties.

[...] Sir C. Douglas & others say that Newdegate's late speech on Disraeli's church policy & principles was equally severe & effective. Quite eloquent at times – & very earnest – he seems to have made Disraeli wince. Is Newdegate the nemesis, raised by Peel's ghost, to take revenge for Disraeli's attacks? This, if so, were odd, indeed. The speech referred to was delivered on the bill relating to R. Catholic chaplains in prisons.[69]

[...] the £50,000 grant towards a memorial to the late Prince Consort. It was futile to oppose this folly of the Queen's at the cost of the Nation. I felt quite certain that Ministers had an understanding with the opposition on the subject. Today it appears that Disraeli was at Windsor just before the vote,[70] & he complimented Ministers thereupon. * Note. I do not mean to insinuate that Disraeli was influenced by the invitation. Rather that he had an opportunity of judging of the state of Her Majesty's mind. I have no doubt he acted honestly. The truth is, Ministers & ex-ministers are equally nervous about the Queen's health. So I gather * [...]

Friday, 24 April: Very serious words were uttered by different members on the subject of our differences with America. I sadly fear that we shall have war. Horsman, Cobden, Horsfall, the Solicitor

[69] 20 Apr. 1863, *H* clxx. 436–43. Disraeli had spoken in favour of the bill, denying that it posed any danger to the position of the Established church: ibid, cols 429–34.
[70] For the significance of Disraeli's visit, see Monypenny and Buckle, *Disraeli*, ii. 119–27.

general,[71] Collier, Cairns & many others were speakers – chiefly, on Maritime Law. The American question completely divides political parties. No man knows, as of yore, with whom he sympathizes.

At an interview with Dr. Foster & Sir C. Douglas it was finally agreed that the Church Rates battle will be fought on Wednesday. The plan of throwing responsibility on Ministers, as a screw upon Gladstone's section, is not approved of. Miall[72] thinks that Govt. might fasten on the Country an injurious or unsatisfactory measure.

Members tried to prevent further applications for grants of Parliament in aid of her Majesty's designs for a memorial to her late Consort. It is reasonably feared that this will be a permanent source of cost to the Nation. The Queen's taste seems to be quite Barbaric & oriental. It is believed by many that her grief has eccentricities – which may raise serious anxieties for her future health & happiness.

Monday, 27 April: [...] If Gladstone have one quality more predominant than another, I should say it is a pedantic regard for symmetrical thought. A want of coherence between different portions of an argument would usually be as painful to him as a false note in music. How can he defend his position on Ch. Rates after proclaiming loudly his entire adherence to the doctrine of equality of religious opinions as before the law? Read hereon his late speech on Hadfield's Qualifications for office bill.[73]

[...] Disraeli has taken the Church of England into his care.[74] But not *all* the Church party are satisfied. Newdegate seems to be unhappy.

When the House met, it was announced to me that Lord Alfred Churchill was going to give notice of an amendment in Committee to my bill – such amendment embodying, in effect, Lord Ebury's plan.[75] This notice will, probably, determine a few waverers to vote with me. It was arranged with Col[onel] Taylor[76] that the division on next Wed[nesda]y shall not take place till 5 pm; so that persons, who are bound to go up with deputations to the Prince & Princess,[77] may be able to attend & vote. I got together some of my materials for the fight, wh. will be a grand one. A knightly courtesy prevails.

Douglas cannot give me very sanguine hopes of winning. We may lose & can hardly win by more than a very bare majority [...]

---

[71] Sir Roundell Palmer.
[72] Edward Miall, editor of the *Nonconformist* and a prominent member of the Liberation society.
[73] See above, 4 Mar. 1863.
[74] Cf. Monypenny and Buckle, *Disraeli*, ii, 83–114.
[75] Abolishing the compulsory power to levy church rates.
[76] Conservative chief whip.
[77] Of Wales.

Tuesday, 28 April: Gen[era]l Lindsay moved on behalf of certain distinguished service Colonels affected in precedency by changes in the system of promotion. It was clear that Govt. would not be able to sustain itself agt. him, tho' the Marquis of Hartington[78] contended that the case put forward was not well founded, so Palmerston (amid laughter) offered to appoint a Commission to inquire into the matter, whereon Lindsay withdrew – a victor! He is pro tanto Minister for war. If he was right, why did Govt. oppose him? If wrong, why did Govt. give way? There is no minister for the Public at large. We are governed by interests – & the military interest is very powerful & closely allied to the governing families [...]

Wednesday, 29 April: [...] 6 $\frac{3}{4}$ pm. I attended & brought on my bill[79] in a speech of 40 minutes, rambling enough & not well arranged. In some respects it went pretty well – at least, the thin House kindly received it. Hardy was good in reply & spoke fluently for about one hour & 10 minutes. Mitford seconded him. Hastings Russell seconded me.

[...] Hardy was very civil to me – he is a pleasant foe, &, by the way, how fortunate I am in my foes who lead! Nearly all have been respectable & able men – I speak of past motions.

My brief reply was heard good naturedly enough. I fear that we lost some men thro' dividing[80] a little too soon, as 5 was to be our earliest hour. I did as much as would have been permitted to me in order to gain time. But a speech in a full House in reply must be a succession of tersely-put points, or must cease, on pain of one's being deemed too great a bore to be endured [...]

Thursday, 30 April: [...] Sir C Douglas & I discussed our defeat & its causes. The Tories worked with a will & brought up within one every man they counted upon. Never was better management.[81] Perhaps, had I talked agt. time for a few minutes more, I shd. have got one more vote – that of Maguire. But really the House heard more than I had a right to expect in hearing me for a few minutes in so large an attendance. I have said to many persons that I now retire from the conduct of the question. This for many reasons. Wear & tear of mind & body compel me to take this course. I must lighten the

---

[78] Recently appointed under-secretary for war.
[79] Church rates abolition, 2nd reading.
[80] 285:275 against the bill.
[81] The Conservative whip claimed that 'We got Eleven from the other side': T.E. Taylor to Sotheron-Estcourt, 30 Apr. [1863], Sotheron-Estcourt MSS, D1571/F367. Disraeli was informed that ten Catholic M.P.s, formerly supporters of the bill, had deliberately abstained; Monypenny and Buckle, *Disraeli*, ii, 100 and n.

ship. My private affairs begin to give me anxiety enough. I have proclaimed my opinions such as they are, & they have not found enough favour. Whether I have been in the right, or those whom I have addressed, remains to be seen.

[...] There was a division on Collins' bill for uniformity of measurement of boundaries of boroughs.[82] The measure, at first, appeared to be worthy of support as tending to extend the suffrage. On conversation with tried liberals, I found that the probable object of the bill was to bring territorial influence to bear on householders in towns. Country voters would mostly be under pressure of local landlords or their agents. Why shd. not ground to be newly included in boroughs remain under its present system of county representation & be contented therewith. It seems to me to be a case of suspicious meddling. Colins was defeated[83] – I had paired with the Hon. W. Addington all night [...]

Friday, 1 May: No house. Some newspapers have an analysis of the Ch. Rates division. There were 285 to 275. Absent liberals 46. Do Tories 10. Pairs 17. Vacant 1. Speaker 1. Tellers 4. Total 656. It appears that 18 liberals voted agt. me & 5 Tories for me.

Speeches in reply, in a full impatient House, just before division & on Wednesdays, get scant notice, unless the speaker possesses a high reputation. Thus it happens that scarcely a line of report is ever given of what I say in reply to speeches agt. my bills [...]

A man of colour, Thomas Arthur by name, went with his English wife to attend service at St. Peter's Ch[urch] in Eaton Sq. The woman in attendance refused to let him have a seat altho' the woman in his company stated that the black man was her husband; so both went out, but, trying another door, got seats. A Mr. Baldock noticed that which occurred & all attended in the vestry & complained to Mr. Fuller, the Minister, who asked the doorkeeper or verger why she did not give the people places? She replied, because she took the man for the white lady's black servant. Mr. Fuller, thereupon, told her not to refuse a seat in such a case in future. Thomas Arthur at my advice sent a petition to Parliament complaining of the grievance & praying for redress. * I advised him to send it to his representatives, but he preferred to intrust it to me.[84] * Before I presented it, I called on Mr. Fuller, who, in substance, corroborated Arthur's account. But Mr. F.

---

[82] The great reform act allowed freemen to vote provided they lived within seven miles of the borough, but various methods were used of measuring this distance, so that certain freemen were disfranchised.

[83] 182:139 against entering into committee.

[84] Presented on 29 Apr; *The Times*, 30 Apr. 1863, p. 8.

said that he had reprimanded the verger, now this Arthur will not admit. Mr. Fuller has written to the 'Times' & gives his version of what happened.[85] It struck me that the feelings of the white woman especially deserved consideration, for it must have greatly annoyed her to find that her husband was subjected to indignity. T. Arthur strikes me as a very intelligent & respectable person.

Monday, 4 May: [...] Gladstone's eloquent defence of the part of the budget which applies Income tax to charities. Much discussion. Sir Stafford Northcote is very favourably mentioned on account of his performance. Gladstone was compelled to give way. Very powerful corporations opposed him with great vigour & nearly with unanimity. So I gather.[86]

I paired with Sir W. Verner & got a quiet night. It seems to me that members who attended in their places must have lived a week in one night, such was the excitement.

I saw Dr. Foster & told him that I resigned my conduct of Church Rates matters. My reasons are numerous. At the same time, I said that I would render such aid as I could in the ranks, & would assist him with my counsel if consulted. Yesterday, I observed to Mr. Hardy that he had just put an extinguisher on me. The truth is the Church Rates difficulty shd. be dealt with by a government upon an understanding with the opposition. It will not suit me to be the annual exponent of an impossibility. Parliament, in both Houses, has decreed agt. me. Time will shew who is right. There will be many a bitter fight in the Vestries, & the clergy will be constantly in hot water, which Hardy says they rather like.

Tuesday, 5 May: I was unfortunate this day in losing a division on one of Walter's education resolutions – that other than certificated masters shd. receive grants from the State.[87] I should have followed Lowe agt. Walter – the Public ought to have all due certainty that its large contribution towards education shd. go to properly-selected persons. It leaked out that Walter would, in some instances, leave the selection of shoolmasters to the discretion of clergymen. Why, in this way the schoolmaster would be merely a subpriest of the Anglican Church!

[85] Ibid, 1 May 1863, p. 6.
[86] Earlier that day Gladstone had received a deputation led by the Duke of Cambridge and the archbishops of Canterbury and York, and including many other clergymen, M.P.s and private individuals. *The Times*, 5 May 1863, p. 10, observed that it was 'one of the most influential deputations, and certainly one of the most numerous', that had ever attended upon a minister.
[87] *H* clxx. 1227; defeated, 152:117.

[...] Bulwer is a curiosity. He arrays himself as he might have done in order to walk in Bond St. in the time of George 4th's youth. His appearance is very singular. Last night he listened, with one hand to his right ear, to Walter's very tedious speech & lengthy quotations on the Education question – & then went away. As he departed, someone asked him if the debate would go on long. He replied that he did not know, but a good many persons in the House seemed to want education. Of course, I only give roughly what I can remember, but somewhat in this way his questioner reported what passed, whereat we both laughed.

Gladstone's speech on Monday night on taxing charities was a grand effort. Brand says that it turned 25 men. This speaks volumes. I am glad I paired for him before the speech. Gladstone's argum[en]t is that, if men at their death (say) be allowed to tie up property capriciously and often to the injury of relatives, there is no reason why such property shd. not pay something towards its protection. Many great Corporations have derived advantage from measures lowering duties on commodities. It were but fair that these bodies shd. pay Income tax. If all charitable gifts were wise & benevolent, it wd. be proper to exempt them from taxation. But exemption is, after all, in principle aid from the State. Now we know what objection many members have to the Maynooth grant [...]

Thursday, 7 May: [...] a brisk debate was on foot, which was well sustained, on the Prison Ministers bill[88] – several Tories opposing [...] I paired with Lord Bective for the night [...] We are, apparently, on the eve of great changes in the positions of various religious communities. If it be right to pay Catholic chaplains in Gaols on the ground that, otherwise, prisoners would want religious advice & consolation, why should it not be right to pay Irish priests for ministering to Irish poor in Liverpool? The cases are not exactly parallel, perhaps, because prisoners are under duress & cannot pay for ghostly aid. But the want of it exists in either – & Henley says we shd. do 'as we would be done by' – wh. Pakington echoes. I heard Kendall make a slipshod speech, wh. excited laughter from its obsolete bigotry. 'The Times' says the bill is the thin end of the wedge[89] – & so it is. Yet there is no help for it. H[er] M[ajesty] has a large number of R. Catholic subjects – & many are in the Army & Navy. We profess to govern on constitutional principles – self-taxation, freedom of worship & other such phrases are household words. How can we ask R. Catholics for money for Protestant chaplains & refuse to allow money

[88] 172:141 in favour of going into committee.
[89] *The Times*, 8 May 1863, p. 8.

for R Catholic? I fear on these & many questions we are at sea for leading principles. 'Hand to mouth' govt. is the regime under wh. we live.

Morritt made a straight-forward speech in favour of the bill – his debut. Disraeli was delighted – & looked round to cheer him with more effect. D. is a little unpopular just now with his own extreme men such as Bentinck, Palk, Kendall & Newdegate. A. Morritt to the rescue was, therefore, welcome [...]

Friday, 8 May: [...] One of the officials about the House + The doorkeeper, Mr. White + mentioned to me that on Thursday Disraeli was rather roundly taken to task by the dissenting radicals Peto, White & such for using religious questions as means of political aggrandisement. Disraeli has a happy time of it betwn. his own extreme men & ours. The state of affairs must greatly delight the Whig party [...]

Tuesday, 12 May: Soon after my arrival at the House, Mr. Pope Hennessy put interrogatories to Viscount Palmerston on the subject of a certain despatch from Mr. Odo Russell,[90] who has had some sort of awkwardness with the Count of Montebello[91] with reference to certain Italian bandits clothed in worn-out French uniforms & allowed to escape across the Papal frontier into the realm of Sardinia. This despatch has not been published; Lord P., instead of giving a direct reply, descanted on the occupation of Rome by 20,000 French troops, who were really governing & were, therefore, responsible for the escape of the bandits. His lordship roundly described the Pope as 'the puppet' of the French govt. & made a very bold speech; of wh., it may be, we may hear more.

Lord John Manners, rather self-sufficiently, reiterated Hennessy's complaint that his question was not answered, speaking in a somewhat indignant tone of remonstrance, whereon Lord P. again rose &, with a few abrupt & nonchalent words – as if he had been answering about the weather – said he would look into the despatch & see whether there was anything in it to prevent its being displayed on the table (great laughter).

Then we had Roebuck's motion for papers on the dismissal of two judges * Sir Geo. Marcoras & Sir Typaldo Xydras * in Corfu for no other known reason than the expiration of the period for which judges usually serve in those Islands, tho' dismissal, under such circumstances, would ordinarily be held to be an injustice. R. brought their

[90] British ambassador in Rome.
[91] Commander of the French garrison in Rome.

complaint forward in a very pointed speech of 20 minutes.[92] He said some very good & clever things; but his description of Gen[era]l Sir H. Storks[93] as a rough 'ill-conditioned soldier' was disapproved of by a majority. So were some witty invectives agt. the Duke of Newcastle.[94] * R. said that in this country great men are picked up by chance. In another part of his speech, in allusion to the D. of N., he said that experience makes wise men wiser, but it never makes a fool a wise man. Several pleasantries of this sort were dotted about his speech, which, if somewhat rough, had some genuine metal in it. * His ridicule of Gladstone, on account of his proceedings at Corfu,[95] was permissible enough & not objected to. Gen[era]l Peel spoke favourably of Storks. Lord Stanley answered Chichester Fortescue;[96] who, by the way, met Roebuck's case in a speech of 40 minutes – good in parts & pungently dealing with Roebuck's taunts, but strangely evading the merits of the case. * Fortescue proved that the right to dismiss judges was a legal right, the question of justice he did not touch. * A few others spoke. Then I left, as the papers were granted.

Stanley's speech was excellent. The fact is the case is a very bad one. The dismissal of blameless judges, who have served well for very many years, is no light matter.

The confidence & fluency of Hennessy[97] are astonishing. He looks but a boy, yet speaks as if he had been a debater of 30 years standing. He is a slight dark man, with jet black hair, bright intelligent eyes, & a remarkably short nose, as if an inch of it had been cut off. He puts all his points with great clearness & in irreproachable English, barring brogue. He has, I think, one or two words which he pronounces in a manner quite his own; these I forget at the moment. Pope H[ennessy] is a great hero among Poles, & recently received quite an ovation at Cracow. Truly the H. of C. is an allsided body. It is not the Parliament of England merely. It is the Parliament of the world [. . .]

Wednesday, 13 May: Roebuck is today the general theme. The sympathy of the upper classes is generally with Storks. For my part, I forgive a great deal to a man who speaks so much bold truth as R. has spoken on this occasion [. . .]

---

[92] Arguing that the judges were being punished for their opposition to the proposed cession of the Ionian islands to Greece; *H* clxx. 1586–90, 1609–10.

[93] Lord high commissioner in the Ionian islands.

[94] Colonial secretary.

[95] He had been Lord High Commissioner Extraordinary for the Ionian islands, Nov. 1858 to Mar. 1859, but his plans for constitutional reform had been rejected by the Ionian assembly; *Gladstone Diaries*, V, lxix–lxx.

[96] Colonial under-secretary.

[97] Trelawny is reverting to the debate on Italy.

Friday, 15 May: [...] Many topics on the motion for supply. Govt. was vehemently reproached for not replying to the speeches of members who moved resolutions – quite a scene, for a part of wh. I arrived in time! [...] The truth is Palmerston is dictator by general consent. In the above case the excuse of Layard[98] was that, if he had attempted to reply to each speech on an amendment, he would have been out of order. This was described by Seymour Fitzgerald as a misconception. As I understood him, he said that each particular speaker might have been dealt with, & then a speech might have been made on the main question – that the Speaker leave the chair. In my opinion, Ministers feel themselves strong enough to do what, if they were in opposition, they would not let their opponents do.

Monday, 18 May: [...] The Catholic Ministers Bill came under debate – & we divided on Black's amendment, when govt. won by 29 votes[99] [...] the danger was of the effect of an union of votes of Scotch members and of the bulk of the independent Tory party. Those of the Tory leaders, who foresee difficulties in office, vote in several instances for Catholic chaplains.

Tuesday, 19 May: A multitude of minor debates arose, mostly on the question of adjournment over Whitsuntide, before Dillwyn could come on with his Irish Church motion.[100] He began at $\frac{1}{4}$ past 8, & spoke for 2 hours nearly. His manner is wholly devoid of art or method. He repeats himself frequently, & uses colloquialisms too familiarly. Also, his speech was just by one half too long. Yet, with all these faults he had a fair hearing upon the whole, altho' at moments the House could not quite endure his indiscreet announcement of more matter for perusal. I was his seconder, & work enough I had to keep him well on his legs. Osborne's asides were very frequent, & not undiverting. O. is very friendly to Dillwyn's cause in principle, tho' O. has an amendment from his point of view[101] but he could not bear the delay wh. destroyed his chance of speaking. When Dillwyn talked of others following, 'yes', but said O, 'you leave us no time' (a laugh). This hint produced little fruit, though it was heard all over the House. Dillwyn, arguing that the alleged compact at the Union, tho' a bar, perhaps, to dealing with the Status of the Irish Ch[urch], was no bar to dealing with its temporalities, with wh., indeed, we had been

---

[98] Foreign under-secretary.
[99] I.e. 3rd reading of the Prison Ministers bill passed, 196:167. Royal assent, 28 July. *P.P.* 1863, iii. 535.
[100] For a select committee to inquire into the present distribution of religious endowments in Ireland; *H* clxx. 1988.
[101] He brought forward his own motion on 26 June.

dealing. O. exclaimed, that we had not only been dealing but shuffling. Dillwyn hit the Whigs very hard on account of their course in upsetting Peel on appropriation[102] & then being contented to hold office without fulfilling the compact by wh. they got it. I observed that newly instead of appropriating the revenues of the Irish Church, the Whigs had appropriated to themselves the salaries of office.

Whiteside was unusually merry & triumphant. Dillwyn's promise of an early return to office to the Tories, put W. in high feather, & his jests at Dillwyn's expense made even the victim share in the general merriment. As to W's logic, the less said the better for him. The gist of the case, & the difficulty of the future were left to that future [...] Eventually, the debate was adjourned.

Thursday, 28 May: We resumed & were soon in full cry on Walpole's motion with reference to the vote, on the report of supply, on the Dover contract with Churchward,[103] charged by a Committee of the House of Commons with having resorted to 'corrupt expedients' in order to the obtaining such contract. A former contract held by C. would have expired in June 1863. Before it expired, the Tories at the admiralty in 1859 corruptly gave him a new one to date from 1863 to 1870, but it was conditional on a vote of Parliament. The Committee reported in due form. Capt[ain] L. Vernon moved that the contract shd. be fulfilled, & was beaten by 45 votes.[104] The Whigs therefore & their party decline to ask for more money for C. than necessary to pay him in respect of the contract end[in]g in June 1863 – & the limitation accordingly appears on the face of proceedings – that is, of £250,000 wanted on a/c for various kindred purposes, it is expressed that no part shall go to Mr. C. except in respect of the uncondemned contract. Walpole moves to omit the limiting words as, in effect, unconstitutional, since the limitation am[oun]ts to a tack; & the Lords may reject a vote with a tack. W. assumes that the limitation will appear in the appropriation act; &, generally, contends that the course of government is unconstitutional & trenches upon the privileges of the Lords, who, altho' they cannot alter a money vote, may reject the whole, & will, he thinks, do so in such circumstances.

Walpole spoke very well. It was the best speech I have ever heard him make. Gladstone replied with considerable point & effect, & said some good things. He mentioned a precedent, as he considered it, for his course – dating from 1767, at wh. the Tories laughed – too soon,

[102] In Apr. 1835.
[103] Joseph George Churchward, contracted to convey mail from Dover to Calais and Ostend.
[104] 162:117, on 27 Mar. 1860; H clvii. 1131–1419.

for he immediately twitted them with their newborn dislike to be led back to the wisdom of our ancestors (laughter). He derided Walpole's superstitious regard for forms, on which as well as substance Gladstone contended the mover was wrong. John Manners replied, with zeal & courage rather than with prudence. Lord R. Cecil was more effective & brief, & all expected a division before dinner. But, for a reason at first unexplained, Fitzroy Kelly got up, &, amidst incessant interruptions by members collected below the Bar, who wanted to keep their prandial engagements, spoke against time in the driest & most forensic style. All wondered at so able a man wasting his hold on 'the ear of the House'. At last, a friend near the door exclaimed loudly 'the pigeon is come'. On asking for an explanation he told me Kelly had been speaking agt. time till some one of his party could get back from the pigeon match. My informant said he wished he had a pigeon in his pocket to let go in the House. One the news arriving it was evidently conveyed to Kelly immediately. Some say Disraeli kicked him. Loud were the laughter & cheers – & cries of the 'pigeon is come' – & so we divided 205 to 191. Govt. winning [...]

Two learned gentlemen sitting near me fell into an argument on the contract – A. & C.[105] A. was rather of opinion that it ought to be carried out. The other demurred. A. said 'what is to be said of the Tralee business?' He meant that O'Connell was induced by a lucrative place to resign Tralee that a Govt. law officer, O'Hagan, might get a seat[106] [...]

Monday, 1 June: [...] Some of the Irish members appear to be greatly alarmed lest Dillwyn shd. not divide on the Irish Church question. Sir P. O'Brien, in conversation with me, was very earnest about this. He represented that some of the Tory Catholic people, like Hennessy, would find themselves out of a serious difficulty, if we shd. not divide, for, if H. oppose us, he will lose Catholic voters; if he support, Church of England men. I assured Sir P. that Dillwyn would divide; indeed, he told me he would. Let us have no half-hearted measures. O'Donoghue has sounded me in a similar manner. I suppose there is dread lest we be 'managed'!!

Tuesday, 2 June: [...] There is a great pressure exercised on members to induce them to vote for Somes's bill for the prevention of the sale of intoxicating drinks betwn. Sat[urda]y night & Monday

---

[105] Possibly Sir John Acton and W.H.F. Cogan.
[106] Daniel O'Connell II had been appointed to a special commissionership of income tax. His vacant seat was filled by the Irish attorney general.

morning. Some succumb agt. their consciences; some, more shabbily, resort to evasive courses.

Wednesday, 3 June: I reached the house about 2.20 p.m. & found Horsfall speaking. Somes's bill was his theme. A brisk debate. Graham's nephew, W. Lawson, did not speak badly. Sir Geo. Grey was at once brief, exhaustive & effective. We divided 278-103.[107]

It seems that the boasted canvas of large towns has been a canvas of householders, omitting the bulk of the working classes, who have petitioned in immense numbers agt. the bill. Sheffield, Halifax & other places instance this. To condemn the workman to drink sour beer on Sundays, bought overnight & put on a shelf, is quite puritanical. To tell a workman, who for once affords his wife & children a sniff of sea air at Brighton, that he must carry provisions with him, might be to tell him to remain in his dusty, ill ventilated attic & watch the increasing pallor of his children's faces & the despair of their careworn mother [...]

Thursday, 4 June: [...] There was a Gladstone hunt during the evening. A speech of his in a past debate was alluded to in a manner wh. is at variance with our rules. * He had spoken of a committee on Holyhead Harbour as not being impartially constituted.[108] * I do not mention details. I only note the tendency there is to teaze him. He is, sometimes, provoking from his very crushing power & command of words, wh. is more remarkable than his command of temper. Not that he is ill-tempered; rather incapable of restraining the torrent of his declamation.

Friday, 5 June: [...] D. Fortescue brought on the very scandalous case of ill-treatment of Sergeant Major Lilley & others by Col[onel] Crawley of the 6th Inniskilling Dragoons. The House was evidently very indignant & not satisfed with the course taken either by the Com[mande]r in chief[109] or the governt. Lilley is dead, his wife is dead & his two children.[110] Yet, Crawley is in command on probation, probably, till he has vexed & hunted 4 more people to death, & the

---

[107] Against the 2nd reading.

[108] 1 June 1863; *H* clxxi. 241–3.

[109] The Duke of Cambridge, the Queen's cousin.

[110] Lillee, who was due to give evidence at the court martial of paymaster Smales, had been arrested by Crawley and confined for forty days in a small space during the height of the Indian summer. His wife, confined with him, was dying from tuberculosis. At a court martial held in England in Nov–Dec, Crawley was acquitted of charges of unbecoming conduct. See the *Annual Register* for 1863, part 2, pp. 312–28, for an account.

reparation is a pension (or its equivalent) to Lilley's relations. (This intimation provoked ironical cheers – & some bitter laughter.) By God! I would hang some one. The Commander-in-Chief seems to have acted like a fool. The Minister for War must have been weak; & as to the Minister for India, it is not easy to say how far he is to blame; but it seems to me he must share with the rest [...]

Monday, 8 June: [...] I voted on Gregory's motion to open Edinburgh botanic gardens after divine service on Sundays. Gregory made a good speech, & was supported in a speech of at least equal merit & of much point by Stirling of Keir. Lord Palmerston expressed his concurrence in the abstract with Gregory, but dwelt on the practical evil of outraging the undoubted feelings of a large number of Scotch people. Several Scotch members deprecated the motion – Mure, the Lord Advocate,[111] Kinnaird & Black, for example. Stirling's quaintness & quiet satire created much amusement. Gregory & he shewed how, in order to defeat the motion, signatures & petitions had been extorted from little children either by clergymen or laymen with ecclesiastical tendencies (a laugh): The House was, $\frac{3}{4}$ths at least, in favour of the motion, which, however, was defeated. Almost the only voice heard agt. it in cheering any speaker was Kinnaird's, wh. circumstance speaks volumes. * Kinnaird is a smug goodnatured & doubtless well intentioned man reputed to be a sort of organ of Low Church opinions. He is evidently well satisfied with the world & his place in it. Also, he is so certain of the correctness of his principles that he would, I think, gladly impress them by force upon the rest of the world. A particularly narrow sentiment is almost sure to raise his cheer, often his alone – in a voice which I recollect K. Macauley describing as redolent 'of tea & muffins' (dissenting preacher's fare). I believe Kinnaird would vote for stopping clocks on Sundays. * Division 123 to 107. I was, of course, in the minority, in wh., also, was my colleague, A. Russell [...]

Tuesday, 9 June: For nearly three hours I listened to a debate on C. Buxton's motion to relax the stringency of subscription to the Prayer book & Articles of our Church.[112] He introduced his motion in a temperate & sensible speech lasting 55 minutes. Monckton Milnes moved an amendment; he desired to continue subscription to the 39 articles, as at present. Sir Geo. Grey indicated that, but for Milnes's amendmt., Sir G.G. would move the previous question. Milnes withdrew his amendmt. & so that question was carried without division.

---

[111] James Moncrieff.
[112] Arguing against a 'prescribed code of doctrine', *H* clxxi. 574–87.

The debate was long & interesting. Most of the regular defenders of the Church spoke. Opinions are surging up. The most Conservative people know there is something wh. must be dealt with, &, yet, they deprecate each form of action proposed. Young men, of active minds & honest purpose, are beginning to avoid clerical life. The heads of the Church are puzzled by their own teaching & are unable to answer criticisms from philosophical laymen; &, unconscious of their incapacity, expose themselves to ridicule. Meanwhile, the clergy cannot suppress their doubts, or stifle their consciences. Where is the end of all this? Statesmen may draw distinctions, & divines may utter menaces; but, meanwhile, opinions grow & harden. Almost every speaker expressed or implied something favourable to the principle of Buxton's motion, & the strongest point agt. it was the vagueness of his object.

Wednesday, 10 June: [...] Hunt introduced, & carried thro' a 2d. reading, a Bill to prevent improper proceedings relating to the withdrawal of Election petitions.[113] These are often got up for purposes of extortion, & withdrawn for money consideration [...]

Thursday, 11 June: [...] There was a brisk conversation on the want of a day for the Irish Ch[urch] question. In my opinion to blink it will be to risk the Empire at no distant time. I seconded Ward upon it twenty years ago, & I think now much as I thought then.[114]

Friday, 12 June: [...] Early in the evening there were attempts to force Ministers to name a day for the Irish Church motion. Palmerston, wanting Monday next for the Exhibition business, begged that Hennessy would postpone the Polish question. Hennessy was ready to do this provided Govt. would get him another hearing. On this Osborne adroitly pressed Dillwyn to make a stipulation for a day for the Irish Ch[urch] question, suggesting, aside, that he shd. notice the priority of Ireland's claim. Dillwyn did not succeed in catching the Speaker's eye, & was subsequently indisposed to rise, doubting I suppose how far he could properly interpose, or, at least, advantageously make terms. On this I inquired publicly whether he meant to bring on his motion next Monday; &, upon his reply & its connexion with the comparison alluded to above, some of us below the gangway raised vehement & protracted cheers in order to mark that we would not allow the Irish question to die out. I did not think Dillwyn could

[113] The election petitions bill was referred to a select committee, but defeated on the motion to enter into committee of the whole house on 2 July.
[114] I.e. he favoured disestablishment; 2 Aug. 1843, *H* lxxi. 175–81.

come on on Monday – my object was to shew to Ministers that this Irish Church question is a serious one, & I think I succeeded. + The Whigs rose to power on the wings of Irish hopes, &, happy in warmth & sunlight, have left their deluded clients to rot beneath. +

Talking of the Irish Ch[urch] I note a remark of Cobden's related to me that any '40 quakers' would have effected more ere this towards getting rid of it than the whole Irish party. Of course, I can only give his idea in my words. I mentioned this to Roebuck, who seemed to be amused.

I hardly know whether I have said before in this diary what I now say – that we have in my opinion to choose one of 3 courses: either to abolish the Irish Church, repeal the Union or pay the Irish Catholic priests. These last ought to be induced to look to the Empire rather than to any foreign potentate. It will be a terrible thing, if, after the American war shall have concluded, an Irish body of trained soldiers & staff officers, intolerant of quiet life & without pay, put themselves in communication with disaffected people in Ireland. Say what we may, the Irish difficulty remains, like the Polish, unsolved.

Speaking one day recently to Monsell, I said that if the Irish Nation endured the Church much longer, they would be unfit for constitutional govert. He hoped that I would say this openly.

Monday, 15 June: The great Exhibition question is before us.[115] In former times we had a courtier govt. & a fierce opposition – now, we have a courtier govt. & a compliant opposition. Disraeli & Gladstone seem to be at one in ministering to royal wishes inspired probably by a jobbing set of schemers, contractors, secretaries & officials desirous of permanent posts at the Public cost. This is my reading of the astounding proposal about to be submitted to the House of Commons. Parliament teems with great contractors, whose conduct is often most suspicious. The fortunes of these men are sometimes made before their political morals. They are little better than politician soldiers & sailors, who almost always support proposals involving more cost. We are governed by cliques. the working classes are not represented + except that Government condescends to spend their earnings. +

We met as usual; &, after some altercation relating to precedency – in wh. altercation Osborne, Hennessy, Ld. Palmerston & others had shares – the Speaker left the chair, & Lord P. moved the first resolution of a series prepared for carrying out the scheme of purchase & building at South Kensington, the said resolution ostensibly binding the Nation

[115] The plan to purchase from the commissioners for the exhibition of 1851 the building and adjoining land at Kensington used for the International exhibition of 1862, in order to establish a permanent exhibition site.

to pay £67,000 for 17 acres of land, but involving, by implication, a far larger object.[116]

Osborne & Gregory, sitting side by side, evidently acted together. Palmerston had a bad case in hand & he recommended it badly – that is, at almost every sentence his descriptions of the project in hand admitted of ironical or derisive cheers. The temper of the House seemed to be strongly agt. more than the purchase of the land. Gregory made a long & clever speech – still it was just a little too long & too much charged with written matter such as the carpings of engineers not employed, like one Mr. Mallet, whose letter he read [...] I paired with + the young bear + Edward (Ellice)[117] & so my name will not be in the division list. It was quite understood that the purchase of the land will involve the Country in a heavy outlay. Still, the menacing tone & aspect of the House has, probably, warned Ministers to beware. Perhaps, they wished to give H. Majesty a notions of their difficulty. The next step will be taken on thursday week. Is this defeat? Division 267 to 135[118] [...]

Tuesday, 16 June: A morning on Irish Fisheries – a bill of wh. my knowledge is zero.[119] I hear it is the subject of interminable talk, & that it has one advantage that it is a sort of safety valve for the passion of Irish members [...]

Wednesday, 17 June: Dillwyn withdrew his endowed schools bill,[120] after intimating his intention to reintroduce it. He took occasion to declare that he had no idea of injuring the established Church by means of this or any other bills – & he glanced at the attacks made upon him from time to time. Selwyn seconded the motion for discharging the order, & commented briefly & civilly on Dillwyn's course – &, particularly, contended that the House had never thus attacked D. And so all was ending pleasantly amidst mutual compliments, when R. Lowe,[121] influenced I suppose by hot weather & aware of the absence of his chief, deemed it to be prudent & statesmanlike to lecture Dillwyn on the effect of his policy in repeatedly

---

[116] Palmerston estimated the total cost of the land, the building and the alterations to it, at £484,000.

[117] Edward Ellice junior; his father had been a fur trader in Canada, acquiring the nickname 'bear Ellice'.

[118] For ministers.

[119] The object was to assimilate the Irish law on Salmon fisheries to that in England. Royal assent, 28 July.

[120] His annual bill to allow dissenters in certain cases to act as trustees of Church schools.

[121] Vice president of the education board of the privy council.

introducing measures on ecclesiastical topics – & said that, if his end
was the promotion of *tolerant* views betwn. Churchman & Dissenter,
his course tended to defeat it, for that the Council of Education had
great difficulty in securing a reasonable *toleration* of the Dissenter,
whilst Churchmen were able to point to examples of unfair aggression
on his behalf. This called up Lord Henley & W.E. Forster – the
former, in support of Dillwyn's measure; the latter in considerable
dudgeon at the use of the word *toleration*, inasmuch as equality is the
Dissenter's object. Lowe's course was very much criticized. He cannot
command his temper, & is by nature overbearing, tho' he means well
& really has some difficulty in obtaining for dissenters fair dealing.
Forster seemed to be a little soothed by some private explanation of
Lowe's in this sense.

　　Sir J. Hay moved the 2d. reading of his Bill for the more ready
recovery of Naval prize money.[122] I heard the debate at length, &
was much interested. Govt. noting the tone of the House yielded,
& Hay won without a division [...] Ministers urged the risk &
inconvenience of hasty & partial legislation. Their opponents charged
the admiralty with repeated delays & broken undertakings. The
House seemed convinced by the opposition – so C. Paget[123] yielded
&, at the same time, deprecated the system under wh. the House thus
takes upon itself responsibility more properly belonging to Government. Why then do not Ministers resign? [...]

Monday, 22 June: This was to have been Hennessy's field day
for Polish affairs. Lord P[almerston] had promised it to him &,
accordingly, moved the postponement of previous order of the day.
Beaumont, Kinglake & Enfield deprecated discussion pending negotiations. On a division (165 to 110) P's motion was negatived.
Horsman was very indignant. One of the members assailed (Enfield)
defended himself. Lord R. Cecil was savage as usual. Lord Palmerston
stated the 6 points contained in the despatch to Russia[124] [...] My
disabled limb kept me at home; that is, I offered to attend, if required,
in order to support Ministers on Poland, but I received notice that I
might remain at home all night.

　　It was a curious case. Palmerston was under a pledge to Hennessy
& the House would not fulfil it. It seems, then, that P. does not lead
the Commons? [...] Of course, it was very agreeable to Ministers to
be defeated. This I infer from the votes of many friends of theirs.

---

[122] Restoring to naval officers the right to appoint their own agents to represent their
interests with regard to prize money, rather than having to rely, as they had since
1845, on the accountant general. Royal assent, 28 July.

[123] Parliamentary secretary to the admiralty.

[124] Urging liberal concessions to the Poles; *B.F.S.P.* liii. 897–901.

Wednesday, 24 June: [...] There was a good deal of discussion on the admiralty & its mode of management, division of responsibility among various officers & kindred topics. Dalglish was leader [...] Stansfeld has displayed activity & power in his office,[125] & earned compliments from various quarters. The government seems to have made a hit in winning over 'young Vergniaud'[126] [...]

Thursday, 25 June: [...] Palmerston has the gout, & hence postponement of the vote for fortifications & for the Exhibition. Osborne took the opportunity of a question relating to the Wellington funeral car & its wicker horses, exhibited to the Public at some 6d. a head in St. Pauls', to laugh at British art & our art minister, Cowper [...] Osborne was more than ordinarily rampant. His asides are more diverting than Senatorial. Notice was given of postponement of the fortification & Exhibition votes to thursday next; on wh. he exclaimed in his seat, loudly enough to be generally heard, 'two jobs together!' (laughter.) Alluding to Cowper's reply to Cavendish Bentinck on the subject of the funeral car, O. said 'there spoke the genius of the Brompton Boilers!'[127] (Shouts of laughter.)

It struck me that Ministers shewed to poor advantage in their chief's absence. Gladstone looked pensive & half asleep; neither leading the house, nor led by his chief. I think he chafed within. Grey & Cardwell talked in undertones, gloomily. I suspect they begin to foresee the beginning of the end. Cowper, assuming to direct Science & art, speaks to be laughed at. T.G. Baring[128] answered Gen[era]l Peel on Army finance with rather a boyish confidence, & without weight enough to satisfy the House. Hartington[129] is too cool, easy & flippant. He regularly fenced with Coningham,[130] in a way which looked disingenuous & studied for the concealment of something he was ashamed or afraid to tell. For once Coningham catechized a Minister & seemed to have the best of it.

Friday, 26 June: Twice the house sat. In the evening the Guards' Ball & a Conservative banquet took place. We were afraid lest we shd. fail in keeping together 40 members. Being very anxious to be of use to Osborne & Dillwyn in the promotion of the cause they have

---

[125] He had been appointed a lord of the admiralty in Apr. 1863.

[126] The *Saturday Review*, 13 Apr. 1861, p. 365, had compared Stansfeld to Pierre Vergniaud, the girondin leader.

[127] The early buildings on the exhibition site, made of corrugated iron.

[128] Under-secretary for India.

[129] Under-secretary for war.

[130] Over the court martial of paymaster Smales and the impending court martial, in England, of Lt. Col. Crawley; *H* clxxi. 1437–43.

jointly in hand,[131] I made two journeys in cabs to Westminster & remained in attendance for a considerable time [...] to me there were no hopes of progress on the Irish Ch. question, so, to save my health, I paired & retired, nor had I reason to be sorry that I retired, as nothing but speeches occurred. Osborne's speech was witty & cogent enough – very damnatory to the Whigs in passages quoted. But, as to making any impression on them, he might as well flog a tanned buffalo's hide. Luckily for O. Lord Palmerston was absent, or the laugh might have been the other way.

Monday, 29 June: There were more questions on the Crawley & Smales cases.[132] Lord Hartington is learning his lesson. I said to Hugessen 'Thirty years hence Lord H. will reply in far briefer terms'. Also, I think he will not be so easily ruffled [...]

Tuesday, 30 June: [...] Roebuck [...] moved his resolution proposing to take diplomatic steps towards recognition of the Confederate States in America. I read his speech which was deemed to be a clever one & amusing, but I do not think that he will have a great many followers. On my return Gladstone spoke, & lectured R. on the policy he had avowed and the language in wh. it was couched. Bright's was, I am informed, a fine piece of declamation; &, by the way, I think Lord R. Montagu was far from being ineffective.[133] [...] Roebuck rather startled the house by his account of his interview with the Emperor of the French.[134] Certainly, R. takes extraordinary steps. Bright described him as being not an ambassador extraordinary, but *most* extraordinary – & insinuated inaccuracy in the version given of what passed. Luckily, Lindsay will be able to confirm R, or set him right, if his memory has been fallacious.

Palmerston is still an absentee.

Wednesday, 1 July: I voted today for Ewart's bill in favour of the decimalization of our metrical system. Cobden's speech on behalf of it was very practical & excellent. Gibson[135] was afraid of adopting a compulsory measure. Yet, without some penalty, no scheme of the

---

[131] Osborne's motion for a select committee to enquire into the present ecclesiastical settlement in Ireland; *H* clxxi. 1560–82.

[132] See above, 5 and 25 June 1863.

[133] Opposing Roebuck, and calling for strict neutrality; *H* clxxi. 1780–97.

[134] Roebuck recounted his and W.S. Lindsay's recent audience with Napoleon III, who had expressed his willingness to act with Britain in recognising the confederate government in America. The Emperor had claimed that his earlier direct approach to Britain had been leaked to the Americans. *H* clxxi. 1771–80.

[135] President of the board of trade.

kind could ever come into action. The choice remains between an obsolete & highly inconvenient system on the one hand, & an effective reform purchased by some temporary trouble on the other. Ewart was the mover. Henley chief opponent, with Hubbard as second. Adderley spoke ably in favour of the bill, which, also, had the voice of Sir Minto Farquhar – & in the end we beat Ministers.[136] The bill, if it shd. pass, would come into operation in 3 years. In the interim, a subtle body of mathematical or mercantile critics, would certainly raise all tenable cavils at the new law. Little would be risked except the affirmation of a principle already in full operation elsewhere. English workmen in France soon learn French notation & measurement. At the great exhibition much inconvenience was felt by foreigners & Englishmen thro' the difficulty entailed by our varied & complex modes of determining & describing relative values. The debate was most instructive [...]

Thursday, 2 July: Roebuck must have greatly misunderstood the Emperor of the French. Layard[137] flatly contradicts both the statement that any proposal since Nov[embe]r has been made to our governt. towards recognition of the southern States, and the statement that the French despatch hereon was communicated to Mr. Seward[138] by our foreign minister. In fact, Mr. S. was made acquainted with it by M. Mercier.[139] The whole business is a puzzle. Has R. been dreaming? In any case, it is a great pity that he has mixed himself up in the matter. If he considered that our Ministry had lost opportunities of useful action in concert with France, shd. he not have moved a resolution in that sense? I suppose time will explain the business. At present conjecture is at fault.

A very remarkable debate was held on Gladstone's motion for £105,000 to purchase the Exhibition Buildings. The House was very boisterous and resolved. Many members spoke. Government was charged with disingenuousness – in gaining a vote on the last occasion[140] without truthfully describing the exact effect of the contract to be entered into. The House, at last, would hear no minister or ex-minister. + Sir S. Northcote was put aside with some contempt, a good lesson for him! & he required it. He puts himself a little too forward sometimes, I think. + Disraeli even succumbed to the typhoon. R. Lowe was at once shut up. Gladstone had a like fate. Old

[136] 110:75 for the 2nd reading; no further progress made.
[137] Foreign under-secretary.
[138] American secretary of state.
[139] French ambassador in Washington.
[140] See above, 15 June 1863.

Henley's telling ridicule of the whole project was in his happiest manner, & he became a sort of leader. A friend told me that a supporter of the scheme had observed jocosely that all the right hon[oura]bles were in one lobby & in the other neither right hon[oura]bles nor hon[oura]bles. + This putting the best face on the matter. + Ayes 121 Noes 287 and served the Ministry rightly.[141]

In the tumult, when Disraeli failed to get a hearing, Lord R. Cecil succeeded, by an appeal, in restoring order for a few moments, when D. was enabled 'in all humility' to put forth a few audible words. A friend recalled this to me with some glee; Lord R.C. is supposed to be a sort of recalcitrant agt. D's dictatorship. Perhaps, office may reconcile the two rivals. It has done more difficult feats.

Friday, 3 July: [...] It is noteworthy that W.S. Lindsay in 'the Times'[142] confirms Roebuck's version of their conversation with the Emperor. All this is very odd.

The sun gets hotter – & debates follow suit. Coningham & Osborne have been fighting over Crawley's case.[143] O. interrupted C. on a supposed point of order. C. doubted whether O. was sober. O. doubted whether C. was sane. C. advised O. to confine himself to the Irish Ch[urch] question & get up the facts better – & he expressed a hope that Ministers would find him a place somewhere in the outskirts of government to keep him quiet. The two combatants damaged themselves, & the House. Meanwhile, I suspect that the Whigs had no objection to the gist & effect of the amenities interchanged.

Monday, 6 July: Palmerston entered early, looking pale, reduced & somewhat broken. I noticed that he very frequently coughed. The Ministerial bench looked fagged, & scarcely ever engaged in conversation. Ayrton made a strong speech on a motion for closing the a/c of the Commiss[ione]rs of the exhibition &c. Much of his speech was very bitter, & elicited severe comments from R. Lowe. I could not vote with Ayrton, as it is hardly a reasonable course to interfere with the rights of the commiss[ione]rs by way of resolution of the H. of C. So I voted with Ministers.[144] It appears to be abundantly shewn that the property entrusted to them has greatly increased in value in their hands, & there is no case for the extraordinary measure recommended by Ayrton. Ayrton appears to rise in estimation; &

---

[141] Brand's report to Palmerston shows that 101 Liberals supported the motion and 129 opposed. As for the Conservatives, they 'jumped at the opportunity of giving Gladstone a slap in the face'; 4 July 1863, Broadlands MSS, GC/BR/19.

[142] 4 July 1863, p. 7.

[143] See above, 5 June 1863.

[144] Ayrton's motion defeated, 165:42.

deservedly. He takes great pains & does not speak as frequently as he formerly used to do [...]

Wednesday, 8 July: A morning on small birds. Paull moved the 2d. reading of a bill to prevent their destruction. A debate of interest to naturalists & farmers followed. French experience was referred to. As usual, Henley made useful criticisms. Caird, a learned agriculturist authority, spoke amusingly & sensibly. The balance of opinions was that destruction of birds by dangerous poisons was not an unfitting subject of legislation; but few approved of Paull's bill as it stands. He got his 2d. reading, with an understanding that the bill would be much altered in Committee.[145]

[...] I note that one portion of my oaths bill, viz, that which extends the principle of Locke's act of /61 to Scotland, is rapidly becoming law by Craufurd's bill.[146] He waited till my larger measure was defeated. Thus we turn to windward by alternate tacks.

Thursday, 9 July: Attending about 5 p.m., the topic of fortifications soon engaged the House, when Sir F. Smith moved, adversely to the 2d. reading of the bill, a very speculative resolution.[147] It appeared to me that as some of these defences are nearly completed & the rest more or less in progress, it was too late to stop them – so I decided to support the bill,[148] understand[in]g that they are conceived for the protection of our main arsenals & the places first liable to attack, so that an invader must be embarrassed with a heavy siege train or stay away. America & the future are arguments for precaution; &, after all, the executive must be trusted to some extent. I paired with Harvey Lewis (till 11).

Afterwards, on my return I had an opportunity of voting for the sale of the Chancellor's benefices bill.[149] There appeared to me to be no sufficient reason, why Churchmen shd. not make arrangements calculated to produce better livings for the clergy in many small parishes. Several Voluntaries thought & voted differently. [...] My friend Dillwyn seemed almost too paradoxical when he affirmed that he opposed the Benefices Bill in order to benefit the Church. I believe

---

[145] The poisoned grain etc. prohibition bill received the Royal assent on 28 July.

[146] Permitting affirmations in lieu of taking oaths in criminal cases; Royal assent 28 July.

[147] Opposing further expenditure on that part of the scheme based on the assumption that the enemy would besiege Portsmouth and Plymouth; *H* clxxii. 442–9.

[148] 2nd reading passed, 132:61.

[149] Lord Westbury's augmentation of benefices bill, selling the Crown's patronage in the case of 320 small livings and applying the money to increase the value of other small benefices. Royal assent, 28 July.

he thinks so, but some few in the House cried 'oh! oh!' suspiciously. Indeed, it seems to me to be a dog in the manger opposition. This is the way Dissenters fail, they ride their hobbies too far. Every Dissenter always seems fearful of being behind hand in discovering one occasion more for disagreement. So it becomes a race in nonconformity. At last, sound friends of Free thought become disgusted & turn their horses heads the opposite way.

Friday, 10 July: [...] At the ev[enin]g sitting at 6, Sir James Ferguson, mov[in]g the adjournmt., appealed to Roebuck to abstain from pressing the debate on North & South.[150] Palmerston backed the request to his 'Hon[oura]ble & learned friend' &., evidently speaking to be read at the Tuileries, made many remarks most flattering to the Emperor, at the same time deprecatory of amateur diplomacy – observing that Englishmen would be debarred from the advantage of freely availing themselves of the Emperor's 'abandon', & courteous frankness of communication, if his conversation were thus conveyed to the H. of C.

Kinglake seemed to think that, as we had a communication, it could hardly be considered as if it had never been. Osborne believed Roebuck's statements, but doubted his discretion. Gregory, R. Cecil, W.E. Forster & Coningham spoke – I shd. say rather threw some venom at each other, Cecil relieving himself of his due share, & Coningham lashing himself into a fury. He begins quietly. Gradually, the House interrupts. Then he gets off his balance, & for the time seems almost insane.

I believe I give the general sense & tone of what I heard; but, as Palmerston's words were guarded & evidently well pondered (as if they were a State paper), it were safer to refer to Hansard.

Roebuck & Lindsay made a great mistake in going to Fontainbleau [...] * During the last interview that Roebuck & Lindsay had, the Emperor enquired how long they intended to stay in Paris. Lindsay cut in before Roebuck could answer, & said they were obliged to leave Paris that ev[enin]g. When they came out, R. nudged Lindsay & said 'Why did you say that? he was going to ask us to dinner.' 'I know he was', said Lindsay, '& I knew you would accept, & I knew you went to dinner too often in Vienna; so I stood between you & your falling virtue'![151] Roebuck tells the story. *

[...] A friend (O[sborne]) mentioned to me a trait of Palmerston. He was coming to the House stick in hand, with his jaw down,

---

[150] I.e. the question of the recognition of the confederate government in America.

[151] See R.E. Leader, *Life of John Arthur Roebuck*, (1897), pp. 285–93, for his increasingly pro-Austrian leanings.

looking very ill & broken. Suddenly he noticed O. & immediately discontinued the use of his stick & made three most vigorous strides, determined, if possible, that O. shd. not think his dictatorship over yet. O. may find P's jaw in its right state & quite up to its work whenever its owner is attacked [...]

Monday, 13 July: [...] Roebuck moved that the order for the adjourned debate on recognition of the South be discharged [...] R. said that he withdrew in the interest of the good government of his country by Lord P[almerston]. Lindsay put the House in possession of more facts & excuses, & charged Layard with imputing to him the fault of being a busybody, when, in truth & in fact, he had been employed by Ministers, at his cost & inconvenience, to do their work in endeavouring to modify the views of the French govt. on trade & maritime affairs.[152] It seemed to me too late for Ministers to lecture Lindsay after allowing him to have intercourse with the Emperor for the advantage of England. Certainly, L. was, at least, an informal ambassador. Palmerston hoped that experience would prevent similar instances of unofficial action betwn. members of the H. of C. & foreign potentates. but P forgot that, in several cases, ministers have lately thrown responsibility on the House for acts & things which ministers deprecated & disapproved of, thereby abolishing regular channels for the conduct of Public affairs & transferring responsibility from the executive to a representative chamber.

The O'Donoghue spoke shortly from the disaffected Irish point of view – & took care to be very civil to both North & South. Suddenly, he could not call up his next ideas, & stopped. The House, rather ill-naturedly, cried 'agreed agreed' – & O'D had still more difficulty. The moment he attempted to articulate, the watchful House interrupted with cruel skill. This went on till he seemed on the verge of sitting down, when, luckily, a sudden inspiration befriended him & he wound up with about a couple of rather unmeaning, but pretty well worded, sentences. His point of view does not suit the English H. of C. However, it was a painful spectacle, & not creditable to members.

Returning at a later hour, came an amendmt. moved by Sir M. Peto to omit the item for Spithead forts. There seemed to me to be so much doubt of the wisdom of constructing these forts that I was induced to vote agt. them[153] [...]

Wednesday, 15 July: At my entrance, I found Lord Hotham opposing certain expensive recommendations of the Dining Rooms Com-

---

[152] He had been thus engaged for the past three and a half years, *H* clxxii. 663–8.
[153] The vote of £25,000 carried, 135:52.

mittee. Osborne & I spoke shortly. The hot weather seems to increase our garrulity, a thing to be greatly lamented. However, we succeeded[154] [...]

Thursday, 16 July: A great deal of debating took place on Railway bills. The Speaker might have saved much time had he read at an earlier moment one of our standing orders, which applied to 2 bills.[155] A third stood on a diff[eren]t footing – the Morayshire Railway bill – on this I voted with Massey,[156] whose opinion on conformity to routine is almost of papal authority. We must, in general, support rules & Committees.

[...] The Brazilian question[157] occupied many hours – I thought Seymour Fitzgerald carried his interruptions in debate, during Layard's speech, far beyond what the Speaker shd. have allowed. There is a growing feeling that he does not keep order; indeed, he seems hardly to attempt it.

[...] Much talk in private with Lord A. Churchill on his Ch. Rates bill.[158] My object is to smooth his path. I mentioned to him that 2 prelates, one Henry of Exeter!, in the Lords have recommended that, in extreme cases, Clergymen shd. break the law & take the consequences – this was on the question of a part of our burial service[159] where, even in cases of avowed infidels or hardened sinners, hopes are expressed of their joyful resurrection. Suppose a dissenter conscientiously object to pay Ch. Rates? Would this be a case for defying the law? [...] I am bound to say that I concur with the Bishops & think that our Burial Service is in harmony with a true conception of primitive Xtianity.

---

[154] French's motion to carry out recommendations to enlarge the dining rooms, withdrawn. Trelawny remarked that members should be satisfied with a 'plain dinner', that they would next want to have their washing done for them, and that the proposal 'would be a step towards giving wages to members'; *H* clxxii. 825–6.

[155] The Great Eastern and North British railways (steamboats) bills had to be recommitted as the companies' plans to acquire steamboats were not permissible unless recommended by the committee; *H* clxxii. 864.

[156] Chairman of committees, who pointed out that the bill violated another standing order in that the acquisition of steamboats was not part of the original bill, but had been added in committee. His amendment to exclude steamboats from the bill was carried, 85:56; *H* clxxii. 866–8.

[157] Fitzgerald's motion for a copy of the manifest of the barque the 'Prince of Wales' to be laid before the House; *H* clxxii. 879–95. Withdrawn. Brazil had withdrawn her ambassador as a result of the dispute with Britain; see above, 6 Mar. 1863.

[158] Abolishing the compulsory collection of church rates. 1st reading given on 10 July, but no further progress made.

[159] 13 July 1863, *H* clxxii. 619–20, for the bishop of Exeter; 1 June 1863, *H* clxxi. 161–3 for the bishop of London.

Friday, 17 July: [...] I spent most of the night till towards $1\frac{1}{2}$ at the House – watching for a New Zealand guaranteed loan, wh. was, after all, withdrawn [...] I was engaged in preparing for the defence of the Public purse agt. Colonial harpies, & asked a question in a threatening spirit & doubt not that we, in part at least, scared the Colonial undersecretary from proceeding with the job of wh. we had heard.

Monday, 20 July: I left town for the season [...]

Tuesday, 28 July: Parliament prorogued.

SESSION OF 1864

I have paired till after Easter, & shall therefore not transcribe what may be found in the Journals of the House.

Monday, 4 April: I attended at the House. Debate on the estimates. Wordy & ineffective as usual. Nothing noteworthy except Stansfeld's resignation.[1]

Tuesday, 5 April: [...] It is generally thought on our side that Stansfeld acted wisely, & justly by his party. He becomes a voluntary offering to save the Ministry; but he shd. have pondered on his own antecedents before he compromised a cabinet by becoming its subordinate charged with combustible matter.

[...] Palmerston looked older. He was, however, wide awake, & sat listening attentively,[2] his mouth wide open; to aid his hearing, I think.

Thursday, 7 April: I heard 2 hours of the budget speech. Gladstone made merry with the Protectionists & paid Cobden a graceful tribute. Good news from France, wh. is about to relax on rags.[3] Gladstone dilated with his usual fecundity, albeit with a more practical manner than usual & less of mere declamation. Bentinck was bilious – Henley prosy. Malins, probably, vexed his chiefs by praising the main features of the scheme, tho' he deprecated details. Gladstone's eloquence failed in keeping Palmerston awake. Debate ended tamely – the enemy found little to find fault with.[4]

Monday, 11 April: Today there was at first a sparse attendance owing to a great crush in the streets to see Garibaldi, who made his entrance.[5] The Govt annuity bill[6] came on &, after debate, was

[1] Following revelations that his London home had been used as a forwarding address for letters to the exiled Italian revolutionary nationalist, Mazzini.
[2] To the debate on the Lisburn election committee.
[3] I.e. its export duty on rags supplied for British papermaking.
[4] Gladstone had taken 1d. off the income tax and reduced the duties on sugar; *H* clxxiv. 536–93.
[5] The Italian nationalist leader was in England from 3–28 Apr.
[6] Allowing smaller sums to be accepted by post office savings banks for deferred government annuities, and abolishing the restriction that only those buying deferred annuities could obtain life insurance; Royal assent, 14 July.

referred to a Select Committee. Ayrton acutely & usefully criticized that measure & Gladstone replied to him – with less of that insolence of power & overweening confidence which I have noticed in him in former controversies with the same antagonist. Sheridan, perhaps, has been a good instructor to Gladstone.[7] A fall now & then makes a man cautious on ice.

Returning about 9 p.m. we were taken into various regions of debate – e.g. the relative cost of the British & French armies & the Crawley case.[8] In the former, that rising speaker, Mr. O'Reilly, distinguished himself; in the latter, Lord Hotham – who, in his way, is a pattern member. Fine old independent soldier! – &, at the same time, he may be described as one of the noblest specimens of the class of English country gentleman.

Lord Hartington[9] speaks a little too low & is, perhaps, too free & easy & slipshod. At times it struck me that he has not all the knowledge of facts & readiness we have a right to expect in an administrator whose business it is to ask us to vote £15,000,000.

The military Colonels, as usual, fussy. These prigs fancy they are the patrons of the British army. What they want – if there be any logic in their system of proceeding – is a military head of the War department. Civilians can know nothing, the Colonels seem to think. But 'of evils choose the least'. How would the Public like to meet with favour every demand which instinct of caste might cause a military chief to make? Perhaps, a standing army would, in consequence, be swept away [...]

Tuesday, 12 April: [...] Lord R. Cecil moved a resolution on suppressions of parts of reports of Inspectors of schools[10] & made a bitter speech agt. Lowe; who is accused of garbling these reports & of only publishing facts or opinions favourable to his preconceived views. Lowe replied that the resolution contained two facts (he meant assertions) & 2 opinions. He undertook to prove that the assertions were untrue & the opinions absurd (a laugh).

Lowe was evidently very warm – his assailant very ferocious. Cecil had twice distinctly declared his inability to adduce his evidence in full, with names of informants, from fear of vindictive measures on Lowe's part. Lowe was by no means ineffective in reply. How much of the charge he deserved is doubtful. There appeared to be a case

---

[7] Sheridan had carried a resolution for the reduction of the fire insurance duties late in the previous session; 14 July 1863, *H* clxxii. 798–815.
[8] See above, 5 June 1863.
[9] Under-secretary for war.
[10] *H* clxxiv. 897–902.

agt. him. But the remedy seemed worse than the disease. Cecil, interrupting, demanded if particular passages in reports were not even sent back 'marked'. 'No' said Lowe. Whereon Cecil passed a paper to a neighbour, as tho' to convict Lowe of mis-statement.

Lowe dwelt on the inconvenience of permitting controversial matter, on religious questions, to be, as formerly, inserted in reports & the necessity of laying down rules. W.E. Forster was for having these reports in full & was, I thought, a little incautious. Where would reports end if a war in print, at the Public expense, could be waged betwn. Protestants & Catholics – high & low Chuch? Sir Geo. Grey made a brief & weighty speech in this vein. Ministers were, however, defeated [...] 93 to 101.[11] This is a rather serious shake. I supported Lowe.

Wednesday, 13 April: Augustus Smith was the hero of the day, having by Tory aid, vanquished Locke King, who proposed his county franchise Bill.[12] Poor Reform! to what a low ebb hast thou arrived! Even this pittance refused! A series of dull speeches, and several, neither very convincing or ingenious, were delivered &, after a few words from Visct. Palmerston, we divided, 254 to 227. The young Conservative gentlemen, such as Knightley, Collins & so forth, could, it would appear, afford to scoff at our party & opinions. America, the conduct of metropolitan members,[13] & such like gibes were hurled at us; and, except by Hibbert & Pease, no good matter was propounded in reply. And, indeed, it is only by some sort of galvanism that the old liberal warhorse can be got upon its legs again. I could not help asking Bright what I was there for? He said nothing could be done while Palmerston lived, to which I replied that we were come to a pretty pass if constitutional govt, after all, had landed us in subserviency to an accident like one man's long life. Of course, I do not give our exact words, but substance. We were walking thro' the division lobby.

People think we shall get thro' the Session – without dissolution.

Thursday, 14 April: 'Bitter-Sweet'. These words respectively headed the columns of the list of pairs inside the door of the right hand division lobby. 'Bitter' meant malt tax repeal – 'sweet' lower sugar duties –

[11] Trelawny mistakenly gave the figure for the minority as 92. Lowe's defeat occurred on a snap division while many members were absent unpaired at dinner; William White, *The Inner Life of the House of Commons*, (ed. Justin McCarthy, 1897), ii. 19–21 (23 Apr. 1864).

[12] To assimilate the county and borough franchises.

[13] Who, according to Bentinck, were constantly making 'piratical' attacks on the public purse; *H* clxxiv. 943–6.

and 'sweet' won. Colonel Bartellot's speech[14] was a remarkably modest & straightforward appeal delivered in a good, quiet, firm & self-possessed manner. Two new members followed. Surtees was far too egotistic & personal. Defective taste, evidently. Thirty years of hard work – a few heavy falls – & plenty of derision may together effect an improvement in him – i.e. if the materials be inherently good. J. Peel, the new MP for Tamworth, provokes no severe comment & was, at least, quiet & unpretending. The dinner speakers – those who are content to shine as minor stars & in the absence of brighter luminaries – were B. Stanhope, Dering, Lord R. Montagu & others. Cobden spoke[15] after Ducane. I heard Gibson (who I think is, for a speaker from the Treasury bench, sometimes rather dull & laboured), also, Gladstone & Disraeli. We soon divided 347–99 – & sugar won. Malt came in a 'questionable shape'. Had it come, disembarrassed of the budget, it might have had a different fate. But we wanted to carry the budget, & to take out a great brick, like sugar, might have been fatal.

The great Bentinck is becoming a stupendous bore. He speaks almost daily. He thinks he is a leader of the country party & sneers at the front benches on both sides. I forgot to mention Cobbett's speech in favour of the poor man's beer, which he confidently described as a necessary of life. C. is a very pleasant & skilful speaker. He speaks rarely – always courteously & to the point. Indulging in no personalities, he deals calmly with facts, & arguments. It is one of our model styles for the House – & deserves study.

The malt tax will probably fall one day. Many of us wished it no good. The truth is the sum is too large to be dealt with at any moment – nearly £6,000,000. A partial reduction would effect little good; the cost of the excise would remain as before. 'Kettle brewing' at the houses of poor men would, it is said by Bass & others, be very dear brewing – & few could afford it. A reduction on the sugar duties would benefit more consumers – & afford more wholesome sustenance. Cobden is for reducing the tax & so I suppose it will go one day. I was 'sweet'.

Friday, 15 April: [...] It is rumoured that Lowe has resigned. Disraeli called Lord P[almerston]'s attention to the number of under-secretaries sitting in Parliament – being in excess of the number allowed by act.[16]

---

[14] Moving to give priority to the reduction of the malt tax; *H* clxxiv. 972–9.

[15] Sympathising with Bartellot's cause but arguing against mixing up the two issues; *H* clxxiv. 1021–8.

[16] No more than four could sit in the Commons, but for a time there had been five which raised doubts about the position of the newest, Lord Hartington.

Monday, 18 April: $4\frac{1}{4}$. Signs of a breeze. The Tories have mustered early. Whiteside, Disraeli & many more in active talk. Most of the benches below the gangway and the opposition side are retained by cards. Bruce's appointment[17] announced: a motion for a new writ. Sir W. Heathcote doubts whether the question relating to the 5 secretaries may not be involved. He moved adjournment of the debate on the writ. Disraeli was sitting just below Sir W. Heathcote, and doubtless set him on. Headlam replied & was followed by Whiteside. The murder is out. The attorney general[18] then spoke in favor of issuing the writ. Full house already. All seemed charged with speeches. A party business evidently. Disraeli to order – he thinks that, in the absence of the chief minister, he had better not argue the question of privilege. He raised a new point, viz, that Bruce was not yet of the privy council; and again suggested postponement. (Attorney general hurriedly turns over a book. All are in a fluster.) Grey acceded to adjournment; a strong government can afford to concede anything.

The whole story of Lowe's retirement was brought forward. Lowe spoke at length and made a strong impression. His blindness was alluded to with a voice slightly tremulous with emotion. It is clear that his physical infirmity was in some degree mixed up with the abuse which, in spite of orders, has continued to prevail with respect to marking reports of inspectors. Lord R. Cecil excused himself as best he could. Lord Palmerston gravely rebuked Cecil's carelessness, & praised Lowe [...] Some say Lowe should have stated on a former occasion all he knew about the former practice relating to sending back marked passages of inspected reports. In that case the victory would not have been obtained by Cecil the other night, & Lowe would not have resigned. It seems that Lowe actually expunged matter because it was too favorable to the office. The debate did Cecil's reputation no good. He does not seem to have kindly instincts or the spirit of fair play. A committee is to inquire into the case made against Lowe.

Disraeli taunted ministers with inadequately supporting their colleagues. A new writ issued for Merthyr Tydvil, on Bruce's vacating his seat. Whether Lord Hartington is or is not legally a member remains for a committee, which is to sit thereon. It appears that he is liable for penalties for every case in which he has sat and voted.[19] The attorney-general maintains that undersecretaries of state are not

[17] To replace Lowe at the education board of the privy council; his transfer from the home office reduced the number of under-secretaries in the Commons to the legal limit of four.

[18] Sir Roundell Palmer.

[19] The select committee reported on 27 Apr. that Hartington had not vacated his seat; *P.P.* 1864, x. 577. An act was later passed indemnifying him against his 'illegal' votes.

officers under the Crown, but officers under the secretaries. Why then have undersecretaries ever vacated their seats? Palmerston was never more joyously impudent than in his reply to Disraeli's charge that the first minister was chiefly in fault for allowing the House to fall into error about a fifth undersecretary. He vigorously counter-charged the opposition with neglect of their duty of finding fault. What did they exist for but to find fault? &c (great laughter) [...]

Thursday, 21 April: Kinnaird put a question to Gladstone amidst impatient remonstrants – was the rumour true that Garibaldi's intended departure was in any way influenced by apprehensions of discontent in the mind of Napoleon at the great man's reception? Gladstone strenuously denied the rumour as ridiculous. Several near my seat agreed that the question lowered the dignity of the House & ought not to have been asked.

Gladstone & Sheridan had a good contest on Fire Insurances. The former carried his motion.[20] Yet, Sheridan has much to say for his proposal; but unfortunately, the budget is too complex a matter to be disposed of, bit by bit, & by irresponsible advisers. We have accepted a reduction on the Income Tax & on the sugar duties with other changes. Let us 'rest & be thankful'.

The house filled early: Garibaldi was expected. Several rather bronzed & sallow young men soon entered the upper gallery, where diplomatic people usually sit. But Garibaldi was not among the number. His sons I understood were. A little while afterwards, the great man came, & in a very quiet manner proceeded to occupy the front bench behind the Serjeant's chair. He wore a sort of light gray cloak which was thrown over his chest & shoulder, so as not to exhibit, except accidentally, his red blouse or shirt. All eyes scanned him, whilst in a calm, contemplative, unostentatious way he surveyed the house & members, who, generally, were careful not to stare long at him at a time. There was some ridiculous hero-worship, which some of us could not help noticing. Old Briscoe placed himself (not sitting, but standing) in the narrow passage leading towards the division lobby &, turning his head from side to side, seemed to watch every gesture of the general as of a more than mortal being. It looked a little, however, as if Briscoe thought he had first discovered the hero's great qualities. But Briscoe is a chartered oddity. Scully, in his asides, sneered from the Catholic point of view – inquiring which was Mazzini, whether he was present or some such question – the exact

---

[20] 170:117 against Sheridan's amendment for a wholesale reduction in fire insurance duties rather than only on that for stock in trade; *H* clxxiv. 1439-46.

purport of wh I forget. B,[21] a very clever man near my seat, observed it was not an intellectual countenance (Garibaldi's). Very soon the general rose abruptly & left as quietly as he entered [...]

Monday, 25 April: A considerable hubbub among 'advanced' liberals on account of the police putting down a Garibaldi meeting on Primrose hill.[22] Sir Geo. Grey observed, in reply to a question put by Harvey Lewis, that this had not happened in consequence of any special instructions to the Police. Dolus latet in generalibus. It turns out that a large body of police were in attendance. By whose order? We have not heard the last of this matter [...]

Tuesday, 26 April: Arthur Mills moved for papers relating to New Zealand.[23] His voice was low & manner lachrymose: he speaks with his eyes shut mostly. Being one of the few interested in his subject, I took every pains to obtain him a good hearing by cheering from time to time – and, eventually, succeeded. Buxton seconded the motion. Cardwell[24] replied skilfully &, in a great degree, satisfactorily [...] The plan presented by the Minister involves a new guaranteed loan & gave me an opportunity of reminding Henley of the manner in wh. he & others on a committee had been deceived by Mr. H. Sewell some years ago, when a £500,000 loan was to be guaranteed[25] [...]

Thursday, 28 April: Great debate on the case of Tuscaloosa. Collier delivered an excellent speech,[26] in the best taste, to a full house – the best thing he has done in my presence. I paired all night with Sir Wm. Verner. Govt. won.[27]

The Tories mustered in great force. Whiteside replied to Collier. Cairns battled with the attorney gen[era]l.[28] Smaller men fought, with varying success, in different parts of the arena. Bovill, Denman & M. Smith were among the combatants.

I took pains to get a reprint of a Parl[iamentar]y paper dated July 7/59 exhibiting the mode in wh. Parliament was induced to guarantee

---

[21] Possibly E.P. Bouverie.

[22] See the letter from the secretary of the working men's Garibaldi committee to *The Times*, 25 Apr. 1864, p. 7.

[23] I.e. the policy of confiscating Maori land adopted by the New Zealand legislature; *H* clxxiv. 1625–33.

[24] Recently appointed Colonial secretary.

[25] See above, 10 May 1858.

[26] The solicitor general, defending the colonial office against Peacocke's complaint about the arrest of a barque, captured from the federals by the confederates, renamed the 'Tuscaloosa' and used as a tender; *H* clxxiv. 1777–83.

[27] 219:185.

[28] Sir Roundell Palmer.

a loan to N. Zealand of £500,000 in 1857. Labouchere was Minister. H. Sewell came before a committee, as minister from N. Zealand, & made a gross mis-statement to that committee – wh. was exposed by me – & is a warning how we agree to Cardwell's intention to propose to guarantee a new loan. Cardwell told me he had no objection to the reprint desired. Willoughby & others have been set on the scent by me.

Friday, 29 April: A curious story was related by H. Berkeley, the case of Mr. Bewicke, who, partly thro' his own perversity, partly thro' perjured witnesses, became a felon & underwent penal servitude. Subsequently, by the energy of his housekeeper, who sought the aid of Serj[ean]t Shee, steps were taken which demonstrated Mr. Bewicke's innocence. The charge had been the use of a loaded pistol agt. Sheriff's officers employed in consequence of his refusal to pay costs in a suit wh. he lost. The officers, a set of perjured ruffians & proven villains of the deepest dye, laid agt. him the accusation. Subsequently, they were in turn convicted of perjury & punished. But, meanwhile, B's goods were seized by the Com[missione]rs of Greenwich Hospital – & he has lost thousands. The case is a very hard one. But the difficulty is how to deal with it without setting a precedent which would involve many cases every year. Not cases so bad, but failures of justice amounting to ruin of innocent people. The attorney gen[era]l spoke well, as he always speaks; &, for one, I followed his advice not to incautiously adopt Berkeley's resolution,[29] wh. might have been an awkward precedent. Yet, some remedy appeared to be called for & up to a certain point – viz, as to part of Mr. B's pecuniary loss – Govt. were disposed to refer his complaint to a committee. Berkeley, however, buoyed up by Disraeli & others divided & won by 2.[30] But his main resolution was defeated, & Ministers carried their amendmt.[31] and a committee will consider the case [...]

In my judgment Berkeley was judicious in describing the victim as a country gentleman of ancient family.[32] I doubt if so much interest in him would have been otherwise raised. The modified proposition was, I think, adopted by Ministers in consequence of a dismal report

[29] For the House in committee to consider compensation for Bewicke; *H* clxxiv. 1917–23.

[30] 120:118 for Berkeley's amendment to the question that the Speaker leave the chair, on the House entering into committee of supply.

[31] 148:100 for Sir George Grey's amendment to Berkeley's amendment, for a select committee.

[32] Bewicke owned Threapwood hall in Northumberland.

from Brand,[33] who wedged himself in next to the chief law officer & communicated with him. His countenance told of probable defeat, and I could easily guess what he said. The treasury bench all in a flutter, & frequent & rapid 'asides' took place from under Sir Geo. Grey's hand (wh. was over his mouth & face) to I. Butt sitting behind – and from 2 or 3 other Ministers. I judge that Butt either offered to back them, or they were making suggestions to him. This bye play I distinctly watched from the opposite gallery & called R[oebuck]'s. attention to it. Butt is a man of great abilities, and appears to be often useful at convenient times.

Disraeli scented humiliation for the Whigs & forgot the future difficulty of sitting at the Home Office. Hardy, who was once under-secretary thereof, spoke with becoming foresight & voted agt. his chief!! This is human nature.

[...] The dissenters are in a great state of excitement on account of a threatened extension of Church rates in district parishes.[34] Wait a little, and the Church itself will move agt. this nuisance. The greater & more complex it becomes and the wider its net, by so much the stouter & more general will be the opposition to its continuance. The best general in the camp at present is 'general' election.

Tuesday, 3 May: [...] Palmerston is still absent. Sir G. Grey seems to hold the position of leader.

Thursday, 5 May: [...] In the course of the evening I took occasion to mention the necessity of providing measures to protect soldiers near large towns from some contagious diseases & several members confirmed my advice. A committee was suggested by me & it seems that Hartington will very likely announce one.

Friday, 6 May: [...] How Hartington mumbled his words last night! – and indeed he mumbles at all times. He appears, however, to possess good plain abilities & average common sense. O'Reilly shd. be employed by ministers – he shews useful qualifications; especially, in military matters. The worst of Hartington is that only those opposite can hear him. O'Reilly may live to retrieve the blunder of com-manding a papal force.

[...] The feeling for the Danes[35] in the House seems to wax stronger.

---

[33] Government chief whip.

[34] The church buildings acts consolidation bill would have extended church rates to newly created parishes; withdrawn.

[35] Who were at war with Prussia and Austria over the disputed duchies of Schleswig and Holstein. On 25 Apr. a conference of the Powers had convened in London, but there was no cessation of hostilities; see David F. Krein, *The Last Palmerston Government*, (Iowa, 1978), pp. 119–44 for the background.

A speech of Cecil's in this sense was received with loud cheers. It is to be hoped that members and the Public will not go into a war with precipitation & have to repent at leisure. Not one in a million understands the Danish case. And who foresees, even dimly, the relative positions of nations at the next great peace? Meanwhile, there are threats of war, war, almost everywhere. Of course, I am not in opposition to just war, only for God's sake! let us know what we are about.

Monday, 9 May: There has been much jealousy of the conduct of some of the authorities in putting down a meeting on Primrose Hill when Garibaldi was here. Another meeting has been held there[36] – & there are things in the case which do not bear a good appearance. Ministers will incur more censure.

[...] Osborne elicited information of a victory of the Danes over the Austrians at sea, near Heligoland. Cheering was general, enthusiastic & protracted. We learned this evening, also, that a suspension of hostilities for one month had been agreed to at the Conference. It sounded curiously, when Sir Geo. Grey spoke of a telegram dated 2 p.m. announcing the battle and another dated 4 p.m. announcing the result – & this within about $\frac{1}{2}$ an hour from the time last mentioned.

Mr. May (one of our clerks) agreed with me in thinking that Ministers will live over the Session. The suspension of hostilities & the increased chances of peace seem to him to promise this.

Tuesday, 10 May: A most tedious speech on finance delivered by J. White. It occupied more than an hour and a half. The incidence of taxation was his theme.[37] Great was the patience of the House. Pollard Urquhart followed, sustaining his moderate reputation. Gladstone then commenced: unfortunately my time of staying was exhausted. The evening passed without division. White & the radicals who act with him appear to me to misunderstand the principles of taxation altogether. Heavy taxes ought not to be charged with the sufferings of needlewomen. A new, sudden & oppressive tax creates much hardship, but rarely can such hardship be mainly due to any old established system of finance. The adjustment must long since have been made in population. There is no space here for unfolding this doctrine, wh.

---

[36] *The Times*, 9 May 1864, p. 8. The eventual result was the foundation of the Reform League in Feb. 1865; Frances Elma Gillespie, *Labor and Politics in England 1850–1867*, (Durham, North Carolina, 1927), pp. 250–3.

[37] Motion for a select committee to consider ways of achieving a more equitable adjustment of the burden of taxation; *H* clxxv. 261–73. Withdrawn.

is trite enough. White's speech, delivered with an air of a person propounding obvious truth & applauded by Bright who sat behind (with Cobden), is a good evidence among others of the unwarranted confidence with which advanced Reformers (as they call themselves) are contented to speak on finance.

Wednesday, 11 May: Noon – debate in (almost) darkness – & then lights were lit. There must have been a heavy bank of cloud & smoke from the East end. Baines brought on his Electoral franchise Bill for boroughs.[38] He proposes to add 240,705 electors to the 487,000 now holding the right – or 49 percent. Instead of 1 in 5, 1 in 3 adults would vote. Baines was calm, earnest, & practical – his handling of figures 'luminous' (to use a word of Gladstone's uttered subsequently).

Cave groaned dolefully agt. the Bill – moving the previous question. His manner, like Baines', is rather too like that of a dissenting parson. Marsh seconded him, ominous of our defeat as Marsh sits on our side. Cave had been in America, whence he drew some of his strongest arguments. He warned us of the fate of the man who had for an epitaph 'I was well – I would be better – here I lie!'

Gladstone supported Baines with warmth & energy. Disdaining paltry tactics & expediency, he boldly cast upon his opponents the 'onus probandi' of shewing the unfitness of the working man to vote – & roundly expressed, or obviously implied, the rights of man. (Ironical cheers.) Gladstone smilingly said he would 'not provoke more inarticulate reasoning' (laughter). Bright's sympathy with Gladstone, or jealousy, would hardly let him keep his seat. There was a curious hiatus on the Ministerial bench, while Gladstone was making a Chartist speech. Where was Grey, Wood & the rest? Brand, Luke White, Baring, Layard & a few non ministerial men sat on the front bench but a long space was empty on Gladstone's left. Will he break up the cabinet? Has he kicked over the traces?

Whiteside came next – declamatory, plausible, jocose, wordy, caustic & inconsistent. Ed. Forster's speech I missed. Bass could not get much of a hearing. Lord Fermoy [...] then spoke: and received scant attention. Cries of 'divide', 'read', 'agreed', 'Bar' &c drowned the voices of most other orators of whom two at one moment stood up, side by side, awaiting a preference – on which the humorous House shouted 'both'.

Division agt. us 272 to 216.

The old high-dried Whigs will be frantic. What will happen?

Thursday, 12 May: [...] The speech of Gladstone is an historical

---

[38] To create a £6 household franchise.

event. Rousseau is, apparently, in communication with our Chancellor of exchequer thro' some medium. Will Gladstone go further & throw upon owners of estates the onus of shewing their titles to exclusive possession? I suggest no argument agt. his views; I merely inquire how far he would carry them [. . .]

Friday, 13 May: Lowe recurred to the subject of his disputed accuracy in the matter of the reports of Educational Inspectors. The House was very much moved in his favour, thinking him hardly treated. Lord R. Cecil shd. have withdrawn his charges & apologized. He is content to abide the result of the coming inquiry by a Committee. The noble Lord seems to me to wage political war with the ferocity of a red Indian [. . .]

Thursday, 19 May: [. . .] One hears whispers that Palmerston has been worse than usual when gout attacks him. Our position is curious. The Queen is in low & desponding spirits, which, perhaps, in a subject would receive a different name. An octogenarian first minister,[39] who cannot attend, leads Parliament. A Ministry we have which is too weak to do justice to its own subordinates such as Lowe &, perhaps, Stansfeld. Is office worth having on such terms?

Gladstone's speech on Baines' motion is still a topic much discussed in society. What will it lead to? Most of the Whigs, who will eat any amount of distasteful food to retain office, will, I presume, take up Gladstone's opinions. Some of the more timid of the party will take the opportunity of joining the Conservatives.

Friday, 20 May: Palmerston was received with much cheering on his return after his illness. He looked thinner, but not much worse than usual. Agt. Baxter, who called attention to our intervention in Chinese affairs & to the consequences, in his view, of such intervention, his Lordship stoutly defended the principle of interventions by numerous modern instances – e.g. those of Spain, Belgium, Greece, Turkey & some others. How about Poland, Cabul, China, Africa, Japan? Some of these names suggest doubts at least. P. spoke in his usual manner for 20 minutes – boasting, bantering, jesting &, to the wonder of all observers, gaily holding his own at 80! The war in Ashantee[40] was afterwards the subject of debate – Pakington calling attention thereto. This business is another fruit of the rule of the D[uke] of

---

[39] Not quite; Palmerston was 80 in Oct.
[40] See below, 17 June 1864.

Newcastle in office.[41] This nation will, I think, be ruined by some Duke.

L[awson] a connection of the late Sir J. Graham brought me back in his hired cab; &, on my calling P. a 'grand old man', my friend strongly deprecated the phrase, saying 'grand old humbug' would be more appropriate: and he alluded to the celebrated suppression of dispatches, in Macnaughten's time, in the Cabul business. Dunlop, it will be recollected, brought the matter before Parliament a session or two since.[42] My friend said that Graham (who was in bed when the debate took place) was most interested in it – & said to L. that Palmerston was the only man who could have done such a thing – ie, garbling public documents to suit the exigencies of a Ministry in danger of impeachment – &, I think, probably deserving it. The Cabul massacre will never be forgotten in India, or England. A minister, who could have prevented it & did not, wd. deserve hanging. Courtesy kept back what was on my lips – to ask what Graham would have had to reply to Palmerston had he reminded G. of the opening of Mazzini's letters to please the Austrian government[43] [...] I explained that by 'grand old man' I meant to express that P. had many great qualities, physical & intellectual, and, indeed, few men could arrive at his position without some great qualities. Also, I cautioned L. agt. a too severe judgment on a man governing a constitutional country – and I asked him if he ever drove 4 horses. A British minister drives a team far more numerous &, possibly, of a lower denomination [...]

Thursday, 26 May: [...] On attending at 4 p.m. I met Brand, who consulted me upon my wishes & intentions with regard to my notice of motion.[44] My reply was that I was only concerned to see government move in the matter. He thought postponemt. for a week would enable Clarence Paget to introduce 2 bills he has prepared & get them read a 2d. time & referred to a Select Committee. I assented – & postponed my resolution for a week. Brand observed 'we are with you'. So much the better. My trouble will be saved – & the cause promoted.

Hennessy moved 3 resolutions on the Polish question.[45] He made a clever &, in parts, an eloquent speech. It seemed to me that, in some of his accusations, he made out an unanswerable case. In particular, he charged Ld. P[almerston] with the having, despite professions of

---

[41] He had resigned as Colonial secretary, on 2 Apr., due to ill health.

[42] See above, 19 Mar. 1861.

[43] When Graham was home secretary in Peel's ministry.

[44] On contagious diseases.

[45] To the effect that the government was no longer bound to recognise Russian sovereignty in Poland; H clxxv. 636–51. Rejection of the resolutions agreed on.

interest, neglected several excellent opportunities of aiding Poland –
when, for example, France, or Austria, has been willing to combat
for that nation, or when circumstances have been peculiarly favourable. Lord Palmerston seemed shy of the points which told most agt.
him – yet, he was forcible enough in reminding Hennessy that, when
he moved before,[46] he distinctly said he did not ask for war. Seymour
Fitzgerald followed Lord P. and gave increased force & point to
Hennessy's charges. It was clear to me that H. has made good use of
his recent interview with the Emperor of France. Hence the knowledge
exhibited of French despatches.

Grant Duff could not get a hearing. What an odd little intellectual
ferret it is! Clever, cultivated & industrious (as I fancy) – why does
he not succeed? Is he conceited? or does he not read his House well?
The House is like a woman – 'uncertain, coy & hard to please'.
Hennessy, near dinner time, announced that he shd. not divide; but
Scully persisted in crying 'no'. However, he found no seconder (much
laughter) [. . .]

The Queen's German leanings were distinctly alluded to in the
Lords by Lord Ellenborough.[47] Very ominous this! Earl R[ussell]
accepted the full responsibility for all which has been done. I do not
generally comment upon language used in 'another place'. But when
Earl Grey talks of one of Earl R's despatches as written in the style of
a schoolboy's theme, & describes him as uttering threats which might
be compared to the scoldings of an important old woman,[48] it seems
to me something is looming in the field of political combinations.
Certainly, Lord R. would have wisely avoided menace, had he foreseen the lame conclusion to which events would reduce him. He
certainly hinted at war in his despatches to German powers, and
roundly rated Prussia in a manner not likely to be endured. Denmark
has, perhaps, some reason to complain.

Friday, 27 May: [. . .] Northcote, on going into supply, moves a
resolution on Prize money & delays of distributing such money – he
proceeds in an easy flow of self satisfied monotony & learned prose –
wh. soon shuts the eyes of Disraeli & Whiteside (the latter sleeps with
a remarkably pleasant smile on his countenance. By the way, a
member of the House shd. acquire this faculty of looking well in sleep.
Some men twist themselves into most ungraceful attitudes – their
chins fall – & their faces assume idiotic expressions. If unpleasant
sounds be added, some friend is compelled to sacrifice himself &

[46] On 27 Feb. 1863; *H* clxix. 879–92.
[47] With reference to the Schleswig–Holstein dispute; *H* clxix. 606–10.
[48] *H* clxix. 616–17.

awaken the sleeper, who rarely thanks his benefactor). Palmerston promises reference of Northcote's case to the Court of Admiralty. In point of fact, that case was a good one; &, had N. divided, I think I shd. have supported him. He is a painstaking man, & must rise.

[...] When I returned at 9.30 pm, I found a joyful club in full sitting. The Speaker was in his private room taking refreshment, so members on both sides merged their differences & all were laughing & talking together. All sorts of odd coteries were formed. Strangers are resting their muscles by standing up. The ladies must be greatly bored. Two more, in gorgeous bournous, have just entered behind the grating. Mr. May (the only clerk at the table) is still, as usual, at work – (order, order) Mr. Speaker returns, & every one is in his place in a second – business proceeds [...]

Monday, 30 May: [...] Col[onel] Stuart astonished himself by beating Ministers on a vote of £4,000 towards a Lunatic asylum for the Isle of Man. The House took almost a savage satisfaction in rejecting the vote,[49] which certainly was an outrageously impudent proposal. Why cannot the Isle of Man as well provide for its lunatics as Devon or Cornwall? Of course, my vote was with Stuart [...]

Tuesday, 31 May: Cobden made a great speech in support of a policy of non-intervention in China. I think I never heard him speak to greater advantage. The impression he made on the opposition was most remarkable, & from them he obtained much cheering. Very skilfully he cited the authority of the D[uke] of Wellington in favour of non-interference with the Chinese government & he produced a written order [to] Lord Napier, then in China, (that is in 1835) laying down very precisely the rule on which he was to proceed [...] Cobden praised the Chinese as an industrious & frugal people – & added that they had been Free traders very early & constantly – adducing a proof + that they actually allowed a cargo of rice (I think) to come in duty free+ which sounded to me very like evidence the wrong way – since to let in a foreign commodity, duty free, on the ground of its being favourable to some interest, however numerous, is very like the protective system. But perhaps my reasoning on this is rather hazy. Cobden sketched a policy which he deemed suitable to our interests in China.[50]

[...] Brand conversed with me on the subject of my notice – that relating to soldiers & sailors in barracks. Lord C. Paget is to await

---

[49] 95:73.
[50] He favoured the setting-up of a number of free ports on islands off the Chinese mainland; *H* clxxv. 916–33.

my pressure, & then introduce his bills, & refer them to a Select Committee.

Wednesday, 1 June: University tests Bill – Committee. Trefusis moved the amendmt.[51] in a short fluent speech – evidently learnt, but not amiss. Go on, young man! but don't presume upon a partial success like this. The maxim for the House shd. be '*Labore*'.

Leatham's speech was clever & full of point. His style is evidently influenced by Bright's – who is his near connexion by marriage. C. Clifford of the Isle of Wight followed. He appears to be rather clever & well read – judging by his quotations [...]

Walter Morrison was, as usual, above the average of young speakers, & will almost certainly succeed. A member (Scully, I think) kindly reminded the House that M. was a first class man at College. M. was modestly pleased – I watched his happy face, which appeared half-ashamed of its happiness. Northcote – don't you speak too frequently, most worthy & painstaking Gentleman? Are you not a trifle too fluent? Roebuck put the sense of the question tersely & well; tests were a web wh. caught the little flies & let the large flies pass thro'. Scully was lengthy, funny & theological. He criticized the formularies of our prayer book – & was nearly caught tripping by Cecil. Scully was not quite certain whether one of the creeds (the apostles, I think)[52] was in our ritual. Cecil interrupted ('order') to convict him of ignorance, if possible. Scully slipped away in a little cloud of jests.

Neate's prepared attack on Cecil, founded on a recent Tory meeting at Oxford, of which the supposed object was to unseat Gladstone, was very brilliant & epigrammatic. Cecil, who had received notice of it from Neate, was not infelicitous in reply &, having been challenged to repeat in the House what he had said at Oxford, boldly repeated the words used; which words, I think, were that no one could be a good Churchman who was not a Conservative. This was thought to be a great scandal. However, the whole episode was irregular, & Scully afterwards complained that, whereas the Speaker noticed Scully's alleged deviation from the subject under debate, no notice was taken of a dispute which was obviously irregular & disorderly. The Speaker observed that, had Scully seen reason to complain of anything out of order, he shd. have noticed it at the time (laugh). But why did Mr. Speaker notice one deviation & not the other? Division – Ayes 236 – Noes 226.[53] I voted with the ayes. The Speaker looked much pleased at his repartee to Scully – and, also, cast some rather

---

[51] Against Dodson's bill to abolish the religious tests required of persons taking degrees.
[52] Impossible to ascertain from the report in *Hansard*.
[53] For going into committee on the Oxford tests bill.

sour looks at him. But Mr. Speaker should not desire this kind of success. What if he got the worst of an encounter? The dignity of the House, wh. he represents, would suffer disparagement. If *Mr. Denison* has no sense of dignity, it might not be (comparatively speaking) of much Public consequence.

Monday, 6 June: [...] The sitting commenced tamely. A few questions (one by Osborne, on the Conference)[54] were put to Ministers. Then came Col[onel] Sykes with a story of breach of faith to the late Indian army in the arrangements arising out of altered circumstances after the mutiny. Sir C. Wood replied in a long & dull speech. A few others supported Sykes' case, when, suddenly & unexpectedly, Lord H. Lennox recalled attention to Denmark & asked Osborne if he was satisfied with Lord Palmerston's reply to the question O. had put to him. This produced a pungent & humorous answer from the MP for Liskeard in the negative, whereupon Disraeli, seeing discord & a chance of increasing it, spoke ably for some 25 minutes. Lord P., briefly & at first under some signs of irritation, followed, but declined to enter at length on a subject whereon he professed that he was tongue-tied [...]

By the way, I noticed that Palmerston coughed frequently during his brief speech (of 5 min[utes]). Early in the even[in]g he brought messages by command of H.M. His walk up the House was evidently scrutinized by the watchful Tories. Hats off – & the Speaker reads each paper commencing 'Victoria Regina'. One, recommends a grant of £20,000 to Sir Rowland Hill; the other, £1,000 a year to Lady Elgin.[55] The Liberal party chiefly cheered the former; all cheered the latter proposal.

(Palmerston was riding about London on Sunday. I met him twice; once in St. James St, once in Pall Mall. Aug[ustu]s Smith told me P. nearly rode over him.)

[...] The point made by Disraeli on the conference was that Ministers had departed from the understanding which had been the basis of the reticence & moderation of Parliament; viz, that the ground on which England took her stand was the London treaty of 1852, whereas now quite new proposals of partition are under discussion.[56] He contended that an understanding had been violated, and he seemingly insinuated that a vote of censure might be the consequence [...]

---

[54] Inquiring whether the London conference on the Schleswig–Holstein dispute had led to any result; *H* clxxv. 1262.

[55] Widow of the late viceroy of India.

[56] Whereas the King of Denmark was originally to have held both of the duchies, it was now proposed that he should only have part of Schleswig; Krein, *Palmerston Government*, pp. 153–4.

Wednesday, 8 June: The Permissive Bill.[57] Lawson amusing and personal. When he attacked Roebuck for lately saying 'I spit upon' a member's plan, Lawson raised a clapping of hands in the gallery. This was instantly suppressed. Bass & Sir G. Grey were successively passed in review with much humour and point. The application of 'canting hypocrite' retorted upon Roebuck who lately used the phrase in the plural was a mistake, as Lawson will find out before the sun shall go down. Bright argumentative and philosophical. He thought the bill departed from the real doctrine of representative government, viz that the elected should deliberate and decide, not the elective body; and he deprecated violent discussions in every district – & probable injustice. He suggested the giving powers now held by justices to Town councils, but he believed more in education. Roebuck very calm and logical. After rebuking Lawson, he discussed Bright's plan.[58] The House paid the true orator the evident compliment of leaving their seats in considerable numbers the instant he ceased. At $5\frac{1}{4}$ p.m. the Speaker went out to luncheon – we talked over the speeches: suddenly Scully came in smiling and saying he had come from the refreshment table, where he had found many supporters of the bill taking sherry and other intoxicating drinks; he told them he should mention their names in the House; to which they replied that the bill would never pass (much merriment). The Home Secretary[59] briefly analysed the measure, criticizing it skilfully & temperately. Others followed – C. Buxton, Wykeham-Martyn, Humberstone, C. Forster, & such like (Divide, divide & impatience). The house wants to come to Bass's music & organ grinder Bill, lower down on the notice paper. Scully told his story above mentioned, to the House (much laughter). Lawson gracefully apologized to Roebuck (Hear). House divided 292 to 35. This, I trust, is a settler. It was urged in debate that were Lawson's bill law, refreshments could not be sold in the Commons' House, if $\frac{2}{3}$rds of the ratepayers of Westminster disapproved. Yet we might all get drunk by going over Westminster bridge. Again, ratepayers are not the working classes for whom the ratepayers would legislate.

Friday, 10 June: [...] Lord R. Cecil made a speech in which the present mode of conducting private business legislation was his theme.[60] Upon this point the noble lord holds several confident

---

[57] To give ratepayers control over the granting of licences to publicans.

[58] Arguing that it would cause much local political dissension, and preferring to leave the matter in the hands of magistrates; *H* clxxv. 1408–13.

[59] Sir George Grey.

[60] Cecil's amendment called for the work of committees on private bills to be 'discharged by some tribunal external to this House.' He argued that attendance on such committees was burdensome for M.P.s, and that the system was considered expensive and inefficient by chambers of commerce and other bodies; *H* clxxv. 1545–51.

opinions & indulged in some rather careless assertions. Wilson Patten easily dealt with him. Lord Stanley spoke usefully, as usual, & earned universal commendation for the indefatigable labour he had taken upon himself, thro' two whole sessions [. . .]

My motion for a committee on solders &c has given me a great deal of anxiety & careful thought. Yet, perhaps, it may not be necessary to speak for more than a few minutes. The danger is not so much in what to say as in what to avoid saying.

Monday, 13 June: [. . .] $4\frac{1}{2}$ p.m. Most people expected that there would be an announcement of a resolution hostile to Ministers.[61] Nothing of the kind came to pass, tho' one still hears that the Tories mean mischief.

Osborne sparred with the Premier on the subject of the Conference. Was a certain statement in the Morning Post true? Palmerston had not read the Morning Post (a laugh). Mr. Kinglake required specific confirmation of another statement. Lord P. had not heard of it, and was not inclined to believe it (laughter). Of course, if members really swallow every story brought to them & then ask questions about it, Government is sure to make game of them.

Followed, next, Mr. Smolletts motion on the case of Azeem Jah,[62] wh. seemed as bad as possible. It is a case involving the honour of England & was in substance unanswered.

Smollett's speech was a very remarkable one. He seemed to be under feelings of strong indignation & used very angry & bitter language. Yet, it is but due to him to say that the grievance seemed to justify it – if truly stated, it was an infamous case of spoilation of a Native Prince, enjoying under treaty certain property – which treaty our Minister at the time,[63] with an almost cynical dishonesty, set aside. Smollett's manner is odd, witty & effective. His arguments were forcible; & urged in bold & denunciatory language. No doubt, he was very personal, but so must any one be who attacks delinquents. It was understood that Lord Stanley & Fitzroy Kelly were watching Wood & the Attorney gen[era]l & this was, I believe, actually true. It was a droll position. The assailants over-reached themselves by their tactics – & hence a division was taken in haste about seven or eight o'clock, when Ministers won (45 to 62).[64] Unfortunately, I lost this during my brief absence [. . .]

---

[61] On the Danish question.

[62] Who had been deprived of his right to the title of Nawab of the Carnatic by the abrogation of the treaty signed by his father and the East India company in 1801; *H* clxxv. 1641–55.

[63] Vernon Smith, president of the board of control in 1857.

[64] Trelawny mistakenly wrote 67.

Wednesday, 15 June: [...] instalments of Law Reform. One was introduced by Mr. Charles Forster & purported to abolish forfeitures to the Crown for felony.[65] This led to much useful analysis of questions relating to the rationale of punishmt. Roebuck, Whiteside, Malins & others advocated Forster's proposal. Also, the Attorney gen[era]l,[66] though under caution as to details. Roebuck cited Bentham with good effect – that, if a fine of one penny would prevent crime, no higher punishment would be justifiable, as being unnecessary pain. How long a fallacy outlives its formal exposition! There is a certain body in the House which requires to hear the tritest truths afresh every time the related question arises.

[...] It is rumoured that the Conservatives are not prepared for battle in serious earnest. A close observer, likely to be well informed, told me that there were supposed to be 70 Tories who will not let Disraeli have the position he aspires to fill, & hence no vote of want of confidence [...]

Thursday, 16 June: [...] Ferrand ranted for an hour or two on the Charity Commission; its faults, its cost, & the mode in which its offices have been filled up. He was very personal, & might have carried a resolution if he knew how to speak within, instead of beyond, his facts. He met with a reverse.[67] This vote I did not share in, &, perhaps, so best, as allusion was made to Mr. Boase's supposed conduct towards me at the Liskeard election,[68] &, tho' it was not true to say that he was my agent & deserted me, it was true that Boase, Grey & their party were all bound to abide by a certain scrutiny – which they threw overboard.[69] In fact they committed a direct breach of faith. Boase & Wm Grey, subsequently, received valuable appointments. W. Grey had been Lord Palmerston's private secretary. Boase was Grey's election agent & thus, at the Public expense, all parties concerned were comfortably provided for.

When I returned, supply was under discussion. One or two divisions of little moment occurred: in one, involving a principle – viz, that the

---

[65] 2nd reading of the forfeiture of land and goods bill agreed to; no further progress made.

[66] Sir Roundell Palmer.

[67] Motion for a select committee of inquiry rejected, 116:40. Ferrand had described the commission as 'a snug nest of Whigs'; *H* clxxv. 1841–64.

[68] In Mar. 1854, when Trelawny had been defeated by William Grey. Boase's letter to *The Times*, 15 Feb. 1864, p. 5, failed to refute Ferrand's charge that he owed his appointment as a charity commission inspector to the fact that he had been Grey's election agent.

[69] The *Plymouth Journal*, 30 Mar. 1854, p. 5, confirms that an incomplete canvass of the Liberal voters had yielded a majority of 54:33 for Trelawny, but that Grey had refused to withdraw.

Public in England ought not to be called on to pay for magistrates all over the districts we have acquired at the outposts of the Empire, but rather the natives, I was made a teller with Mr. Hennessy. The special sum was £450 for the 'residing magistrate' at Anguilla[70] [...]

Waiting till nearly 2 a.m. my notice on Contagious Diseases came into play at last, but too late to admit of a speech in support of it. So I was obliged to content myself with an indication of my object. Lord C. Paget, then, tendered to me a promise of a bill on Monday, & a committee thereon, so I withdrew on those terms & I am content [...]

Friday, 17 June: [...] House met again at 6 pm, and soon came Sir J. Hay moving his resolution expressive of regret on account of losses on the Gold coast.[71] He made a long, &, in parts, rather violent speech. The truth is he shd. not have been mover. A man who has lost his brother, thro' alleged misconduct in a department, should not be the person selected to lead an opposition. Herein the Conservatives wanted tact. Sir J. Hay might during the debate have spoken briefly, & with proper caution & reserve. As it was, it was next to certain that he would mar his case; and he did mar it. Hartington[72] was put up to explain facts as regards provisions for the soldiers & other details. And here Ministers made a blunder. Hartington is a well informed young nobleman who speaks unexceptionably, but would not be likely, from want of experience, to make in such a cause a comprehensive defence on the merits. Hence an impression seemed to grow up that Ministers had no defence except in the shape of replies to arguments founded on details. An old official should have taken his stand at the outset upon some broad principle & the party shd. have maintained it throughout the discussion, whereas it was not till very late that Cardwell spoke & then he spoke briefly & not with very much effect. As to Chichester Fortescue,[73] that exceedingly self-conscious young man, rather damaged than served his party by his flippancy and conceit. Danby Seymour opposed the Government. Pakington carped in his style of diminutive criticism. B. Cochrane spoke pretty well in his (almost) falsetto voice. Pity, however, that his energy & feeling are often disproportionate to the importance of the argument he is advancing! Palmerston blustered and bragged and launched at his foes vague charges of untruth and was easily foiled by

---

[70] Vote passed, 45:34.
[71] *H* clxxv. 1950–63. An expedition sent from the Gold Coast, to punish the King of Ashantee for making incursions into British territory, had been ravaged by disease.
[72] Under-secretary for war.
[73] Colonial under-secretary.

Disraeli. On dividing Ministers won by 7 votes. Numbers 233[74] to 226. Tremendous and protracted cheering & counter cheering followed, lasting for several minutes.

I felt constrained to vote with Sir J. Hay. The New Zealand case is nearly as bad or worse, and the principles which guide me in that case cannot be in consistency renounced in this. One friend expressed his concurrence with me in opinion, but said he shd. vote with Ministers & spoke of the Duke of Newcastle as a dying man – as if this were reason enough for voting with his late colleagues. There were and are a good many dying men among our soldiers in Africa. Who will have killed them? People who, thro' ambition, aspired to offices for which the aspirants were unfit thro' want of knowledge and want of commonsense. The Duke of N. was Minister for war when the Crimean struggle commenced!

General Peel made a scathing speech agt. the Government.

Henceforth, I shall be deemed to be almost an opponent of the party with which it has usually been my fate to act.

More notes. Danby Seymour seconded Hay, & spoke, as he generally speaks, well. S. declared that the resolution was not a vote of want of confidence, merely a complaint of a particular act of the administration; and added that surely an independent member might reasonably make such a complaint without implying more. G[ilpin], a subminister, seeing me near the table on which lies the list of pairs, came & chatted. He observed that S. wanted office. G. evidently wished that I would open my mind to him. He was not gratified.

During the debate Clarence P[aget][75] defended his party & his particular department and very frequently, as it is his trick to do, used the words 'I say frankly' or, at all events, the word 'frankly'. Each time, Osborne called the attention of his neighbour to this; when P. said 'frankly' O. echoed 'frankly'. Men shd. unlearn tricks, presenting pegs for criticism. P. is not deemed to be very frank.

Denman rather lost his head at one moment in debate. Pakington was speaking. D. considered that P. was misrepresenting some thing. D. cried 'no' in a stentorian voice. P. good humouredly noticed the interruption & went on. Again, came a very loud 'no' wh. was repeated several times. At last, Denman rose to explain ('order, order'). A member can only explain who has spoken. Else there is nothing in order to explain, as mere interruption is disorderly. How could a practiced lawyer make such a mistake, and one of form too? Later, he recurred to his interruption, but no doubt thought, afterwards, he had better, when he had nothing to say, have said '*it*'.

---

[74] Trelawny accidentally wrote 333.
[75] Parliamentary secretary to the admiralty.

As I left the House on dividing, among the first, I heard in sad & rather reproachful tones these words 'Oh! Sir John!' I do not know whose they were.

The rumour ran that the division would be within 10; and that 500 would be present in the House.

Monday, 20 June: The subject of the arrangements for taking away troops from the Gold coast was mooted by Sir J. Elphinstone, who, so as to be in order, moved the adjournmt. Lord C. Paget described the plan of the Govt. as altered. The late debate had its effect, then? So much the better for our sick men!

Others used the advantage of Elphinstone's motion. Osborne put questions on the Conference[76] &, likewise, Disraeli; & there were complaints of Palmerston's absence, in the midst of wh., as Lord J. Manners had just said it was the duty of the noble Viscount to be present & was in the middle of a sentence, Palmerston walked in & found the House loudly cheering. It required some minutes to communicate to him what had passed. Lord J. Manners, being on his legs, restated Disraeli's 3 inquiries & was so accurate that the inference was obvious that the whole business had been arranged beforehand – at least, so far as the opposition front bench was concerned [...]

Tuesday, 21 June: [...] At the evening sitting the Ballot was feebly introduced by Berkeley, who, according to his whim, spoke from the Conservative front bench. Disraeli faintly smiles at the droll mover, & other leading tories made room for him.

John Locke, briefly and amid interruption, spoke for the Ballot. Lord Palmerston opposed that measure – & division was taken. Of course, I voted for Ballot, as usual[77] [...]

Wednesday, 22 June: [...] Many rumours are abroad to the effect that the Ministry is weak. The Cabinet, it is also thought, is divided – for & against warlike proceedings.[78] It does not seem to me that the Public realize to themselves an idea of a great war, and less than a great war can hardly be contemplated if war break out at all.

The Conference has broken down, the newspapers say. Today, more authentic news will probably be forthcoming. It will not surprise me if Ministers resign or dissolve.

War would be at this crisis very dangerous to us. We have an army committed in New Zealand. There is the Ashantee business. Napoleon

---

[76] In London, on the Schleswig–Holstein question.
[77] 212:123 against the 2nd reading.
[78] Cf. Krein, *Palmerston Government*, pp. 157–60.

is looking out for an opening. Spain is becoming more powerful and ambitious. Russia has not forgotten Sebastopol. The Turkish question is unsettled.

Thursday, 23 June: At 4.25 I entered the House, wh. was rapidly filling [...] Numerous questions were put to Lord Hartington & Clarence Paget. Both were a little prolix in reply & too defensive. Cardwell's style of response was far more skilful, going to the point & no further; courteous; impassive as marble. At length questions came from Disraeli on the termination of the Conference & the upshot. He got nothing beyond assurances that on Monday i.e. after the conference shall have finally closed (it will close on Saturday), full details of the proceedings shd. be made known. The House by this time was full to an overflow. Peers & persons allowed to enter the ambassadorial bench were present in considerable numbers [...]

Friday, 24 June: [...] Three rather factious divisions, in a thin House, were taken on the Irish Chancery Bill,[79] which seems to excite an immense amount of feeling. Whiteside was never more voluminous or voluble than of late, or Hennessy more pertinaciously active. Longfield, also, is very busy. There have been several sittings on this Bill. Are Irish opposition lawyers anxious to make their powers incontestable in the judgment of those who will, probably, be dispensers of offices a short time hence? or, seeing a case for practical Reform, are they resolved that the credit of it shall not fall to the Whigs? Perhaps neither. It may be that these Irishmen in opposition have better motives than, at first sight, one would be disposed to attribute to a body whom no Englishman can comprehend.

Much will be the general impatience between this and Monday night. War or peace? every one asks. The Tories are confident – ready for a spring. The Whigs are nervous and depressed. Their very followers speak of their expected dissolution. Let no one be confident. Palmerston has had a move ready when it has been least expected. We are not behind the scenes, and see thro' a glass darkly.

Monday, 27 June: [...] On Sunday one heard statements to the effect that whatever Ministers have decided upon, their decision has been unanimous.[80] It is to me inconceivable that they shd. continue in office; & if they be wisely advised, they will, I think, announce their

---

[79] In committee; the bill was withdrawn on 11 July.
[80] Only in so far as the Cabinet had agreed, on 25 June, not to engage in war for the sake of the duchies. There had been a majority of 8:7 in favour of using the British fleet in defence of Copenhagen; Krein, *Palmerston Government*, pp. 161–2.

resignation. They already hold a position upon sufferance & one otherwise too degraded to be endured. The opposition can eject them whenever they choose so to do. On the other hand, being out of office the liberal party may be recast & acting together, with full effect, may compel Lord Derby to govern on terms imposed by us. Ministers were evidently in this dilemma. Had they proposed war, their own party would have been divided. In the choice of a peace policy, they encounter the opposition – not because the opposition is committed to war, but because it can frame & carry a resolution involving censure on men who have compromised the honour & prestige of England. In the Danish business we have done too much or too little.

4.20. On attending I found the House crowded in every part. A very unusual buzzing prevailed. No business remained appropriate to the moment. Presently, Palmerston entered. Great cheering welcomed him. He made a good stout walk to the bar & then brought up 'papers by command of Her Majesty' wh. papers contain the proceedings of the Conference. He then moved some formal resolution wh. I could not hear – I think it was 'that they be printed' &, in moving, made a speech of 55 minutes in wh. he humorously described the general course of events in the Danish business and the conduct of government. The House very calmly heard his narrative & all might have ended pretty creditably had not P., after stating the views of H.M.'s advisors, uttered renewed threats to the Germans of the conduct to wh. we might be driven in certain events. This was too much. Every one saw the mistake. Friends & foes were alike conscious of an increase of ridicule attaching to the Nation, in a case in wh. it appeared before that more ridicule was hardly possible. Of course, Disraeli seized the opportunity & assailed his antagonist with great power & sarcasm.

Disraeli looked deadly pale & ill. I noted that Palmerston threw on Denmark the blame of being first in the wrong.[81] But Disraeli did not fail to remind him of the promise that in certain events she would not stand alone. It is a bad business.

Disraeli complimented P. on the perspicuity of his statement. This compliment was eminently deserved. Few living men could have told the tale in words so few and well-chosen.

A liberal, speaking privately to me late in the evening, observed it is a pity that Lord P. is so fond of blustering & Earl Russell of lecturing. Between the two the dignity of the Nation is apt to sink.

[...] The prevalent impression is that Ministers will win by a small majority. It may be that my opinion has been rash. I must yield to

---

[81] King Christian IX, on ascending the throne in Nov. 1863, had endorsed a new constitution which virtually incorporated Schleswig with Denmark; ibid, pp. 127–8.

the verdict of events. Very few of our side will oppose govt. and many on Disraeli's side will refuse to follow his lead. So men say.

Tuesday, 28 June: [. . .] Beginning my attendance at 6 p.m. I heard Disraeli read his notice of a motion of censure.[82] Kinglake rose, but during the cheers which greeted D., K. was inaudible. Many cried 'Kinglake, Kinglake' after he had sat down, as they desired to know what new element he had to throw into the cauldron. He rose a second time & gave notice of an amendment, of which he would state the terms at our next sitting (oh & cheers). Meanwhile, Osborne was busy. He seemed to be desirous of sounding his neighbours with respect to the coming contest, & expressed his own judgment audibly & with his usual freedom. O. & K. are, apparently, acting in concert. Politicians, as much as any other men, shd. desire to see themselves as others see them. We work in a chamber full of hostile observers & jealous critics. The best motives are often misunderstood – the worst easily discerned & promptly attributed. Rumour does the rest. Men, out of office & seeking it, cannot be too considerate in their judgments of Ministers, as the enemy very soon blasphemes.

Disraeli's resolution is true enough in words – but as to spirit, time, justice – the case is not so clear. It seems to me that those who vote agt. it, will vote on confidence or no confidence. It is said there will be a majority for govt. There was a majority agt. them on Doulton's motion relating to spaces round the Metropolis – the division took place after I left.[83] It is difficult to say how one ought to have voted in this case. How is it the duty of governt. to provide open spaces round London – unless the same duty have a wider area – as, for instance, round all our great hives of industry? Is Mr. Doulton prepared to support centralization to its fullest extent? Is the State to do everything for us? Surely, London is rich enough to be able to pay for its own health & recreation! On the other hand, Doulton might ask me if I be prepared to refuse all votes now given for special benefits to particular places – to reject proposals for the purchase of pictures, for National Museums & such like Institutions. The subject is full of difficulties. The case is hardly one in which any rigorous or dogmatic teaching is applicable, but one of degree & circumstance.

Wednesday, 29 June: Soon after the House met, Hennessy moved

---

[82] Regretting the failure of the London conference and observing that, in its failure to maintain its policy of upholding the integrity of Denmark, the government had lowered the influence of Britain in the councils of Europe and thus diminished the securities for peace; *H* clxxvi. 750–1.

[83] Resolution carried, 79:40. *H* clxxvi. 431–4.

the 2d. reading of a Bill for assimilating the principle of the Irish to that of the English Poor Law, the latter only, at present, affording out of door relief. It seemed to me that his case was good. Englishmen have an interest in the question because, if our system be more liberal than the Irish, we create a motive inducing them to emigrate to this country. I voted with H. The Irish landlords were strongly opposed to his scheme. Hennessy had only 24. A very large majority was agt. him.[84]

[...] Lastly Bass's Street music Bill[85] drew together a very full House – & we had 5 divisions. My votes were given in favour of mitigation of penalties. Much amusement was created by the discussion, which admitted of a facetious treatment. But it struck me the dignity of legislation was hardly consulted. Practical difficulties occurred to several; among others, to Ayrton, the Attorney-general[86] & Gladstone. I ventured to express some doubts & spoke of a danger of 'peddling legislation'. At the same time I admitted that an evil existed & to mark this I voted agt. an amendmt. for reporting progress.

Many members are embarrassed by the coming vote of censure. If we support Disraeli's motion, we affirm the truth, and something more – that is to say we throw out Ministers and, perhaps, produce war. If we oppose D's motion, we seem to exculpate governt., who are justly chargeable with breach of faith to Denmark. Kinglake's amendmt.[87] leaves the conduct of governt. untouched, at the same time deprecating war. The Tories, in voting agt. K., virtually affirm that war ought to be resorted to. All this is very complicated. But there may be another motion. Dillwyn is not favourable to Ministers; &, acting partly on an observation of mine that a more skilful resolution than Disraeli's might be drawn (were it an object to do so) retired to a lobby & framed one, of which he subsequently gave me a copy – having shewn it to some other members. His difficulty, like mine, is that our honour is compromised. We induced Denmark to give up material advantages in hopes of our aid. We now not only fail to keep faith with her, but reproach her with priority in wrongdoing. Dillwyn is for war. I am for peace if possible. Both for the Honour of England. What is to be done? Perhaps, there may be no division. It often so happens. It is thought that Ministers will win by a fair majority – say 25 or 30. If they win, the Session will soon expire of inanition.

[84] 201.

[85] In committee; the bill required the metropolitan police to order street musicians to move on if a single complaint about noise was made; Royal assent, 25 July.

[86] Sir Roundell Palmer.

[87] Expressing satisfaction that there was to be no armed interference by Britain in the Schleswig–Holstein dispute; *H* clxxvi. 1300. Drawn up with Cobden's aid.

Friday, 1 July: Great is the interest felt in the coming struggle. One is sounded on all sides upon one's intentions. My friend R[oebuck] told me that he heard some one at a club describe me as one of the War party. This I denied, saying that I was of the opposite opinion – unless, indeed, it could be shewn that we were committed by words used or hopes held out. This is, of course, merely the sense of what fell from me. He said Rumour had it that the majority would fall short of the 20 supposed – that now it is said it will be no more than 7 & that the Tories were sure of 304. It will be curious to compare facts with presumptions. White, the doorkeeper, understood that Ministers would win by a small majority [...] Dillwyn is still very keen agt. government & for war. He has shewn his motion to many – some on the opposition side who approve of it. Kinglake's amendment is considered to be very clever. Those, who shall vote agt. it, will be or seem to be committed to a war policy. Those who shall vote for it to peace. It will, probably, produce an odd confusion of parties [...]

Monday, 4 July: It is said neither party is sanguine. The 'Times' is evidently prompted to warn members that a defeat of Ministers will mean dissolution of Parliament.[88] A member told me yesterday that 11 was the majority then expected. No one can very confidently guess how it will be. So many & diverse are the issues involved; such as peace or war – Tory or Whig – Dissolution or no Dissolution (I would add Honor or Dishonor, if the addition were not ridiculous). Many members are, I believe, still doubtful.

8.7 p.m. After hearing Disraeli for $2\frac{3}{4}$ hours – when he finished – I returned home & now hastily describe what has passed.

At $\frac{1}{4}$ before 4 the House was nearly full – a rare thing! After prayers, the Speaker, beginning to count, saw the absurdity of doubting whether enough members were present, & so, instead of counting further, he said 'forty' &, smiling, took his seat (Hear, Hear & some laughter). We had attended in order to get places; which an attendance at prayers earns.

Before the debate commenced, I took occasion to consult 2 of the clerks; also, Bouverie, Roebuck, Osborne, Bright & others as to the Speaker's inconsistency in deciding differently in 2 parallel cases when his casting vote was given. The cases were those of the University Test Bill & Church Rates abolition Bill.[89] Some were of opinion that the

---

[88] *The Times*, 4 July 1864, p. 8.

[89] On 1 July the 3rd reading of the University tests bill had resulted in a tie, 170:170. The Speaker cast his vote in favour of the bill, so that the House had an opportunity to vote again on the question 'that this bill do pass'; *H* clxxvi. 677–8. On this vote, the bill was defeated by 173:171. See above, 19 June 1861, for the Speaker's different conduct on the church rates bill.

difference deserved a question, some thought that, tho' the decision in the Church Rate case was erroneous, it would be too much to expect the Speaker to confess that he had acted inadvertently[90] [...]

Disraeli's speech was a serious one for Ministers. Earl Russell, who was under the gallery, tried to look calm & superficially tranquil, as if the efforts of the rhetorician were a real amusem[en]t to him. But by degrees the Earl looked more & more grave, & his arms & hands were in use to disguise the play of his mouth. Earl Grey & some other peers had, I think, encroached a little on our usages by crowding on to the seats in the gallery at right angles to that part of it wh. diplomatists occupy. In fact, Earl G. & others were among the representatives of the people & I thought the all-seeing Speaker was looking at them with a severe expression.

I attended again in the even[in]g and heard the last part of Gladstone's magnificent declamation; which received loud & long contin[ue]d applause. Many members congratulated him. Both he & Disraeli are obliged to use stimulus as I take it to be frequently. Kinglake, too, on commencing put something into his mouth. I fear the physical part is not equal to the strain put on the intellectual in these times. All are trying to live several lives in one. Lord Russell looked much gratified at Gladstone's success. The grave look had left him.

Tennyson was in the House this evening, also, the Duke of Cambridge, Bishop of Oxford & several other celebrities. The Speaker had permitted the crowding already alluded to.

[...] My vote will probably be with Kinglake. No one can doubt that Ministers acted bona fide in their endeavours to save Denmark & keep peace. That their endeavours were not very skilful and that the result is humiliating are true propositions. After all 'Humanum est errare', and the greatest general makes many mistakes. There is something, which is not quite satisfactory in telling the world that the influence of England is lowered; it may be true, but there is no pressing necessity for propounding such truth. Also, if Disrael's case be accepted we are, I think, under a pledge to go to war in order to protect the integrity of Denmark. Indeed, that is his case. To vote for it then were to involve war – ie, England would be compelled to combat enemies of unascertained power & number because our foreign Minister has made indiscreet undertakings. Is this sophistical? Is it the effect of conversation? Am I succumbing to example? There is still in my mind a wrong without a satisfactory remedy in any of the resolutions tendered to us; yet, it will be something if the net result of a week's talk be that we remain, after many blunders, at peace. These are my

[90] Trelawny did not raise the matter in the House.

present thoughts. But at this moment, I know not what vote I shall give.

Tuesday, 5 July: Cobden began the debate – & spoke with very great ability for one hour. While he, in effect, supported Ministers, his speech in reality bitterly impeached them. Lord R. Cecil followed with less than his usual effect on account of the multitude of papers he read. Ed. Forster, H. Vane, Roebuck, Horsman, Seymour Fitz-gerald & Butler Johnstone spoke. I heard Cobden only. Government take little by the speeches even of those who will vote with them. Sitting in the gallery opposite the Treasury Bench, I closely watched the effect of Cobden's dreadful blows. First, there were curiosity & interest. Then occasional remarks from one to the other, especially betwn. Gibson & Layard. Collier took notes. By degrees one affected to go to sleep, then another & at last there was scarcely one who was not either actually asleep or pretending to be. Wood was really asleep from fatigue, as people do not often feign sleep to the length of being ridiculous objects and he certainly was – with his mouth opening & shutting. The fact is the Ministry have very few supporters, tho' the division may be favourable to things as they are. Palmerston is very deaf. One of the most amusing points in Cobden's speech was that in which he described Palmerston as doing Tory work better than Lord Derby would & likely, in the event of his political death, to make the Conservative party his residuary legatees. Hereat there was great laughter. At the sound Palmerston leant towards Grey to hear what was the cause of it. On learning the cause, he threw up his head & laughed heartily. But I noted that the whole of Cobden's sentence could not have been conveyed to him in the time taken by Grey in explaining – & infer that some of P's deafness is affectation. Very little that is worth hearing actually escapes P. He sleeps like a duck – with one eye open. Earl Russell is the Minister who will have suffered most by the debate. Horsman's is an awful speech to fall from one whose vote will be friendly. The hardest hits the government has received are from behind or, rather, in flank. Roebuck's was a very remarkable effort: some of his sayings will be heard of very far off. Epigrams don't die young. They have kind nurses in the friends of the butts. His description of Prussia was excellent – part pedagogue, part drill sergeant, & part highwayman.

Thursday, 7 July: Layard[91] opened the Ball & made a power-ful speech in defence of Ministers, contending that they had not threatened any one; that their policy had been inevitable & shared

---

[91] Foreign under-secretary.

by nearly all their chief accusers; that warlike despatches had been peaceful & peacefully intended; that they had made no promises which had not been performed notwithstanding the descriptions of their words or deeds given by their opponents; and that the honor of England had not been tarnished. In the course of his speech he charged Disraeli with 'falsification' of cited papers, & certainly used very unparliamentary language. This passed at the moment, but not unnoticed by Disraeli & his friends; one of whom Hardy called attention to them in his speech, and hereupon arose a rather exciting episode; crimination and recrimination succeeding each other with much heat & personality. Palmerston & Osborne, among others, took part, & the Speaker, apparently, had some difficulty in reducing the House to tranquility; when the debate proceeded Hardy & the attorney-general,[92] after Layard, were the chief heroes of the evening. The Government were evidently in high delight at hearing so good a defence from Layard, who would, however, have been infinitely more effective had he been more temperate, diplomatic & classic in his choice of words. It is easy to say that an accuser has disingenuously described despatches, misplaced dates & omitted to state material circumstances, without charging him with 'falsification'. The Suaviter in modo lends force to the fortiter in re. The introduction of language such as 'skedaddled', perhaps a trivial matter, rather jarred upon one, tho' it excited mirth. Still, Layard did his party excellent service; &, if speeches alter the intentions of members, he will have gained at least a vote or two. Now, a vote or two will be of vital consequence. The 'Times' even speaks of an estimated majority of 4.

[...] Again & again, members have inquired how I mean to vote. My reply is that I have not yet heard all the debate, which seems always to produce amusement. Why? That it should have this effect is no laughing matter [...]

Friday, 8 July: Arriving at $\frac{1}{2}$ past 4 I found a full House and almost immediately Osborne began his speech. He spoke for one hour and 35 minutes &, perhaps, never more successfully so far as wit, sarcasm & felicitous fancy can produce success. Perhaps, there was a shade too much expansion of the Danish question & details on family succession & the Duchies. He was most effective in his personal allusions to men in various parts of the House: – Roebuck, Horsman, Newdegate, & many others shared his notice. The Ministry and its component parts were the subject of much pungent satire. A quotation from Gladstone agt. Palmerston from a speech delivered in former times created much amusement, as those two sat side by side – &,

[92] Sir Roundell Palmer.

certainly, the passage cited was very severe. No one seemed more amused than P. himself, who looked round to Gladstone; & both laughed heartily. *Gladstone looked very grave at the comparison of Lord R. Montagu & Cobden to Righteousness & Peace kissing each other and, also, at the verses from Don Juan about Donna Julia.[93]* No one seems to know what is to be the result of the division. Dillwyn is still uncertain for one. Some say Ayrton will walk out.

Osborne's manner was that of a consummate comic actor. Some one near me compared him once or twice to Buckstone;[94] but it is dangerous to amuse the House so much. You are tempted to indulge the sense of success in this way, & then Scientific Statesmanship becomes more difficult. *Some amusement was created by Lord H. Lennox who, after Osborne's success, went over to him & evidently loaded him with compliments. Some one near me in the gallery said 'See there is Lennox embracing Osborne'.*

About $\frac{1}{4}$ before 10, when I came back to my work, I found that a few dull speeches had been delivered. Soon, however, came Walpole, Palmerston & Disraeli & the House rung with peals of cheers till men were almost hoarse & the cheers took a higher & higher key so as to enhance sound as much as possible. *I did not hear Disraeli speak of Horsman as 'the superior person' of the House. That will live.* P. particularly dwelt upon the general success of his policy and, in a very significant way, alluded to the probable judgment of the Country at large even if the House shd. decide agt. the Government.

Some thought the majority would be 6 or 8. Few dared hope for 15 or 18; This, however, was about the number I had expected – yesterday I named to Fonblanque[95] some number between 15 & 20. I tried to convince D[illwyn] & he voted with us – whether I had an influence over him I know not. But he was clearly dissatisfied with Ministers as regards their conduct towards the Danes. W.[96] inquired, just before division, how I meant to vote. I think I had some slight influence with him: indeed, he formally consulted me, & I gave him my reasons for voting with Ministers.

Newdegate was very obstinate but finally gave way on his war amendment. He wanted to divide. The House made a tremendous uproar. The question was put & we were on the point of dividing. *Almost the whole House would have gone into one lobby agt. Newdegate.* To meet the difficulty – where so many could go without

---

[93] 'A little still she strove and much repented, / And swearing "I will never consent" – consented.' From Byron's *Don Juan*, (1821–4).

[94] John Baldwin Buckstone, a popular farceur of the day.

[95] Albany Fonblanque, proprietor of the *Examiner*.

[96] Possibly James Wyld of Bodmin.

confusion – the Speaker directed that the larger (expected) body shd. turn, after getting thro' the lobby on his right, to their right into the great lobby outside the doorkeeper's chair. So I understood. Luckily, we only had one division, & that led to no particular inconvenience, this was on Kinglake's amendt. Numbers 313 to 295. Tremendous was the cheering & waving of hats. Palmerston was in an ecstacy of delight, as, leaning forward, he caught the news brought up the House by one of his under officials.

As I went thro' the lobby, Massey said to me 'Ah! you are a dark horse'. I laughed & said 'I like to hear a debate before I decide'. J.,[97] who was in a state of *very* great exhiliration, could not restrain his feelings. He said he knew I should vote with them – he had won £2 by me &c &c.

We left the House thro' a long lane of people assembled in Westminster Hall who vociferously cheered & waved their hats. It was then 2 a.m. on Sat[urda]y the 9th.

Saturday, 9 July: As we really sat till 2 a.m. this morning I head my page accordingly. The Bishops generally supported Ministers in the Lords. There were, I believe, only 2 exceptions.[98] Twenty one Irish liberals opposed Ministers in the Commons. It is said that priestly emissaries from Card[inal] Antonelli[99] were exerting themselves in the lobbies in order to influence votes. Ayrton, G. Clive & Osborne forbore to vote. Disraeli was funny enough in his allusion to Roebuck, whom he described going about with his enormous lantern to find an honest man. + & finding Horsman. + I noted that Lord P[almerston] had rather more than usual difficulty in his elocution. In one sentence he became so embarrassed that he recommenced it not less than 3 times; &, but for a certain tenderness for the (all but) octogenarian, there would have been some laughter. Indeed, I think a slight titter was audible. A[rthur] R[oebuck] observed to me today that Palmerston should retire this winter if he desire to do his fame full justice. Brougham's example shd. be a warning. Roebuck said of Earl Russell something of this sort – that nature had intended him for a schoolmaster: accident had made him a cabinet-minister. Osborne reminded R. of Arnold[100] who could be both. A member of the chess club (who I believe is connected with Govt.) told me that O. is fond of private theatricals: if this be true, it perhaps bears out a little a comparison already given herein.

[97] Unidentified.
[98] The bishops of Oxford and Bangor. Lord Malmesbury's censure motion was passed by 177:168.
[99] Secretary of state in the pontifical government.
[100] I.e. Thomas Arnold of Rugby.

Monday, 11 July: Old P[almerston] received a hearty cheer on entering the House from the door behind the Speaker's chair. Disraeli & his friends on the opposition bench put the best laugh on they could command [...]

Wednesday, 13 July: We had a discussion on Bouverie's Bill for amending the act of Uniformity – & a division – the liberals suffering a severe defeat.[101] Of course I voted with B.

Then the Scottish Episcopal Clergy Bill[102] came on – & passed, after conversation, without division.

[...] Walpole was mover agt. Bouverie's Bill, which would have relieved of tests certain persons in our Church. Sir W. Heathcote was for allowing to Scottish Episcopal Churchmen facilities beyond those now held for holding benefices in England. Now it happens that these clergymen are more free from tests & less hampered than English clergymen; & Heathcote so far is at direct variance with Walpole & with Heathcote himself. Surely an English Incumbent or Minister ought to be at least as free as a Scottish Episcopal? Bouverie had some triumph over Heathcote; &, in passing out in front of Locke King, B. very audibly congratulated himself on his smartness. This boast might have been as well omitted. It is, however, not fair to dwell on asides. The Papers call Bouverie a prig; I wish we had more such prigs [...]

Thursday, 14 July: Disastrous news has arrived of a defeat in New Zealand.[103] May members ponder on it before the debate shall begin!

A brisk debate on Arthur Mills' amendment on the 2nd reading of the New Zealand Loan Guarantee Bill[104] [...] On division Mills was defeated – numbers being 92 to 55. Whalley created much amusement by an ominous suggestion that a deep cause was at the bottom of the war in the Colony; members – particularly, Osborne – at once guessed that the Pope was indicated & had hardly uttered his name, when Whalley confirmed their suspicions, the Jesuits were at work in New Zealand (great laughter).

[...] Lord Stanley stoutly opposed guarantees of loans. Roebuck declared that the Brown man must of necessity disappear wherever

---

[101] 157:101 against the 2nd reading of the bill to repeal those portions of the act of Uniformity which required subscriptions of loyalty from those seeking fellowships at Universities; *P.P.* 1864, iv. 581.

[102] A Lords' bill, removing the restrictions which prevented episcopal clergymen from holding benefices or officiating in the Church of England. Royal assent, 29 July; *P.P.* 1864, iv. 175.

[103] Cardwell, the colonial secretary, announced the defeat of a British force at Tauranga, on north island, with the loss of many officers; *H* clxxvi. 1469–71.

[104] Involving £1,000,000.

the white man sets his foot. Cobden said Roebuck's ideas were more worthy of a Parliament of Thugs [than] of a Christian People. Cardwell did his best to prove that the New Zealand colonists were intitled to aid from the British Taxpayer and urged that the Income of the Colony was good & its prospects bright, altho' the City merchants paid little attention to offers of unguaranteed Colonial Stock. Aytoun described the transaction respecting the £500,000 guaranteed loan of 1857 – & Sewell's conduct.[105] Trelawny amplified this topic & mentioned the fact that Sewell had a vote of £1,000 for his smartness in obtaining the Imperial guarantee – & how he did it.

Monday, 18 July: [...] the New Zealand Guaranteed Loan Bill came on; whereon I moved an amendment &, after an useful debate, we divided. Of course Ministers won.[106] But the debate left us, I think, in a fair position [...] It sounded to me like music when Walpole called the New Zealand war 'an unrighteous war'. Similar phrases fell from many. Consciences are awakened.

Tuesday, 19 July: A morning sitting, whereat passed in committee the Contagious Diseases Bill. Ayrton made a long & excellent speech in which he stated numerous objections to the scheme. The committee, being in a singularly practical state of mind & determined to abate a nuisance if its abatement were possible, went thro' all the clauses without division.[107]

[...] evening attendance [...] One division occurred on reporting progress upon the order being read for the New Zealand Loan guarantee Bill.[108] Hennessy is beginning to busy himself herein. By degrees I shall have got quite a pack of hounds in full cry. It has taken years to effect this & much pertinacity.

Wednesday, 20 July: [...] One or two bills were discussed & withdrawn – particularly, a bill relating to private worship in Public Schools.[109] The ever-active dissenter was ready here & was represented ably by Hardcastle. The session is flickering out.

The Church sees an opening. Many Public schools in connection

---

[105] See above, 10 May 1858.

[106] 79:32 against the amendment for a select committee to inquire into the financial relations between Britain and New Zealand; *H* clxxvi. 1681–2.

[107] The bill received the Royal assent on 21 July. It provided that, in 11 scheduled towns, magistrates could order prostitutes suspected of being infected with venereal disease to undergo an examination, and to have them detained for up to three months if they were infected; *P.P.* 1864, i. 493.

[108] Hennessy's motion for adjournment, defeated 30:5; *Commons Journals*, 1864, p. 441.

[109] Collins's facilities for divine service in collegiate schools bill.

with her at their foundation have become useful training institutions for the middle classes. Attendance at parish Churches was not objected to by dissenters. But private worship enforced in school chapels is another thing & might have the effect of deterring parents from entrusting their children to particular masters.

Thursday, 21 July: [...] Hennessy means to oppose the New Zealand guaranteed Loan Bill tonight. He reported that Disraeli approved of his course. I asked 'But where is Disraeli?' & added 'He's a pretty fellow!'

[...] Hennessy, after a brief speech, moved the rejection of Guarantee Bill. We divided & were defeated by more than 2 to 1.[110] I was a teller. While I was telling, a loud cheer came in with the posse of members opposed to Ministers. These members were still in one of the lobbies or corridors thro' which we pass in dividing. Soon the reason of the cheer appeared. Sir W. Dunbar, a minister,[111] had accidently voted with us. Hennessy observed soon afterwards in mock triumph that such had been the effect of the discussion that one of the Govt. had voted agt. his friends (a laugh). It is well there is still a laugh possible in the midst of this New Zealand business [...]

Friday, 22 July: [...] White (Doorkeeper) told me that when Stansfeld was in the admiralty, his knowledge of business produced almost a revolution. He showed immediately how thoroughly he understood business. Previously a debtor & creditor account had been a thing quite new to many of the officials. Taking stock had not been practised theretofore. Stansfeld's merits deserve future notice [...]

Monday, 25 July: [...] A Bill for giving effect to a convention with Prussia for mutual surrender of Criminals led to some rather strong remonstrances & denunciations. Prussia is not popular, & Mazzini's name was mentioned. It was said that, were he a Prussian subject, he could be given up under such a Bill. Hennessy, Locke, White & others spoke. Palmerston detected a rising storm, & postponed the measure – till the terms of some other treaties now in force shd. have been referred to (a laugh).[112]

Soon after, Lord Palmerston moved & carried a resolution rescinding a resolution passed on Ap[ril] 12th. on the mutilation of Education

---

[110] 75:32. The bill received the Royal assent on 29 July, but the terms of the loan proved unacceptable to the New Zealand ministry.

[111] A lord of the treasury.

[112] The bill was withdrawn on 27 July.

Inspectors Reports.[113] Thus R. Lowe is rehabilitated. The House had done him injustice. It has now, so far as it could, retraced its steps [...]

Friday, 29 July: Prorogation. The Queen's speech makes a poor show [...]

[113] Resolution agreed to.

SESSION OF 1865

Tuesday, 7 February: [...] Sir H. Williamson moved & Mr. Hanbury Tracey seconded the address. Sir H.W. spoke with considerable fluency & self-possession for 20 minutes. He received very good attention – & his speech was not bad, indeed rather good. It was a little too fluent. Ars est celare artem. H. Tracey was not so well heard. His speech might have been better than it seemed to me to be, who judged less by what I collected of it, than by its reception. The seconder has a disadvantage in finding topics preoccupied.

Scully refreshed the House by a speech in his quaint manner – & moved an amendment[1] [...]

Wednesday, 8 February: Scully pressed his amendment to a division & had some 12 followers[2]– a few being English liberals. I opposed him – thinking that, altho' the state of Ireland is not satisfactory, the terms of Scully's amendment, especially regard being had to the speech in which he explained it, would tend to commit the National Exchequer [...]

Friday, 10 February: Sir John Walsh made a rather pompous speech on the situation of affairs in America. The notice to [terminate][3] a certain treaty relating to the lakes betwn. Canada and the U. States and the naval power to be kept on foot by each contracting party was his prominent topic. It did not strike me that Sir John was very judicious in the language he used unless he think that we ought to declare war.

Lord Palmerston anticipated other speakers who were evidently on the point of rising – Bright & Watkin, I mean – and in a few adroit sentences entirely took the sting out of Walsh's speech. Perhaps, the Premier was never more successful in dealing with a difficulty under the deepest responsibility. Bright was evidently aware that another speech would only mar a good effect[4] [...]

---

[1] Regretting the unsatisfactory condition of Ireland and the continued need for Irish emigration; *H* clxxvii. 84–8.
[2] 67 opposed the amendment.
[3] Trelawny accidently wrote 'determine'.
[4] Walsh's amendment, for the production of papers, withdrawn.

Monday, 13 February: [...] Gladstone amused some of us by a visit to members below the gangway. He perched betwn. Cox & Al[derman] Salomons, & shook hands very warmly with several. What is up?

Tuesday, 14 February: [...] I do not think the Conservatives have opened their mouths – at least not on any subject suggestive of combined action on their part. This is curious & unusual.

Wednesday, 15 February: The attendance of today was very meagre. A Bill introduced by Lord Naas for facilitating a system of creating mortgage debentures on land was the subject of a debate.[5] Lord Naas spoke with considerable ability; indeed he generally speaks with ability. His style is easy, natural and unpretending. Scully followed (after a few remarks from others); and, after a lengthened and elaborate analysis of the plan of the mover, delicately and skilfully approached the point, which he had reserved for the end of his speech. That was the fact that Lord Naas and Col[onel] Greville were interested, as Directors of a Public Company, in the measure before the House. It never appears to have occurred to Lord Naas that the Bill shd. have been introduced by some impartial person – or that it was his duty to make a clean breast before he asked the House for its interest. Had Roebuck or Scully moved the introduction of a Bill for putting money into his own pocket, what an outcry we shd. have heard! A Lord can do many things that a 'common fellow' must not dream of. Yet, Lord Naas never imagined that he was acting indiscreetly – at least till Scully came to the end of his speech, when for a moment I noticed a graver expression on Lord N's countenance. Did the idea then first occur to him?

Thursday, 16 February: [...] *Lord Palmerston paid a very beautiful tribute to the memory of Mr. Gregson & dwelt much on the merit of members who work hard on private business, unostentatiously and without some of the incentives to exertion which stimulate Public men. Palmerston's careful speech was a marvel of appropriateness in thought and expression.*

Cardwell announced the arrival of despatches from New Zealand. These are very important. There is a new Ministry there, & it professes an entirely new & self-reliant policy. How will the news affect Mills' resolution?[6] Our action in the Home Parliament has certainly influenced affairs in the colony – &, I think, beneficially[7] [...]

[5] 2nd reading agreed to, and referred to a select committee; Royal assent, 29 June.
[6] It was not moved.
[7] Cf. Rutherford, *Sir George Grey*, pp. 516–38, for the reality of the new government.

Monday, 20 February: [...] Augustus Smith moved the abolition of one Parl[iamentar]y Secretary under the Poor Law administration. He did not seem to be entirely borne out in his view of the case. At first his proposal seemed to be plausible. But the labour of the Department added to the duty of attending the House & replying to questions on the notice paper or arising unexpectedly is very heavy & I doubt whether aid in the House does not increase the checks which tend to insure a wise administration of the Poor Laws. Gilpin[8] was the subject of pointed allusion, as being connected with several firms. Both he & Villiers stoutly maintained their side of the argument. Both were a little waspish. Gilpin's reply about Public Companies in effect was – 'that's not your business – any more than the Scilly Isles are mine'.

Villiers fastened his fangs on Smith for having made his proposal without knowing all the circumstances which it behoved him to know and this Smith had in truth admitted. He was no match for the sarcastic President – & Gilpin twisted the barb in the wound. V. who looked ghastlier than usual – he always looks very ill and I believe has long had lung disease – observed that he did not speak in his own interest as it was not likely that another year of his work would leave any question of importance to him (a laugh), but in the interest of the future. Of course this was the substance of his remark, not his exact language. My vote was agt. A. Smith.[9]

Thursday, 23 February: The plan for new Law Buildings and the concentration of our Law Courts made good progress this day.[10] It is quite curious how quietly business moves. When will the fray begin? or is the Session to go out like a lamb as it came in?

I gave notice of a question regarding an unfit selection, that of Lord de Ros for the Colonelcy of the 4th Hussars. He already holds a sinecure office as deputy L[ieutenan]t of the Tower worth £746.15 a year. The case is deemed in military circles to be a very flagrant job. It is said that he signally failed as Quartermaster gen[era]l in Turkey & never saw service before an enemy [...]

Monday, 27 February: [...] The Irish motion of Hennessy was resumed.[11] This led to an animated debate. Roebuck made a very remarkable speech. It is clear that his whole political tone is changed.

---

[8] Parliamentary secretary to the poor law board.
[9] Motion defeated, 193:17.
[10] The courts of justice building bill received the Royal assent on 19 June.
[11] From 24 Feb., regretting the decline of the Irish population and calling for measures to stimulate employment in Ireland; *H* clxxvii. 661–73.

He has turned his back upon himself. The Irish have, he thinks, no grievance. Their nurses taught them that they once had, & the fancy remains after the reality has ceased. The Church establishmt. was not so much as mentioned by him – at least not that I can recollect. Roebuck wants a certain stability of judgment, and in his speeches forgets that he is observed not merely by his hearers but by numerous persons who have watched his course during 30 or 40 years. If the Church of Ireland be no grievance to the Irish Catholics, is the Church of England no grievance to the Protestant Dissenters? If not, why does Roebuck oppose Church Rates? He may say, because the evil they produce is greater than the benefit their value adds to the Church's strength. Probably, that is his answer.

Pitt intended to pay the priests. This was the complement of the Union policy which took away the Irish Parliament. The bigotry of Geo. the 3rd. prevented the success of a great scheme of settlement when settlement was possible. We shall pay for this [...] Hennessy's motion was rejected on a division.[12] I was absent, nor did I care much. In my judgment something might be done for Ireland, and we ought to do that some thing. Still, knowing the vagueness of H's words and to what he would have committed the Exchequer, I shd. have voted agt. him.

Thursday, 2 March: Henry Baillie moved a resolution by way of amendmt. on going into supply. His object was to condemn the govt. for not having more efficiently armed our ships. It did not seem to me that the motion was much more than a party attack. There was a division in a thin House.[13] I was absent at the time.

Henry Baillie's subject shd. be very lively, since his style is deadly dull. Slow, ponderous, methodical – he certainly does not please his audience. That he is painstaking is tolerable evident. At one part of his speech – when he was most effective – his voice suddenly failed & dwindled away to a thin squeak. Some one suggested water. 'No thank you' and the orator tried to go on. In vain – voice still worse & worse – even after trying water, wh. after refusing, he had accepted. Luckily some one handed him a lozenge, which suddenly restored to him his voice in moderate force, & he went on with his speech.

Friday, 3 March: My question on Lord de Ros's appointment elicited from the Marquis of Hartington a reply which seemed to be studiously illogical. *I suspect the old jealousy betwn. the Civil & Military administrations still exists. Otherwise why did Lord Har-

---

[12] 107:31.
[13] Resolution for a select committee, defeated by 57:22; *H* clxxvii. 962–82.

tington put his military colleagues in the wrong?* Lord de Ros is to
have both appointments, because he began to hold the Dep[u]ty
Lieut[enan]cy of the tower before the new rule agt. holding 2 such
appointments came into play. But why was it necessary to offer him
a second appointment at all? He has no military claim to it of adequate
foundation. The Public will bear this shameful abuse as it bears many
others. It is clear to me that the Duke of Cambridge[14] has no fears of
control by the Secretary of State for war,[15] who is not, I suspect, a
very strong man.

Newdegate moved his resolution on religious houses.[16] He was very
earnest and stated his case well. How he has improved! Recollecting
his reception on many occasions some 20 years ago, I shd. scarcely
have believed he could ever have obtained the ear of the House. But
time and perseverance, with honesty of purpose & courage, effect
much in Parliament as elsewhere. His motion took 79 followers.[17] I
paired with Henry Baillie agt. it. The case did not seem to warrant
special action. As Sir Geo. Grey[18] put it, laws can not effect much agt.
moral agents. Still there is a growing impression that some measure
is wanted in order to prevent interference with Public liberty on the
part of persons acting under orders from a foreign Bishop. The small-
ness of the majority may be a warning to these priests, who are after
all pretty much alike. As one set find the secret of terrifying mankind
more effectually than the rest, these last make a general outcry 'what
odious tyranny!' In Scotland, no one in certain parishes dares to do
any work or take any pleasure in Public on Sundays. This is tyranny
of Presbyterians – and so in other cases [. . .]

Monday, 6 March: When I arrived there was much hubbub on the
subject of certain heavy defalcations in the accounts of Mr. Edmunds,
clerk to the Patent office and late clerk of the House of Lords [. . .]
The Chancellor,[19] who has appointed his son to the clerkship of the
Lords, is in rather bad odour. As yet, it is difficult to visit him with
any positive censure. But the Public mind is in a suspicious state.

[. . .] Ferrand begged for higher pay for Dockyards-men. Ferrand
represents Devonport. He was seconded by Sir James Elphinstone
who represents Portsmo[uth]! I think a more impudent piece of
electioneering was never perpetrated in a rather impudent age. Chil-

[14] Commander-in-chief.
[15] Earl de Grey and Ripon.
[16] For a select committee to inquire into monastic and conventual establishments in
Britain; *H* clxxvii. 1045–64.
[17] 106 opposed the motion.
[18] Home secretary.
[19] Lord Westbury.

ders[20] replied and asked how could govt. give more wages, as requested, when they were pressed by numerous economists to curtail expenditure. Augustus Smith & I repeatedly cheered Childers on this part of his argument, and this, as old economists, *we* were warranted in doing [...]

Tuesday, 7 March: [...] There is still a great disturbance of the minds of men in the clubs on the business of Edmunds' delinquencies [...] People, I think, do not like his getting a pension of £800 a year from a committee of the Lords at a time when the Chancellor knew that Edmunds was a defaulter. There is more whispered than has yet appeared in print, so far as I can discover.

Wednesday, 8 March: We had a rather animated debate on Lord Robert Montagu's project for the preservation of our rivers from all sorts of befouling causes.[21] This excited the members for Cornwall, whose mines were endangered. Altho' Lord R[obert]'s plan would not be suitable, he decidedly made good his case agt. Ministers, with whom lies the duty of presenting a law calculated to prevent a grievous nuisance and a waste of National resources. Lord R.M obtained and deserved great praise for his pains. His speech was good. Yet there is some important quality wanting in his mind. Why make a vehement attack on Ministers whom it might have been wise to conciliate? The measure is not a party measure. All concur in thinking that legislation is necessary. It is the difficulty which stands in the way. The debate will do good. Much interesting matter was brought under Public notice.

Lord R.M. withdrew his bill on condition of a 2d. bill on a kindred topic being read a 2d. time.[22]

Thursday, 9 March: [...] Our select Committee on the qualification for offices Bill reported in favour thereof.[23] Perhaps, ultra-conservatism never was in a sorrier plight than when it was defended in that Committee by Mowbray & Ld. R. Montagu agt. Bright, Ed. Forster & F. Peel. The defenders were absolutely crushed. Bright entered the room late – & had not heard many preliminary facts. In a few minutes he was quite at home – & with a few telling inter-

---

[20] A lord of the admiralty.

[21] The river waters protection bill would have created local protection boards and an inspectorate appointed by the home secretary.

[22] The sewage utilisation bill; Royal assent, 29 June.

[23] I.e. Hadfield's annual bill for the abolition of oaths required of dissenters who became members of municipal corporations. Trelawny was a member of the select committee appointed on 1 Mar. The bill was defeated in the Lords on 1 May.

rogatives, to which no consistent or tenable reply was forthcoming, reduced Mowbray to absolute silence. Forster's inquiries – to say nothing of F. Peel's – only further developed the nakedness of the land. It was altogether a refreshing exercitation in dialectics [...]

Friday, 10 March: [...] The leading topic of the evening was New Zealand. Arthur Mills concluded without a motion. Roebuck repudiated the obligation of the Queen to keep her word (under the treaty of Waitangi[24] wh. he ridiculed). * As a contract made with 'the ignorant & rude'. Lord R. Cecil rebuked him and trusted that for R's own sake he would never have to interpret his obligations under contracts with the 'ignorant & rude'. (a laugh). * Stanley sketched a vague kind of policy meaning little new or to the purpose, I think. Cardwell[25] welcomed an escape from a very awkward position, due rather to good luck than merit in a Ministry which endorsed the robbery of the Waitara block, produced a miserable & expensive war, & then endorsed the restoration of the plunder. See hereon Cardwell's last despatch.[26] In short the subject dropped. Are we becoming more cynical?

I watched – half intending to speak. No good opportunity presented itself. The policy now on foot is substantially in agreem[en]t with that which I have preached, & it were idle to endeavour to gather 'spilt milk'. The executive in Colonial affairs appears now to be doing well, & it were doubtful wisdom to weaken its power.

Roebuck's doctrine is one which would be but little strained if taken to cover repudiation of a National debt, in cases where the lenders exhibit ignorance and want of civilization. The Natives are now little more ignorant than an average English peasant, and I fear that we are inferior to them in moral tone. At least Roebuck's doctrine has not yet been broached, I believe, in a New Zealand Runanga.[27] It would be deemed very smart in Pennsylvania.

The Edmunds business[28] may be a serious source of weakness in the Cabinet. The Chancellor's private affairs have been a leading subject of gossip for some time. The great services he has rendered to the cause of Law Reform will hardly float him on if Public opinion be outraged by his domestic conduct. After all, he is the keeper of the 'Queen's conscience'. The sensitiveness about Edmunds' case is greater

---

[24] Of Feb. 1840, by which the Maori chiefs recognised British sovereignty and were promised undisturbed possession of their tribal lands; *B.F.S.P.* xxix. 1111–12.
[25] Colonial secretary.
[26] Rutherford, *Sir George Grey*, pp. 510–11.
[27] Tribal council.
[28] See above, 6–7 Mar. 1865.

in consequence of a certain predisposition in the Public mind to believe the worst.

Monday, 13 March: [...] There was a most important debate on the danger of war with America and the defencelessness of Canada. Several good speeches were made. Lowe's was very remarkable, chiefly because he recommended the prompt withdrawal of our troops. Bright made a powerful speech in favour of the North and in justification of A[braham] Lincoln. His great power of thought and expression never struck me more. He fascinated friends and foes. I watched the effect on Lord Palmerston's countenance, which was that of a delighted hearer. Almost every party in turn received rebuke from the caustic orator. Roebuck, Cecil, Earl Russell, Palmerston, and, above all, our Press were severely handled. The words 'lies' of 'the Times' might as well have been omitted. But Bright does not affect reserve. Putting Bright's opinions aside his speech was almost the most powerful I ever heard. He is, in my judgment, our greatest orator. He is more terse than Gladstone. Not so wordy and diffuse. Gladstone's escapes from the mazes of his own verbiage are wonderful feats. The difference is that Bright does not become involved in the difficulty. His sentences are short, and incisive. No time is lost in his lunges. He gives you in the highest degree a sense of present power, and indomitable courage; fearless as to whom he attacks, or in what company, or how numerous his foes. His asides are admirably telling; his exuberant fancy must work. Bright has over Cobden one great advantage – he has a more powerful voice & better health. Cobden would, I think, be safer in council. The two, in unison, would almost realize perfect political force.

I could not wait for Palmerston's speech, which was brief & politic.

Tuesday, 14 March: A very important division was taken on 'the Lancashire & Yorkshire &c Railway'. The stage was that of the 2d. reading. The bill was defeated.[29] Of course, my vote was in favour of it. A perilous precedent has been set of refusing a reference of a Bill to a committee in the usual way. It would appear that interest for existing companies was the cause of the victory. But the Public will suffer. Wholesome competition would have lowered prices and enforced careful management. Safety to life would thus have been increased [...] A noble lord canvassed openly for votes agt. the Railway Bill. He asked for my vote in the cloak Room, where he stood in waiting. I have since heard a conjecture that he thus obtained some 50 votes, and the explanation has been added that he is largely

[29] 162:121.

interested. Since I voted, he met me & asked how I had decided. I told him what was my uniform rule. He said 'it is too bad'. In this speech, he said what it might have been on the tip of my tongue to say to him. Many members, I think, regret their votes on this question.

Thursday, 16 March: Today it was my lot to take a rather more active part than usual of late. I asked Cardwell, on the motion that the Speaker leave the chair, whether a certain proclamation dated Dec[embe]r 17th/64 by Gov[erno]r Sir Geo. Grey in New Zealand, offering the Maories certain terms in the event of submission,[30] would be scupulously adhered to. To this question I received an affirmative reply.

Soon after the Speaker left the Chair. Lord Hartington then moved the Army estimates. Gen[era]l Peel & many others commented thereon. I attacked the appointment of Lord de Ros,[31] & drew down on myself an avalanche of military declamations. All the Colonels that ever were spoke, some agreeing with me.

One division took place on the pay of the Major Gen[era]l attached to the Foot G[uar]ds. This was on my motion.[32] Numbers 47 to 27. Of course, we were the minority.

Hartington made a very good opening speech & we mostly commended him.

[...] The reason which induced me to put my question to Cardwell was this. Roebuck recently ridiculed the treaty of Waitangi as a bargain made with the ignorant & rude; he compared it, I think, to a contract made with a child of seven years old for disposing of its inheritance. Most of the natives of New Zealand distrusted us before. Roebuck's speech will be translated by European schoolmasters or clergy & some of the chieftains will be apt to say, when Sir Geo. Grey's offer is under consideration, 'how about the fulfillment of the treaty of Waitangi? Can we trust the Pakeha?'[33] It struck me that an authentic statement by the Secretary of State in Parliament might be of use at this time. The war has mainly arisen out of the contravention of the Treaty of Waitangi, which conferred upon the Maories the rights of British citizens. The treatment dealt to W. Kingi by Governor Gore Browne set aside those rights, Gore Browne using a British military body for the purpose of effecting by force a contract with Te Teira for the sale of lands on which Kingi had unadjusted claims on

---

[30] Cf. Rutherford, *Sir George Grey*, p. 520.
[31] See above, 23 Feb. 1865.
[32] To omit the vote of £691 19s 7d.
[33] I.e. the white man.

behalf of his tribe.[34] This fatal mistake has sadly marred a great exper[imen]t in colonization.

Monday, 20 March: An evening on Army estimates [...] I asked questions relating to the uniform observance of the Queen's regulations now notoriously set at nought in the guards – & on the unbecoming language in wh. some officers Publicly address soldiers on duty. Lord P. evidently prompted Hartington to ask for a specific instance, to which I replied that I would give one in private & I did this. The case was that of Gen[eral] Pennefather, who said to some corps 'I wish you were in hell and that the Engineers were making you permanent barracks.' (Lord H. laughed greatly.) This story was mentioned to me by an officer of the Guards. Curiously enough, when I had spoken, a cavalry officer came to me & inquired whether my question referred to Gen[eral] Pennefather, who seems to be notorious for his rough language [...]

Wednesday, 22 March: [...] There was a Cabinet council. Will Ministers dissolve? Were it not well to take the opportunity & thus gain time for the budget? The defeat on Fire Insurances[35] is very humiliating, for Ministers have in fact received an instruction from the House of Commons. And it is very likely they will be defeated on the Canada Fortification question.

I have a notice of three questions relating to the army on going into supply. It has struck me that a few preliminary observations would be appropriate. The Army may be looked upon as an Institution which is improvable, or as an Institution which is doomed. Many liberals seem to me to leave it unnoticed as a thing which is rotten & must perish. However, if any amendment can be made in it, why not? It is a very serious matter that the power of the F[ield] M[arshall] Com[mandin]g in chief has so greatly increased. The Army, Navy & ordnance in 1835 cost about £13,000,000. Now the army alone costs £14,348,000 (or thereabouts). The influence thus wielded by the Duke of C[ambridge] must be very great. As he is virtually a permanent officer, every step he gains in the way of encroachm[en]t on the authority of the Sec[retar]y of State for war is probably maintained. If beaten by one resolute Minister, the Duke regains his lost ground with the next weak one. It is rumoured that he strives to

---

[34] See above, 1 Mar. 1861.
[35] On 21 Mar. Sheridan had carried against ministers, by a majority of 137:65, a motion to extend the previous years' reduction in the duty on fire insurances to houses, household goods and all insurable property; *H* clxxviii. 35–7. Trelawny was paired in favour of the government.

gain even the Militia under his auspices; or at least that he interferes with it at times, altho' politely informed that this course is not within his instructions. [...] My three questions are chiefly upon the old subject of the privileges of the g[uar]ds and distribution of Colonelcies of reg[imen]ts.[36]

It appears to me that, as we must have a large force, it were prudent to substitute 15,000 marine artillery for linesmen. In this manner the force at the disposal of the D[uke] of C[ambridge] would be diminished, and a constitutional objection partly met. If we do not look out, we shall drift into the condition of a German province. Our Royal family is not English at heart even now. Our sea force ought to be that on which we should chiefly rely. Colonies must defend themselves internally. Ships and sea artillery will be more wanted than land forces if we be wise: so it seems to me.

Friday, 24 March: [...] Lord Hartington was obliged to explain his recent speech in reply to my questions on the Guards & on the Army generally. It appears that he gave offence to the Inspector of Infantry and some com[mandin]g officers of depot Battalions.[37] Good will, I think, come out of the imbroglio. + The Queen's regulations ought to be followed throughout the army. The Inspector gen[era]l took care that this should be so in depot Battalions, but L[ieutenan]t Col[onel]s at Head Quarters sometimes found the men coming from these too perfect & in fact a reproach to the listless or capricious system in vogue there. Hence, no doubt, the abolition of the office. The Public interest seems to lie on the side of the Inspector-gen[era]l. + [...] Hartington's admission in the late debate raised by me of his unacquaintance with the internal arrangem[en]ts of reg[imen]ts gives me a right to speak again on the subject, as it is time he shd. learn that which is awanting to complete his education for the post of undersecretary of State for war, which I am bound to say he upon the whole fills well.

I notice that the Edmunds scandal excites great interest. The Lord Chancellor has been exam[ine]d at length.[38] Will not the affair cause a motion of censure and, possibly, a defeat of Ministers? They seem

[36] On 23 Mar. Trelawny inquired as to the expediency of abolishing the grade of Lieutenant Colonel of the foot guards, of abolishing the system whereby captains of guards' companies were ranked as Lieutenant Colonels and not required to reside in the barracks, and of appointing colonels of army regiments mainly according to seniority; *H* clxxviii. 86–9.

[37] Hartington explained that while he did not consider the depot system necessary, his speech on 23 Mar. had not been intended as a slur on depot officers or the Inspector general; *H* clxxviii. 241–2.

[38] By a select committee of the House of Lords; *P.P.* 1865, ix. 1.

to have eaten the leek presented to them by Sheridan.[39] In fact, he may be deemed to be Chancellor of Exchequer.

Monday, 27 March: Villiers moved the 2d. reading of the Union Chargeability Bill[40] in a long & able speech. He appeared to be ill – his voice being even weaker than usual & he had a suspicious cough. I fear we shall lose him. However, standing up nobly agt. fate, he did a good work in the interest of the Poor and unprotected. There was a long debate. The Tories, under Knightley's conduct, opposed him with vigour, but sustained a disastrous defeat. The numbers on division were 131 to 203. Ma[jority] 72. I paired with Mr. W.G. Wynne [...] I heard almost all Villiers' speech, wh. was quite conclusive. The arguments on this subject have been notorious any time in these 30 years. It will have been a most unpopular course to oppose the bill & this will be found out at the hustings, I suspect.

Failing to hear Villiers' voice where I sat, I went into the gallery opposite to him. Grey sat on one side of V. and Gladstone on Villiers' right hand, leaning back with his eyes upturned & with a certain expression of wearied impatience, which Gladstone, when not in action, has. Villiers was rather humorously adverting to the obstacles always thrown in the way of Reforms by men who harp upon the want of 'more time', 'more facts, more opportunity for deliberation generally', meaning some form of ignorance, indolence or interest – tho' not always. At this moment a smile of pity, or contempt, or derision played on Gladstone's features, as much as to say, 'what a hopeless task it is to battle with stupidity!' It strikes me that Genius shd. be tolerant, or not make stupidity more obstinate by intolerance even in a look.

Mr. Speaker and some members were again a little in hotwater this evening.[41] If he be wise, he will take his peerage & retire at the end of this Parliament.

Tuesday, 28 March: [...] Darby Griffith [...] complaining that only Peers can hold the office of Postmaster general. Every form of interruption was used to put him down, it being avowed that he was not indisposed to stand in Dillwyn's way. His slipshod & undignified twaddle stopped at last and the Irish Church question, brought on

---

[39] See above, 22 Mar. 1865.

[40] Making the union, rather than the parish, the financial unit for poor law purposes, and abolishing removability from parish to parish within a union so as to end the abuse of 'close parishes' with no poor. Royal assent, 29 June; *P.P.* 1865, iii. 557.

[41] Numerous irregular speeches in committee of supply, with the Speaker admitting that he had been inconsistent in his rulings; *H* clxxviii. 359–63.

by Dillwyn,[42] occupied the remainder of the night. I paired with Col[onel] Packe, & retired. A division took place on adjournment & the debate stands for May 2d.

Though Dillwyn's style is too colloquial, his speech does not seem to be a bad one as it is printed. Some of it I heard. Gladstone's was, perhaps, the most important speech of the debate. An admission that the state of the Irish Ch[urch] is unsatisfactory, by a Minister, who is thought to aspire to the leadership of the liberal party, is a great fact. A dozen speeches like those of Grey, Hardy and Whiteside will not annul it. The Irish, beginning to believe in the possibility of success, will be on the highroad to it – and may they reach the goal!

Wednesday, 29 March: [...] In the evening I attended Mr. Speaker's levee.

Later, at a private party, a member was talking with me on Ld. P[almerston]'s extraordinary powers at 80, and his habits of sporting which he still keeps up; walking for 2 hours ashooting & also, sometimes, riding to hounds. This led to other evidences of his vitality and courage. In further discourse the member said that he went to his Lordship to obtain a promise of a nomination for a lad not yet 21 to an office – and the age was the difficulty, as he is too young by 2 months. Lord P. adverted to this difficulty; and, with evident allusion to his own time of life, said jocosely that it was a sort of race agt. time. I suspect that the hunting & shooting are partly talk – for stage effect.

Thursday, 30 March: [...] *A liberal below the gangway mentioned to me that he was going to dine with Lord P. Subsequently I asked what sort of a dinner they had. He did not give a very highly-coloured description of the evening's entertainm[en]t. About 16 dined. Each person, after shaking hands with the host passed into the circle, but had scarcely any opportunity of exchanging a word with him. At dinner he spoke a little to his two neighbours, but little to others. A few minutes only were spent in the drawing room, and the whole affair was soon over. His lordship, no doubt, saves himself for more important matters: some 20 years ago he did the honours with almost unrivalled skill & tact. I dined, in my former career of 9 years from 1843 to 1852, once with his lordship. Of late, I have avoided such things. It may be that it is wrong to avoid Ministerial civilities, if it be understood that they commit you to nothing. However, these things are matter of feeling and it certainly would be agt. the grain

---

[42] Declaring the present position of the Irish Church to be unsatisfactory and calling on the government to give early attention to the matter; *H* clxxviii. 384–92.

to severely criticize today the goodnatured and genial host of last night.*

A very exalted official (The Speaker) new to his office and doubting his ability to fill it well, hinted his fears to a servant * Tho[ma]s Vardon* of the House employed in the Library who replied 'you must dine them well'. The advice is followed. In fact, the banquet is an important part of constitutional govt.; members, who would, perhaps, never speak to each other elsewhere, enter into familiar and unreserved conversation at official dinners. Am I right, then, in my course?

Friday, 31 March: [...] The greatest portion of the evening was expended on Irish tenant right. Maguire spoke ably hereon. Many members on both sides supported the motion.[43] Roebuck charged Ministers with pusillanimity in not endeavouring to lead the House instead of watching speeches made in order to escape from a difficulty. R., hoping little good from tenant right, still thought that a committee would 'eviscerate' the subject and do no harm; perhaps, some good. cries of 'Palmerston, Palmerston' and 'Peel'. 'Repeal' said one member mildly & sotto voce. Palmerston hesitated. Monsell arose & spoke briefly. Then, his lordship met the case by a compromise – that of referring an act of 1860 to a select committee. I was in attendance till late, and was much struck by the altered tone taken by members, who were temperate, unprejudiced and anxious to be informed.

I forgot the interpellations of Lord P. by Newdegate, in the early part of the evening, on the subject of a speech of M. Bonnechose[44] in the French chamber relating to the Pope's supposed idea of residing in England.[45] P. spoke with studied care in reply. There are several persons who will jealously weigh his words, among others the Emperor and some English Protestants. Newdegate, on rising, was received with rounds of applause, as much as to say (ironically of course) 'you have got now a really vital matter in hand'. His observations produced great laughter; which, it strikes me, was rather forced. Some people are really afraid of the Pope, while the Irish Catholic members generally take the line of wondering what men can be alarmed at [...] Palmerston's course must be specially interpreted at present by the light of the approaching general election. This remark applies in part to his speech on tenant right, and on the subject of the Pope's possible preference of our hospitality to that of the Emperor of the French.

[43] For a select committee to inquire into the more equitable adjustment of the relations between landlords and tenants in Ireland; *H* clxxviii. 570–85. Withdrawn.

[44] Cardinal de Bonnechose.

[45] In the event of the French garrison abandoning Rome.

Lord P. has just been making an adroit speech at a Workingman's (South London) exhibition over the water.

Monday, 3 April: Sad news, indeed! Poor Cobden is dead. He died yesterday about $\frac{1}{2}$ past 11. This came upon us like a thunderclap. It is likely that his premature journey to London a short time since, in order to give his counsel on Canadian defences, killed him, yet his health has for long past been very feeble.

In rapid succession 4 active & useful men have gone – Gregson, Wentworth Buller, Willoughby & Cobden.

[...] The House subdued & mournful – general sympathy with Cobden's friends. Palmerston's speech of 10 minutes was simple, feeling and effective. Perhaps, in respect to Free Trade, a shade too triumphant & controversial. Disraeli, in 7 minutes of skilful and elaborate rhetoric – avoiding points of difference – concentrated his remarks upon points in Cobden's character which are the foundation of common admiration. Bright followed: overcome with emotion, he could only articulate in a speech interrupted by distinct pauses at every 3 or 4 words, so that he might keep going at all. Those which he managed to say, were loving and most appropriate. Cobden's earnestness and other high personal qualities were dwelt upon with admiration, and the whole House united in cheers of the speakers.

[...] Dodson & some of the Committee on naval estimates appeared to be a loggerheads.[46] The rules of debate are very strict, and will only work well when applied with tact & discretion. These are indispensable on one side at least. Palmerston lectured Hon[oura]ble members pretty severely – & some deserved his remarks.

Tuesday, 4 April: [...] John Stuart Mill & Cobden have privately interchanged letters lately.[47] Mill has the privilege of Genius to be unlike the rest of the world. There are doubts how far he would be able to work with practical men. The word 'practical' is, I fear, in bad odour – connoting, perhaps, some surrender of opinions or profession of opinions not really held. Mill is for Universal suffrage, women inclusive!

Thursday, 6 April: It is noteworthy that the 'Times' of this date has found out the vicious system of promotion on foot in the War office. A chief clerk dies. All the departments recommend. The best man in

---

[46] A dispute between the chairman of committees and M.P.s, notably Torrens and Cecil, regarding the order of discussion of certain items; *H* clxxviii. 733–43.

[47] Cobden disagreed with Mill's views on proportional representation; John Morley, *Life of Richard Cobden*, (1881), ii. 462 n.

merit may not fit the vacant post. He goes upwards a grade in pay, but keeps his situation. Clerk No. 2 in the department wanting a new head is promoted without more pay. On this plan increased trust gets no more pay; & higher pay is awarded to an officer for duties wh. a cheaper servant could well discharge. This is the 'Times' description in few words.

The information received by me from good authority is that the F[ield] M[arshall] commanding in chief is gradually working his way into the War office. Many of the officials are military men responsible as such to the chief.

[. . .] There was a meeting of delegates to the Metropolitan members on the opening of Museums &c on Sundays. At first, it was in the Tea Room, which at last was wanted for members– and I heard that Gen[era]l Forester would not give the delegates another room – so they adjourned to one of the smaller lobbies. For some time delegates had to wait for the Metropolitan members, &, during this interval, Gregory & I conversed with the persons present [. . .]

Friday, 7 April: [. . .] More bad news from New Zealand[48] – Parliament seems to be resolved to know nothing it can help of the state of that Colony. 'Out of sight out of mind'. The Duke of Newcastle, in endorsing the conduct of Gov[erno]r Gore Browne in the case of the Waitara, caused the war; and to this hour dust is thrown into the eyes of the Public to hide this fact. All sorts of reasons, but the true one, are invented.

It is not yet clear that J.S. Mill will stand for Westminster – I found some trouble in finding any organized body to which I could give my name as Committee-man – & offer £26.5 towards expenses.

[. . .] The delegates of trades, in the matter of the proposed opening of Museums on Sundays, were skilfully *managed*. I hear that Gregory quieted them. The Metropolitan members fear the loss of their seats as the Sunday question creates divisions in every camp.

Monday, 24 April: Parliament reassembled [. . .] I have been ill for more than a fortnight, & have passed my holydays in bed. The question again assumes importance – what course ought I to pursue? – shall I resign? I feel that I am unequal to hard work.

Thursday, 27 April: With considerable trouble I succeeded in attending to hear Gladstone bring on the budget. The House was pretty full. Many peers were present, including Earl Russell [. . .] Gladstone spoke for 2 hours and twenty minutes; then I left. In this

---

[48] Cardwell announced that the war had recommenced; *H* clxxviii. 893–4.

time he had stated all material points.[49] The 'Times' says he spoke for 2¼ hours. Certainly this time is shorter than the time he occupied.

The House received with smiles the preliminary announcements of alteration in twopenny halpenny taxation with which the orator kept us in suspense. The reduction of the Income tax was received with some enthusiasm. The tea duty reduction passed muster; certainly the argument for it was stronger than that for the reduction of the malt Tax; on which, however, he had reserved a slight sop to cerberus. Some thought the timber duty (on raw material) shd. have been lowered.

Gladstone was strong in the argument on Malt – that to gain a ¼d on the quart of beer the Public would have to surrender £2½ millions of Income, and that the duty on wine, spirit, and tea was in each case far higher than on beer; the great bulk of which is consumed by adult males.

He gave in to the House on Fire Insurances; tho' he did not fully satisfy Sheridan, who could only call the surrender an instalment.

It is premature to express a strong opinion for his plan as a whole. We have had several prosperous years. May not a bad cycle come? Is he not a little experimental? How about our debt? Be this as it may, the budget will be a difficult nut for the Tories to crack. A large class will be pleased at the diminution of the Income Tax: another, still larger, will approve of the taking off of 6d. in the lb. of tea: a third will highly approve of the change as to Fire Insurances.

I noticed that Palmerston was not in his place. It has been stated to me that he has been a severe sufferer from gout for some days past. Bright's usual place, too, was not occupied by him. Still he may have been present, tho' I think not.

Gladstone very eloquently dwelt upon Cobden's character & merits.

Monday, 1 May: I hobbled in to hear speeches on the motion for an address on Mr. Lincoln's assassination. It was unfortunate that Palmerston was unable to manage this delicate business. Grey moved and Disraeli seconded. Grey spoke better than usually, but made a manifest blunder instantly perceived by the House & evoking disapprobation from a large section sitting below the Conservative gangway. The blunder was that of giving an opinion that the great mass of Englishmen were on the side of the South. *I believe he

---

[49] I.e. the reduction of the income tax by 2d. to 4d., the halving of the tea duty to 6d. per lb., and the reduction of the duties on fire insurances to a uniform rate of 1s. 6d. with a 1d. stamp in lieu of the 1s. duty on insurance policies; *H* clxxviii. 1084–1128.

said 'North'? See how this is in Hansard.[50]* However, he adroitly restrained his dangerous Pegasus and converted disapprobation into something like approval in a sentence or two. There is no saying what a sentence of Grey's may end in when fully elaborated. In this he resembles Gladstone. Both use a good many words & hearers tremble when the effect of words may be to embroil nations, one of which is already nearly mad.

On the whole, Grey was eloquent & hearty in sympathy, & evidently gave satisfaction to Federals below our gangway. He spoke for 11 minutes. Disraeli was very studied. His speech of about 9 min. was a work of art and so appeared; however he suited our men below the gangway, but I think he had no cheers from any of our Ministerial people, nor many from his own side. In alluding to the uniform failure of assassins to alter the inevitable destinies of Nations, a remark or two he made sounded to me as slightly materialist and necessarian. I doubt if his ideas suit the school of the Henley's, Walpole's & Pakington's. If all phenomena be results of natural laws which science may unfold, special Providences are nowhere, and even assassinations might be predicted. Without giving opinions on this question, it seems to me that Disraeli's tone sounded too like Buckle's[51] and that of the Utilitarians. Be this as it may, he cautiously abstained from any remark likely to offend the Americans of either side [...]

Tuesday, 2 May: Captain Jervis, in a good speech, advocated the claims of a large body of officers in India to redress of their alleged grievances arising out of the recent amalgamation of the 2 armies, the Indian & the Queen's.[52] Had I heard Jervis only my vote would probably have been with him; but it seemed that Sir C. Wood made good his countercase for the authorities. It became quite a party struggle. Never did I observe more pairing. By the way I paired with F. Powell. Ministers lost the day by 13 votes: 49 to 36.[53]

A good deal of uncertainty hangs over technical questions of the kind under debate and such a revolution as we have achieved in India can hardly ever be accomplished without some cases of hardship. It seems to me that a complaint must be very well supported, which would warrant a course, such as the officers have adopted, that of appealing for redress from govt. to the House of commons. Very soon that House will be drawing to itself, insensibly, the actual admin-

---

[50] Grey did say 'North'.

[51] Henry Thomas Buckle, author of *History of Civilisation in England*, (2 vols, 1857–61).

[52] *H* clxxviii. 1318–27.

[53] Brand advised Palmerston that it would be possible to rescind the vote by threatening to dissolve parliament, but this course was not taken; 3 and 5 May 1865, Broadlands MSS, GC/BR/24–5.

istration of the merest details. What will become of the Crown & the H. of Lords? I pronounce no opinion, only wishing to indulge in a little speculation.

Wednesday, 3 May: Six hours of excited talk – ending almost riotously. Our theme the Bill of Baines for a £6 franchise in boroughs, a plan wh. would add about 240,000 to the electoral body. Baines, who must have known that the enemy meant to prevent a division today, talked as it were agt. himself by occupying about an hour and a half in a dreary, but respectable re-statement of his case. His voice and address are not very lively: too much in the style of a dissenting minister, whose tones in moral exposition are such as are conventionally used in the language of prayer. The habit cannot be shaken off. Bazley seconded him in a speech of reasonable length and displaying his usual good sense. Lord Elcho, in a long and able speech delivered with his usual ease & confidence, moved the previous question. Leatham eloquently replied to Lord Elcho and well sustained his reputation. Lowe made a very remarkable speech agt. Baines – a speech which shd. be studied. His allusions to science must have puzzled country gentlemen, whose knowledge of abstruse mathematics is not extensive. The tendency of the smallest molecules to aggregate & crystallize, with the greatest force, in illustration of the tendency of the labouring classes to unite for particular objects, might come more within the mental horizon of the House. Osborne & Stansfeld rose – as, also, the Lord Advocate.[54] Great cries were raised for Osborne. The Lord Advocate entirely failed to obtain a hearing, even of one word. The Speaker did not appear to think that the decent conduct of debate was a matter in which he was in the least concerned. The Lord Advocate gave way and Osborne spoke rather to the disappointment of his audience, who expected an epigrammatic speech and heard little new or pungent. In short, it had been better for him had the House not expected so much of him; or had he not been called for. But it would have its toy.

The end of all was that the clock pointed to the hour at which by the rule of the House the debate closed,[55] and hence the wrangle, with respect to another day for its continuance, died a natural death.

Palmerston's absence is a serious evil for the government, which can hardly exist without his tact and ready knowledge of the mode & time of giving way.

It is abundantly clear that the plan of Baines would be no settlement, and raises no enthusiasm in its favour among the so-called

[54] James Moncrieff.
[55] A quarter to six.

working classes – that is, the bulk of artisans & day labourers. He is like an architect, who, called upon to build a house, presents a single gable. The Conservative party feel that they are masters of the situation, as they may safely say that no one petitions earnestly for the scheme. Unless a great principle, involving, theoretically at least, the co-ordination of taxation with representation be tendered, the democratic party will view our proceedings with apathy.

It strikes me that Lowe's contemptuous mode of dealing with the claims of the labouring classes and his tone of ridicule applied to their most cherished prejudices will not in the long run strengthen the position of those who desire to stand upon the Reform Act of 1832. America is nearer than it was, in point of time, and almost every working man has a relative or friend there. Will there be no interchange of ideas on forms of government? *Will not cheap literature generate betwn. the two great Anglo Saxon nations a constantly growing interest in each other's condition? A few years ago labourers in England knew very little of America. In the recent great struggle almost every Englishman had formed an opinion for the North or South.*

Workmen are learning to combine; they thus learn their power. Were it not well that their ideas should generally be known at the earliest moment in the H. of C?

Elchos and Lowes may sneer, but tide will rise nevertheless.

Thursday, 4 May: The budget was the topic of the day. We were all under great pressure from the grocers,[56] who demur to the abruptness of Gladstone's proposal with reference to the Tea Duties* and desire that the diminution of the duty by 6d. per lb shd. not take effect till June 1st. so that existing duty-paid stocks may be got rid of without loss.* It seemed likely that Gladstone would adhere to his project. Moffatt brought forward the case of the grocers temperately and judiciously, and was seconded by Cave. The Chancellor made a clever speech, and then, in substance, gave Moffatt what he asked[57] – to the enormous discontent of the Conservatives who, with liberal aid, would infallibly have placed him in a minority. It strikes me that he shd. recollect the lesson not to use so many unnecessary words. He is, or affects to be, obliged to give up about £100,000 this year, because in a former statement – I think in 1863 – he used language raising the impression that the change then to be made in the Tea Duties would be (at least as H.M. Ministers were concerned) likely to be undisturbed[58] – language which was quite uncalled for.

---

[56] Who had sent a deputation to Gladstone; *The Times*, 2 May 1865, p. 12.
[57] Moffatt's amendment, delaying the reduction in the duty until 1 June, agreed to.
[58] 16 Apr. 1863; *H* clxx. 200–51.

His speech was a masterpiece of adroitness. He appears to enjoy a difficulty as an opportunity for the exercise of his marvellous suppleness & versatility.

He has been fairly terrified by 165,000 grocers; whose organ in the House hinted at the approach of a general election. Talk of representation! Why, in a day or two this body was all but present in Downing St., and acting together as one man! *We hear of plans for the protection of minorities from vast numbers. Shd. there not be a scheme for the protection of numbers from minorities? These last amply compensate for weakness by activity & organization, and very often have the best of it.* [...]

Friday, 5 May: [...] It is said that Lord Palmerston has exhibited more languor than usual during his fit of gout. It is thought that he will return to the House on Monday next, which is Baines's day for the continuation of the debate on the franchise.

The gravamen of the charges agt. Lord Westbury is that he allowed the House of Lords to give Edmunds a pension without stating known evidence of his disreputable conduct in the Patent office; and it is thought that the resignation of one of his posts was so managed that the Chancellor had the first chance in soliciting it for his son. As to this point, inference with regard to motives is the question & these cannot be proved. On the whole, the government is considerably damaged in Public opinion.

Monday, 8 May: [...] the debate on Reform was revived[59] by Gregory who ably followed the line of Elcho & Lowe. Sir G. Grey expressed whig hollowness on the whole question. A few minor speeches occupied time; the great speech was that of Horsman[60] whom the House preferred to Disraeli, & he closed the debate. Majority of some 70 for the Anti-Reformers.[61] I paired with Lord Henniker.

Friday, 19 May: Still very weak & barely able to crawl[62] I attended in my place in order to support Ministers agt. the attempt of the Attorneys, thro' Denman's aid, to escape a small annual tax to which they are liable. Denman spoke for an hour and at last wearied the House. 'Move, Move' was the cry. Collins' patience was exhausted &, at last, he gave the cue, in loud tones; hiding his face immediately by a sharp turn away from the Speaker. Collins had planted himself

---

[59] From 3 May.
[60] Opposing the bill as a step towards universal suffrage; H clxxviii. 1674–91.
[61] 288:214.
[62] Trelawny had been bed-ridden for several days, owing to gout.

on our side near the gangway, so that Denman could not see him. This may be an useful, still it is not a dignified function. Still Collins' post is one which has its effect [...] We divided & suffered a defeat by some 2 or 3 votes[63] [...] The whole thing was very disreputable. A barrister, just before a general election, moves for a bonus to the purveyors of briefs, and a barrister speaks for it,[64] both, in effect proffering a grant from the exchequer to the class most active & powerful at elections.

[...] Palmerston looked very thin & weak. His face is quite changed – & his hand in a sling. His voice strong as usual. It struck me that he looked dejected, as well he may! He suffers much, I fear.

Henley's late course, in order to defeat the Union Chargeability bill, by outbidding its provisions in an amendment in favour of the entire abolition of the Law of settlement,[65] was not a course which can easily be rescued from an imputation of insincerity even by a plea of infirmity of temper. The landed gentry are found out; & hence, in their bitterness of rage, they have forgotten all decency & respect for Public opinion. The measure, offered bona fide, was good. But its object was to make Villiers' projected substitution of Union for parochial rating as unpalatable as possible to the Lords. It is possible Henley may urge reasons which do not occur to the world at large. Maybe he will say that parochial rating & chargeability checked undue increase of the population, whereas the check of Union rating is inappreciable; and, that if so much progress be made towards a National rate, it were not worth while to maintain a complex law for so small an advantage.

Kekewich moved an amendment to substitute 1 for 3 years as the period which shd. hereafter entitle a pauper to irremovability. Villiers agreed. It seems to me that we are on the highway to National rating.

Monday, 22 May: Col[onel] Dawkins' case came on, irregularly, on a motion for adjourning the House by Darby Griffith.[66] I voted with him as an exceptional mode of proceeding necessary under pressure of circumstances. Dawkins is to be gazetted out on half pay almost immediately. It appears that he has received unfair treatment; altho' it is true that he has some faults of temper, and is not fit to command

---

[63] 146:143 for Denman's amendment, abolishing the certificate duty of £9 in London and £6 elsewhere; *H* clxxix. 564–70.

[64] P.S. Humberstone was a solicitor.

[65] 18 May 1865, *H* clxxix. 492–6; amendment defeated by 184:110. See above, 27 Mar. 1865, for Villiers' bill.

[66] Dawkins, a Lieutenant Colonel in the guards, had been imprisoned for eleven days without trial, and then dealt with by a secret court of inquiry; *H* clxxx. 641–6. 172:112 against the adjournment.

a reg[imen]t. [...] Many Tory Colonels & others supported him. I declined to bring on his case for reasons which were, I think, sufficient.

Friday, 26 May: Dawkins again! Darby Griffith spoke, moving for papers. He made a ridiculous speech & materially injured his client. Even Dawkins could not help laughing, in sympathy with the House, at some of Griffith's absurd remarks. The most amusing circumstance was his inability to see their effect. And he exhibited this in several instances. The House gave him, as a recognized bore, no mercy.[67]

[...] There was a tedious evening: no division. Palmerston was present for a short time, looking ill & in pain. At one time his hat was over his eyes, his head drooping, his arm in a sling – & he looked much to be pitied. Yet, if he leave the House, no one can maintain a decorous conduct of business. Grey, Wood, and Gladstone are all unfortunate in manner. The Speaker interferes too much or too little, and without the late Speaker's[68] tact, and that kindly smile which took away from rebuke much of its sting and, nevertheless, enforced obediance. On the other hand, many members are very provoking.

Friday, 2 June: [...] Gladstone's plea at Chester for his son, who is a candidate for that city, contained a regular liberal programme[69] and was, no doubt, intended to be a reply to Disraeli's manifesto[70] – a document which had the faults of being weak, inflated and ungrammatical. The Reader, newspaper, well exposes the last fault. The Tories are doing their best to ensure their own defeat. We can stand upon Ch. Rates abolition, & Union Chargeability at least, which the Tories have stoutly opposed [...]

Friday, 9 June: [...] Members are kept in town with much difficulty. Politically speaking, each of us may consider that he lives with a halter round his neck. The question is upon whom the noose will be tightened. For my part, it would be a kindness to kill me, as life in Parliament is to me slow death [...]

Monday, 12 June: I paired, after hearing nearly the whole of Dis-

---

[67] Rejection of Griffith's motion agreed.

[68] Shaw Lefevre, 1839–57.

[69] Favouring 'a sensible extension of the franchise to the working man'; *The Times*, 2 June 1865, p. 5.

[70] To his constituents, emphasising the defence of the Church and favouring a modest measure of parliamentary reform along the lines of the Conservatives' bill of 1859; Monypenny and Buckle, *Disraeli*, ii. 145–6.

raeli's speech on Monsell's oaths bill[71] with Col[onel] Calcraft; & went
home [...] Disraeli's argument was laboured & curious. In finding
reasons for opposing Monsell, Disraeli destroyed the whole case of his
party. He contended that oaths were no security; and that, whether
they are or not, there shd. be one form only. Speaking of the difficulty
of governing in the face of the two fanatical bodies ultra Catholic &
ultra Protestant, he used a happy phrase when he spoke of the 'gulf
stream' of common sense which luckily intervened. Clearly, he wanted
to defend a wise policy without losing the confidence of his own bigots,
and bid for support from the Catholics by flattering their religion &
its head. But his speech will not please any one. The Papal party will
not like his sneer at the 'Bull in coenae domine', from which he said
he did not recollect having suffered any evil consequences (a laugh).
The Tory party will not relish his treatment of the oaths guarantee
question on principles of a man of the world & utilitarian philosopher.
It was very noteworthy that not a soul cheered except when he said
that oaths were as good as useless either for the security of the Church
or Monarchy – & then the cheers were from a few who are called
sometimes philosophical radicals. Could this have pleased Whiteside
or Newdegate?[72]

Wednesday, 14 June: 12 o'clock. Goschen made a very able speech
in moving the 2d. reading of the University Tests Bill.[73] I paired till
4 p.m. with Col[onel] Somerset. At about ½ past 3 I returned & heard
a witty speech of Scully's.[74]

Hardy was one of the leading orators of the day: it is difficult to
believe that so clever a man does not know better than his speech
betokened.[75] Gladstone had spoken before I returned: he produced an
unfavourable impression on his party – he was apparently inconsistent
with his line last year[76] and, in consequence, he was taunted as if his
proceedings were intended to affect the coming Oxford election. The
vote, said Scully, was an Oxford test in more senses than one. On a

[71] Committee stage of the Roman catholic oaths bill, altering the oath required under
the relief act of 1829 so that catholics no longer had to disclaim any intention of
deposing the Queen or of subverting the protestant church and protestant government
of the realm.
[72] Lord Derby secured the defeat of the bill in the upper house on 26 June.
[73] To abolish oaths for those taking degrees at Oxford.
[74] Supporting the bill, and trusting that British Liberals would support the O'Donoghue's bill for a Catholic University in Ireland; *H* clxxx. 240–2.
[75] His opposition to the bill was no doubt influenced by his intended candidature for
Oxford University.
[76] Gladstone now opposed the bill because of the tone adopted by its promoters, who
desired to separate education from religion; *H* clxxx. 217–23.

division we won by 16. Numbers 190 to 206[77] [...] The whole debate was very damaging to bigots on both sides. The Rationalistic school had many a laugh [...]

Friday, 16 June: [...] Evening sitting at 6 p.m. On the question of going into supply, Seely moved agt. the custom of appointing naval officers as superintendents of dockyards and limiting the tenure of such posts to 5 years, and defeated the govt. by 2 votes.[78] This was a motion in substance similar to a motion for which I was responsible some years ago, when we stood in a minority of three persons besides tellers.[79] The three were Ayrton, Pilkington & Gilpin. Ayrton was at that time very angry with me for placing him in so small a minority [...]

Tuesday, 20 June: A morning sitting at noon. I attended, think[in]g there might be difficulty in making a House. At length, forty were wheedled in, and business commenced. Immediately, a process of depletion left only 24 [...] Old Brougham was under the gallery. He talked rather too loudly, & stood up. Several went to shake hands with him, Sir George Grey, Gladstone & others. B. called out to the Lord Advocate, who was going out at the bar, to come to him & his voice might have been heard all over the House. But he is privileged. His fame in the Commons makes the place, as it were, his own; &, as he was generally on his legs, when he was a member, the posture was natural.

[...] 6 p.m. The O'Donoghue spoke well in favour of his motion. His object was to obtain for R. Catholics in Ireland a fairer share than they now enjoy of collegiate education.[80] Virtually, Ministers acceded to his wishes, undertaking, at least, to give them favourable attention.

The O'Donoghue is wise in pressing Irish grievances just before a general election. Ministers are disposed to be civil & the opposition fear to thwart them.

Wednesday, 21 June: [...] Brand has work at Lewes, I hear. It will be curious if our whip be defeated.[81] The Session is virtually over.

[...] Layard was replying yesterday to a question from a member

---

[77] For the 2nd reading; the bill was later withdrawn.

[78] 36:34 for the amendment, but on the question that Seely's words be added, he was defeated by 60:33.

[79] 18 May 1857; *H* cxlv. 457. 215 opposed Trelawny.

[80] He pointed to the grievance arising from the fact that conscientious objections prevented many Catholics from using the Irish university system; *H* clxxx. 541–7.

[81] Brand held his seat.

on our side, &, to do this, turned round, when Disraeli exclaimed, rather loudly, & with emphasis, 'speak to the House – speak to the House'. Disraeli rarely interrupts a member by exclamations [. . .]

Thursday, 22 June: My stay at the House was short as I had an engagement to attend a meeting on behalf of John Stuart Mill, candidate for Westminster. At 8 o'clock we assembled at the Pimlico rooms, Winchester St. – & many excellent speeches were made. The chairman called upon me out of the regular order of movers & seconders, and, then, I made a clumsy speech and am consequently much dissatisfied with myself.

The 'Times' of the 23rd reports some of my observations, which were, no doubt, of the kind required as far as they go[82]

Monday, 26 June: 'The Times' has a scathing leading article upon the Leeds Registrar business. It seems to be certain that the sale of an office was negotiated – & that £500 passed.[83] The case is compared to that of the Duke of York & Mary Anne Clarke. Can the Chancellor, the keeper of the Queen's conscience, retain his post? – or can the Ministry remain in office with him? [. . .]

Tuesday, 27 June: [. . .] Evening sitting. 6 p.m. [. . .] Monsell had a question wh. he intended to put, when arose Longfield to put questions relating to the Leeds delinquency. This course being rather demurred to, he said he would move the adjournment of the House & then proceeded to pour forth a flood of invective agt. the Lord Chancellor, whom he deliberately accused of conniving at crime for his own advantage and that of his son. The charge, stated in [illegible] terms, was pressed home with vigor. Again & again, was the House reminded that the arch offender was the 'keeper of the Queen's conscience' – & the accuser declared that he was ashamed of his profession when he became aware of the conduct impugned, & had never, in a long experience, known a worse case. Had the Chancellor no shame? or, if he had none, could he not have affected shame? Such were a sample of the bitter questions put.

[82] Trelawny, who was 'announced as a personal friend' of Mill, defended him against the charge of being an atheist and presented him as a friend of the working man; *The Times*, 23 June 1865, p. 7.

[83] The Lord Chancellor's son, Richard Bethell, had received money from a Mr. Welch in return for using his influence to obtain Welch's appointment as registrar to the Leeds court of bankruptcy. The former registrar, H.S. Wilde, had been pensioned off by Lord Westbury under suspicious circumstances. A select committee was appointed to investigate the matter. *Annual Register* (1865), pp. 138–43.

The Attorney general[84] replied, & dwelt for some time upon the indignity & cruelty of dilating upon unpublished evidence, when the accuser must have known that, in 2 or 3 days, all necessary materials would be in the hands of members. At this point, I was compelled to leave the House.

I recollect that the attorney-gen[era]l spoke with evident emotion – indeed, it seemed as if he was about to burst into tears – crocodile's? Women & lawyers always have a reservoir at command. Several members followed. The Chancellor's defenders were more courageous than successful. Hardy's speech I had not time to read. Lord Cranborne was effective in his viperous style. Interruptions in mitigation only elicited cutting retorts. He is certainly a very able man. Lord Palmerston could say little, & obviously felt that the less said the better [...]

Wednesday, 28 June: [...] I yesterday noticed Palmerston's face while he endeavoured to catch every word of Longfield's speech. Like all the Ministers, whom I observed particularly, he looked serious and anxious. Gibson's face & Cardwell's struck me. The Lord Advocate was no less frightened, I think. He was in reserve & spoke by way of support to the attorney-general. Disraeli studiously avoided the expression of any feeling, but listened attentively. Pakington chimed in at one moment very eagerly. Now & then a savage laugh among the Tories expressed their incredulity when any good motive, or absence of evil, was suggested in favour of the accused.

Altogether, the case is one of the worst we have had in our time, & brings back to the remembrance of abuses supposed to be quite out of date. It is difficult to imagine that the Chancellor can remain in the government [...]

Thursday, 29 June: On this day I went to Tavistock [...]

Friday, 30 June: + I held a meeting and was rewarded, for 17 years of hard work, with an adverse resolution at a Public meeting.[85] It is amusing. +

There will be a tremendous row about the recent proceedings of the Lord Chancellor. Hunt has given a notice of a resolution thereon.

Sunday, 2 July: I am summoned to London by Brand: no less than 3 lashes to the whip. It seems to me that the fate of the government is involved.

---

[84] Sir Roundell Palmer.
[85] *Western Daily Mercury*, 1 July 1865, p. 5.

Monday, 3 July: I returned from Cornwall. A very large number were collected. Hunt made a long & dull speech.[86] He had a clumsy way of handling his papers & his story was too disjointed. Still he was moderate & just, & what he did was done with proper gravity. I did not hear the Lord Advocate[87] who moved the amendment, more or less affirming the report of the committee,[88] & holding out a promise of a better check in future on the system of granting pensions.

But even this implies censure. Can we not trust the Lord high Chancellor, the keeper of the Queen's conscience! Bouverie gave early notice of an amendment which differed little from the motion of Hunt. Hunt's language was a little equivocal, and might have seemed to imply the Chancellor's corruptness. At 12 o'clock (about) Lord P[almerston] proposed an adjournment on the ground of unexpected circumstances. Time forsooth was wanted. (Laughter & oh!) Disraeli would not permit this, and we divided.[89] The division list expresses nothing certain as to opinion because it was not taken on the merits. However Palmerston proposed to accept it as if it had been on the merits. I voted for the adjournment. I wanted to hear the whole case. The main question (Hunt approving of Bouverie's words)[90] was carried nemine contradicente – a very serious matter. The Chancellor must go.

Tuesday, 4 July: I resigned my candidature for Tavistock & explained my reasons in a letter to J. Pearse.[91] The electors did not attend my meeting & therefore gave me a hint to quit; which I took.

Lord Palmerston announced that the Chancellor would retire on Friday, after having signed documents necessary for calling a new Parliament. After this even Palk could not keep members in their places & they went in shoals. I forgot to mention, in my account of the debate of the 3rd, Denman's speech which was a lawyer's speech as it were from a brief & made little impression. He dwelt on too many small matters. Bouverie noticed this & dealt very severely with the Chancellor. But Bouverie made a mistake in adverting to rumours flying about to the Chancellor's disadvantage; as if a man's character

[86] Condemning the 'highly reprehensible' conduct of the Lord Chancellor in the light of the findings of the committees on the Edmunds and the Leeds registrar cases; *H* clxxx. 1045–71.
[87] James Moncrieff.
[88] I.e. that Lord Westbury was guilty of no more than haste and want of caution with respect to Wilde's pension, but recommending that further checks were needed over the system of granting pensions; *H* clxxx. 1072–91.
[89] 177:163 against adjournment; Moncrieff's amendment was then negatived.
[90] Criticising the Lord Chancellor's 'laxity of practice and want of caution'; *H* clxxx. 1135.
[91] Chairman of the meeting at Tavistock.

should be damaged by rumours. The Attorney-General very severely commented on this. The Attorney General spoke well, yet some of his more audacious arguments were received with ironical derision & scoffing incredulity. The House was determined to ruin the delinquent [...] Returning to the division, Palmerston took several votes by accepting the division on the main question; but this course was not fair to many of us who wanted to hear more before giving a judicious vote.

Wednesday, 5 July: + I wrote my retiring address & forwarded it to Tavistock for publication. + At the 4 o'clock sitting (it was arranged to be at 4. although the day is Wedn[esda]y) the Speaker attended in the Lords to hear the Royal assent to several bills. Soon after 5, the Chancellor who had been chatting with one or two Lords, rose & moved in a stately manner a few paces from the Woolsack, to his left, & then spoke for 10 minutes, announcing his resignation. He said that he had repeatedly tendered it before, but his view of his duty had been over-ruled by his noble friend at the head of the Government; who urged that, if everytime a Chancellor was attacked, he resigned his post, it would be only necessary in order to get rid of a Chancellor to accuse him of some crime. The manner of Bethell[92] was admirably good. His finished diction & measured appropriateness, his calm power & felicity were never more fully exhibited. He studiously avoided self defence on the charges, chiefly dwelling on the measures he had introduced, the absence of arrears of judicial business, and his intentions to work as a private member in effecting law reforms. He said, also, that if he had by language or manner offended, he heartily begged pardon of noble Lords, having reason to complain – & then he gracefully concluded & returned to the woolsack [...]

Thursday, 6 July: The Queen's speech was rather long. The Chancellor did not read it. Lord Granville was H.M.'s mouthpiece; prorogation is to the 12th & dissolution will now at once take place.

Thus ends, I think, my public life.

[91] I.e. Lord Westbury.

INDEX

Details of the constituencies represented and offices held by individuals are confined to the period covered by the diary. Further information may be found in *Dod's Parliamentary Companion*. General elections took place in March–April 1857 and April–May 1859. Parliament was again dissolved in July 1865, at which point the diary ends.